SPANISH PERU

1532–1560

James Lockhart SPANISH PERU

1532–1560 *A Colonial Society*

The University of Wisconsin Press

Published 1968

The University of Wisconsin Press

Box 1379, Madison, Wisconsin 53701

The University of Wisconsin Press, Ltd.

70 Great Russell Street, London

ISBN 0-299-04664-8

LC 68-14032

To PEDRO DE SALINAS

notary

CONTENTS

ILLUSTRATIONS

MAP

TEXT TABLES

APPENDIX TABLES

ACKNOWLEDGMENTS

This book is in very large part an attempt to interpret for today's scholarly public the records of sixteenth-century Spanish Peruvian notaries. Those who aided me in the task, absorbing but arduous, have my heartfelt gratitude. I wish to thank José Federico Sánchez Regal of the National Archive of Peru for introducing me to paleography; Professors Manuel Aparicio Vega of Cuzco and Eduardo Ugarte y Ugarte of Arequipa, for opening their archives to me beyond the requirements of formality, and sharing their special knowledge with me; Professor Enrique Otte of Berlin, for my orientation in the Archive of the Indies and for specific information from his research there; Vicenta Cortés and Miguel Maticorena in Seville, for bibliographical help; and above all Professor John L. Phelan of Wisconsin, under whose supervision the book was written as a doctoral dissertation, for encouraging independent thinking and research. In matters of financial support, I am indebted to Professors Phelan, Philip D. Curtin, and E. R. Mulvihill, all of Wisconsin, for their instrumental action, and to the University of Wisconsin and the Ford Foundation for assistance in the form of an Ibero-American Ford Grant to the University of Wisconsin. And for aid and support at all levels from research to editing, I would like to thank my wife Mary Ann.

In the illustrations section, Plate 1 is reproduced by permission of the Library of Congress, Plates 2 and 7, by permission of the Archivo Nacional del Perú, and Plates 3 and 4 through the courtesy of the Archivo General de Indias. The signatures reproduced in Plates 5 and 6 come from materials in the Library of Congress, the Archivo Nacional del Perú, and the Biblioteca Nacional del Perú.

SPANISH PERU
1532–1560

I INTRODUCTION

The reader has before him a description of the Spanish society that grew up in Peru during the conquest and civil war period, about 1532 to 1560. For all its remoteness of locale, the conquest of Peru was a major episode in the sixteenth-century Spanish occupation of America, equaled in significance only by the conquest of Mexico occurring ten or fifteen years before it. Like Mexico, Peru had an impressive Indian civilization and mineral wealth; like Mexico it quickly became the main center of Spanish civilization and government in a whole continent, and retained that position throughout the colonial period. Peru, richer in silver, less fortunate in its governors, its terrain more difficult, was by far the more turbulent of the two during the first decades. Yet a varied civil population was pouring into the country, creating lasting social and economic patterns, building a nation in the midst of political chaos.

Spaniards reached Peru as explorers in the 1520's, but the consecutive history of Spanish Peru begins in 1532, when Francisco Pizarro's conquering expedition entered the country from the north and captured the Inca emperor Atahuallpa at Cajamarca. Within a year the Inca capital of Cuzco was taken, within another year Quito. There was hardly time to found a Spanish capital at Lima on the coast in 1535, before the newcomers were engulfed in a country-wide Indian rebellion, involving a year-long siege of Cuzco in 1536–37. Pizarro's partner and rival Diego de Almagro, returning in 1537 from his expedition to Chile, lifted the siege but did not bring peace.

Almagro's claim to Cuzco set off a major civil war among the Spaniards, the first in a series which was to continue with little respite for

3

TABLE 1 A CHRONOLOGY OF PERU, 1532–60

GOVERNORS OF PERU	WARS, REBELLIONS, AND LANDMARK DATES	FOUNDING OF CITIES
Francisco Pizarro, governor and Adelantado, 1532–41	Capture of Inca Emperor Atahuallpa at Cajamarca, 16 Nov. 1532	Piura, 1532
	Spanish occupation of Cuzco, 15 Nov. 1533	Jauja,* 1533
		Cuzco, Quito, 1534 Lima, Trujillo, Puertoviejo, Guayaquil, 1535
	Great Indian rebellion and siege of Cuzco, 1536–37 "War of Salinas," 1537–38, between the Pizarros and the elder Almagro, ending in the latter's defeat at Salinas, 26 April 1538	La Plata, Chachapoyas, 1538 Huamanga, 1539 Arequipa, 1540
Licenciado Cristóbal Vaca de Castro, governor, 1541–44	Assassination of Francisco Pizarro, 26 June 1541 "War of Chupas," rebellion of the younger Almagro, 1541–42, ending in his defeat by Vaca de Castro at Chupas, 16 Sept. 1542	Huánuco, 1542
Blasco Núñez Vela, viceroy, 1544–46	Gonzalo Pizarro rebellion, 1544–48. "War of Quito," 1544–46, ending in defeat of Blasco Núñez Vela at Añaquito, 18 Jan. 1546	
Licenciado Pedro de la Gasca, president of the Audiencia with authority to govern, 1547–50	Gasca's campaign against Pizarro, 1547–48, ending in defeat of Pizarro at Jaquijahuana, 9 April 1548	La Paz, 1548
Don Antonio de Mendoza, viceroy, 1551–52 Interim rule by the Audiencia, 1552–56	Rebellion of don Sebastián de Castilla, 1553 Rebellion of Francisco Hernández Girón; war between him and forces of the Audiencia, 1553–54	
Don Andrés Hurtado de Mendoza, Marquess of Cañete, viceroy, 1556–60		

* Moved to Lima, 1535.

more than fifteen years. These wars, not readily reduced to comprehensibility, were at first very largely personal and factional feuds between the Pizarrists and the Almagrists, but they were also conflicts between the rich and the poor, the well-established and the newly arrived. As time went on the factional element grew weaker, and the element of discontent and rebellion grew stronger. After the initial episode, in which both sides had an arguable legal case, the civil wars were fought between supposed loyalists and supposed rebels, and even to some extent between the sedentary coastal region and seditious Upper Peru.

The first war, the "War of Salinas," ended with Almagro's defeat and execution in 1538. In revenge, the Almagrists assassinated Francisco Pizarro in 1541 and, under the leadership of Almagro's son, held much of the country until defeated in 1542 in the "War of Chupas" by Governor Vaca de Castro (allied with the Pizarrists). Both the Almagro wars were formidable affairs, but the most serious uprising of all came in 1544 when Gonzalo Pizarro, Francisco's brother, rebelled against the first viceroy of Peru, Blasco Núñez Vela, and the restrictive New Laws.* Pizarro attracted to himself not only malcontents, but a large body of the most powerful men in Peru, and proceeded to hunt down the viceroy, defeating and killing him in battle near Quito in 1546. To cope with the situation, the crown sent Licenciado Pedro de la Gasca, who, after amassing the largest forces yet seen in Peru, brought about Gonzalo Pizarro's fall and execution in 1548. After this there were no more rebellions by senior and powerful figures, but in the early 1550's Peru increasingly filled up with impatient claimants of honors, some of whom briefly seized control in the southern mining area in 1553 under don Sebastián de Castilla. The period of major wars came to an end in 1554 with the defeat of Francisco Hernández Girón, who, though he never counted the powerful among his followers, for a year dominated much of the Peruvian highland and even once advanced to within a few miles of Lima.

Where, in this picture of turmoil, is there room for peaceful colonization? It is small wonder that many observers have assumed that real

* The Spanish crown promulgated the New Laws of 1542–43 (amended in 1545–46) at the instigation of humanitarians, with the principal purpose of hindering the rise of a powerful aristocracy in the colonies. No new encomiendas would have been granted, encomiendas would not have been inheritable, and those who held even minor royal office were not to be encomenderos. In addition, the New Laws would have penalized those who had participated in the Peruvian civil wars, that is, most of the conquerors of Peru. (For an explanation of the encomienda system, see p. 11.)

development of the society and economy began later, either with the
rule of Viceroy Toledo in the 1570's, or at earliest in the later 1550's
after the end of the civil wars.[1] The fact is, however, that to a certain
extent basic development is compatible with war, political chaos, and
bad governors. Had there been peace and good government, no doubt
marvels would have been accomplished; but much was done in any
case, and indeed the wars at many points served as a stimulus to commerce, artisanry, and navigation. All the main population centers of
Peru, all the main economic and social trends, had taken shape by 1545
or 1550, and in many cases much earlier, in the course of a spontaneous, undirected development concurrent with the conquest and civil
wars.

A quick glance at some aspects of Peru in 1542, just ten years after
the capture of the Inca at Cajamarca, and a year after the assassination of Francisco Pizarro, will serve to show how much was done in a
short time toward building up Spanish Peru. Lima, which was then,
as it always afterward remained, the center of the Spanish occupation,
was a quite imposing city, full of the large, sometimes palatial Spanish-
style houses of the encomenderos, with artisans' and merchants' shops
lining the square and central streets. Around the city lay a garden area
where intensive Spanish irrigation agriculture was carried on, mainly
by Negro slaves, to supply the local market. Encomenderos from the
highlands, leaving retainers behind to care for their interests, spent
much of their time in the capital. Lima was the Peruvian headquarters
of merchant firms, based ultimately in Seville, which traded along the
route from Seville to Panama, Lima, Arequipa, and the highlands, importing goods and sending back silver. The coastal cities contained
strong elements of a civil population, including merchants, artisans,
mariners, large numbers of Negro slaves in various stages of acculturation, and more than a few Spanish women married to encomenderos
and artisans.

In the highland settlements Spanish civilization was less dense, but
all the elements were everywhere present; the southern highland area
had already come to provide the basis of the Spanish Peruvian economy through the production of precious metals, though the then important sites of Carabaya and Porco would be replaced a little later by
Potosí. The cities of Quito, Puertoviejo, Guayaquil, Piura, Trujillo,
Huánuco, Lima, Huamanga (Ayacucho), Cuzco, Arequipa, and La
Plata (Sucre) had been founded, and occupied positions relative to the

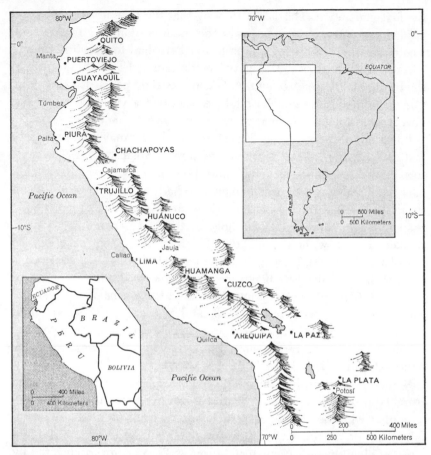

Greater Peru in the conquest period. The smaller map at left shows modern national boundaries in the region. (Map by the University of Wisconsin Cartographic Laboratory.)

whole that were to be permanent; each town was dominated by encomenderos whose families were to continue their sway for a generation and in some cases for centuries. In 1542, an Hispanic Peru existed that was still recognizable one hundred, two hundred, or four hundred years later.

The present study centers primarily on the precocious civil society which coexisted with the conquest and major wars, in the time from the 1530's until 1555, but for some purposes the time span has been extended, in order to give scope for treatment of the unfolding lives of the first generation. This is not to deny that the time around 1555 and 1556 does represent in some ways the inauguration of a new period. The civil wars were definitely past, and Peru had for the first time in Viceroy Cañete (1556–60) a governor determined and able to rule in the traditional sense. A *buen republicano,* as the Spaniards called him, Cañete built bridges and hospitals, established a viceregal court and guard, and brought the town councils more nearly under obedience.

But even in Cañete's time, formal government remained a secondary matter, compared to the informal structure of Spanish Peru. The same social trends continued as before, and the same people remained dominant in all walks of life—usually men who had the enormous prestige of being conquerors or first settlers. Only after Cañete did more basic changes begin to occur, as the hold of the first generation began to weaken. Therefore the terminal date for this study is the year 1560, the last of Cañete's rule. Indicative of the kind of change then going on is the appointment of some new types of people to the town council of Lima in 1561: a physician, a merchant, and three sons of conquerors.[2] The thirty-year period before 1560, and particularly the core of it, about 1538–55, constitutes a real unit, which may well be called the conquest period in a broad sense, the time when Peru was effectively occupied and included in the Iberian world.

Numerous sources, but above all the Peruvian notarial records, were searched through for the present study with the general purpose of determining who the settlers of Peru were and what they did. What resulted can be considered social history, and it is here organized into a series of chapters on various social groups. The categories, dictated by common sense rather than logic, follow closely the labels used by the Spaniards of the time, when they attempted to classify themselves in legal records, chronicles, and ordinary speech. Emphasis is on a broad picture of society rather than on social theories or concepts; a few rough and ready concepts such as "the seigneurial ideal" are merely tools of expression, meant to be defined mainly by their use in the body of the book. Each chapter aims to give a general description of the characteristics and functions of a group, as well as to outline the lives of some typical or otherwise significant individuals. The scheme comes close in many ways to a *vie quotidienne,* but mainly one will find here, rather than the furnishings, the architecture of men's lives, their careers in months and years rather than days.

Though organized by social groups, this study contains much material on the economy and other substantive matters. In the Spanish Indies even more than in most societies, function determined status; consequently, if one is interested in who the settlers were, there is no other way, and no better way, to describe them than to tell what they did. Each of the chapters therefore can be read as if, instead of being organized around a group, it were about that group's principal function. "Encomenderos" could be "The Encomienda System," and "Merchants," "Commerce."

But the book stops far short of being a total history of Peru from 1532 to 1560. It contains no systematic treatment of administrative, military, or intellectual history. These are matters which have received some, if not definitive, study in the past. A further limitation is the almost exclusive focus on an internal view of Peru and what the Spaniards did there. While some attention is given to the Spanish regional and social origins of the settlers of Peru, comparisons with Spain and other parts of the Indies cannot usually be made explicit, desirable though that would be. Presumably many or most of the developments here described have their origins and parallels elsewhere, but works on the other areas are not yet available, not even in the case of Spain itself.

The study perforce confines itself to Spanish Peruvian society proper, the world of the Spanish and the Hispanized, leaving out the great mass of Indians. Except for a short section summarizing the effect of the Spaniards on the Indian mass, Indians appear only insofar as they were a part of Spanish Peru. Unacculturated Indians lived apart from, though not unaffected by, the Hispanic society which was concentrated mainly in the cities, and, as a result, the archival sources which are the basis of this study contain little about them. Certainly the materials are lacking for the intimate view which the notarial archives make possible in the case of the Spaniards. For such a view of the Indians, different sources and different techniques are required, so that history and anthropology are once again, despite good will, split over the question of the written word. Meanwhile, until more sources appear, it makes sense to treat Spanish Peru and Indian Peru as separate entities, for they have continued for centuries to exist independently, and Peruvian history is the story of the action of the one upon the other.

The Indians in the Spanish towns, however, are a very different subject from the Indian mass. Though they stand out as the only people in Spanish Peruvian society (and therefore in this book) who were not intruders or the sons of intruders, their acculturation, beginning during the first generation, has a larger relevance to the book's main subject. Peru through the centuries was Hispanized to the extent that it was by example rather than by teaching, by bringing increasing numbers of Indians into direct daily contact with the Spanish life emanating from the cities. The Peruvian Indians living on the margins of Spanish society in the first thirty years after the conquest were the focal point of a process which was to transform the country. To study Spanish Peruvian society is to study not only a fascinating group important to the history of Spain and European expansion, but the principal instrument of the Hispanization of Peru.

II ENCOMENDEROS
AND
MAJORDOMOS

The encomienda, as is well known, was the basic instrument of Spanish exploitation of Indian labor and produce in the conquest period.* Since the encomienda system was also central to the economic and social organization of the Spaniards themselves, it is well to begin by telling who the powerful group of men holding the encomiendas were, and how the system functioned in Peru.

As scholars have already begun to realize, not every Spaniard in the Indies was an encomendero.[1] Generally Spanish governors and captains seem to have created the smallest number of encomiendas and the largest individual units feasible at any particular time and place. Where conditions were bad, that is, where difficult geography cut up the country into small fragments, where the Indians were organized in small political units and were therefore hard to control, the governors granted many small encomiendas. Where the Indians were organized

* An encomienda is generally described as a royal grant, in reward for meritorious service at arms, of the right to enjoy the tributes of Indians within a certain boundary, with the duty of protecting them and seeing to their religious welfare. An encomienda was not a grant of land. In Peru the grant came from the governor or viceroy, the crown taking no active part in the process, and particularly in the first years after the conquest, the terms of the grant went beyond the right to collect tributes, specifically entitling the encomendero or grantee to use the Indians in mines or agricultural enterprises. In practice, as will be discussed in the course of the chapter, grants were assigned not only to reward service at arms, though that was usually a prerequisite, but also for social and political considerations. And the encomenderos, leaping over technicalities, made their encomiendas the basis of great estates even if they did not legally own the land. Historically, the encomienda is situated on a line of development leading from the march lord domain of the European Middle Ages to the Spanish American hacienda or large estate of the seventeenth century and later.

in large political entities, making it possible to control a larger encomienda by using Indian traditional authority, the governors granted
whole regions to the most eligible individuals.

An abrupt change in the nature of encomienda grants occurred between the area of southern Central America, from which Peru was conquered, and Peru itself. The great city and province of Lima, encom-
passing at its founding perhaps a third of present-day Peru, had far
fewer encomiendas and encomenderos than the city of Panama, with
only a fraction of Lima's area and population and incomparably less
wealth. The determining factor in establishing the difference was not
Spanish policy, but the Inca empire. Within its borders, few and large
encomiendas were the rule. Outside it, the Spaniards reverted to small
and numerous encomiendas like those of Panama. Puertoviejo and Guayaquil, making up a relatively small, poverty-stricken, wet tropical
area, had nearly as many encomenderos as large provinces like Cuzco
or Lima. Chile, with its indomitable Indians, again had a dispropor-
tionately large number of encomiendas.

In the whole of greater Peru, including all the more closely inhabited
parts of twentieth-century Ecuador, Peru, and Bolivia, there were
never more than five hundred encomenderos, that number being substantially attained by 1540 and thereafter remaining quite stable. Whatever exact proportion of the Spanish population the encomenderos
represented, they were certainly a small minority. To give a rough
idea, the 500 encomenderos may be compared with at least 2,000
Spaniards in Peru in 1536, the time of the great Indian rebellion; with
contemporary estimates of between 4,000 and 5,000 Spaniards in Peru
in the mid-1540's, and with an estimated 8,000 in 1555.[2]

Where so much wealth was granted to so few men, its recipients naturally sought help in the work of tribute collection and exploitation. In
the area of former Inca domination, every encomendero had at least
one Spanish steward, called a majordomo, who resided among his Indians a large part of the year, to collect tributes and supervise other
enterprises carried out with cheap or free Indian labor on the encomienda. Large encomenderos had networks of servant-employees ad-
ministering a maze of economic undertakings, in which the common denominator was the land and population of the encomienda, for even
though all knew that the encomendero did not own the land, his monopoly on labor made the land of little use to anyone else. Hiring
Spaniards to exploit encomiendas naturally had social as well as eco-

nomic implications. In their own eyes as in the eyes of others, the encomenderos were something like feudal lords with a court of hired Spanish retainers and Indian vassals.

The first encomenderos of Peru were the members of the conquering expedition of 1530–32, and the first city founded was Piura or San Miguel, in 1532. Before going on with the main body toward Cajamarca, Pizarro left behind about forty Spaniards in Piura, mainly the older men and the sick, giving almost all of them encomiendas. The citizens of Piura therefore lacked the prestige and failed to get the riches which were the part of those who went on to Cajamarca. Older men already in 1532, many of them were long-time veterans, even original conquerors, of Panama and Nicaragua. By the mid-1540's Piura and neighboring Trujillo (where some of the more prestigious citizens of Piura had managed to transfer) were towns dominated by old married men.[3] Having missed their chance at Cajamarca, hardly any of them ever succeeded in getting an encomienda in richer areas like Lima, Cuzco, and Charcas.

In the other cities of Peru, as in Piura, the pattern of possession of encomiendas for many years reflected the historical circumstances of their founding, though in more central areas there was nothing like the almost complete fossilization of Piura.

Each of the 170 men involved in the capture of Atahuallpa at Cajamarca was entitled by his presence there to a good encomienda in a central area, if he desired one. Those of the men of Cajamarca who survived and stayed in Peru became the largest encomenderos of Lima and Cuzco (and later on Huamanga and Arequipa), and held posts of honor as alcaldes and city council members until they could no longer walk to the town hall. They came from all kinds of backgrounds except the high nobility. There were hidalgos of good standing and men from poorer families with some hidalgo connections. There were no less than ten trained notaries, most of them with some half-valid pretension to hidalgo rank. There were artisans and other plebeians: three tailors, a swordsmith, a sailor, a crier or executioner, two trumpeters. It was a group with an impressive degree of education among its leaders, but a strong overall numerical predominance of the humbler elements of Spanish society. Whatever their origins, their association with Cajamarca lifted these men into the highest rank. Many became encomenderos of Jauja, later Lima, while others preferred to take citizenship in Cuzco.

Shortly after Cajamarca a new group of around 200 men under Almagro arrived in Peru, apparently of much the same social composition as the first contingent. The new men, plus most of the veterans of Cajamarca, went on to take Cuzco and found a Spanish city there in 1534. The taking of Cuzco, with spoils as rich as those of Cajamarca, also had a transforming effect on the participants, though less strong than the miracle worked by that first decisive event. Cuzco was the last city founded in Peru where essentially all those who wanted encomiendas got them—not that literally everyone there became an encomendero, for Cuzco was founded with only eighty or ninety encomiendas. All along the way from Piura to Cuzco there were merchants and merchants' factors accompanying the conquest, men who did not expect and did not receive encomiendas. A still larger consideration was that the conquerors of Cuzco were so rich that a good number were willing to relinquish their claim to an encomienda in order to get license to return to Spain, where they could buy seats on the municipal councils of their home towns and live in splendor for the rest of their lives.

Up to this point, political considerations had not been of basic importance in the selection of encomenderos, since, given the small number of Spaniards, the immense size and wealth of the Inca empire, and the desire of many conquerors to return to Spain, any combatant who wanted an encomienda could get one. After Cuzco, politics came more into play. Francisco Pizarro and other governors after him gave the best and the largest number of encomiendas to their relatives, their aides, and men from their own regions in Spain—three criteria often united in one individual.

Pizarro's home region was primarily Trujillo, and by extension an area of northeastern Extremadura stretching from Plasencia in the north, through Trujillo and Cáceres, to La Serena in the south. Beyond these limits the Pizarros felt little regional affiliation, and Badajoz in western Extremadura was as least as foreign to them as Ciudad Rodrigo or Talavera de la Reina. Before he died in 1541, Pizarro had given the Trujillo region representation among the ranks of encomenderos far exceeding its numerical strength among the conquerors. Since there was a strong tendency for encomiendas to be perpetuated among friends and relatives regardless of legal succession, it is doubtful that the over-representation of the Trujillo region had been completely overcome even by 1560.

When Quito and Trujillo were founded in 1534 and 1535, the non-encomenderos already outnumbered the encomenderos. Also, the men responsible for giving out the encomiendas in these cases, Sebastián de Benalcázar and Almagro, were from Córdoba and Ciudad Real respectively, and cared nothing for Trujillo. This was one of the main reasons why Quito later became the area of strongest resistance to Gonzalo Pizarro's rebellion (1544–48).

The age of miracles was already over by 1536–37, the time of the country-wide Indian revolt. At Cuzco fewer than two hundred Spaniards stood off the whole remaining force of the Inca empire in its heartland, in an action more heroic and hardly less decisive than the capture of Atahuallpa. But though the participants long boasted of and were honored for their deeds, the event did not make encomenderos of those who were not. There were merchants, artisans, and notaries in the siege of Cuzco who long stayed in Peru practicing their trades, and no one became an encomendero merely because of his performance there.

Another element was added to the constantly rising standards for encomenderos when the group that accompanied Pedro de Alvarado to Peru began to receive encomiendas in the years 1535–38. While many of Alvarado's men were no different from the Spaniards already in Peru, they included a new social stratum, closer to the high nobility than anything seen previously. In the group were the first two men in Peru to bear the title "don" by birthright, don Gómez de Luna from Badajoz and don Pedro Portocarrero from Trujillo. Alvarado himself, who brought with him many relatives both near and distant, belonged to a distinguished family with branches in Badajoz and Burgos. The older branch in Burgos, though without the title of "don," was definitely considered a noble house, and members of it had worn the cross of Santiago. There was also a contingent of men from Badajoz, Alvarado's own region, who had connections with the court of the Count of Feria, a prominent nobleman of Western Extremadura. Garci Laso de la Vega, one of these, was a great-grandson of the first Count of Feria. With men like Garci Laso entering the competition for encomiendas, new arrivals of humble origins no longer had a chance.

The years 1537–38 saw further basic change in the process of granting encomiendas. The Pizarros won the battle of Salinas over Almagro, and for the first time encomienda grants were geared to conduct in the civil wars. Captains and other important men fighting on the side of the Pizarros were rewarded with new or better encomiendas, and the encomiendas of enemies were taken away. Only captains and cavalrymen were in serious running for new grants. Thenceforth, tales of encomiendas for infantrymen were told only to greenhorns.

No important new developments occurred then until the end of Gonzalo Pizarro's rebellion (1548), when the victorious Pedro de la Gasca carried out a major redistribution, a large number of Peru's encomenderos having been killed in the war. Gasca reassigned encomiendas all over Peru, with only one criterion, the importance of a given individual's contribution to his own campaign against Gonzalo Pizarro. Ignoring his home town, his retainers, and many of his supporters, Gasca gave the largest encomiendas to the former captains of Gonzalo Pizarro who had handed over Pizarro's fleet to him in Panama, making his campaign possible. The best encomiendas were now those in Upper Peru, near newly-discovered Potosí.

Peruvian Spaniards drew the obvious conclusions from Gasca's policy: until 1555, Peru saw a series of small and large mutinies, often deliberately started in order to be betrayed, in the hope that the traitors would be rewarded by encomiendas, as indeed they sometimes were. However, there were no large shifts until the arrival of Viceroy Cañete in 1556.

Viceroy Cañete (1556–60), without having the opportunity to reassign nearly as many encomiendas as Gasca did, still began a new era. He ended the policy of rewarding captains for destroying their own rebellions. He gave encomiendas to some of the old supporters of Almagro, whose seniority by this time earned them respect regardless of the side they had fought on. In Cañete's following was the largest contingent of high nobility yet to reach Peru, sons and nephews of counts or dukes. Cañete gave some of them encomiendas, raising the social standard for encomenderos as high as it could go. Now the only men eligible for encomiendas were courtly nobles, captains from the civil wars, and men in Peru since before 1540.

Another innovation of Cañete's was the relatively large-scale use of pensions. This had nothing to do with the New Laws. Though the king's allies always won in the civil wars, the king's legislation was soundly defeated, and Peruvian encomenderos continued, up to 1560 and long after, to be the well-nigh absolute masters of their encomiendas, making liberal use of all kinds of personal service by their Indians. Cañete's policy was of a more limited nature. Encomiendas fell vacant from time to time, and Cañete left some of them unfilled, appointing hired administrators to collect the tributes. He could then satisfy two or three individuals with pensions taken from the tributes of a single encomienda.

By 1560, the roll of encomenderos was a mixture of the new and the old. The imprint of Francisco Pizarro and the early conquest period was still visible; in Lima, fully half of the encomiendas were held by the same men, or sons of the same men, who held them in 1538. Next strongest was the effect of Gasca and the aftermath of the Gonzalo Pizarro rebellion. Having been originally appointed under such different circumstances, encomenderos were socially a very uneven group, but despite some friction treated each other as equals, because humble origin could be offset by seniority in the conquest. The most powerful and prestigious figures of the late 1550's were, predictably, those who combined seniority with good birth and education.

To list the criteria for picking encomenderos in Peru, then, they were: seniority in the conquest of Peru, social background in Spain, military action in the civil wars, and connections with the governors or the royal court. Standards for selection were constantly revised upwards after about 1536, when the quota of encomiendas was nearly filled and new claimants, of ever higher social degree, continued to arrive, attracted by Peru's reputation of wealth. But seniority never lost its primacy over all other considerations.[4]

A strong factor operating in the determination of encomenderos was a tendency to self-perpetuation, over and above the legal devices for inheritance. Legally, either an encomendero's legitimate heir or his wife could succeed in the encomienda. If the heir succeeded, continuity was assured, because the dead encomendero's friends and retainers, as guardians of the successor, would operate the encomienda as before. But in the case of complete vacancy, the encomienda was regranted to a new claimant, and if the encomendero was succeeded by his wife, custom and the insistence of the governors forced her to remarry quickly, her new husband becoming in effect the encomendero. When either of these things happened, strong pressures were brought to bear to assure that the new encomendero was a friend or relative of the old one, or at least someone from the same region in Spain.

In a sense a man did not hold an encomienda for himself alone, but also for a block of relatives, friends, and retainers who gained their living from it as he did. Removal of the encomendero from the scene meant that the whole group lost its livelihood, so there was naturally an attempt, often successful, to regain what was lost. An encomienda was also part of the rough balance of power in any given city between various political groupings, particularly groups based on Spanish towns or regions. When an encomendero from Trujillo died, other encomenderos from there would ask that he be replaced with one of their own.[5]

It is possible to give an account of how one group of Basques managed to hand on an encomienda from one to the other through three successions. The Basque Lope de Idiáquez was a figure of some importance who came to Peru after having held governmental posts in Santa Marta, and at some time before 1541 received an encomienda in Arequipa. In 1542, after the war against the younger Almagro, Idiáquez decided to return to Spain, and arranged for Governor Vaca de Castro to grant Idiáquez' encomienda to his friend, business associate, and fellow Basque, Miguel de Vergara.

After enjoying the encomienda in Arequipa for several years, Miguel de Vergara was killed in a battle against Gonzalo Pizarro in 1547. When peace came, the encomienda went to an infantry captain named Juan Pérez de Vergara, Miguel de Vergara's relative. Juan Pérez in turn soon fell mortally ill, and to keep the encomienda in the family, he resorted to a common legal trick. On his deathbed he married a young lady recently arrived from Spain, making her thereby his successor in the encomienda, and extracted from her a promise to marry Juan de Vergara, a relative of both the preceding encomenderos. The governor then granted the encomienda to Juan de Vergara, conditional upon his marriage to his relative's widow. At this point the stratagem failed. The young widow broke her promise to marry Juan de Vergara, marrying instead a man from her home town of Avila, and the encomienda was lost to the Vergaras and the Basques.[6]

From time to time various Spaniards, mainly disappointed aspirants, raised the cry that encomiendas were going into unworthy hands, by which they generally meant that artisans were becoming encomenderos. The attitude of the Spaniards toward artisans as candidates for encomiendas was complex, but, with some reservations, in the end flatly unfavorable. There were artisans among the men of Cajamarca who, transformed socially by their participation there, received large encomiendas. But for various reasons, within a very few years all of the known artisans either died or returned to Spain. During the short period of flux before the social situation became more rigid after 1537, other practicing artisans became encomenderos. The latest case to appear in the records is that of Pedro de Valmaseda, still a blacksmith in Lima in 1536, who received an encomienda in Quito.[7]

After 1537, there were still scattered examples of new artisan encomenderos, but only in a restricted meaning. The encomiendas they received were too small and poor to support even the principal recipient, much less the tribute collector and the houseful of guests without which a man was not really an encomendero. The only artisans who got larger encomiendas came from a special class. Silversmiths and armorers were highly skilled men, often wealthy and quite well educated, and it is not surprising that a few of them should have entered the ranks of encomenderos at a fairly high level, with incomes of as much as 1,000 pesos.[8]

In one way the Spaniards' attitude toward men of artisan background was relatively liberal. The actual practice of a mechanical trade in Peru itself generally excluded a person from consideration as an encomendero, but the mere fact of having come from a family of artisans and having received an artisan's training did not have such severe limiting significance, particularly in the 1530's. It is to be assumed that a good proportion of the original encomenderos of the major cities were of artisan stock. A Spaniard born of artisan parents could come to Peru, live for a time as someone's guest, buy a horse on credit, and go on the first expedition or campaign that offered itself, thus becoming a candidate for an encomienda, at least in some out-of-the-way region.

A pair of brothers living in Lima illustrates the sharp distinction the Spaniards made between potential and practicing artisans. Martín Pizarro, from Trujillo but no direct relative of Francisco Pizarro, was with the expedition of 1530–32, and took part as a footman in the events at Cajamarca. He received an encomienda in Lima, and went on to become an alcalde there on various occasions, despite his illiteracy. His brother, Juan Pizarro, came to Peru in his wake, by 1536 or 1537 at latest, and though there was nothing obvious to prevent Juan from associating himself closely with Martín and attempting to emulate him, he did not do so. Juan Pizarro set up a shop in Lima, and worked there as a shoemaker until he died in 1548. Of course Juan never received an encomienda, or any honorary posts. Juan's son became a merchant, while Martín's children were part of Lima's aristocracy. Since Spanish artisanry usually ran in families, there is hardly any doubt that Martín came from a family of shoemakers, and was probably trained as one. But neither did Juan's trade pull Martín down from his high position based on his presence at Cajamarca, nor did Martín's position suffice to lift Juan out of his status as an artisan, once he had so proclaimed himself.[9]

In Peru the ultimate scandal was the sale of encomiendas. The practice was so contrary to the ethos of granting encomiendas for meritorious service and so hideous in the eyes of those who failed to become encomenderos, that sellers, buyers, and the governors who permitted the sale did the utmost to hide what they were doing, but there is no doubt that on certain rather infrequent occasions encomiendas were sold. The most usual reason for sales was the permanent return of an encomendero to Spain, an event that did not occur in Peru every day. Most men who had the degree of success indicated by the possession of a good-sized encomienda had little desire to return to Spain permanently; they could be rich and respected in Spain, but hardly the masters of whole valleys and the most powerful men of their country, as they were in Peru. Though quite a few encomenderos went to Spain for a year or two with special permission, to see home again, to marry or bring their wives back, and to raise their relatives a notch in society by their new wealth and prestige, only a small minority decided to give up their encomiendas and return for good.

The sale of an encomienda generally took the legal form of selling its appurtenances at a greatly inflated price. One such transaction is known in some detail because a principal participant confessed to it. Captain Francisco de Godoy, a large encomendero of Lima and an important man in the conquest and civil wars, decided in 1542 to return to Spain, after having amassed great wealth. He sold some lots in Lima and two pieces of agricultural land, for 9,000 pesos, to two young men named Hernán González and Bernaldo Ruiz. The actual value of the lots and land was about 500 pesos. Captain Godoy then negotiated with Governor Vaca de Castro to get his encomienda granted, in halves, to González and Ruiz. In all probability Godoy gave the governor part of the 9,000 pesos.

González and Ruiz were not implausible candidates for encomiendas. They had been in Peru since 1535 or 1536 and had fought against both Indians and Spaniards. On the other hand, they were very young, had no particular social qualifications or military accomplishments, and were rather too directly involved in commerce, especially Ruiz, who in origin was doubtless a full-fledged merchant, though he never called himself that in Peru. By buying their way into the encomendero class, the two laid the groundwork for eventual great success. While their encomiendas, taken individually, were not large, and neither of them ever distinguished himself in the civil wars, they built up their wealth in various ways, spent money on charitable works, and by the early 1560's were two of the most honored citizens of Lima.[10]

A set of binding legal obligations was part of the framework of an encomendero's life. He was obliged to keep a horse and arms for defense against Indians or rebels, to reside in the city in whose jurisdiction his encomienda fell, and to maintain a house where he had to receive and feed guests when the need arose during military emergencies. These were serious duties, not the dead letters so often found in Spanish legislation. Even in the early days when the prices of horses were prohibitive, the authorities insisted that every encomendero have a horse, and sent a notary around periodically to inspect and make sure that those temporarily without a horse had definite plans to acquire one. In Lima in December, 1535, there were only seven encomenderos who for one reason or another had no horse.[11]

There was in any case very little problem in getting the encomenderos to fulfill their duties, because the duties were almost identical with their universal ambitions. The only trouble which arose had to do with the actual physical residence of the encomendero in his own city, for the highland encomenderos struggled to spend a good part of every year in Lima, so that the authorities had to be content with a rather lax fulfilment of the residence requirement.[12]

Central to both duties and ambitions of the encomendero was the *casa poblada*, an occupied or peopled house. This simple term meant something very definite to the Spaniards of the time. It implied a large house, a Spanish wife if possible, a table where many guests were maintained, Negro slaves, a staff of Spanish and Indian servants, and a stable of horses. The casa poblada was the largest single element in the dream of a lordly life which all Spaniards shared. Other things important to this ideal were fine clothing, ownership of agricultural land and herds of livestock, and holding office on the municipal councils.

Encomenderos in Peru began very early to realize this pattern of ambitions. Even before the great revolt of 1536 there were encomenderos, particularly in Piura and Trujillo, who had sent for their wives and children, built stone houses, and were growing Spanish varieties of plants on surrounding land. With the years, the establishments of en-

comenderos became ever more imposing. By 1553, one large encomendero of Lima was feeding forty people daily at his table.[13]

The encomenderos provided the framework for all Spanish social
and economic activity. A high proportion of the Spanish population
lived in the encomenderos' large compound houses; not only were
friends, relatives, and compatriots their more or less permanent
guests, but many other people lived on the premises as renters. The encomenderos' ostentatious spending was the life's blood of Spanish artisans and merchants. The labor of their Indians was essential to construction, agriculture, and mining. When any change of the encomienda system, such as the New Laws, was suggested, the Spaniards of
Peru replied with curious circular arguments which merely described
the system as it was; the encomenderos were so central that life could
not be imagined without them.[14]

To support their seigneurial life, encomenderos could rely on several
sources of income. Most basic were the produce and labor which their
Indians gave in tribute. (Nominal tribute income remained the usual
standard of value for encomiendas when they were assigned, rather
than size, number of Indians, or actual gross income. Anything falling
below 1,000 pesos yearly was generally sneered at. The ordinary large
encomendero would have a nominal revenue of perhaps 5,000 to 10,000,
though some had less. Captains and great encomenderos might have
revenues above 15,000, soaring after the opening of Potosí to as much
as 50,000 for certain prize encomiendas in Upper Peru.) But hardly
less important were what the Spaniards called *granjerías* or ancillary
enterprises, generally but not always agricultural in nature. An encomendero would, with approval of the municipal councils, acquire land
on his encomienda and raise either indigenous or Spanish products for
sale, using both tribute labor and the labor of slaves. Encomenderos
also invested money in the ventures of merchants and artisans, and
owned livestock and real estate, as properties which brought them both
income and prestige. And, of course, they participated both directly
and indirectly in mining. Whatever form an encomendero's activities
took, he operated all his interests as a single unit, giving some attention
to the coherence of the whole. The encomienda proper was often not
the largest element in an encomendero's prosperity. One encomendero
of Lima spent 6,000 or 7,000 pesos yearly to maintain his state, the tributes of his encomienda amounting to only 3,000 pesos.[15]

Encomenderos needed to find managers for their estates, but in the

first three or four years of the conquest, it was very hard to get anyone
to accept such work, since there were still so few Spaniards and such
unlimited opportunities for all. During this period many encomenderos
tried to alleviate their situation through "companies" or partnerships.
Partnership was a living institution among the Spaniards; they made
partnerships in every conceivable activity, from fighting to preaching.
Most common of all, in the early years, was a generalized partnership
between two relatives or long-time friends who lived and ate together
and owned all their property in common. Such partners often received
in common an encomienda which was not formally divided in any way.
Other partnerships in encomiendas were more deliberate arrangements
between two neighboring encomenderos, with the idea that when one
was away, the other could care for both their interests. The formation
of new encomendero partnerships soon stopped, as hired managers became available, but some of the old ones continued for many years.[16]

By 1539 at the latest, the great majority of encomenderos had at
least one steward or majordomo to administer their affairs, and large
encomenderos had several. In the 1530's and 1540's it was common for
the majordomo to get a percentage, varying from a sixth to a fourth, of
the net gain from the encomienda and subsidiary ventures. An increasing number, however, received fixed salaries. The single steward of a
small encomienda might receive 200 or 300 pesos a year; the chief majordomo of a large one could get 2,000 pesos or more. Whatever the
nominal salary, it was understood that the majordomo was free to use his
position to earn more on the side; one man with a 2,000-peso salary
earned 12,000 pesos in three years.

Some majordomos were, in a business sense, fully the equals of the
encomenderos they worked for, a relationship which expressed itself
formally in a partnership agreement. An encomendero of Huamanga,
Vasco Suárez, made a four-year agreement with Pedro del Peso, an
agriculturalist and small entrepreneur of Lima, in which Peso invested 4,000 pesos in cash and was to have full administration of Suárez'
encomienda, estates, and mines. All profits were to be divided equally.
By the late 1550's, some encomenderos were beginning to fall into the
hands of merchants. An encomendero of Arequipa, in order to give security for a large debt he owed to a company of merchants, fired his
majordomo and turned over the administration of his estate to the
merchants.[17]

As a social type, majordomos were an amorphous group. Generally they were of quite humble origins, but literate and able to keep accounts. Majordomos of large encomiendas were figures of some consequence, treated with respect and invited to the social functions of the great. But even the most powerful steward could hardly hope to become an encomendero, having in effect publicly declared himself another man's servant. This did not keep the majordomos from identifying themselves with the encomenderos' interests. When a group of angry encomenderos of Cuzco gathered at the town hall to protest against an ordinance on personal service, the most vocal of them was a majordomo whose employer was absent.[18]

Majordomos provided the Spanish Peruvian economy with a continuity which could not be expected from the often absent encomenderos themselves. It is clear from widely scattered references that even in the worst crises of the civil wars, most majordomos stayed at their jobs, and not merely because of their own or their employers' half-heartedness, but because it was necessary to maintain some control over the Indians and to collect the revenues that supported the wars. In war or peace, many majordomos had a free hand; the encomendero simply turned over the encomienda to the majordomo to get the most out of it he could.[19]

The activities of Diego Ramírez, who managed an encomienda in the Arequipa region in 1546-47, were probably not untypical of the way stewards operated, though he was working for a rebel governor instead of an ordinary encomendero. Like all majordomos, he had to spend a great deal of his time among the Indians. The encomienda had no mines, so Ramírez had to convert the Indians' products, mainly maize and Indian clothing, into revenue. Since the Indians' formal tributes were insufficient, hardly enough, Ramírez claimed, to keep his household going, he placed more emphasis on production organized by himself. Under his supervision, perhaps rather indirect, the Indians produced wheat as well as their traditional clothing and maize, and in March of each year Ramírez personally took a contingent of Indians to Potosí with products to be sold. To keep his operations running, Ramírez dealt directly with muleteers and merchants, even going into debt on occasion. From time to time he reported on his activities by letter, and whenever a sizable amount of money came into his hands, he sent it off to his employer through merchant channels, in lots of 1,000 to 2,000 pesos.[20]

A more specific manifestation of the majordomo was the *estanciero*.

Large encomiendas had several majordomos, and those whose main function was to care for herds of livestock or agricultural holdings were called estancieros after the *estancias* where they worked. Such men also collected tributes. It is apparent that practically no distinction was made between tribute collection and the encomendero's private endeavors, the main reasons for such endeavors being indeed to maximize tributes in a more or less legal fashion.

The estancieros were at the bottom rung of Spanish Peruvian society; while majordomos could be quite respected figures, estancieros were a despised class. Many of them emerged from other groups of low prestige, such as sailors, foreigners, and semi-foreigners; quite a few were from Portugal, Valencia, and the Canaries. Court testimony could be impugned on the sole ground that the witness was an estanciero and therefore mean and base.[21]

From the point of view of the Spaniards, who wanted to be in their cities as much as possible, the estancieros led a miserable existence, staying all year in some Indian village to see to a herd of goats, pigs, or cows. The everyday contacts of the estanciero were with the cacique, the Spanish priest (where there was one), and possibly a Negro, a mestizo, or a half-acculturated Indian. Estancieros' salaries were as low as their status, usually from 100 to 200 pesos.[22]

The agricultural estancieros were a somewhat different breed, including among their number gardeners and farmers who brought real skill to the cultivation of Spanish plant varieties. The properties where they worked could be on the encomiendas, but just as often were on land the encomenderos owned near the city, in which case the estanciero's whole manner of life was transformed. Men of this type were without doubt the originators of the intensive general agriculture, with Negro labor, which flourished near Lima, Arequipa, and other towns. The agricultural employees were ambitious to become independent, and by the 1550's some of them owned gardens, orchards, and grain fields near the cities.

Another type of employee often successful in becoming independent was the coca grower. Highland encomenderos, particularly in Cuzco, raised the Indian narcotic plant coca to be sold in Potosí, using the labor of encomienda Indians, under the supervision of Spanish estancieros. Estancieros on coca farms were not usually skilled, but the coca trade was so lucrative that they found it possible to save money and go into business on their own. Late in the period, some former estancieros had incomes from coca-growing which were equal to the revenue of a small encomienda.[23]

The activity most basic to the Spanish Peruvian economy was silver and gold mining, which encomenderos therefore naturally dominated. Though not all the people owning and operating mines were themselves encomenderos, the remainder were mainly their agents, friends, or relatives, and in any case they used the labor of encomienda Indians and fed their workers with produce coming from encomienda tribute. Many encomenderos had a miner in the same sense they had a majordomo, a man dedicated to searching out and exploiting whatever mineral wealth might be found on the encomienda.[24] But the bulk of mining was done at concentrated sites noted for their richness, a mountain in the case of silver, a river in the case of gold.

The act of discovery of a mining site did not have vast implications for the man who discovered it. The discoverer had only the privilege of staking out the best single vein or position. All the rest was distributed by the nearest municipal council, using political criteria. The council gave out sites first to council members, then to other encomenderos in order of importance, and then to the rest of the populace, if any sites were left.[25] Once in possession of their mines, the encomenderos often entered into company arrangements with mining entrepreneurs or merchants, in which the encomendero put up the mine and Indian labor, the other partner cash, mining equipment, and Negro slaves.[26] Whether the encomendero used the company device or not, actual direction of the mine was turned over to another person, the miner proper.

Miners are the most shadowy figures in the whole range of people who inhabited the Hispanic Peruvian world. In fact they hardly did inhabit that world, for they lived most of the time in remote mining sites or camps where the dense civil life of the cities was lacking. In the early period miners were often amateurs, or nearly so. A Sancho Tofiño, in Peru from 1538 to 1547, was one of the miners who discovered and opened up the Carabaya gold mines in 1542. He had been in Mexico, where he learned something about smelting, making furnaces, and prospecting. In Cuzco he instructed Spaniards, Indians, and Negro slaves in mining techniques, and acted as an assayer. For a time he made his living as a prospector, seeking out mines for encomenderos in return for a percentage of the output.[27] Placer mining for gold always remained an amateurish affair, in which untrained laymen, including tailors and barbers, could act as miners.[28]

Silver mining was more technical, and miners tended to be trained professionals, or at least men experienced with metals, like assayers, founders, silversmiths, or artillerymen. Among them were Germans, Flemings, and Greeks, but not enough is known to estimate what proportion of the total may have been foreigners. An expert silver miner might receive a salary of 1,000 pesos a year, or up to a fifth of the total output of metal. His chief duty, more than extraction, was to see to the building of furnaces and the smelting, refining, and assaying of the ore.[29]

The last of the satellites of the encomenderos were the merchants who made companies with them. Though not working for the encomenderos in a formal sense, such merchants were always the junior partners, investing less money and doing all the active work. In this type of partnership the encomendero sought to gain a large profit without appearing on the scene as an active merchant; the merchant sought to tap a source of capital and to gain influence in the municipal councils, which were dominated by the encomenderos and placed constant restrictions on the commercial population. Occasionally the merchant was a relative of the encomendero. Diego Gavilán, a great encomendero of Huamanga, and possibly himself from a merchant family, went into a large-scale commercial venture through his nephew, a declared merchant in Lima.[30]

To find a case typical of the diverse group of encomenderos is an impossible task; but the career of one encomendero, Jerónimo de Villegas, reveals some significant patterns. Villegas was from Burgos, of a family which had achieved a certain prominence, but was not a noble house like the Alvarados of that region. There was a Villegas from Burgos playing a significant role as a merchant in the Antilles as early as 1510. Jerónimo had a nephew named Antonio de Villegas, who was accountant general for the Council of the Indies around 1560; another relative, Jerónimo's namesake, held the post of accountant general in Chile in 1557. All in all, the evidence indicates that Jerónimo de Villegas was a member of one of those families of Burgos who through wealth, marriage, and education transformed themselves in the course of the sixteenth century from merchants into government functionaries and hidalgos. Just how far down that road the Villegases had traveled is a matter for speculation, but accounting, the family specialty, was the type of government work most closely associated with commerce. In Peru, at any rate, Jerónimo de Villegas always claimed to be an hidalgo, and was accepted as such by all, including other Spaniards from Burgos. He was, at the very least, a literate man from a merchant family with hidalgo pretensions.

When Villegas came to Peru in 1536, he was something over 30 years of age; he seems to have been born around 1504. His age at various stages is an interesting, and not unrepresentative, aspect of his career. At the time he got his first encomienda in 1542, he was perhaps 38 years old; when he acted as cavalry captain in a civil war battle in 1547, he was about 43; when he was made corregidor of Arequipa in 1554, he must have been about 50. Spaniards considered that the prime of life was the age period 30 to 45, not only for administrative tasks, but also for military leadership and even single combat.

Villegas did not arrive in Peru penniless. He already had his own horse and arms in the year 1536–37, when those items were at a premium. In 1538 he accompanied Captain Alonso de Alvarado, like himself from Burgos, on an expedition of discovery and conquest to the province of Moyobamba. Because of Villegas' money and equipment, family name, and the Burgos connection, Alvarado made him one of the expedition's junior captains.

The Moyobamba venture failed to uncover any Indians who could be distributed in encomiendas, so Villegas tried again, accompanying Gonzalo Pizarro on the Amazonian expedition of 1540–42. While they were in the jungles, there was occasion for Villegas to use a very special skill he possessed, for he dabbled in astrology and dream interpretation, and people often called him simply Villegas the astrologer. Gonzalo Pizarro had a vivid dream which Villegas interpreted in a way that later appeared to be a veiled prophecy of Francisco Pizarro's assassination. Villegas emerged from the expedition, which failed notoriously, still without an encomienda, but closely allied to the powerful figure of Gonzalo Pizarro.

Since the men returning from the Amazon in 1542 had missed a whole episode of Peru's civil wars, the campaign of Governor Vaca de Castro against the younger Almagro, they also failed to profit from the distribution of encomiendas which took place at the end of the war. If Villegas had been in Peru proper during the campaign, he would certainly have been a captain or prominent cavalryman on Vaca de Castro's side, and would have received a good encomienda in a central area. As it was, he still managed to enter the ranks of the encomenderos, but only marginally and indirectly.

After recuperating in Quito from his Amazonian experiences, Villegas started out for the headquarters of the governor in Cuzco. On the way he had occasion to stop in Piura, where he found in residence a doña María Calderón, a relative of Dr. Robles of the Audiencia of Panama; her husband had just died, leaving her a small encomienda. Only months after her husband's death and weeks or days after Villegas arrived in Piura, she married him, and Villegas became in effect an encomendero, though he received no legal title.

Exactly what was behind the marriage can only be surmised. While Governor Vaca de Castro may have given his approval, as a gesture to placate Gonzalo Pizarro, the speed of the marriage indicates it may have taken place over Vaca de Castro's head. A widow who succeeded in an encomienda could not remain unmarried, but she had some discretion in picking a mate, and a *fait accompli* was irreversible. Doña María may have been influenced by the fact that Villegas was already at this time a wealthy man, the owner of slaves, livestock, and land. With business sense, a little capital, and influential friends, it was possible to gain wealth in Peru even without an encomienda. Villegas probably kept his livestock at little or no expense on the encomienda of some friend or compatriot like Alonso de Alvarado. One of his main economic activities was money-lending, in quite large amounts of 750 or 1,500 pesos.

Not satisfied with his half-title to a small encomienda in Piura, Villegas went on in 1543 to Cuzco, to court Governor Vaca de Castro. He was well received, living in the governor's house and going on official tours of inspection, but he did not achieve his primary aim, a better encomienda. When Viceroy Blasco Núñez Vela arrived in 1544, Villegas hurried to Lima to press his claims there, and gained the viceroy's confidence.

In late 1544 the rebellion of Gonzalo Pizarro began to take shape in Cuzco. One of the viceroy's measures against it was to send Villegas to Huánuco to gather men and arms. Instead, Villegas was instrumental in the desertion of the men of Huánuco to Gonzalo Pizarro, giving his cause an impetus it then badly needed. Pizarro, when he shortly came to power, sent Villegas to Piura as his lieutenant. In 1545, as Pizarro was coming north in pursuit of the viceroy, he awarded Villegas an encomienda in Cuzco, and allowed him to go back south to take possession of it, while Pizarro and his force continued northward. In this way Villegas avoided the most incriminating episode in the whole history of the civil wars, the battle near Quito in early 1546 where Pizarro's men defeated and killed the viceroy of Peru. Villegas probably was hoping to avoid too close an identification with Pizarro's cause; Pizarro hoped that he was leaving behind a trustworthy follower who would help to keep central Peru under his control.

Villegas had hardly settled down in Cuzco with his wife in 1545 when he decided to move again. With approval of the rebel officials, he arranged to trade Indians with an encomendero of Arequipa, and moved to Arequipa to live. According to one chronicler, Villegas moved because he had a premonition that his wife would meet a violent death in Cuzco, as she subsequently did. Villegas' practice of astrology lends some plausibility to the explanation, but it is also possible that Villegas preferred Arequipa's climate, or just thought the trade advantageous.

The counter-rebellion against Gonzalo Pizarro which spread across southern Peru in the spring of 1547 thus found Villegas in Arequipa. In June, 1547, Arequipa rose against Pizarro's lieutenant, and Villegas was picked as captain general from among several candidates, apparently in an attempt to convince Pizarro that his best friends were turning against him. Villegas led the men of Arequipa to join the main counter-insurrectionary force, and fought against Pizarro at the battle of Huarina as a captain, at the head of a company of cavalry made up mostly of encomenderos of Arequipa.

Huarina was a disaster. Villegas was wounded and had to escape across country to join the royal forces gathering under Gasca in the north. His wife was taken by force from Arequipa to Cuzco, and there executed by Pizarro's men as a terroristic measure. One of his two children died.

Villegas accompanied the final campaign of Gasca against Pizarro in 1548, though he did not receive a captaincy, because the army had been organized before he arrived. Still, his leadership in the Arequipa uprising was not forgotten, and in August, 1548, Gasca awarded him one of the largest encomiendas in Arequipa. It was no coincidence that the encomienda, Tarapacá, had belonged to the lieutenant of Pizarro whom Villegas had overthrown.

In the early 1550's Villegas lived in great state in Arequipa, with frequent trips to Lima. On the occasion of the rebellion of Francisco Hernández Girón in 1553, he briefly held the post of corregidor of Arequipa, playing a rather ambiguous role reminiscent of his action in the great Pizarro rebellion. Villegas' health was failing, and he died in Lima in 1555, leaving his estate to his seven-year-old daughter, doña Ana de Villegas. Though doña Ana's guardian married her to the nephew of a judge of the Audiencia in order to reinforce her claim to succeed in the encomienda, it reverted to the same man who had lost it years before. Villegas also left a mestizo son, Pedro Ruiz de Villegas, to whom he bequeathed the fairly substantial amount of 2,000 pesos.

The encomienda of Tarapacá and Arica was one of the largest in the jurisdiction of Arequipa, taking in the whole northern part of twentieth-century Chile. Measured on a country-wide scale, it would be only medium large, since many of the grants in Cuzco and Charcas far surpassed it in population and wealth. During the seven years Villegas held Tarapacá, he ran the encomienda as a well-organized economic unit, exploiting its diverse possibilities systematically.

In charge of the whole operation was a head majordomo, who also had the special duty of supervising the operation of eight *chácaras* or farms which Villegas had legal title to, most of them located on the encomienda. The chácaras produced mainly maize, wheat, and barley, and were cultivated by Negroes and *yanaconas* (non-tribute-paying Indian servants) using oxen. Another majordomo resided in Tarapacá, the main Indian town, collecting tributes, trading with the Indians, and selling provisions to passers-by at Tarapacá's *tambo* or inn. Once a year the resident at Tarapacá took a party of Indians on the 250-mile trip to Potosí to sell produce. In another valley on the encomienda, Villegas had a Spaniard caring for about 250 cattle, a thousand goats, 200 Spanish sheep, and an unknown number of pigs. A Spanish miner worked the silver mines near Tarapacá, with the help of some of Villegas' twenty Negro slaves, who included blacksmiths and silver refiners.

Transportation to and from the encomienda was not neglected. In 1548 Villegas tried unsuccessfully to buy a ship in Lima. Finally he settled on an arrangement which not only gave him steady access to his encomienda by sea, but allowed him to exploit the fishing that went on in the waters off its shores. He bought a one-third interest in a company owned by some Spaniards, who with two boats and Negro slaves were fishing along the southern coast and selling the dried fish in Arequipa. Under the arrangement, the fishermen received their food and supplies from the encomienda Indians; they were obliged to transport provisions out of the encomienda for Villegas' table, and mining tools and other supplies into it, as well as to carry personnel whenever needed.

In Arequipa, Villegas lived in a large Spanish-style house with patio and *zaguán*, in which he could quarter fifty men at a time. The house's rich wall hangings and table covers, its golden ornaments and silver utensils, must have been impressive in the big rooms bare of all but the simplest furniture. In addition to his residence, Villegas owned two other compounds of houses in Arequipa, which he rented out for income.

At any given time, Villegas' staff of Spanish servants and stewards must have totaled about ten men. Most of these would change quite rapidly—the resident at Tarapacá was new almost every year—but Villegas' head majordomo, Iñigo de Bocanegra, was with him for the whole seven years. Bocanegra was from Burgos, like Villegas, and probably of partly Italian descent. His salary arrangements were quite complicated; he received 300 pesos a year, one fourth of the yield of all the agricultural work he supervised on the chácaras, and the right to enter into companies with third parties on his own. In the latter case, Villegas received half the profits. Since Villegas actively directed his own affairs, Bocanegra did not have a completely free hand as some majordomos did. Nevertheless he bore great responsibility, and had Villegas' complete confidence. At the time of his death, Villegas owed Bocanegra 5,000 pesos, yet did not hesitate to make him one of the executors of his will. After Villegas died, Bocanegra became an entrepreneur of Lima. In 1557 he was appointed provisioner of a large fleet going to Chile, and in 1560 was prominent enough to head Lima's protest against price-fixing on slaves.

Villegas' retinue did not stop with his stewards. He maintained one and sometimes two priests on his encomienda to indoctrinate the Indians. And above all, he was always surrounded by relatives, his own and his wife's, the names of five of whom are known. The most important were Diego de Villegas, who took possession of Tarapacá in Villegas' name; Cristóbal de Villegas, who was connected with the encomienda for many years; and Juan de Villegas, a nephew. Juan was in a different class from the others, too nearly an equal to be satisfied with a subsidiary role. He came to Peru in 1551 with a royal cedula of recommendation, definitely hoping to become an encomendero. Jerónimo sent him off to serve as an aide to the then Marshal Alonso de Alvarado, his long-standing associate and Burgos compatriot. Juan, failing to achieve his ambitions, settled down in Lima as a permanent claimant for honors and repository for his uncle's cash; at one time he had 5,000 pesos belonging to Jerónimo. After Jerónimo's death, Juan finally obtained a post as a gentleman cavalier of the newly created viceregal guard, so that the name of Villegas lived on for a time in Peru.[31]

The life of Jerónimo de Villegas shows how the civil wars were compatible, to a degree, with peaceful development, how intrigue, adventure, and the bizarre could be combined with methodical and purposeful economic activity in the life of a single man. However, what in Villegas was an intelligent exploitation of all the economic possibilities, was in other cases merely the unenthusiastic carrying out of a set pattern of behavior. Regardless of the characteristics of the terrain or climate, encomenderos insisted on having livestock and herders, mines and miners. Near Potosí they kept herds which died off as fast as they could be replenished; in Piura they continued to hire prospectors. What was of ultimate importance to them was not the viability of their enterprises, but the prestige accompanying certain possessions. Though they welcomed a profit and did everything possible to maximize it, particularly on a short-term basis, they desired wealth only for ostentatious, prestige-bringing spending, and to create patrimonies for the honor of their lineages.

Any time after 1538, the encomenderos of Peru were a widely varying group, reflecting faithfully the historical vicissitudes of the conquest and the civil wars, and also the immensely varied and constantly changing composition of the Spanish population that occupied Peru. Every social stratum, and every region of Spain, must have contributed at least a few encomenderos to Peru. Whatever their backgrounds, all the encomenderos tried in some measure to realize the same specifically outlined social and economic ambitions for a seigneurial life, ambitions shared by the whole Spanish population, but which only the encomenderos could fully achieve. In this as in other ways the encomenderos were the center of the Spanish Peruvian world. They were not, however, all of that world, and particularly essential to their wealth and power were the stewards, more numerous than themselves, who managed their affairs and collected their revenues.

III NOBLEMEN

It is notorious that the high nobility of Spain did not conquer the Indies. As one old veteran of the Peruvian conquest, Juan García de Hermosilla, wrote,

this country of Peru was not won, nor was any blood spilled here, by dukes or counts or people titled "don" or relatives of royal judges, because they didn't come in the time of danger, but by Pedro Alonso Carrasco and Juan de Pancorbo and Juan Fernández and Alonso Martín de Don Benito and Pedro Elgarro and other peasants and ordinary hidalgos, and by Juan García de Hermosilla.[1]

Nevertheless, certain members of the class of Spanish high nobility did come to Peru. They missed Cajamarca and the taking of Cuzco, but began to arrive almost immediately thereafter; some went to Chile with Almagro. Each new governor arriving in Peru brought a contingent of noblemen as part of his following; courtiers who were penniless or out of favor got the king's permission to leave the court and try their luck in Peru. From 1535 to 1548, noblemen were increasingly important in the conquest and civil wars as individuals, and by 1550 they had to be reckoned with as a group.

The Spaniards were such masters of fine social distinctions, and Spanish social history is as yet so little advanced, that before discussing the nobility of Peru, some treatment of Spanish and Spanish Peruvian social terminology is necessary. The Spanish terms for indicating degrees of nobility were in a state of considerable decay by the sixteenth century. A true high noble referred to himself as a *caballero hidalgo,* a cavalier and hidalgo, but this alone did not suffice to define him, for hidalgos far down the scale, particularly those with military accomplish-

34

ments, called themselves the same. Because of the peculiar Spanish hunger for nobility, the term "hidalgo" had come to be applied to many people who in another country would have been considered substantial members of the middle classes. The term *escudero* or squire, which overlapped with "hidalgo" but connoted subservience to a higher nobleman, was dropping out of currency in the first half of the century. It was still used in Panama around 1520, and a few veterans of Panama still called themselves escuderos in the first days of the conquest, but after 1535 the word was no longer heard. This left "hidalgo" with such a wide field of reference that it was, by itself, of little use in defining social status. In Peru, though peasants and artisans were extremely reluctant to claim the name, even if they became prominent citizens, the whole upper segment of Spanish Peruvian society, perhaps a third of all the Spaniards, considered themselves hidalgos. To define his social background at all adequately with the traditional terms, a Spaniard needed about a paragraph, in which he would modify the terms and refer to his actions, morals, and religious character in such a fashion that an experienced judge could place him quite well.

The points of departure for the high nobility in Spain were the royal court and the courts of several great dukes and counts, by far the most important of these, for Peru, being the court of the Duke of Medina-Sidonia in Seville. From the courts, nobility emanated outward, with no definite stopping place. Counts and dukes married their daughters to small feudal lords with lesser titles or without title, and these in turn married into locally prominent families, producing a fluid hierarchy of people with some claim to high nobility. In describing the noblemen who accompanied Almagro to Chile, the chronicler Oviedo establishes a descending order of sons of titled lords, sons of *mayorazgos* (holders of entailed estates), relatives of lords, and hidalgos of lesser rank.[2]

The best mark of the true high noble was the title "don." Centuries of indiscriminate use of that title, both in Spain and America, have obscured the fact that in the mid-sixteenth century the term still had a definite meaning. For the whole generation that conquered and held Peru, the title "don" remained the prerogative of direct descendants of high Spanish nobility, and of those who held certain high governmental and ecclesiastical offices. The original meaning of the word, "lord," still had some force, it being above all the attribute of dukes, counts, and other feudal lords. By the sixteenth century, custom had loosened to the point that anyone whose father was called don could himself use the title. This was a mechanism which could in a few generations have spread the "don" to the whole Spanish population, but it had not yet proceeded very far in the period 1530–1560. Almost all of Peru's dons were sons, grandsons, or nephews of some feudal lord.

The "don" could also be transmitted through the maternal side, a procedure on the face of it perfectly valid, since the title "doña" was merely the feminine equivalent of "don". A strange fact of Spanish social practice, however, made inheritance of the title through the mother a little dubious. Spaniards had for many years used "don" more conservatively than "doña." While the title "don" established a presumption of close relation to some feudal lord, almost all women of any prominence were called "doña." Doñas must have been from five to ten times as numerous in Spain as their male counterparts. Even in Peru, with so many more men than women, "doña" was the more common term by far. The sons of an ordinary local hidalgo would be untitled, but his daughters were doñas. The use of "doña" indeed comes close to overlapping completely with "hidalgo," but actually "hidalgo" was somewhat broader. There were some petty or recent hidalgos whose women were not doñas, and usage seems to have been more strict in some areas of Spain than in others. The mother of Hernando Pizarro was not a doña, even though the Pizarros were feudal lords of a small village to the south of Trujillo.[3] "Doña" is, nevertheless, a useful tool in arriving at estimates of social rank during the period of the first half of the sixteenth century. If a man's mother and sisters were doñas, it is almost certain that he was an hidalgo of good standing; if not, it is still possible that he was some kind of an hidalgo, but not a very high-ranking one.

The widespread use of "doña" meant that there was no distinction in title betweeen the daughter of a duke and the daughter of a municipal council member of some provincial city. If the duke's daughter married an hidalgo without a "don," in order to transmit her father's "don" to the grandson, all concerned had to remember that her title of "doña" was something special. The most firmly established dons were those whose father and both of whose grandfathers were dons; next, those whose father and paternal grandfather were dons; and last in line, those who had no other claim than that their maternal grandfather was a don. A good many of Peru's dons were of this latter type; they were the sons of fathers who were important hidalgos, but not dons, and mothers who came from really high nobility. For example, don Miguel,

don Martín, and don Pedro de Avendaño, three brothers in Peru and
Chile at various times, were the sons of Martín Ruiz de Avendaño,
who was a nobleman and the head of two noble houses, but did not
bear the title "don." The brothers derived their right to the title from
their mother, doña Isabel de Velasco, daughter of the Duke of Frías.[4]

Whatever the basis for a nobleman's claim to the title of "don," it
was an invariable element of his name. In this as in other matters, sixteenth-century usage varied profoundly from that of the twentieth
century. Today "don" is an optional courtesy title, almost always omitted on occasions of ultimate seriousness. In the sixteenth century it
could never be omitted, even in baptismal documents or testaments.
Don Martín de Avendaño y Velasco usually titled himself only don
Martín de Avendaño, and could be called just don Martín without dis-
respect, but to omit the "don" was unthinkable, even in ordinary conversation. So ingrained was this custom in the Spaniards that they
would refer to "Antonio de Ribera" and "don Antonio de Ribera" without its ever occurring to them that anyone might not realize two people
were involved.

Once the important principle of invariability of usage is established,
some exceptions may be admitted. At the time of the greatest success
of Gonzalo Pizarro's rebellion, in the years 1544 to 1546, there was a
great deal of extravagant talk about crowning Pizarro as king and making dukes and counts of his captains. In this spirit, and half in jest,
Hernando Bachicao, one of Pizarro's greatest supporters, called himself
Count don Hernando Bachicao, and Pizarro's lieutenant in Arequipa
was once referred to as Adelantado don Pedro de Fuentes.[5] No one
ever seriously addressed these men as "don;" not even Gonzalo Pizarro
himself ever laid any claim to that title.

It could also occur (Thayer Ojeda points out an example) that a
young man with the right to use the title came to Peru poverty-stricken
or with few acquaintances, and refrained from calling himself "don"
until he had wealth and a position consonant with his title.[6] What happened essentially was that the nobleman remained incognito for a time.
Once assumed, the "don" was an invariable element.

Uncertainty of usage did creep in with the ceremonial "don" that accompanied certain high titles. The titles of Adelantado and Marshal
carried with them the right to use the "don," but no one was sure
whether the "don" adhered more to the man, and therefore had enno-
bling social significance, or to the office. Peruvian Spaniards proved

rather more conservative than the royal chancellery in this matter. Whereas the Spanish court always included a "don" with the title Marshal as a matter of course, Marshal Alonso de Alvarado did not usually call himself "don" (although he was one of the most presumptuous men in Peru), and his contemporaries could never quite decide whether to do so or not; sometimes they would change their minds about it in the course of a single letter. Pascual de Andagoya held the title of Adelantado as governor of a region to the north of Peru, but he apparently took the view that the title applied only when he was actively governing, for in Peru he used neither Adelantado nor don. In any case, men holding these titles had to use the full title if they wanted to make use of the "don;" that is, Andagoya had to say "Adelantado don Pascual de Andagoya" and could not be called just "don Pascual," like a born nobleman.[7]

Only the two great old men of the Peruvian conquest, Francisco Pizarro and Diego de Almagro, received the compliment of having their countrymen call them simply "don Francisco" and "don Diego," which meant that in the public mind they had truly become the equals of the high nobility. It was primarily Almagro who was called in this manner, not because there was less respect for Pizarro, but because Almagro never quite held a title or position corresponding to his true rank, while Pizarro was called first "the governor" and then "el Marqués."

Holders of high ecclesiastical office also had the right to use a ceremonial "don." With bishops and archbishops the right was undisputed and invariable; the title of the archbishop of Lima was "don fray Jerónimo de Loaysa, arzobispo de Los Reyes," and the "don" carried real weight, but nevertheless, Loaysa was always called "the archbishop," and never "don Jerónimo," though "don fray Jerónimo de Loaysa" was possible. Lesser dignitaries such as deans, treasurers, archdeacons, and canons, were sometimes allowed a purely formal "don" to accompany their titles, but this was optional and the "don" could under no circumstances be used apart from the title.

If the Spaniards of the conquest were very reticent about appropriating titles to themselves, they lost much of their reticence when it came to their sons. The first slight indications of this appeared with the sons of the Adelantados. Though the "don" of the Adelantados was so strictly tied to their office that even the titleholders could not use it freely, and it certainly was not inheritable, the sons of Adelantados were regularly called "don." The first of these was don Diego de Almagro, Almagro's mestizo son, but Almagro was an exceptional case in every way. Another was don Antonio de Garay, in Peru from 1541, son of Francisco de Garay, who had held the title of Adelantado in the Caribbean.[8]

Giving the "don" to sons of Adelantados was really only a minor change, hardly a cheapening at all; the crown had always given the title to new noble houses. A major devaluation came only in the 1550's when sons of Peru's encomenderos began to reach maturity and claim a right to the "don." Apparently the encomenderos made an analogy between their sons and the hereditary nobility of Spain, as groups inheriting great feudal estates. Why the sons of some encomenderos took the title and others did not, remains unknown. Many young men who inherited large encomiendas did not become dons, even though descended of well-born parents on both sides. Some of those who did take the title had no apparent qualifications. The son of Francisco de Londoño, who had far from the largest encomienda in the area of Quito, and whose wife was not even a doña, became don Juan de Londoño.[9]

Even with this major change in the meaning of "don," it is not to be thought that the Peruvian Spaniards became completely irresponsible in its use. No one except the son of an encomendero was eligible, and even there a strange process of consensus was at work which allowed the title in some and denied it to others. The new dons also retained a curious conservatism and honesty of usage about their forbears; that is, they did not confer titles on their fathers and grandfathers ex post facto. Though it was somewhat humiliating, don Juan de Aliaga freely admitted that his father was just Jerónimo de Aliaga, and his grandmother plain Isabel de Zamora, this last a pretty violent contrast.[10] The practice of transcribing unchanged the names of past generations long continued. Garcilaso de la Vega, writing in the early seventeenth century, still retained the usage of the age of the conquest perfectly, when discussing that period. Only later in the seventeenth century did genealogists begin to confer posthumous "dons" on the ancestors of prominent people, something they still do, to the detriment of social history.

The true dons, the men who came from Spain already bearing the title by birthright, may be considered the contribution of Spain's high nobility to the conquest and occupation of Peru. It was not a great contribution. All the true dons in Peru up to 1560 probably did not much exceed 150 in number. They were undeniably from the fringes of their class, third sons of small feudal lords or the grandsons of counts, all of them poor and some of them illegitimate. Nevertheless, they were perfectly capable of transmitting the customs and values of the high nobility; the youngest son was as much a member of his class as the firstborn who received the patrimony, and many of Peru's nobles had lived in the royal court or the courtly atmosphere of Seville.

In the 1530's, dons were so rare in Peru that they found little difficulty in receiving encomiendas, provided they wanted to stay in the country. About five or six of them were granted encomiendas in the early years, and began careers little different from those of other encomenderos. Those who lived on into the 1550's had a kind of prestige which could not be matched, combining as they did high nobility with seniority in the conquest.

The arrival of a high nobleman in Peru in the 1530's was a momentous occasion. When don Alonso Enríquez de Guzmán, from Seville, came to Peru in 1535, he was one of certainly less than ten dons then in the country, and a knight of the order of Santiago. As he approached Lima, the whole population came outside the town to greet him, an honor generally reserved for bishops, governors, and viceroys. Francisco Pizarro gave don Alonso 2,000 pesos to help him meet expenses. In Cuzco, Hernando Pizarro made him the nominal second in command during the siege of that city.

Don Alonso Enríquez was a very unusual man, definitely pathological in some ways, but in other ways more typical of Spanish court nobility in Peru than his fellows who settled down to help occupy the country. He was the only Spaniard in Peru in the whole period 1532–60 who is known to have written a volume of memoirs, or diary, a book which unfortunately for many years spread confusion more than it divulged information, because it was taken to be a variety of picaresque novel. Gradually scholars saw that the work was authentic, as it indubitably is, but misleading conceptions of it were left over from the social implications of the genre of the picaresque. Even Raúl Porras, the best critic of the chroniclers, was still dominated by such ideas, calling don Alonso a bastard nobleman, in the face of the fact that both don Alonso and his father were legitimate, and the distant illegitimacy in his family involved kings and dukes, with whom even an illegitimate connection was an honor. In the character of his person don Alonso bore some resemblance to a pícaro, but there is no comparison between the social position of don Alonso Enríquez de Guzmán, knight of

Santiago, personal acquaintance of the Spanish king,, and a pícaro's rock-bottom social status. Don Alonso was in every way a valid representative of Spain's high nobility, except that he was quite desperately poor, in the sense that he could not live in the proper state on his income.

It was to remedy this situation that don Alonso came to Peru. His stated purpose was to get rich quickly and return to live a more honored life in Spain, that being the ambition of the great majority of Peru's nobles:

My intention is to bring back 4,000 ducats or 40,000, depending on the lay of the land. If it turns out 4,000, I'll take a thousand and repair my houses and increase my flock of sheep, because I have 500 and they tell me that I should have a thousand, because 500 cost just as much to maintain and bring less profit; another thousand ducats to redeem my life grant of 70,000 maravedis in income, to get 14, 15 or 20 per cent out of it if possible; 1,500 ducats to buy a seat on the council of Seville; and the remaining 500 ducats to buy horses, hose and shirts. If it turns out to be 40,000 ducats, things will go as they desire, because I won't presume to force and subjugate such a multitude.

The noble courtier, then, desired just the same type of seigneurial life as other Spaniards (a large house, livestock, position on a municipal council, fine clothes), but the nobleman was more than ordinarily determined to enjoy it in Spain, near the court of Valladolid or Seville.

In the civil wars, don Alonso was an unsettling influence. The king of Spain did him an injustice in assuming that he was the sole root cause of all the conflict; he was, nevertheless, utterly out of place in Peru's civil wars, which, particularly in the 1530's, were fought by grim, taciturn, realistic men over the basic issue of who was to have Peru. Don Alonso treated the whole affair as if it were a rivalry between two court cliques for the favor of the king; he talked and whispered interminably, and wrote long letters full of puns, conceits, and subtle taunts. When don Alonso returned to Spain in 1539, he had marked out a trail which many courtly nobles were to follow after him.[11]

As more and more dons arrived in the course of the 1540's and 1550's, the Peruvian Spaniards became somewhat more inured to them, and the recognition given dons was channeled into certain special areas. Aside from being prime candidates for encomiendas, they were given captaincies in the civil wars if they had the slightest military ability, and they were frequently chosen to be envoys to governors or to the royal court.

Still, the old patterns persisted. The equivalent of don Alonso Enríquez in the 1550's was don Martín de Avendaño (whose ancestry is given above, p. 37). Don Martín was a Basque nobleman and a gentleman of the royal court who came to Peru in 1550 in the footsteps of his sister, the wife of Peru's Marshal Alonso de Alvarado. From 1551 to 1556 he rejected one generous offer after another from governors in Peru and Chile, as not commensurate with his rank and merits. Finally, to get rid of him, Viceroy Cañete paid don Martín 8,000 pesos in a lump sum and he returned to Spain, complaining.[12]

Even holding encomiendas did not cure the dons of their tendencies. Don Pedro Luis de Cabrera, a nobleman of Seville who was in Peru from 1542 to 1556, was a caricature of a loquacious *bon vivant*. Years of overeating and drinking had made don Pedro so fat that five half-grown boys could stand comfortably inside one of his doublets. He kept jesters, and loved to tell and listen to ribald tales; he used to retire to his large encomienda in the Cuzco region with twenty friends, relatives, and servants, to carouse for months at a time. Though his girth would not suffer him to mount a war-horse, don Pedro was a cavalry captain in the Gasca campaign of 1548, on the strength of his birth and political influence.

After the war his son-in-law, an encomendero of La Paz, returned to Spain as Gasca's messenger, leaving don Pedro to care for his encomienda, but don Pedro consumed the whole of its revenue himself. In 1554 don Pedro rejected an appointment as captain in the army of the royal Audiencia, insulted that he had not been named commander-in-chief. Half-exiled for tumultuousness, half wanting to return, don Pedro went back to Spain in 1556, there to sue constantly for permission to stay in Spain while retaining rights to his encomienda. He died at court in 1562, still pursuing that object.[13]

To find dons who played the same kind of constructive, stabilizing role as the ordinary large encomenderos—that is, to find men who participated in the municipal councils, exploited seriously the economies of their encomiendas and in general took root—one must look beyond Seville and the royal court, to the Spanish provinces. Don Pedro Portocarrero, a figure of first importance in Lima and Cuzco, was from Trujillo, the son of an untitled mayorazgo there. Don Antonio de Ribera, repeatedly alcalde in Lima, was connected with the local nobility of Soria. Don Juan de Sandoval, important in Trujillo (Peru), was the grandson of a feudal lord of Segovia. It appears that those who had once tasted the life of the great courts could not resign themselves to remaining in Peru.[14]

Aside from presumptuousness, love of the courtly life, and other trouble-making qualities of the dons, their mere presence in the country was a source of tension. Because of the associations between the title of "don" and feudal nobility, any don in Peru without an encomienda or a high post like corregidor was a sputtering fuse. Peru's encomiendas had been given out to reward seniority and service in the conquest as well as social rank, but newly arriving dons saw only that men who in Spain would be their inferiors were here acting the part of feudal lords. As long as most dons could receive encomiendas, there was no serious problem, but after Gasca's 1548 redistribution, even the most resplendent high nobleman could expect to wait five or ten years before receiving gratification.

Discontent among the dons was the more serious because they were the natural leaders of their own regional groups. A major revolt broke out in 1552 in Upper Peru under the at least nominal leadership of don Sebastián de Castilla, from Seville, a son of the Count of Gomera. Inspired by several young, ungratified noblemen of Seville, among them three dons, and including some nobles from Badajoz (for the nobility of Seville had multiple connections with the court of the Count of Feria in the Badajoz region), the rebellion spread quickly to all kinds of other discontented groups, but had the backbone of its support among merchants, tailors, and other relatively humble people from Seville and Badajoz.[15]

Rebellious dons continued to be involved in mutinies, including the revolt of Francisco Hernández Girón, until the arrival of Viceroy Cañete in 1556. Although Cañete brought into the country the largest contingent of dons yet to arrive, perhaps doubling their number, he was able, if not to make them happy, at least to control them. He was himself, as don Andrés Hurtado de Mendoza, Marquess of Cañete, a high-ranking member of their own class, and he set up a viceregal court where the dons could display their qualities to better advantage than theretofore. Above all, Cañete was a strong political leader. He exiled some of the most troublesome dons to Spain, gratified as many as he could, and sent the rest on an expedition, under the leadership of his son, to pacify Chile.

One avenue always open to dons was to make advantageous marriages; because of their prestige, they could often achieve wealth or an encomienda in this way, if they were willing to marry partners rather far down the social scale. Don Antonio de Ribera came into one of the largest encomiendas in Peru by marrying doña Inés Muñoz, the widow of a half-brother of Francisco Pizarro. Doña Inés was originally of peasant or other humble stock, and had her "doña" only by royal decree, to reward her close association with the Pizarros and her presence in Peru in the early 1530's. Don Pedro Portocarrero married certainly Peru's richest woman, María de Escobar, who was not a doña at all. This match between a man with the maximum title of "don" and a woman without the minimum title of "doña" struck everyone as bizarre, and for a time, immediately after the marriage, there was an attempt to call María de Escobar "doña." But her name was already too familiar in its unadorned state, and the Spaniards could not bring the "doña" to their lips, so the outward indication of the discrepancy between the origins of man and wife was allowed to stand.[16]

The above marriages may not have been between social equals, but the female partners to them were at least prominent women, respected for other attributes. Don Martín de Guzmán, from Salamanca, allowed himself to be persuaded to marry the mestizo daughter of a wealthy encomendero, in order to acquire the large fortune of 20,000 pesos that she brought as her dowry. Don Martín then quickly squandered the money, or, as he claimed, spent it in the service of the king, before returning to Spain.[17]

Though the title "don" was roughly coterminous with high nobility, nobility did not stop short at that landmark. As the result of the pattern of intermarriage, as dealt with above, dons had cousins, uncles, and nephews, in most ways their equals, who were without title. Particularly the royal court was a tangle of groups of varying origin, all with some claim to nobility. Basically there were two kinds of people connected with the court, high nobles and functionaries. But since the two constantly intermarried, distinctions tended to be lost, and the son of a high functionary was likely to be also the son of a noblewoman; at any rate, he had grown up at court, and had all the qualities and pretensions of a don.

There were families near the court which, from a start at the small functionary level, had come to provide the crown with bishops, royal council members, ambassadors, and corregidors. In each new generation these families made more impressive marriages, with the goal of merging into the high nobility. Such a family was the lineage of Avila

which supplied Peru's first viceroy, Blasco Núñez Vela. Blasco
Núñez had a brother who was a bishop, and he himself had been corregidor of Málaga, inspector general of the border of Navarre, and
captain general of the Indies fleet, before becoming viceroy. He acted
and was treated like a great cavalier; his wife was from the true high
nobility, and his children were called "don." A little further down the
ladder from high nobility, but just as powerful, were the Carvajals,
based in Talavera and Plasencia. One of them, the bishop of Lugo, was
on the Council of the Indies, and two of his brothers came to Peru, one
as royal factor.[18]

A claimant to an encomienda who was connected with some of these
families, for they were intertwined, was in a better position to be
gratified quickly than many dons. The governor of Peru was always
anxious to please the Council of the Indies. Pedro Hernández Paniagua,
a member of the municipal council of Plasencia, was a cousin of Cardi-
nal Loaysa, president of the Council of Indies, and of Archbishop
Loaysa of Lima, and was moreover related to the Carvajals. With this
background, Paniagua received a large encomienda almost immediately after his arrival in Peru in 1547.[19]

Men like Paniagua, who was more of a provincial hidalgo than a
court figure despite his connections, were no different from the ordinary encomenderos in the way they ordered their lives. The secondary
nobles who came directly from the great courts were a different matter.
While in one sense all dons made up a unitary group distinct from
other types of nobility, in another sense the dividing line was between
the court and the province, the provincial nobles, dons or not, proving
tougher and more stable than the men of the court, whether the latter
were sons of counts or sons of functionaries.

The most profligate family to have anything to do with Peru in the
conquest period were the Beltráns of the royal court. They were headed by Dr. Beltrán, a successful court lawyer named to the original
Council of the Indies in 1524. He, his wife, and all his sons were heavy
gamblers. When the king reviewed the Council of the Indies at the
time of the New Laws in 1543, Dr. Beltrán was dismissed from his post
for graft, but he had already moved to assure the livelihood of his sons.
His oldest son, Ventura Beltrán, was high constable of Lima and an encomendero there. His second son, Bernardino de Mella, had an encomienda in Cuzco and a seat on its municipal council.

With these positions, Dr. Beltrán's sons should have been settled for

life. Instead, Ventura Beltrán died in Spain, convicted of his wife's
murder. His brother Bernardino de Mella committed the unusual folly
of leaving a rich area for a poor area, selling his encomienda, giving up
his post on Cuzco's council, and going to Chile. After a disappointment
and return to Peru, he went back a second time and had better luck,
finding gold mines on his Chilean encomienda. The quite unbelievable
shortsightedness of the courtly types is typified by Mella's manner of
exploiting his mines. The earth or ore from the mine was more than
half gold; he left it completely unprocessed in a large coffer until he
needed 200 pesos to gamble with, whereupon he simply washed out as
much of the earth as was required for the moment.

Just how close these families of courtly officials were to the high nobility is shown not only by the Beltráns' pattern of behavior, but by the
fact that Dr. Beltrán's third son actually appeared in Peru as a don,
don Antonio Beltrán, who went to Chile in the following of his older
brother Bernardino de Mella. How the title was acquired is a mystery.
Perhaps Dr. Beltrán got a royal cedula to permit its use, or perhaps he
was married a second time to the daughter of a don. It is always possible, however, that the Beltráns simply thought that the family had
reached a sufficient level of power and prestige to begin to assume the
"don," at least in far-off Peru. When one reads contemporary complaints of the misuse of titles in the Indies, it is this kind of premature
inching over the line that is to be understood, rather than any deep or
sudden change in the manner of addressing merchants, artisans, and
peasants.[20]

A special group related to the nobility were the members of the military orders, who were titled *comendadores*. There were several orders, but one of them, the order of Santiago, had much more fame and
prestige than the others. Many ordinary people in Peru were unaware
that any order other than Santiago existed, and members of orders like
San Juan and Alcántara to a certain extent masqueraded as knights of
Santiago. While the highest nobles of Spain aspired to belong to that
order, membership was also given quite freely to lower-ranking hidalgos and functionaries, as a reward for achievement. Viceroy Blasco
Núñez Vela and Governor Vaca de Castro both wore the cross of Santiago. In Peru, membership was granted to Francisco Pizarro and several other first conquerors who could claim some hidalgo connection.
Generally the comendadors who came to Peru were marginal figures,
from orders other than Santiago, and about half of them were Portu-

guese. There probably were not more than twenty or thirty in Peru in the whole period.[21]

Dons, comendadors, court functionaries, and other pretenders to nobility formed a tightly knit unit at the top of Spanish Peruvian society, held together by blood relationship and marriage. The chronicler Garcilaso, anxious to tell all his father's connections, gives us a good idea of the extent of this kind of interrelation. Garci Laso de la Vega, from Badajoz, the great-grandson of a Count of Feria, but no don, was a great encomendero of Cuzco, once corregidor there. He had a first cousin who was a don, don Gómez de Luna, encomendero in Charcas. Garci Laso also claimed a certain relationship to don Pedro Luis de Cabrera, from Seville and encomendero of Cuzco (see above, p. 42), because don Pedro's mother was of the house of Feria. Antonio de Quiñones, Garci Laso's brother-in-law, was a nephew of the chief almoner of Prince Philip, and an encomendero and council member of Cuzco.[22]

By the later 1550's, the interrelated class of dons, nobles, and hidalgos of very good standing had practically preempted the high society aspect of the Spanish Peruvian world, as seen in the viceregal court and public ceremonies. In Lima in 1559, pompous funeral ceremonies were held for Charles V, and six of Peru's encomenderos were chosen to carry the royal insignia, in what amounted to the purest kind of test of social prestige. Of the men picked, two were dons, three were hidalgos with noble connections, and only one came from the ranks of the plebeian conquerors so important in the early 1530's.[23] But the predominance of the nobility in Peru was more appearance than substance. A measuring-stick for the six men, truer than their social rank, is their seniority in the conquest of Peru. Among the six there were three men of really great wealth and power, who varied in social origin from nobleman to hidalgo-noble to commoner, but all of whom were in Peru by 1535.

In 1560 the courtly dons held some encomiendas and were in a better position than any other group to receive new ones, but were very far from dominating a picture that still reflected basically the grants of Francisco Pizarro before 1541 and the Gasca redistribution of 1548. After thirty years of rising social criteria, a majority of Peru's encomenderos in 1560 were probably hidalgos even by peninsular standards, but they were for the most part ordinary local hidalgos. The largest and richest encomiendas belonged to senior provincial noblemen like don Pedro Portocarrero and noble hidalgos like Garci Laso, or to first conquerors.

The same groups dominated the powerful municipal councils. The council of a large city like Lima or Cuzco would typically include first conquerors both hidalgo and plebeian; provincial and lesser nobles; some men with legal training; and by 1560 conceivably a non-encomendero merchant; but never a courtly don. Whether the dons chose not to serve in the municipal councils, or were excluded, is not clear. Dons would not have automatically rejected such service. The Spaniards were the heirs of the Romans in identifying municipal office with nobility, and there was hardly a nobleman in Spain, except the titled lords, who would not have been honored to sit on the councils of cities like Seville, Córdoba, or Toledo. Perhaps the high nobles had their eyes too firmly fixed on the councils of Spain to want to hold office in Peru. Perhaps the men who ran the Peruvian councils deliberately excluded the dons, from a sense of rivalry or in view of their poor record for civic responsibility.

Courtly dons, along with other nobles and near-nobles from the great courts of Seville and Valladolid, were out of their element in the Peru of the conquest and civil wars. They arrived late, fomented unrest by making excessive demands, took no interest in developing the country, and returned to court life in Spain at the earliest opportunity. Only after the creation of a lasting viceregal court in 1556 did the courtly nobles begin to find a role for themselves. Interrelated with the courtly nobles were a class of provincial dons and hidalgo nobles who played a very different role, providing Peru with an element of stable leadership through the whole period, from 1535, when such men began to arrive with Pedro de Alvarado, to 1560. Both types made an important contribution, by their presence, to the reproduction of a complete Spanish society on Peruvian soil.

IV PROFESSIONALS

In 1537 a single versatile man, Bachiller Garci Díaz Arias, later bishop of Quito, was serving Francisco Pizarro as chaplain, legal adviser, and private secretary.[1] In performing the three tasks at once, Bachiller Díaz showed the close relationship between the three main groups comprising Spanish Peru's professional class: churchmen, men with degrees in law and medicine, and notary-secretaries.

The professional class was a single group, yet twice divided. On the one hand, the clergy stood as a body distinct from the rest; on the other hand, law, medicine, and the church were each divided into an upper stratum of university men with diplomas, and a lower stratum of men with a grammar-school education or less, whose skills were learned through direct practice or apprenticeship. At both the upper and lower levels, many basic common traits crossed the lines of the disciplines. The priests and friars who held degrees in law or theology, and were ambitious to occupy bishoprics or benefices, had a great deal in common with the titled lawyers and physicians. They came from the same kinds of backgrounds, local hidalgo or substantial middle class, and even their training was so similar that a transfer from one field to the other was always possible. Licenciado Pedro de la Gasca spent most of his life in administrative positions, including the governorship of Peru. Yet he was an ordained priest, and finally received a bishopric. The connection of physicians with the other two groups was more tenuous, but it existed; physicians too had a mainly formalistic education, and laymen in Peru, following an old tradition, invited all three types of professional men into councils of war and peace.

On the lower levels, social similarities were just as pronounced,

though training varied more. Ordinary priests, untitled attorneys, notaries, and surgeons all emerged from the same strata of Spanish society, being connected with families of artisans, small merchants or, occasionally, petty hidalgos. Practical surgeons, however, were a rather
different group, falling, in popular conception and often in fact, completely out of the professional class and into the class of artisans
through their collateral trade of barbering and their tendency, as a
group, to be illiterate.

The horizontal split among the professional people was reflected in
their regional origin. Though both the upper and lower professionals
diverged from the standard patterns for the Spanish Peruvian population as a whole, they varied in different ways. Ordinarily, in Peru, Andalusia was the best represented of the great regions of Spain, with Extremadura second. In its contribution of notaries and ordinary priests,
Andalusia, according to a sampling, was even stronger than usual,
while Extremadura, as one of Spain's most backward areas, fell far
below, contributing hardly more than a tenth of the notaries (though
when it came to priests, Extremadura recovered its normal position).

While the lower levels of the professional class were strongly Andalusian, the striking feature about the upper levels is the number who
came from the north of Spain. In most regional groupings, Old Castile
was in third place. In a sampling of the origins of titled lawyers and
doctors, Old Castile rose to first place among the regions, and New
Castile and León had a larger proportion than usual. This fact is apparently to be explained by the presence in the north of the University
of Salamanca and the royal court, usually at Valladolid or Madrid.
Like their secular colleagues, over half of the churchmen with degrees
seem to have come from the north (see Appendix Tables).

Secular and clerical, titled and untitled, the whole professional class
was united by its thoroughgoing formalism and legalism. An attorney
or notary could move from a secular court into an ecclesiastical court
and hardly notice the difference. Chapter meetings in monasteries and
cathedrals followed the same procedures as the meetings of municipal
councils. All professionals wrote their books, treatises, ordinances, and
protests, when they were of any length, in the same capitular scholastic
style; not even the chroniclers could divest themselves of the eternal
Item.

Ecclesiastics began to move into Peru in the early, military stages of
the conquest. Not long after the founding of each Spanish city, it ac-

quired a church manned by one or more secular priests, and one or two monasteries; reports from the early years more often express surprise at the number of churchmen in Peru, than complain of their absence. Everything indicates that secular priests were more numerous than friars, from beginning to end of the conquest and civil war period. The repeated complaint was that the friars, who were best fitted for the work of converting the Indians, were scarce, while secular priests, who were there in numbers, were interested in nothing but economic gain.[2]

A very rough idea of the top limit on the number of ecclesiastics in Peru in the period 1530–60 can be inferred from an estimate made in 1563, that there were then no more than 350 ordained priests, both secular and religious, in all of greater Peru.[3] This figure seems on the face of it too low. Perhaps an adequate explanation is the strange ability of the Hispanic countries to appear priest-ridden while actually low in ecclesiastical manpower, but the extreme frequency with which clergymen appear in all kinds of sources would seem to imply a larger number than 350, even by 1550. In the documentation, priests are literally too numerous to count.

Secular priests came to Peru individually and, except for those already appointed to some benefice, on their own. Friars came in organized parties, often subsidized, and twelve at a time, if possible. The two orders of primary importance until 1550 were the Dominicans and the Mercedarians. The Franciscans were well established only in the fringe area of Quito, where they carried out a program, exceptional in Peru, modelled on patterns learned in Mexico. The Franciscans and Augustinians moved into central Peru very late, in 1548 and 1552 respectively, but made rapid progress in the Spanish towns; loyalties built into the Spanish populace made it possible for them to spring into existence as equals of the older orders almost immediately.

The central duty of the church in Peru was construed to be the conversion of the Indians; not the town Indians, who were quickly converted through social pressure, but the mass of encomienda Indians. The activities of the missionaries therefore escape the present study to a great extent, in part for lack of information, in part for lack of relevance, for the missionaries, like the estancieros, the miners, and the encomienda Indians themselves, lived and worked beyond the limits of the Spanish Peruvian world.

Missionary work in Peru was tied to the encomienda system. Each encomendero was legally obliged to maintain, that is, to employ and feed, a missionary, whether secular priest or friar, who was to reside on the encomienda and devote himself to the conversion of the Indians. Through most of the period, the ideal of a priest for every encomienda was very far from realization, because of the lack of qualified people, their involvement in the civil wars, and their reluctance to carry out a task that was the ecclesiastical equivalent of the estanciero's, involving low status, low pay, and isolation from the Spanish communities. The same documents which contain hundreds of agreements between encomenderos and majordomos produce only two or three contracts with *doctrineros,* as the missionaries were called, though there must have been many more missionaries than that ratio indicates.

In the absence of ecclesiastics, encomenderos were supposed to hire lay missionaries. It may be easily imagined how they discharged this duty; they introduced into contracts with their majordomos a clause empowering the latter to instruct the Indians in the faith. In 1548 Gasca attempted to make the lay missionary a more meaningful institution, and a few encomenderos hired Spaniards specifically for that purpose, but even these men became in effect additional majordomos, with duties of tribute collection.[4]

To keep a priest, who was an educated man with multiple potentialities, at the unappetizing work of a doctrinero, substantial salaries had to be offered, higher at least than the 100 to 150 pesos an estanciero received. The average salary for doctrineros seems to have been about 300 pesos a year, with side benefits such as those enjoyed by the majordomos. At times, demand drove salaries higher; in Quito in 1547, the usual salary went up to 400 pesos, because priests would not take 300. In Cuzco in the early 1550's, one encomendero went to the prior of the Franciscan monastery there and said he would pay a doctrinero 500 pesos plus food, if the prior would find him one, but the prior failed to find a priest who would accept these terms.[5]

From the point of view of the encomendero, the missionary priest was another member of his feudal retinue like the majordomo. Encomenderos openly called the doctrineros their chaplains, and sometimes took them along as followers during military campaigns. In the contract of one doctrinero, there was only one specifically stipulated duty, to say weekly masses for the souls of the two encomenderos who were hiring him. Not only were the doctrineros counted among the majordomos, in several instances they actually became majordomos, assuming responsibility for the economic exploitation of the encomienda. A

Basque doctrinero of Cuzco, Fortún Sánchez de Olave, was a career estate manager.[6]

A doctrinero, alone on one of Peru's county-size encomiendas, or even responsible for two or three encomiendas, could not make a serious effort to cover his whole region. Generally he relied on the method of intensive instruction of a group of children whom he requested from the cacique. The doctrinero resided in the area's largest Indian town, where his encomendero might have a church built, and where there was likely to be a majordomo or estanciero. Isolated in the country, the priest and the estanciero became close companions, and the priest would manage things and guard the estanciero's possessions when the latter had to be gone. Many doctrineros also had a Negro slave who was aide, servant, and companion.[7]

In addition to their salaries, doctrineros received a certain allotment of direct tribute labor and produce to support themselves. They attempted to maximize the value of this tribute in the same way the encomenderos did, employing the labor to care for livestock and cultivate plots, then selling the increment on the city markets. Such activities brought them heavy criticism both from laymen and church authorities, but nothing else was to be expected, in the context, and the practice continued despite official countermeasures.[8]

Getting doctrineros to stay in one place for very long was a major problem. While some areas are known to have had the same doctrinero for ten years, many priests took a position as doctrinero only as a stopgap, to support themselves until something better appeared. Doctrineros were inclined to move around the country from one Spanish city to the next, searching for a benefice, vicarage, or other steady urban employment; particularly men with degrees were impossible to hold long as doctrineros.

When the hierarchy finally began to exert some pressure on the doctrineros in the 1550's, it resorted to an extreme measure to try to keep them on the job. The bishop would seize the priest's original titles and give them in safekeeping to the encomendero, to assure that the priest would not absent himself before serving a minimum three years. But sporadic implementation by the authorities themselves kept this apparently foolproof device from being effective.[9]

Of course many doctrineros were not priests but friars. What the proportions were is, for the present, a mystery. The traditional view was that the regular clergy were particularly predominant in missionary work during the early period, but wherever the records provide a glimpse of a sample of doctrineros, this is not borne out. On encomiendas held by the crown or temporarily vacant, the royal treasury paid the doctrineros' salaries, and many of the records still exist, showing a predominance of priests over friars.[10]

Friar doctrineros were at any rate better organized than the priests, who, practically unconnected with the hierarchy, were in no position to offer resistance to the encomenderos, and could be dismissed at will. The friars, sent out in twos, were under the protection of the monasteries in Spanish settlements. Even so, a powerful encomendero could assert himself, like Diego Maldonado, the Rich, in Cuzco, who expelled the Franciscans from his encomienda; but this took a major effort. The sources do not make the relationship between the encomenderos and the friar very clear. It remains uncertain whether the encomenderos invited the friars in, or whether the orders expanded according to their own plans and possibilities; also whether the encomenderos made payments to the friars or to the monasteries (more likely the former).[11]

Most friars probably were equipped something like two Dominicans who set out for the new settlement of Jaén in 1557 with saddle mules, a pack mule with provisions and religious necessaries, a Negro slave, and new habits. A pair of friars was assigned to a vast area of two, three, or even four encomiendas, where they seem to have operated in much the same fashion as the priest doctrineros, except that they spent more time in traveling and less time seeing to their economic interests.[12]

The results of the type of effort thus sketched out, measured in conversion of encomienda Indians, were apparently quite meager. Two contemporary authorities claimed that by about 1550 practically nothing had been accomplished.[13] Conversion of the Indians seems to have been a major casualty of Peru's prolonged civil wars. During the wars majordomos kept at their work, merchants and artisans made war profits, and mines flourished, but the clergy was drawn into the conflict, and its activities suffered. Churchmen were in constant demand to serve as peace-negotiators and messengers; they were taken on the campaigns as chaplains, confessors, and a source of moral support. In the years 1544–48, the Mercedarians and part of the secular clergy gave their active support to the Gonzalo Pizarro revolt, while the Dominicans did everything they could to oppose it.

Secular priests, or "abbots" as the Spaniards sometimes called them, were for many years completely free agents, able to come and go at their pleasure, and responsible for their own livelihood. Only in 1552, in the course of Peru's first synod, was a general order issued to the effect that all priests be assigned to missionary work and not be permitted to wander about the country or occupy themselves in other enterprises. But even after that, the old trends long continued.[14]

While some priests arrived with royal appointments to benefices, and a few carried cedulas providing that they be paid a small salary by the treasury if they devoted themselves to missionary work, many came on their own initiative, and were thrown upon their own resources. In this situation, they made their livings in any way they could. Even if they found modest positions as parish priests, chaplains, or sacristans, they could not in this way earn a subsistence wage.[15]

During the early years of the conquest there was to be seen in Peru a breed of priest-entrepreneurs who enriched themselves in that atmosphere of fantastic wealth, then quickly returned to Spain. In 1533 at the town of Cajamarca, two priests named Juan de Asensio and Francisco de Morales contracted a universal partnership, agreeing to divide equally all income from their activities in war or peace, anything they earned from their profession or alms, and any shares given their horses, for in the conquest of Peru horses got shares as well as men, and a noncombatant could speculate on future divisions of spoils by letting someone else ride his horse to war. In conjunction with a company of professional merchants, the two priests loaned money, and sold horses and other merchandise to the conquerors. They had great success. When Juan de Asensio died in Jauja in 1534, he was a rich man, and the next year, 1535, Francisco de Morales returned to Spain carrying 14,500 pesos, at that time a fabulous amount, and far more than most of his traveling companions who had had a share of the booty of Cajamarca.[16]

Not nearly all priests were so overtly commercial, even in the early period, and as time went on their activities became more discreet. They did not, by and large, deserve the unmeasured criticism heaped upon them by the friars, who were under no such necessity to make a living. Nor were they all determined to get quick wealth and go back to Spain on the first boat. Their aim was to find some honorable and stable ecclesiastical employment, and failing that, to go home with a sufficiency. Priests' economic activities were almost always such that they did not have to become too actively involved. Typically, they loaned money, owned real estate and livestock, and invested as silent partners in merchandise or other ventures, making good use of their ecclesiastical connections as a business network, particularly important for debt collection.[17]

Friars did not earn their own living, nor did they need to. Only the Mercedarians, as a non-mendicant order, permitted their friars a certain restricted commercial activity, mainly the buying and selling of horses for personal use, and small loans. Both mendicants and non-mendicants supported themselves primarily through corporate holdings of real estate and agricultural land, either directly donated or bought with donated money. The two oldest orders, the Dominicans and Mercedarians, also held encomiendas in several parts of Peru.[18]

The Mercedarians' notoriety in the Gonzalo Pizarro rebellion, and their admitted position as the only non-mendicants, have given rise to the impression that they were the only order to hold property and encomiendas.[19] Actually, the most blatant buyers and owners of income property were the Augustinians, who went so far as to invest in a ship. The Franciscan order was the most reluctant, but did own houses to be rented out. The main economic distinctions between the orders in Peru were two; first between the Mercedarians, who did not receive governmental subsidies, and the mendicants, who did; and second, between the early arrivals, the Dominicans and Mercedarians, who received and long held encomiendas, and the late-arriving Franciscans and Augustinians, who did not. It is true enough that the Mercedarians showed the more businesslike spirit in encomienda exploitation, but the Dominicans wanted very much to keep their encomiendas, and did keep them for a time after the Mercedarians lost theirs in 1548.[20]

Each monastic chapter would select a friar solicitor, or, more often, a lay majordomo from among the town's prominent merchants, who was charged with accepting donations and renting out, selling, or buying property for the chapter. At bottom the holdings were direct donations from laymen, in return, generally, for permanent chapels or chaplaincies, but the monasteries made some effort to consolidate their property, preferring to own a whole row of several stores, or contiguous agricultural land.[21]

The clergy's roots in the Spanish communities were not, of course, merely economic. A great number of churchmen came to Peru, like other Spaniards, because they had relatives there. On the upper levels, a quite typical case was Archbishop Loaysa of Lima, from an hidalgo-functionary family, who was related not only to the president of the Council of the Indies, but to encomenderos and high officials in Peru.

On the lower levels, ties of blood and common regional origin were often a major factor shaping priests' lives. Lázaro García, a priest from Seville who held minor ecclesiastical posts in Peru, was the brother of a Lima merchant with business connections in Arequipa; it is almost certain that García left Lima and settled in Arequipa partly in order to represent the family's interests there. Members of the monastic orders were also affected by such ties; some were related among themselves, and cases are known of errant friars saved from punishment in the civil wars by the intercession of relatives.[22]

Related by blood to other Spaniards or not, ecclesiastics often tried to enhance their positions in the Spanish Peruvian world by marrying their female relatives to prominent community members, thus indirectly participating in the fruits of encomiendas for which they were not personally eligible. This type of involvement could be the expression of personal or family ambition, as in the case of Hernand Arias, cantor of Cuzco's cathedral, who married three sisters to encomenderos of Cuzco, but it also could have strategic or organizational significance. The leader of the first major contingent of Augustinians to reach Peru, in 1551, brought with him his niece, doña Juana de Cepeda, and married her almost immediately to an encomendero of Lima, Hernán González, the same who ten years previously had acquired an encomienda through purchase (see p. 20). González was by now very rich, and inclined to pious charity, but still not satisfied with his social position; he was more than willing to contract a marriage with a wellborn lady and serve as a patron of her uncle's order. First González sheltered and fed the Augustinians in his house, then built them living quarters (where they stayed until 1563), and donated money with which the order could buy income property. Over the years he donated the huge total of 50,000 pesos. The order of Saint Augustine in effect established itself in Lima through an advantageous marriage.[23]

Arranging marriages for their sisters was a practice which brought legitimate reward both to the churchmen and to the Spanish Peruvian world; but it could be distracting and time-consuming in the extreme. Fray Francisco Martínez de Abreo, a Dominican from Seville, resided in the Charcas region in the late 1540's. In 1548 he had his mother and his sister, doña Catalina de Figueroa, brought to Peru, and came all the way across the country to meet them in Lima. There he outfitted his sister with new clothes, and returned to Charcas to arrange a marriage for her with an encomendero of La Plata, while she and their mother proceeded more slowly as far as Cuzco.

With the marriage arranged, fray Francisco rode back the six hundred miles to Cuzco. He anticipated the large dowry doña Catalina would receive from her new husband, and went heavily into debt in order to send her to La Plata in state. When fray Francisco's credit was exhausted, he borrowed 200 pesos from the prior of Cuzco's Dominican monastery, and then drew on the prior's credit. After weeks of expensive delay in Cuzco, fray Francisco and doña Catalina set out, with several horses and mules, a Spanish servant, a Negro slave girl, and three yanaconas. All were newly dressed, and doña Catalina was equipped with a resplendent wardrobe and a new ivory false tooth, made for her by a silversmith. Complete disaster overtook them when doña Catalina fell ill in an Indian village south of Cuzco and died, without having seen the husband arranged for her. Fray Francisco returned to Lima to liquidate her affairs and to see about their father, who was coming to Peru to share their expected prosperity. In attempting to marry off his sister, fray Francisco had traveled well over two thousand miles on horseback, had lost easily a year's time, and was left several hundred pesos in debt.[24]

The general shape of ecclesiastical careers varied considerably between secular priests and friars. For secular priests, a benefice in Lima or Cuzco was what an encomienda was to laymen, a maximum goal, generally unattainable. Most priests reduced their aims to a vicarage in a smaller community like Piura or Huamanga, where they might stay for many years; the backwoods community of Chachapoyas had the same vicar for fifteen years after its founding.[25]

Even qualified men with degrees found it hard to get benefices. Usually they had to be content to hold high but temporary positions as ecclesiastical administrators. Bachiller Francisco Guerra de Céspedes, an able priest, came to Peru from Nicaragua in 1537 in answer to the call for help in the Indian revolt, bringing a ship full of horses and slaves to sell. During the next twenty-five years he served variously as deputy inquisitor, inspector general, and judge, and was vicar general of the dioceses of both Lima and Cuzco. The post of vicar general was a strange one, for while it brought great power, it rarely lasted for more than a year or two, and was hardly ever a step toward advancement. By 1562, Bachiller Guerra was wealthy and respected, but, far from achieving his lifetime ambition of becoming dean of Lima's cathedral, occupied no benefice at all.[26]

Spanish Peruvian priests who succeeded in getting a benefice did so by staying in the close personal following of a bishop, and had to be content with a canonry, because that was as far as the bishop's influence on appointments extended. The crown kept quite firm control over appointments to the higher dignities, which typically went to men who had never been in Peru. Dignitaries generally arrived in Peru in debt after the expensive passage from Spain, but soon began to collect their incomes and settle down to lives characterized by independence and pomp. While bishops had wide hierarchical authority, which in the decade of the 1550's they increasingly exercised, the other dignitaries were urban figures whose duties were mainly ceremonial, although they did have an important role as spiritual advisors in the Spanish community.[27]

The lives of friars fell into characteristic patterns according to their rank. The often illiterate lay friars, a good many of whom entered the orders in Peru, usually spent their lives in a single monastery, as porters or in other subsidiary posts. The monastic chroniclers writing in the seventeenth century still knew of the dedication of some of these men to humble tasks. Some lay friars, however, were forced to enter the orders in the civil wars, under threat of death if they did not, and they naturally did not leave such admirable records. Often they deserted the orders when danger was past, despite their vows. Diego de Fresneda, master of Francisco Pizarro's galleon "San Cristóbal," entered the Dominican order as a lay friar when Pizarro was assassinated in 1541. After a few years he left monastic life and fought on the side of Gonzalo Pizarro against the royal army, for which he was convicted in 1548 and sentenced to exile in Spain. Before 1558 he was back with the Dominicans, probably not having left Peru.[28]

The rank and file of educated, ordained friars were shifted from place to place readily according to the needs of their orders, staying assigned to one monastery for perhaps from two to five years. Over a longer period, the turnover would be almost complete; the Dominican monastery of Lima retained only three friars through the period 1542–53. It was typical that two of the three were the prior and the sub-prior.[29] Two or three well-educated, experienced friars would stay in one monastery all their lives, dominating the priorate, providing continuity, and becoming well-known and venerable figures in the community. Friars as well as other Spaniards respected seniority in the conquest; the great prestige of the veterans of the 1530's made them perennial candidates for positions of honor and authority in the orders.

Three Spanish Peruvian churchmen of the conquest period, a secular priest and two Dominican friars, attained bishoprics. Bachiller Garci Díaz Arias, though perhaps not particularly well qualified, had the whole power of his patron Francisco Pizarro behind his appointment. The two Dominicans, fray Tomás de San Martín and fray Domingo de Santo Tomás, were exceptional, zealous men who alternated as provincial heads of their order. Both were masters in theology, ideologically exponents of a modified Las Casas position, and seriously devoted to the conversion of Indians. Fray Domingo, from Seville like Las Casas, was the more uncompromising, and the better scholar of Indian culture and language, while fray Tomás was a more human figure, who took church construction and organizational matters much to heart.

A picture of other important aspects of clerical activity, such as the internal life of the monasteries and preaching in the Spanish community, must await detailed study of church and monastic archives. The notarial and official records reveal, as was only to be expected, that ecclesiastics were also Spaniards, very much a part of the secular Spanish Peruvian world.

Formally trained practitioners of law and medicine, in Peru as in the home country, held three ascending degrees, the baccalaureate, licentiate, and doctorate, which were expressed in the corresponding titles of *Bachiller, Licenciado,* and *Doctor.* Because of the Spanish love for titles of any kind, the degree titles had great significance as marks of social prestige. Like "don" and "doña" they became an invariable element of the holder's name, never omitted, whether in conversation or in serious documents like wills. And like "don," a degree title was considered to be enough to distinguish an individual from his namesake; the nineteenth-century historian Manuel de Mendiburu once concocted a most improbable biography by identifying a certain Rodrigo Niño with his uncle, Licenciado Rodrigo Niño. Spaniards greatly preferred names of two elements, so the men with degrees were almost always called only by their title and the most aristocratic-sounding of their surnames, losing so completely the Christian name and the plebeian surname which many of them bore, that anyone who is interested in the true original name may encounter great difficulty in finding out what it was. Diego González de Altamirano, who probably had a rather shaky claim to the Altamirano and must ordinarily have been called just Diego González, was transformed upon receiving his degree into Licenciado Altamirano.[30]

The comparative frequency and significance of the titles varied somewhat from law to medicine. The great majority of all titled lawyers in Peru held the licentiate, the baccalaureate having little prestige in law and the doctorate being a rare and high degree, held in Peru only by some judges of the Audiencia. In medicine all three degrees were in common use, but particularly the baccalaureate and the doctorate; the doctorate in medicine, though prestigious, did not carry the overwhelming weight of a doctorate in law.

Degree titles, like many other symbols of social status, were apparently slightly, but not seriously inflated in Peru; some physicians and lawyers found it possible to claim a status they would not have quite dared to claim at home. Alonso Alemán, a physician and pharmacist who left Spain untitled, appeared in Peru as Bachiller Alemán. Though he had not finished his degree, he had indubitably studied at a university, and there was no obvious discrepancy between his ability and his assumed title. Bachiller Juan Guerrero, one of the first lawyers to reach Peru, assumed the title of Licenciado, rather than be submerged among the licentiates who soon began to come into the country, men with essentially no better training than he, since once the baccalaureate in law was achieved, the step to a licentiate was a small one. It was, in fact, possible to acquire the licentiate with no further study at all. Gaspar de Espinosa came to the Indies originally with a baccalaureate from the University of Salamanca, then went back to Spain to hold an administrative post in Madrid. When he decided to return to the Indies, he quickly acquired the licentiate, for its added prestige. Whether he got the degree through political influence, a fee, or a test, is not known, but the chronicler Oviedo, who reports the event, indicates by his skeptical tone that the procedure was suspect. Most of Peru's licentiates in law must have had valid, even if dubious, titles, for the Audiencia and other courts made important distinctions of protocol between the various degrees, and certainly the punctilious Spanish judges must have inspected the lawyers' diplomas.[31]

Lawyers, titled or untitled, were not legally supposed to be in Peru. In one of those visionary measures which plagued legislation for the Indies, the Crown, fearing the bad effects of Spanish litigiousness in a new country, banned all lawyers from Peru as a part of the 1529 agreements with Pizarro.[32] Reality soon repealed the law. Titled lawyers and physicians began to come to Peru in 1534 and 1535, and were significant as a group by 1540. At any given time, there would seem, according to samples, to have been perhaps half as many lawyers and doctors in Peru as clergymen. (Lawyers and doctors must be taken together for purposes of estimate, because very frequently only their names and titles are known.)

The first men of the law came not as court practitioners, but as administrators and entrepreneurs. Several legists who had been governors of areas in Central America and the Caribbean, not satisfied with the modest opportunities there, brought commercial expeditions to Peru, hoping also for a major political role. The horses, slaves, and arms they brought to sell made them rich quickly, but they found that if they wanted to stay in Peru they would have to accept a great reduction in their pretensions. Only one of them stayed permanently, Licenciado Antonio de la Gama, who had been provisional governor of Puerto Rico and Panama. He was at one time or another lieutenant governor or corregidor in Lima, Cuzco, and Quito, and held a medium-sized encomienda in Cuzco until his death in the late 1540's, but he was more a governor's handyman than a power.[33]

Though the age of the legist-governor was over in a few years, there always continued to be, among holders of law degrees in Peru, men who were not primarily attorneys, but candidates for encomiendas, high administrative posts, and captaincies. While persons with law degrees were a middle group in the sense that hardly any of them belonged to the highest nobility or the strictly plebeian classes, the range of their social backgrounds was quite wide; above all, there was no contradiction in the minds of the Spaniards between a law degree and nobility of the hidalgo type. A degree in fact increased the luster of the name.

Licenciado Rodrigo Niño, who came to Peru in 1541 intending to defend the Pizarros against the accusations of a royal investigator, was the brother of a member of the city council of Toledo, and by all odds an hidalgo of very good standing. He brought with him a young nephew, his namesake, and the difference in the careers of the two is instructive. With his title, Liceniado Niño, who never actually practiced law in Peru, quickly made an advantageous marriage, and became an encomendero and council member in Lima. His nephew, only an hidalgo, had to work his way up slowly through increasingly prominent participation in the civil wars, receiving an encomienda only after fifteen years.

Many hidalgo families sent one son to earn a law degree in the same manner they sent one son into the church. Hernán Cortés, the conqueror of Mexico, had been launched on that path, before he abandoned it for other things. An example in Peru was Licenciado Benito Suárez de Carvajal, an important figure during the first two decades of the conquest period. He was one of three brothers connected with Peru in some way. One, Illán Suárez de Carvajal, was Peru's royal factor; another, Licenciado Juan Suárez de Carvajal, was bishop of Lugo and a member of the Council of the Indies. They were, in other words, one of those powerful families of high functionaries with very serious pretensions to nobility. Licenciado Carvajal was Francisco Pizarro's lieutenant in Lima in 1536, and later corregidor of Cuzco; he held a large encomienda and was a captain in the civil wars.

While a law degree said relatively little about its holder's social origin, it did have other connotations. Aside from the legal profession's perennial reputation for trickery (the Spaniards used "bachiller" to mean "trickster"), lawyers were supposed to be men of peace. In overreaction to any implication of unmanliness, Peru's hidalgo-lawyers manifested an excessive bravado. All Spaniards were quick to defend their honor, but the lawyers often went to extremes, the two men mentioned above being good examples. Licenciado Niño, hurling filthy insults, once drew his sword on the archbishop of Lima. Licenciado Carvajal, whose brother had been killed by Viceroy Blasco Núñez, joined the forces of Gonzalo Pizarro and sought vengeance relentlessly, being personally responsible for the viceroy's death after the battle of Añaquito. (His court connections saved Licenciado Carvajal from punishment.) Both Licenciado Niño and Licenciado Carvajal, when they were on Lima's city council, came ostentatiously late to meetings, and said little when they came.[34]

The Spaniards never ceased to comment on the spectacle of lawyers fighting in battles. Lawyers ordinarily participated in the civil wars whenever the occasion arose, and perhaps a score of them were captains of companies at one time or another. Of these, about five or six became through experience real fighters and leaders of men.[35]

After the establishment of the royal Audiencia in Lima in 1544, its four or five *oidores* or judges were at the top of Peru's legal world, and their claims to the prerogatives of nobility were strong indeed. They were generally from well-connected hidalgo-functionary families, had already held high judicial or administrative posts in Spain itself, and brought with them large followings of relatives and servants. While quite a few of the lawyers in Peru brought their families along, judges of the Audiencia were positively expected to do so. Often the judges already had relatives among Peru's encomenderos, and they hastened to strengthen the bonds through marriage. Though the Audiencia functioned quite well at times, its history was marked by the judges' ambitions to lead armies in the civil wars and their wrangling with all and sundry over matters of precedence and honor.[36]

Not all lawyers were hidalgos; many were from families of merchants and notaries which had already begun to rise on the social scale in Spain or other parts of the Indies. Licenciado Miguel de Cuéllar, who was briefly corregidor of Arequipa and remained there permanently as an encomendero, was the brother of Gaspar de Cuéllar, the last important merchant of Burgos to be active in Peru. Even he, however, would no doubt have claimed to be an hidalgo, with some justice, since he was, like Jerónimo de Villegas (see p. 27), a representative of a family long important in the Indies, and ripe for promotion into the ranks of the hidalgos.[37]

Lawyers with less imposing lineages were more content to settle down to court work. For them the ideal was to live in Lima, where they could practice before the Audiencia and find other types of governmental employment in Peru's administrative center. Any time after the Audiencia was established, a sizable colony of lawyers would be residing in Lima. In the provincial centers there was less opportunity, but there would usually be from one to perhaps four titled lawyers in residence in a given city, depending on the time and place. A lawyer could earn a basic living wage of 100 to 200 pesos as legal adviser to the city council or defender of the royal treasury, and supplement it by conducting important law suits (the lesser cases were left to untitled *procuradores*). A titled lawyer's fee varied from 25 pesos for a minor case in the provinces, to perhaps 1,000 pesos for a major suit before the Audiencia, such as one involving rights to an encomienda. Needless to say, lawyers who had the money indulged in the same kind of general capitalistic activity which characterized the clergy and indeed the whole Spanish Peruvian population.[38]

During the whole period from the first founding of the cities until

1556, men of the law alternated with powerful encomenderos as corregidors in Peru's cities. After that, Viceroy Cañete appointed predomi-
nantly lawyers, feeling that they were more easily controlled.

Peru's physicians had fewer pretensions to nobility, and indeed less
of its actuality, than the lawyers. More of the physicians came from
families in which their profession was a tradition. Not a single physician was ever a corregidor or a captain in the civil wars, and only one
or two, late in the period, received encomiendas.

The physicians, like the lawyers, had their age of giants in the early
years, but the differences are indicative. The most famous of them was
Dr. Hernando de Sepúlveda, who left an established position as a physician in Santo Domingo to come to Peru in 1536. In the years
1537–39, when Spanish Peru's commerce had not yet become fully
professionalized, Dr. Sepúlveda was one of the largest entrepreneurs
in the country, selling merchandise and livestock, both wholesale and
retail. He also owned real estate, and a galleon to transport his goods.
Sepúlveda was highly literate and had a good comprehension of the
civil wars (he wrote a long account of one campaign, used by the
chronicler Oviedo), but, though he was included in the councils of war,
he never received the kind of recognition accorded to his lawyer equivalent, Licenciado de la Gama, who held administrative posts and an
encomienda. With all his other interests, Dr. Sepúlveda continued the
active practice of medicine.[39]

Physicians did not have an institutional economic base as strong as
lawyers, who could find one or two governmental jobs in even the
smaller cities. Only in the late 1540's and the 1550's, when hospitals
began to appear, was there at least one steady post for a physician in
most Peruvian cities. Most towns had one or two physicians in permanent residence, who lived from private practice, plus hospital work
where there was any. Lima had the greatest concentration because it
was the largest population center with the most amenities, but could
offer physicians nothing comparable to the Audiencia for lawyers.

The great economic opportunity for physicians was war; they lived
from one civil war to the next. Whenever there was a campaign, most
of the country's physicians were to be found in one of the two oppos-
ing camps, not as combatants like the lawyers, but in a near-neutral
sideline position. In the early years, physicians at battles collected their
fees individually from the men they treated, and this never ceased

completely, but from 1547 there were also official paid surgeons, with
very high salaries. A year's salary for a hospital physician might be 200
pesos. A year's salary for an army surgeon could be as high as 2,000
pesos.[40]

A physician who got his start in civil war campaigns, then reached
real prominence in the community of Lima, was Licenciado Alvaro de
Torres, from Jerez de la Frontera, who came to Peru as a young man in
1542, and accompanied the campaign of Governor Vaca de Castro
from northern Peru to Cuzco. Licenciado Torres arrived in Peru with
few possessions—clothing, a sword, a horse, a case of medicines, and a
case of books on medicine and philosophy—and when a serious illness
befell him in Lima in April, 1542, he was still in debt for the cost of
freighting them from Panama. Serving as a physician on a campaign
could be lucrative, but it was also, like most ventures in the Indies, an
extremely speculative affair. The physician could ordinarily expect to
be paid for treatment only after victory was won, and if he was with
the losing side, he could expect not to be paid at all. After accompanying the royal army from Quito to Lima, Licenciado Torres could
show nothing but 500 pesos worth of debts owed him, and some vague
promises of emeralds and favors. At the same time he owed about 250
pesos to merchants and pharmacists.

Within a month or two Licenciado Torres recovered his health, borrowed a hundred pesos from a lawyer acquaintance, and rejoined the
campaign. Presumably, after the hard-fought battle of Chupas, he collected what was owed him, and earned more. To reward his services,
Governor Vaca de Castro named Torres *prótomedico* of Peru, a mainly
honorific post which carried with it the right to inspect and license
physicians, surgeons, and pharmacists.

Torres then settled down in Lima as one of the town's most prestigious physicians, because of his title, and though he may have accompanied more campaigns, he made his economic way mainly through
private practice in Lima and speculation in real estate. By 1552 he had
accumulated a row of nine houses on one of Lima's main streets, which
he sold to the city for the large amount of 15,400 pesos. This did not
end his dealing in real estate, which continued on a large scale; he
must have been richer than many of Lima's encomenderos. In 1553
Torres made clear his intention to remain in Peru by marrying doña
Bernaldina de la Barrera, from Utrera. Doña Bernaldina had come to

Peru in the guise of a wellborn lady, but in all probability her parents were the same kind of good substantial non-hidalgo people as Torres' family, seeing that her mother bore the plebeian name of plain Catalina Jiménez.

Up to this point Torres' career had been successful within the limits imposed by his profession, but he now went beyond those limits, becoming in 1553 or 1554 the first Spanish Peruvian physician to receive an encomienda. The size of the encomienda, the occasion of the grant, and how Torres managed to get it, are all unknown. One thinks immediately of purchase; or, since little is known about his wife doña Bernaldina, it is possible that she had inherited the encomienda, and Torres got it through marriage. At any rate, he certainly did not receive the grant for military performance, high lineage, or seniority in the conquest. In 1561, just beyond the time boundary of our period, Licenciado Torres attained another first for his profession by becoming one of Lima's alcaldes, but that year also saw other new departures as an age came to an end. Torres lived on in Lima for a great many years. He was still alive and practicing medicine in 1590, when he must have been at least seventy years old.

Licenciado Torres was an exceptional case, but typical of the medical profession in achieving a maximum of success with a minimum of fanfare. His life also illustrates the close connection existing between physicians, lawyers, and well-educated churchmen. In his first year in Peru, Torres had already made friends with fray Domingo de Santo Tomás, the Dominican scholar and propagandist, to whom he meant to bequeath his books of philosophy. A timely loan from a lawyer was a quite crucial event in Torres' career. Since he resided mainly in Lima, Torres often served as a kind of home base for doctors and lawyers who went out into the country and would leave him in charge of their affairs.[41]

The progress of lawyers and physicians in Peru defies any clear separation between an early rough period when professionals were mainly absent and a later more settled period when they became prominent. From 1535 on, the corregidors of Cuzco and Lima were, as often as not, trained and titled men of the law. Doctors and lawyers throve on civil strife. The change is easier to see in the men themselves. Lawyers and physicians in the early years were at least as much captains, leaders, and entrepreneurs as they were professional people. The 1550's saw, along with the maturing of the Audiencia system and the rise of hospitals, the predominance of a type of professional more willing to dedicate himself fully to his calling.

The principal beneficiaries of the Spaniards' inordinate respect for the written word were the bottom rank of the professional class, the innumerable notaries who witnessed every phase of the conquest and occupation of Peru, from beginning to end. Notaries were present without exception on the most adventurous expeditions of discovery, in the smallest towns, in every mining camp, wherever there were groups of Spaniards. To history's gain, there was hardly anything that the Spaniards did not notarize, from the act of taking possession of the Pacific to a rebel captain's declaration that he was fighting the royal army unwillingly. One day in 1544 two shoemakers walked into an office on Lima's square and had an impressive document drawn up devoted to nothing more than the fact of their arrival in Lima. Trials and investigations of all kinds also made large demands on notaries, for Spanish trials were written affairs. A notary took all testimony in writing before the judges saw it; even attorneys' briefs and petitions passed through a notary's hands.

Notaries were not only, or even mainly, scribes. Literacy was widely enough spread among the Spaniards that there was not much demand for scribes, except on a secretarial level, and while some notaries produced masterpieces of calligraphy, others had a poor hand. They were primarily experts in legal formulas and terminology, who could draw up a power of attorney or a testament, and produce an official command, ordinance, or petition in correct form. The notary was the versatile workhorse of Spanish government. Governors' secretaries, court clerks, lower-level treasury officials, untitled attorneys, even chroniclers, were all variations of the notary, and all had the same training. That training was almost completely practical. After grammar school, a notary-to-be was put into apprenticeship in the office of a notary public, and training was complete by or before the age of twenty. The apprentice then negotiated at court for a permanent title as "His Majesty's Notary," which, however, was not the same as the right to set up an office. To do that a notary had to acquire a specific notarial office in a specific city, either through purchase or through political favor.

The relative ease and inexpensiveness of training meant that a notary's career was available to people from an even wider variety of backgrounds than was the case with law and medicine. To some extent notaries' backgrounds overlapped with those of lawyers and doctors. There were notaries who were hidalgos of good standing, their mothers and sisters doñas, their brothers on the council of some (generally small) Spanish city. Others came from families of merchants, both small and well-to-do. Since the trade was learned through apprenticeship, a core of the notaries came from families which had long been handing the notarial office from father to son. Finally, a good proportion of the notaries came directly out of the artisan class, their fathers carpenters or shoemakers. Over the years, the notaries more and more appropriated hidalgo standing to themselves, taking the attitude that where some were hidalgos the rest must be, and also profiting by the close association in the minds of the Spaniards between nobility and municipal office of any kind. The change did not come in a day; in 1541 Alonso de Luque, a notary who was related to Bishop Hernando de Luque, the associate of Pizarro and Almagro, and who became alcalde and encomendero in Arequipa, still claimed only to be a "person of honor." But by 1560 most notaries who were not of frankly artisan backgrounds were calling themselves hidalgos.[42]

The need for, and the great value placed on, the notaries' skills, permitted them, above all in the early period, to carve out careers for themselves hardly less impressive than those of their colleagues with degrees. Notaries who participated in the early military phase of the conquest, at Cajamarca or the taking of Cuzco and Quito, not only received encomiendas as a matter of course, but were prime candidates for positions of honor as alcaldes and council members. The membership of the municipal councils reflected broadly social criteria, but the councils had to be able to function within the framework of Spanish legalism. Not all the members could be chosen, therefore, on the basis of wealth, military prowess, political influence, seniority, and lineage; some of them had to be knowledgeable about legal procedures, which gave notaries a distinct advantage.

Notaries were also well placed to seize every political opportunity. A town's chief notary, who also served as clerk of the council, was particularly close to the source of power, and all notaries belonged to what one could call a courthouse crowd. In the best position of all were the governor's secretaries, who one after the other were granted encomiendas, over the Spanish Peruvians' strong protests. In all, at least twenty notaries who had practiced their trade in Peru achieved the total success marked by a large encomienda and high municipal office. As encomenderos, notaries did not entirely deny their origins, being among the most sedentary and business-minded, and though they did not shirk their military duties, only two or three of them ever became captains, and of these, only one, Nicolás de Heredia, was a major leader with real skill and a following.

The occasional raising of notaries to encomendero status continued through the Gasca redistribution of 1548, but most of the new encomenderos had been in Peru since the 1530's. Alongside those who earlier or later transcended their status were the working notaries, who were active and numerous in Peru from the first moment. As usual, their actual numbers are hard to estimate; a project of counting all references to notaries in the sources of the present study had to be given up because of the magnitude of the task. It appears that they ranked in numbers considerably above doctors and lawyers, but rather below the clergy. At Cajamarca there were ten notaries among the 169 men, and there is little reason to think the proportion diminished later.

On the day of a city's founding it already had a combined council clerk and notary public. As the city grew, more notary offices were added; four to six in Lima, three in La Plata.[43] The number at any given time was legally fixed, and the appointments were made by the crown on a patronage basis, though local authorities retained a large degree of practical control. The notaries' offices were always clustered together on the town square, near or even in the city council building. Notaries tended to rent their offices rather than own them, and often they and their staffs lived in contiguous quarters behind the offices.

The notary did not do the bulk of the writing himself. That was the task of an aide who might be another notary without an established position, but more typically was a young man who had not yet acquired his notary's title. The apprentice system continued in full force in Peru, though only exceptionally as a formal agreement. The young aide or *escribiente* acted as a servant, wrote out the long formulas of the documents as instructed, and after a few years of experience, having worked perhaps for three or four masters, would send to the royal court an application for a notary's title in the Indies. Then he would go off on his own. One result of the comparatively short period of training for notaries, and the continuance of apprenticeship, was that notaries often arrived in Peru at a very early age, in their middle or late teens. This may seem a commonplace, but there are indications that other types of professional people were mainly mature, often middle-aged men when they came, partly because of their long period of education, and partly because they had started careers in Spain before coming, particularly the ecclesiastics.

The office of a successful notary could be quite an establishment, with one or even two associates or partners of the head notary, and one to three apprentice-aides. Such a notary, particularly if he was also the clerk of the city council, might affect a certain pomp in the way of guests, slaves, and horses, and quite a few notaries were married in Peru.[44]

Nevertheless, notaries showed a definite propensity to return to Spain after a certain number of years if they did not receive encomiendas—as hardly any did who arrived after 1540. Even a lucrative position as a notary could not forever hold a man who could return to Spain and enjoy the same status as in Peru, something neither an encomendero nor an artisan could do. Practically the whole Spanish Peruvian population, most encomenderos excluded, harbored some ambition of returning to Spain, but were often frustrated by death and inertia. Notaries were, after courtly nobles and merchants, the group most determined to return. Sometimes this was merely the classic desire of emigrants to spend their old age in the mother country after having invested the prime of their life in the new. But more often, a notary had accumulated enough money, after three to five years of work at his trade and general capitalistic activity, to return and buy a notary's office in Spain.

The notary who was returning sought out and sold his office to someone willing to pay for it, a few hundred pesos for a minor post, and many thousands for a rich one. The old notary then relinquished his office to the new one, promising to secure the crown's approval within a given time. This procedure of confirmation was so slow, and the turnover of notaries at times so fast, that the resignations piled up, the second notary relinquishing to the third before his own confirmation arrived, with ensuing lack of clarity. In 1548 Gasca swept many of these dubious claimants aside, granting the offices as rewards to notaries who had served in his campaign against Gonzalo Pizarro.[45]

The work of notaries extended far beyond drawing up and notarizing public documents. The notary who was town council clerk had other administrative tasks ex officio. All the notaries served as clerks in the courts of the alcaldes, and a large part of a notary office's daily work was the production of trial transcripts, for copies of everything had to go to all the parties, and on to higher courts if there was an appeal. Francisco Pizarro paid 1,200 pesos for a transcript of the voluminous trial of Almagro. Sometimes as part-time occasional work, and sometimes as full-time employment when they held no other position, notaries served as deputy constables, treasury clerks and accountants, clerks of investigating judges, and ecclesiastical notaries.[46]

Governmental work became, however, for a certain number of notaries, more a lifetime career than a sideline. One notary, Bernaldino de San Pedro, gave up his office in Lima to work for the treasury, and was for two years acting treasurer general of all Peru, before deciding to return to Spain rather than accept the position permanently.[47] Court clerks of the Audiencia, administrative assistants, and governors' secretaries tended to stay in their somewhat specialized branch rather than seek to obtain a notary public's office.

Closely related to the notary was the procurador, or untitled lawyer. In Spain, procuradors competed with titled lawyers at all levels, right up to the royal court. They were supposed to have training beyond that of an ordinary notary, but in Peru they were for the most part simply notaries, as some of the better qualified of them occasionally complained. A few of the best-trained procuradors were admitted to practice before the Audiencia. As opposed to the titled lawyers, who took on major cases one at a time, the procuradors sometimes agreed to do all of a client's legal business over a greater length of time for a set fee, and their services were distinctly cheaper. Some procuradors gained a permanent position for themselves in a community not as court lawyers but as caretakers of the estates of minors, widows, and absentee owners.[48]

Though procuradors had potential prestige at least as high as a notary's, their economic base was so uncertain that most of them only worked as lawyers temporarily until they could find something more steady, and would have been happy to accept a notary's office. Each city licensed a number of procuradors to practice in the alcaldes' courts, but they were subject to constant harrying, partly because of their own irresponsibility. They moved from one city to the next with great frequency, and at times were known to conduct litigation on a speculative basis, at no cost to the client, with profits to be divided if the case was won.[49]

A prominent notary of Peru was Pedro de Salinas, twice clerk of Lima's city council, about whose career many revealing details are known, though he can hardly be said to be typical. A notary with his ability, family connections, and seniority should by rights have received an encomienda, but he never did. Possibly he was personally unprepossessing, or made errors in political tactics; possibly a large part of the explanation lies in his extreme youth in the crucial period of the 1530's, for the Spaniards would have been very reluctant to give an encomienda to a boy in his teens.

Pedro de Salinas was born in Madrid around 1518. Nothing is presently known about his family except that one of his brothers resided at one time in the royal court. Pedro considered himself an hidalgo, but was not very assertive about it; all things considered, it is likely that Pedro's relatives were notaries and procuradors in Madrid, and therefore had some court connection, for as Oviedo said, everyone in Madrid was a courtier.

In 1535, a seventeen-year old boy, Pedro came to Peru as the secretary of Bishop Berlanga of Panama, who was carrying out an investigation for the crown. He already had received his notary's title, but his unsure writing hand betrayed his youth. Later, when he reached maturity, he had one of the finest hands in all Peru; his signature with its rubrics was a marvel, fluent and graceful, yet firm. When Bishop Berlanga returned shortly to Panama, Pedro went on to Cuzco, where he was caught in the siege of that city by the Indians in 1536–37. Only eighteen years old, and furthermore, as well as one can tell, not militarily inclined, Pedro in no way distinguished himself (nor did he ever in the later course of the civil wars, though he took part in major battles). Almagro lifted the siege in 1537, and Pedro served for a while as notary for Almagro's alcalde. In 1538 he was present at the battle between Hernando Pizarro and Almagro outside Cuzco.

Late in 1538 Pedro was catapulted into Peru's most sought-after notarial office. Domingo de la Presa, notary of Lima's city council, had advanced to encomendero status, and relinquished the office to Pedro, who was still only about nineteen years of age. Though Pedro was well qualified, the only reason that the post can have gone to him rather than to a more senior figure is that his family and court connections were decisive.

Pedro de Salinas now entered on a five-year period as Lima's chief notary. He got a basic salary of 200 pesos a year for his activities as clerk of the council, and had his own notary public's office besides. One or two aides carried much of the burden of work in the notary's office, from which he was often absent. The aides changed quickly, leaving to seek other opportunities. One of them was a Bartolomé Arvallo, from Huelva, a boy younger than Salinas himself, who was in the office for about a year, left to work for another notary, and then went on his own as a procurador, before finally becoming a small-scale merchant. Another of Salinas' aides was Juan de Salinas, a relative, who stayed with him as long as he was in Peru.

In 1541, the year of Pizarro's assassination, Salinas acquired a partner, the notary Juan Franco, ten years older than he was, who thenceforth took over the daily operation of the notary's office almost completely, leaving Salinas free for municipal concerns and his own growing business affairs. Franco lived, ate, and slept in Salinas' house, and the two soon became very close friends. During Governor Vaca de Castro's 1542 campaign, Franco stayed in Lima to keep the office running, while Salinas went with the army. He spent the eve of the battle of Chupas notarizing wills; what he did on the battlefield is not known. He did not do enough, at any rate, to earn himself an encomienda. Concluding there was no hope, in the spring of 1543 he relinquished his post to Juan Franco, arranged to send his Indian servant woman María and his mestizo son Juan to Spain, and planned to follow quickly.

Salinas was an indecisive man, and the Gonzalo Pizarro rebellion of 1544 found him still in the country. He stayed on, attending to business matters and doing occasional work related to his profession. From time to time he took extended trips to Huancayo in the highlands, where he kept a herd of goats. (Huancayo was the encomienda of his friend Juan de Cáceres, Peru's accountant general, who was from his home town of Madrid.) These trips were partly for business, and partly for pleasure; sometimes Pedro invited friends to come along, and took his Spanish mistress, Juana de Berrío, with him. Once, when he did not take her, he returned to find she had been unfaithful, whereupon he promptly arranged for Juana to marry her lover, himself paying for the wedding. This he did only partly in disgust. He was already thinking of marrying a woman with a higher lineage and greater wealth.

In 1546 Salinas was able, through chance, to return to his post as notary of Lima's council. After a year in office, his partner and successor Juan Franco had in turn resigned, and now in the course of the civil wars the new occupant had entered the Dominican monastery. Salinas and Franco returned to their old partnership, and operated their office as before, while Peru's worst civil war reached its climax in 1547 and 1548.

Lima was still in the grip of Gonzalo Pizarro in May, 1547, when Salinas married a young woman named Isabel Arias, who was not a doña, but her wealthy sister, possessor of an encomienda, provided her with a 3,000-peso dowry, including valuable landed property. The marriage brought Salinas increased wealth and association with the encomendero class, but it may also have finally doomed his aspirations to acquire an encomienda for himself. His new in-laws were enthusiastic followers of Gonzalo Pizarro who changed sides almost too late, and were lucky to retain their encomienda in Gasca's redistribution of 1548. Gasca gave nothing to Salinas, though Salinas was not in disfavor, collaborating with the authorities during the war effort and afterwards.

After the war both partners finally left Peru for good, relinquishing the notary's office to the same man who had it in 1540, and now had left the Dominicans. They wound up their affairs, no triviality, since both owned property and were silent partners in commercial ventures worth thousands of pesos. Franco was first to depart, in 1548. He went to Seville and bought a notary's office there; the documents in his registers reflect the continuation of relationships begun in the New World.

Salinas did not leave until 1550, with Gasca's fleet, having been fifteen years in Peru. On the passage across the isthmus of Panama, he finally, too late, achieved the military distinction that earlier might have won him an encomienda. Gasca was bringing back a great fortune in Peruvian silver, which a party of Spanish renegades from Nicaragua attempted to seize. Salinas was named captain of a company in forces organized in the city of Panama to resist the pirates. After hard fighting the loyalists were victorious and Salinas arrived in Spain as a hero, calling himself Captain Pedro de Salinas. At court he was granted a coat of arms, and got a royal cedula of recommendation to the Peruvian authorities, an indication that he was toying with the idea of returning and having one more try at an encomienda. He thought better of it, and lived the rest of his long life in Madrid, in what capacity is not known, but he continued to testify about the siege of Cuzco until 1585, when he was nearing seventy.[50]

Professional people in Peru were after all something of a middle group. Socially, they occupied a broad middle ground just bordering on the nobility at the top and the artisans at the bottom. They were less firmly rooted in the country than the encomenderos and the artisans, but more so than courtly nobles and merchants. They could neither be called martial, nor strictly peaceful, for all of them, even the clergy, were active in the wars. Pedro de Salinas, a borderline hidalgo, an undistinguished veteran, undecided whether to go home or to stay, was not unrepresentative of the many hundreds of professional men who took part in the occupation of Peru.

V MERCHANTS

The numerous merchants who exploited Peru's great wealth stood out from the rest of the populace, even in a capitalistic world where everyone from viceroy to carpenter's apprentice tried in one way or another to invest in merchandise. The true professional merchants were experts in accounting and interest rates, worked full time at buying and selling, traveled often, and, above all, publicly declared themselves to be merchants. Whether in Peru or in Spain, merchants were far from despised, but there were definite limitations to the kinds of success they could hope to achieve. Peru, though it yielded them untold wealth, was in some ways more unkind to merchants than Spain or other parts of the Indies. In Seville wealthy merchants could hold honorific posts in the municipal government, in Panama they dominated the city council, but in Peru significant municipal office did not go to merchants until after 1560. No merchants became encomenderos except through devious means. Even in the first few years of the conquest, when miracles of social mobility were being performed, most merchants went about their business, neither claiming nor receiving encomiendas, while around them artisans and other humble people were transformed into encomenderos.

It is hardly possible to describe adequately the social position of merchants by reference to their origins in other classes, as with professional men, for merchants were themselves one of the primordial social classes and points of reference. In rank they stood below hidalgos and above artisans, but with some special advantages and disadvantages. As educated, wealthy men, they were accorded some respect, and had much in common with the upper groups; in Peru they moved in the circles of encomenderos, though only on sufferance. On the negative side, merchants had a reputation as cowardly moneygrubbers, and in some ways suffered in comparison to artisans, many of whom were fighting men.

The great majority of Peru's merchants belonged to merchant families of Spain; commercial organizations were built on family ties, and most merchants did everything possible to keep all their sons in the business. Still, the borders of the class were indistinct. Wealthy merchants in Spain often were able to marry the daughters of hidalgos, and their sons, while still merchants, could claim hidalgo status. Lawyers and doctors, themselves sometimes only one generation out of the merchant class, would send a son into a career as a merchant. On the lower levels, there was no clear line between merchants and artisans, since artisans kept shops where they sold their own products and anything else that might bring a profit. The line actually became somewhat clearer in Peru than it had been in Spain. It would be hard to say whether Seville's *sederos* or specialists in silks were more merchants or tailors, but in Peru they were definitely artisans, quite distinct from the merchant class. Artisans in Peru who prospered and became entrepreneurs refused to call themselves merchants, even though their activities proclaimed them so.

Merchants tended to come from the same regions of Spain as the lower levels of the professional class. Though there were merchants from all regions, a sampling of their origins shows Andalusia even more predominant than usual, and Extremadura far below its usual rank. A tiny but influential minority of merchants came from the kingdom of Aragon.[1]

Significant change in the regional origin of merchants took place in the course of the civil war period, at least on the higher levels. In the Caribbean, commerce had been dominated by four different groups, all based in Seville: Italians, merchants from Burgos (representing Old Castile), Basques, and Andalusians. By the time of the conquest of Peru, Italian merchants had dropped out of the picture. Only two or three true professional merchants from Italy are known to have come to Peru, as opposed to the numerous Italian sailors who went into small-scale business. The Basques too were just dropping out of really large operations at the time of the conquest. The last of them was Domingo de Soraluce, a merchant from Vergara and one of the famous thirteen who stayed with Pizarro on the Isle of Gallo. He had built up a great fortune before he died in 1536, but found no successors. The sizable minority of Basque merchants which continued to operate in Peru contained no major figures.

An explanation for the diminishing role of the Italians and Basques must be sought elsewhere, but the fading out of the prominent merchants of Burgos can be partially explained here, because the final steps of the process took place on the Peruvian scene. Merchants from Old Castile were one of the more important commercial groups in Peru in the 1530's, and some still maintained themselves in the 1540's, to fade into relative insignificance in the next decade. The disappearance of the Old Castilians from the high levels of commerce was not simply a case of failure or displacement; it was also the result of their successful effort to transcend their status as merchants. This process began in the Caribbean, where, for example, García de Lerma, who was a member of a merchant family of Burgos, became governor of Santa Marta. Lerma's relative, Pedro de Lerma, came to Peru in 1537 as an hidalgo and a captain. Jerónimo de Villegas, captain and encomendero (see p. 27), was from another of these families. The last important Old Castilian merchant was Gaspar de Cuéllar, a "merchant of Burgos" (actually from Segovia) who had operated in Santo Domingo before coming to Peru in the late 1530's. Around 1545 he was one of the most respected, if not the most wealthy, of Lima's merchants. He had two brothers in Peru, one of them Licenciado Miguel de Cuéllar, corregidor of Arequipa, and the other Diego de Aguilar, a lawyer. In other words, the merchant families of Burgos sent representatives to Peru, but increasingly as professional men, captains, and administrators, rather than merchants.[2]

As the others receded, Andalusians took their place. In the first decade of Peruvian occupation, merchants from Andalusia were but one group among several, perhaps the most numerous, but not clearly the most prominent. By 1550 Andalusians dominated most of the large firms importing goods into Peru from Spain, and remained dominant until 1560 at least. Most of the large merchants seem to have originated in peripheral centers like Huelva, Jerez, or Córdoba, rather than in Seville itself.

Peru's merchants, like others of their time, were determined enemies of specialization, and Peru lost even the limited specialization in such things as slave trading, cloth selling, and money lending which already existed in Spain and the Atlantic. Nevertheless, the principal business

of the merchants, to which all else was secondary, was the importing
and selling of shipments of general Spanish merchandise in return for
the silver and gold of Peru. The merchandise was referred to as "cloth,"
that being certainly the largest single item, but besides domestic and
foreign cloth of all qualities, and finished articles of clothing, it included wine, olive oil, and conserves; iron, horseshoes, mining tools,
and scissors; playing cards and prayer books; rugs and vaulted chests.
The staples of trade did not change much from the early days of the
conquest through 1560, though the quantity steadily increased.[3]

Other major items of commerce, not a direct part of the shipments,
were livestock (particularly horses) and slaves. While Negro slaves
were within the province of the professional merchants (see p. 177),
the livestock which were brought from Nicaragua and Mexico more
often went through other channels, with shipmasters and the stock
raisers themselves playing the most active part. Merchants often owned
the ships and the pack teams which transported their goods, though in
the case of ships they were usually only short-term or partial owners.
Beyond this they took advantage of any economic opportunity that
presented itself, making loans, insuring money remitted to Spain, and
contracting various types of companies with non-merchants. The most
important of these were companies with encomenderos in mining operations, in which the merchant would supply cash, mining tools, and
Negroes.

One thing merchants tried to avoid was extensive investment in real
estate. If they owned more than the house they lived in and the store
where they sold their goods (most did not own even that much) they
opened themselves to the seizure of those properties to enforce debt
collection, and even the most solid merchants were at times many
thousands of pesos in debt, seeking to have borrowed money work for
them as long as possible before they repaid it. Moreover, merchants
were strongly oriented toward Spain and Seville, where the largest
firms were based, and their whole effort was to get a maximum of spe-
cie back to Seville in the shortest possible time.[4]

Most merchants operated under a considerably refined form of the
medieval company or partnership, with its basic idea of a new company for each new investment. Peru's smaller dealers, who bought in Panama to sell in Peru, or in Lima to sell in the highlands, still used this
form of company in its purity. Larger merchants organized companies
based in Seville, with terms of three to five years, periodic shipments,

reinvestment of profits, and the understanding that the company would continue beyond the term if all went well. There were as many kinds of companies as there were opportunities, but the two main types were, first, the large firm with a senior partner in Seville and junior partners in Panama and Lima; and, second, the smaller company with its senior partner in Lima (or Arequipa) and junior partners who went to Panama (or Lima) to buy goods, and to the highlands to sell them. In trade with Mexico, the senior partner was usually based in a Mexican city. Lima representatives of large firms of Seville made secondary companies to sell merchandise in the hinterland. As a rule, the senior partner was the real investor, and the others his factors or agents, but the factors generally invested some amount, at times on a credit basis, becoming partners and earning a share of the profits rather than a salary.

Family ties, and secondarily regional origin, were important in the formation of companies. Peru was the most distant and wealthiest part of the Indies, where governmental authority was weakest. Without the family bond, merchants of Seville could not begin to trust their factors in Peru, whose record, even when they were relatives, was not a good one. The ideal, rarely achieved, was to have the father in Seville, and sons in Panama, Lima, and elsewhere in Peru. When it was necessary to trust someone from outside the family, every effort was made to marry him into it; his new wife's dowry could be left in Spain as additional security for his good behavior. The extra-familial partner would have some young member of the family with him, partly to gain experience and partly to keep watch over the family interests.[5]

Formal commercial arrangements had a strong element of fiction in them. Rather than have the partners formally earn percentages of the profits, which is what they really did, merchants adjusted the nominal amount of their respective investments so that each partner would gain an equal share after recovering his investment. Merchants also thought of prices in terms of percentages, but hardly ever expressed this. They hoped to earn 50 per cent to 150 per cent between Seville and Panama, and the same again between Panama and Lima. In the early 1540's merchants trading between Panama and Lima made 100 per cent profit for three years straight, which leveled off to 30 per cent to 60 per cent in 1544, to rise again when goods became scarce during and after the Gonzalo Pizarro rebellion. The same pattern of fictionalization held in money lending and debt collection. Actually a high rate of interest was charged, but this was expressed as the obligation of the recipient of the loan to pay a fixed sum at a fixed time, under the fiction that he had originally received the whole amount. In 1546, an agent of Pedro de Valdivia had to oblige himself to pay over 20,000 pesos in Chile in order to receive about 3,000 in Lima. For collecting debts for colleagues, merchants received a commission, not written down but understood, of 5 per cent or more.[6]

Under a veil of fiction, constant speculation in currency went on. Through most of the period all the transactions were in gold pesos, though silver was far more common, until in the latter 1550's the term "peso of current silver" was introduced as a gesture toward reality. There was good, bad, and indifferent silver in circulation, some of it having paid the royal fifth and some not. Merchants, who kept in touch with the European money market, and were moreover confident that the more sophisticated methods of refining and assaying used in Spain would give their silver more than its nominal value in Peru, apparently made as much at times from currency speculation as from sale of merchandise. Ordinary payments of all kinds were made in silver bars or in *plata menuda,* odds and ends of silver, which were weighed out at an agreed ratio of silver to gold pesos. Merchants kept their supplies of silver and gold themselves, typically in a strong chest at the foot of the bed. An aid in making payments, and a further matter for speculation, was the practice of transferring debts from one merchant to another, as many as three or four times.[7]

In a wildly fluctuating market situation, merchants generally did not limit themselves exclusively to either wholesale or retail operations. Depending on the state of the market, a large firm would at times sell its merchandise in Panama and quickly reinvest, at times send the goods on to Lima, and then perhaps to Arequipa and Potosí. It was important to have an experienced, responsible man in Panama, though Panama represented, as one merchant said, "more work and more danger" than Lima. Wholesale transactions also took place in Lima, a shipment or store-full of goods costing anywhere from 2,000 to 20,000 pesos. In 1550 two large merchants bought thirteen or fourteen lots of merchandise in Lima and refused to sell it retail, meaning to corner the supply and sell wholesale at high prices to other merchants.

Even the largest merchants, however, kept stores where goods were sold across the counter to the general public. Both poor and rich customers tended to keep an account which they settled periodically, not only from need, but also because the currency was so awkward. Stores were very early concentrated in rows on certain streets, but only Arequipa is known to have had an actual "Merchants' Street." Since supplies came in to large firms only at long intervals, and small stores were liquidated completely before being replenished, there was always a rush when a new lot arrived or a new store was set up. Often the encomenderos, through the municipal council, preempted the right of first choice. Within a few days the best items were sold at high prices, and the rest might lie on the shelves for a long time until, at worst, the goods were auctioned off, or at best, a period of scarcity allowed the sale of the remainder at good prices.[8]

No channels existed in the Indies to which merchants could entrust the communications so important in determining the timing and size of their shipments. Each company was its own communication network; every time any representative went from one place to another, he carried a thick packet of papers which included, along with debts to be collected, long letters of up to fifty pages, full of personal and political news, messages to be relayed on to others, and, above all, reports on market conditions and suggested future plans for the company. Sometimes these messages were in code. The commercial networks were so superior to any others, that non merchants took advantage of them to send letters and money home to Spain, and the relatives in Spain of people who died in Peru used them to try to collect their inheritances. Within Peru itself, the company of one merchant, Francisco de Torres, who was particularly heavily involved in importing mules and horses, and who kept a brother stationed in Cuzco, operated something like a courier service for the merchants of Lima and on occasion even for the governor.[9]

The role of merchants in the wars which rocked Peru was somewhat ambiguous, but mainly they were considered noncombatants, even in the early times of great Indian dangers. In 1534 Francisco de Calahorra, a merchant's factor, was accompanying the small Spanish force of about two hundred men, collecting debts and selling merchandise, but not fighting; the others did not consider him one of the conquerors. Throughout the civil war period, other Spaniards tended to scoff at the merchants' lack of skill with weapons. However, at least a few did fight in battles, though without distinction or reward. Many times in the civil wars merchants received summons to duty, which in fact were invitations to supply arms, money, or men to fight in their place. Mer-

chants enjoyed the status of near-neutrals in the wars, since everyone
needed them and they were not candidates for the encomiendas over
which the wars were fought. When the Almagrists assassinated Pizarro
in 1541, and most of the populace hid for several days in their houses,
the merchant Diego Montesinos was one of the few people who continued to go back and forth openly. After each war, the governors easily forgave the merchants most closely associated with the defeated
rebels.[10]

A yet more basic question concerning merchants in the civil wars is
the extent of war profits. While merchants claimed that the wars
brought them unmitigated disaster, in other accounts the merchants
appear as the greatest beneficiaries, and this latter view seems the
more probable, in view of the fact that at the end of each war ambitious new companies would be set up with capital that could only be
war profits. To help finance their campaigns, governors raised
hundreds of thousands of pesos from among merchants through forced
loans and sales. According to the complaints of merchants, the prices
and interest rates they had to accept were low, but others claimed the
prices were exorbitantly high. However this may be, in other respects
commerce flourished, as demand increased and prices rose for all kinds
of articles, not only arms and horses, but also wine, provisions, and
cloth. To the Spaniards war was an occasion for the display of finery.
When an army was being organized, recruits received lump payments
of from 200 to 500 pesos, much of which they spent on plumes and
silks. Outside the immediate locale of battle, business in Peru went on
as usual during the civil wars, and though some roads were blocked at
times, the sea routes remained open except for a time in 1546–47.[11]

On the margins of the commercial class were small dealers whom the
Spaniards called *tratantes*. They were distinguished from the true merchants by their lack of connection with a network, and by the fact that
they bought locally to resell locally, whereas the merchants always
bought at long distance. Peru's merchants were still the heirs of the
itinerant traders of the Middle Ages, equating their calling with frequent travel. One of them explained his absence from Peru in 1545 by
alleging that being a merchant involved constant travel from one place
to another.[12] Even members of large firms often went back and forth
between Lima and Panama. The tratantes, on the other hand, were
more closely associated with a single community.

A considerable gap in social rank separated the two groups. When sums were collected for civil war campaigns, two lists were kept, one for merchants, and the other for tratantes and artisans. The chronicler Gutiérrez de Santa Clara distinguishes between merchants, whom he treats with respect, and "tratantes and others of little consequence." Many of them illiterate and no few of them foreigners, tratantes did indeed come from backgrounds quite different from most merchants. As always, however, the distinction was not utterly sharp and consistent, either in terminology or in fact. In Spain, the word "tratante" in legal formulas meant the same thing as merchant, and this use is seen occasionally in Peru as well.[13]

In the towns, tratantes sold as much general merchandise as they could afford to buy, but more especially miscellanea and trifles, such as old clothes, playing cards, game, and dried fish. Most kept stores, though some were little more than peddlers, and at least one operated in a tent in the public street. Tratantes, particularly those who were married, doubled as inn and tavern keepers. From 1550 on, the city of Lima awarded tavern licenses as an act of charity to tratantes who were poor, burdened with family, lame, or wounded in war. In the countryside, and above all in the southern highlands, tratantes dealt in Indian products to be sold at Potosí, their specialties being llamas and *ropa de la tierra*, or Indian clothing. But since this business was so lucrative, the tratantes were not allowed to monopolize it, carrying on only the part left them by the encomenderos and the true merchants.[14]

The system of commerce as sketched above grew up in Peru very quickly after the conquest; elements of it were present from the beginning, and by 1540 it was essentially mature. The decade of the 1530's was a period of transition. Until Cajamarca (1532), the commercial aspects of outfitting expeditions in Panama were simply an extension of Caribbean commerce. After Cajamarca, against a background of immense wealth and constant danger, entrepreneurs entered on a several-year period of maximum risk and maximum profits. A single shipment of merchandise brought to the right place at the right time could make its owner wealthy for life. In the 1530's therefore, particularly in the period 1533–38, neither expert knowledge, large capital, nor an extensive network was absolutely essential to commercial success, and professional merchants operated side by side with other kinds of entrepreneurs. Three main types are discernible: (1) expert professional merchants with direct connections to Seville; (2) small merchants without connections, including both true professionals and rough, uneducated men of the kind who were later tratantes; (3) non-merchant entrepreneurs, principally the legist-governors, Dr. Sepúlveda (see p. 65), the royal officials, and the Pizarros, the last acting through intermediaries.

The trade of Peru was always too large, chaotic, and rich to be dominated by any one commercial interest, though the Pizarros, in the person of Hernando Pizarro, made a determined effort to do so. Acting through his majordomos and to a lesser extent through professional merchants, Hernando sold general merchandise to the conquerors of Peru, becoming probably the country's largest single entrepreneur. His business profited from the Pizarros' political position, but the hoped-for monopoly never materialized, and the Pizarros never took any restrictive action to enforce one, goods from whatever source being too badly needed. Hernando's final return to Spain in 1539 marked the end of the Pizarros' active participation in commerce; after that they depended on encomiendas and mines for their financial sinews. At about the same time, the other pseudo-governmental entrepreneurs left Peru or retired from active participation in business, except for Veedor García de Salcedo, whose continuing activities were a scandal.[15] Salcedo's large and barely-disguised business ventures, continuing into the 1550's, show that neither popular disapproval nor the royal sanctions against commercial activity on the part of governmental officials were of themselves sufficient deterrents. The increasing professionalization of commerce was far more important in the gradual disappearance of official-entrepreneurs.

In this context of general commercial activity, with prominent individuals engaging in trade without stigma, while outright merchants were excluded from the encomendero class, some well-educated and ambitious merchants were able to disassociate themselves from their calling quickly enough to become plausible candidates for encomiendas. Felipe Boscán, a merchant from Jerez de la Frontera, came to Peru around 1536 as the senior of two factors of Marshal Diego Caballero, to sell a shipment of merchandise worth 4,000 pesos. But instead of declaring himself a merchant, he appeared in the guise of a gentleman entrepreneur. Through a close association with Hernando Pizarro, he soon became an encomendero.[16]

Merchants had to be quite adaptable to make the transition from the commerce of the mid-1530's, with its bonanzas when spoils were divided, and complete ruin when the Indians annihilated an expedition, to the more orderly business world of the next decade. Some merchants got the mood of the age of discovery so much in their blood that they moved on to other areas as Peru began to settle down.

Others were not able to make the transition even though they tried, for rough practical knowledge of commercial affairs was no longer sufficient in the 1540's, and old hands who lacked education and connections had to retire to the second rank. Seniority had less importance in determining the status of merchants than with any other group. One small merchant who was not helped by his seniority was Silvestre Rodríguez, from the area of Jaén, who accompanied Pizarro's expeditions of discovery in the 1520's and was in Peru proper by 1535. Though he shied away from the label of merchant, he manifestly was one, and was never considered for an encomienda. In 1535, as the factor of a Portuguese merchant of Panama, he took a shipment of merchandise to Cuzco and sold it there as part of the outfitting of Almagro's expedition to Chile. Rodríguez was literate and able to keep accounts, but was no expert on large affairs, and had no connections with any large firm. His closest associates, for whom he sold merchandise on the side, were men like Maestre Pedro de Paredes, a tailor and small entrepreneur of Panama. Rodríguez stayed in Peru for many years, but could not maintain himself among the importers of Spanish merchandise. In 1547, already an old man, he was a small dealer in maize and wheat, which he bought in Arequipa to sell in Potosí.[17]

The early years also saw, however, the beginning of an important trend, the migration of successful merchants of Peru to Seville, which typically did not mean a loss of interest in the trade, for in Seville the ex-Peruvians became senior partners of companies trading with Peru, and sent back their younger relatives to take their places. This movement started as early as 1535, when Francisco Núñez de Illescas, a merchant of Seville who had first operated in Panama and then enriched himself in Peru, returned to Seville, leaving his associate Ruy Díaz de Gibraleón to represent him in Peru. Their company was active in this form through the early 1540's, after which Ruy Díaz also returned, and the two in company with numerous relatives, both in Seville and the Indies, sent merchandise to Peru and Mexico in lots as large as a hundred tons.[18]

In the 1540's this pattern was increasingly repeated. Perhaps the most active firm in Peru in the period 1540–44 was the company of Diego Montesinos, stationed principally in Lima, and Luis Suárez, in

Cuzco and Arequipa. Both were related to, and were to a certain extent the representatives of, merchants in Seville and Panama; Suárez in particular represented his brother, Juan Alvarez, city council member of Nombre de Dios on the Isthmus. By 1547 Montesinos was in Seville, and Suárez had taken his brother's place in Panama, while an in-law of Suárez represented their large company in Lima. The company was, formally, a merger of two separate companies, both of which included Montesinos and some combination of Suárez' relatives, and was typical of the increasingly involved arrangements of the 1540's.[19]

The most spectacular case of migration to Seville took place in 1549, right after the defeat of Gonzalo Pizarro, when five merchants, while still in Peru, organized a large company, with a six-year term and a capital of 45,000 ducats (or 37,500 pesos), to import goods from Seville. They were trained professionals, though not particularly well connected, who had accumulated their large capital during the first flourishing of the mines of Potosí. All had been heavily involved in the Pizarro rebellion; two had been formally accused, and one of them actually convicted, but that did not deter them.

The company's moving spirit was Francisco de Escobar, who had been in Peru since 1537. Merchant relatives of his had helped finance Valdivia's expedition to Chile, then gone there themselves, while Francisco stayed behind, gradually building up his wealth from a small start in Arequipa. By the late 1540's he still traded mainly between Arequipa and Upper Peru, but had diversified interests, and lived usually in Lima, with his wife. In 1549 he organized the new company among his associates, and he and the other two large investors returned to Spain, leaving the remaining two partners, who had invested little, as factors in Panama and Lima.

Enough is known about the organization and subsequent fate of Escobar's company to provide a coherent picture of how a large Seville firm operated. One partner lived in Toledo and visited the fairs of northern Spain, where he sold the gold and silver that came to the company from Peru. Escobar himself lived in Seville in some splendor, occupying a high office in municipal government as *fiel ejecutor*. He and a third partner procured, insured, and shipped merchandise with most but not all of the fleets leaving for Nombre de Dios, making extensive use of credit. In Nombre de Dios a factor-partner received the goods, transported them across the Isthmus by means of the company's boats, pack team, and slaves, and stored them in the company warehouse until time for shipment to Peru or, less often, sale on the spot. The factor-partner in Lima received the goods sent from Panama and had complete discretion as to their disposal. He could sell them wholesale, or in the store in Lima, or transport them by the company's pack team to Arequipa, where another house was maintained. At frequent intervals he made remittances through Panama to Seville.

All three of the major partners in Spain reserved the right to use the company network for the transportation and sale of their own goods outside the company. Escobar particularly made extensive use of this benefit, investing more on the side than he did within the regular framework. The partner in Lima maintained an extra store and a factor to sell Escobar's goods alone. Escobar kept up business contact, through the company, with his relatives in Chile. His wife, now in Seville with him, and his brother-in-law and sister, in Lima, also had small shipments sent, some of which were intended for high officials and must have been in the nature of bribes.

The company proceeded as planned, apparently prospering to judge by a 30,000 ducat (25,000 peso) reinvestment, until 1553. In May of that year news reached Seville of the death of the partner in Panama, a blessing in disguise according to Escobar, for he had used his responsible position to embezzle on a grand scale, retaining merchandise destined for Lima and remittances destined for Seville. The time had come to think of a new company. Over a two-month period Escobar wrote a long letter to his partner in Lima, devoted in large part to the question of future arrangements. He first suggested and then himself rejected two different companies before he finally settled on a third, which was signed by the parties in Seville without awaiting the concurrence of the man in Lima (who was anxious to return to Spain, while the partners in Seville wanted to keep him in Lima, since he had proved satisfactory). For a time it appeared that a large competing Seville firm was breaking up, and that some of the dissidents would join Escobar, thus making the largest concern trading with Peru; but this failed to develop. A source of preoccupation for Escobar was the role to be given the representative in Panama. He thought of selling the pack team and boats there and reducing representation to a simple factor, obliged automatically to send all goods to Lima. In the end he went back to the old arrangement, entrusting the position to a new partner whom he had just met.

In its slightly revised form the company again operated for some years, until major dissension broke out among the partners in 1557. Escobar's firm had never had, except at the lower levels, the extra cohesion supplied in most companies by ties of blood and regional origin. The second partner living in Seville now fled with company funds to Portugal, and turned up in 1558 in Lima, from which refuge both he and the partner stationed there defied Escobar. Both sides started litigation, and the company ceased to function, but Escobar continued to trade with Peru on his own, while the absconder attained at least a local prominence in Lima.[20]

The movement to Seville of merchants from Peru was complemented by the movement to Peru of large, established firms of Seville, some of which started sending permanent representatives to Peru in the early 1540's. Such representatives did not have to go through a long process of accumulating wealth and experience, but took their places in the top ranks of Peru's commercial world immediately. Alonso Pérez de Valenzuela, representing Marshal Diego Caballero and a wealthy man in his own right, came to Lima around 1543 at the age of fifty, and was, from the moment of his arrival until he died in the next decade, one of Lima's largest and most respected merchants. Another great merchant of Seville, Alonso de Illescas, prior of the Consulado and tax farmer of the customs of Seville, sent his son Alvaro de Illescas to Lima in 1543, the same year Valenzuela went, to represent a company dominated by the Illescas family. Despite his youth, Alvaro immediately became a power. In the first half of the decade of the 1550's, the Illescas company became the largest, or at least the most obviously active, in Peru, and Alvaro de Illescas in 1555 became the first merchant to be nominated for alcalde in Lima, though he was very far indeed from being elected.[21]

From early in the decade of the 1540's, then, Seville and Peru were for merchants the poles of a unified, inseparable field of action. More than any other group, the merchants of Peru cannot be understood without reference to Spain, since they were ultimately representatives of firms of Seville and themselves ambitious to move to Seville, an aim which the most successful of them managed to achieve. On the other hand, Seville's trade with Peru needs to be understood in relation to the internal affairs of the colony, for among the greatest "merchants of Seville" trading to the Indies were men who had first made their fortunes as merchants of Peru.

In the dialogue of Seville and Lima, the word of Seville, as the residence of the senior partners and the goal of all, carried much the greater weight, giving commerce in Peru its peculiar character. Peru's import merchants carried on many types of activities, but all had the common trait of being short-term, easily liquidated investments which would make possible an uninterrupted flow of gold and silver toward Seville. There was no equivalent in Peru of the extensive investment in government securities and real estate which Seville merchants used to stiffen their credit. Any such tendency on the part of the Lima representative of a Seville firm brought strong protest. When Alvaro de Illescas bought an interest in Lima's principal carting company and invested in livestock to supply the local meat market, his partners threatened to dissolve the firm, and Alvaro's angry father Alonso demanded that he come to Seville and give an account of himself. Such attempts to invest in the local economy were, however, quite rare, since merchants in the provinces who hoped to move on to Lima, and merchants in Lima who hoped to go to Seville, ordinarily had little incentive to put down roots.

As time went on, though, some merchants finally began to develop closer ties with the communities where they lived. One position in the Spanish community had always been the merchant's monopoly. From the moment of the first inception of monasteries, hospitals, and *cofradías* (the lay sodalities that united all strata of the Spanish population in their membership), the majordomos of these institutions were almost without exception merchants, unless a monastery happened to pick a friar instead. The choice was natural, for merchants were better qualified than others to manage the property which formed the organizations' economic base, and were very willing to fill a post that brought public honor. Social and economic criteria were important; a list of the majordomos of religious and charitable organizations in Lima shows mainly the representatives of large firms of Seville. A sincere philanthropic urge was not lacking among the merchants, however. The large merchant Alonso Pérez de Valenzuela was one of the founders and endowers of Lima's hospital, as well as its long-time majordomo.[22]

In the 1550's there began to appear among the merchants a new breed, who gave up their nomadic aspirations and settled firmly in one community, gaining an influential position as a stable representative of the shifting merchant corps. In Cuzco this dean of the merchants was a Lucas Téllez, in Arequipa a Diego Gutiérrez. They were perhaps not the largest traders in their respective cities, but were undisputed leaders on a local level. In Lima, too large for a single dominating figure, there were several merchants who chose a similar type of career. The goal of all these men, high municipal office, eluded them, though they appeared frequently at council meetings as representatives of the mercantile interests. Only in 1561 did an Aragonese merchant, Francisco Fajardo, become chief constable of Lima, with a seat on the municipal council.

Though large firms dominated commerce, at least between Seville and Lima, the smaller dealers who bought goods in Panama or Lima and sold them in the Peruvian hinterland were just as significant socially, and the biography of one of their number is as representative of the merchant class as that of a great merchant of Lima. Baltasar de Armenta was the name of a merchant from Seville who lived through nearly three decades in Peru, weathering the changes in the nature of commerce with good, though not spectacular success. In Seville the Armentas were *viñaderos*—which might mean vineyard-keepers, small wine merchants, or both—and Baltasar had a cousin who was a trained notary. Baltasar himself, at any rate, was literate and a professional merchant. All his life he maintained contact with his family, sending them money and having several of them come to join him in Peru, but the Armentas in Seville did not take an active part in Baltasar's business, or serve as his base of operations.

Baltasar came to Peru in 1537, and after a few months agreed to accept a position as agent of Hernando Pizarro, charged with helping to sell the lots of merchandise the latter was importing into Peru. This task carried Baltasar to many parts of Peru during the next year or two, until he took Arequipa as his headquarters at the time of its founding in 1539. By that time he had been joined by his younger brother Gaspar, who for some years was a junior partner in all his ventures. Baltasar's primary responsibility was to look after the Pizarro interest in the Arequipa region, but he immediately set about making himself independent. While the details are not known, it is apparent that Baltasar used the then widespread device of including in the large shipments of his employer a small investment of his own. He also gave financial aid to encomenderos of Arequipa, and took commissions for other merchants.

In 1542, while in Lima, where he appeared frequently, Baltasar signed two major contracts placing him in a new, higher category. First, he and his brother entered into a mining company with a large encomen-

dero of Arequipa, the encomendero contributing the mine and the
work of his Indians, the Armentas 4,000 pesos for Negroes, mules, and
mining equipment. When the encomendero was killed shortly afterwards at the battle of Chupas, Baltasar continued to operate the company in the name of his heir, whose guardian he was. Most of the
Armentas' capital went into the mining venture, but the same year
Baltasar became a partner in a medium sized, short-term company, with
a capital of 10,000 pesos, to take merchandise from Lima for sale in
Arequipa. The arrangement was a perfect example of how the merchants of Peru lifted themselves by their bootstraps. Nominally Baltasar
was an equal partner with a 5,000-peso investment, but actually he invested nothing whatever beyond his influence in Arequipa and expert
knowledge of market conditions there. Half of his investment was borrowed from two merchants of Panama; the other half was to be made in
Arequipa, from Baltasar's profits. Baltasar did not even have to invest
much work; the company hired a factor to take the goods to Arequipa
and sell them, Baltasar's only duty being supervision, and responsibility for any decisions to send the goods on to Cuzco or Upper Peru, if
conditions warranted.

Even now, Baltasar remained the representative of the Pizarros,
though he had incurred the wrath of Hernando Pizarro, who may have
suspected that his growing independence was based on graft. During
the period of the Gonzalo Pizarro rebellion, the Pizarros made various
use of the Armenta brothers in the Arequipa region. Gaspar administered the encomiendas of two mestizo daughters of Juan and Gonzalo
Pizarro. Baltasar was so closely associated with the Pizarro regime that
when it was overthrown in Arequipa in 1547, he was one of the very
few prisoners detained as presumably incorrigible.

But he soon emerged from this cloud, thenceforth to be completely
independent of the powerful family which had given him his start. The
new government absolved him of guilt, and gave him the important
temporary mission of helping record the large shipment of silver sent
to the king at the end of the war. In 1548 Baltasar advanced another
step in the importing business by investing 4,500 pesos in a company
with a Corsican merchant to bring goods to Lima from Panama. His
life now assumed a somewhat different pattern, which continued
through the decade of the 1550's. Dividing his time about equally between Lima and Arequipa, and going occasionally to Upper Peru, he
both invested in goods coming from Panama, and bought them whole-

sale in Arequipa. Probably he thought of himself as a merchant of Lima, where he was in some years one of two of the city's receivers of alms, and where he owned an interest in a pharmacy.

In Arequipa, Baltasar's brother Gaspar was becoming much more than a factor. Family relationships were the building blocks of merchant's companies, but inside the family each member, even the younger ones, had individual wealth. As Baltasar became involved in the flow of merchandise from Panama to Lima, Arequipa, and Potosí, Gaspar in a roughly complementary way settled more firmly in Arequipa, and though he still sold merchandise, invested in land and livestock as well. Three or four other Armentas, brothers, cousins, and nephews of Baltasar, were in Peru at one time or another and participated in the family enterprises. The most prominent of them was Alonso de Armenta, who came to Peru in the late 1540's, and made an attempt to rise above the family calling. He fought on horseback in the campaign of 1547, but receiving no reward, continued to serve as Baltasar's agent. In 1554 as Alonso was bringing merchandise belonging to himself and Baltasar from Lima to Arequipa, rebels seized the merchandise, lying partly unloaded in Arequipa's port of Quilca, along with the small ship that carried it. Alonso and the shipmaster, in extreme danger, escaped with the ship and singlehandedly sailed it to Lima. On the basis of this exploit Alonso became a serious candidate for an encomienda or other high honor, but was once again disappointed.

Sometime around 1560 Baltasar, then probably forty-five or fifty years old, wealthy and well-known though not one of Peru's largest entrepreneurs, took a step that proves how deeply some Spanish merchants felt their religious and philanthropic duties, even if it was impossible to integrate such imperatives into ordinary commercial practice. Baltasar entered the Augustinian order in Lima, and was so well received that in 1563 he was chosen to go to Spain and present the order's appeal to the crown for personnel and subsidies. The merchant was still under the friar's habit, however, and when it became known that Baltasar was on his way to Spain, laymen rushed to give him money to take home and messages to relay. By the time he left Peru, after more than twenty-five years in the country, he was so burdened down with private affairs that the Augustinians thought it prudent to send a second friar to accompany him.[23]

The merchants of Peru made both war and peace possible with the iron, tools, cloth, and provisions they supplied. Because of them, the

Peruvian civil wars and the Peruvian cities were good imitations of the Spanish originals. Merchants were a useful, educated class of people, and their private communications networks, the best Peru had, served the whole populace. Yet, though peaceful and substantial, they were, most of them, as rootless as gypsies, traveling constantly, avoiding permanent investments, anxious to climb the next rung of a ladder that extended from Potosí through Lima to Seville. Already inclined to constant migration, the merchants found little possibility in Peru of obtaining the encomiendas and municipal offices which might have caused them to take root more quickly, since the criteria for encomenderos practically excluded noncombatants. Just at the end of the conquest and civil war period, merchants were beginning to achieve wealth and honor within the community, but outside the encomienda system.

Though merchants as individuals had little inclination to stay in Peru, this was far from the whole picture. Lack of opportunity to leave kept many in the country, and those who went to Spain typically left behind relatives to maintain the family interest. Francisco de Escobar, after over a decade of activity in Peru, left to head his own large firm in Seville, but sent back his brother-in-law Lope de Salinas and his sister Juana de Escobar, who stayed permanently. Fray Diego de Córdoba Salinas, a Franciscan chronicler who lived in Lima in the seventeenth century, was Francisco de Escobar's great-grandson. In the commercial world, Seville could not be separated from Peru, and the family provided a continuity the individual would not.

VI ARTISANS

The formidable development of Spanish commerce in the conquest period still left a wide field of action for the numerous, varied group of Spanish artisans working in Peru. The largest single item of commerce, European cloth, was the raw material from which tailors produced most of the clothing worn by Spaniards. Along with the tools and weapons that merchants imported came large amounts of iron to be worked by Spanish Peruvian smiths in whatever form mining, construction, and the civil wars demanded. Peruvian smiths and founders manufactured a large part of such things as horseshoes, hoes, and swords, the bulk of the muskets used in the civil wars, and practically all such large items as bells and cannon. For the construction trades, commerce did not even deliver the needed raw materials. Carpenters and masons were responsible for procuring and processing the wood, stone, lime, and adobe with which they built everything from shops to pretentious mansions in the Spanish cities.

What proportion of the Spaniards in Peru were of artisan stock is not ascertainable even approximately, though it must have been large. Some attempt can be made, however, to estimate the number of artisans who actually practiced their trades in Peru. Research for the present study resulted in a list of over 800 Spanish artisans who were in Peru between 1532 and 1560. There is little room for doubt that they were indeed working at their trades. In the Peruvian notarial records they appear buying raw materials, making contracts, and selling their products; in the treasury records in the Archive of the Indies they are typically being paid for work done. Needless to say, the list of 800 artisans is far from complete. The archives of Quito, Guayaquil, Piura,

Trujillo, La Paz, Sucre, and Potosí were not seen; the notarial records of Cuzco for the period before 1560 have disappeared. Lima and Arequipa's notarial archives contain a mine of information, but only a part of the original documents is preserved, and not all of these could be seen for the present study. In the circumstances, it seems conservative to estimate that there were at least three times 800, or about 2,500, artisans in Peru during the period 1532–60. This is to be compared with a total Spanish population which few would imagine to have exceeded 10,000 before 1560, with a possible maximum of 20,000 Spaniards having set foot in the country through the whole period. It would appear likely that at the very least one in ten of the Spanish settlers was a working artisan. The absolute numbers of artisans increased constantly through 1560, but it is not clear whether or not the proportions changed.

With such fragmentary records, and no basis for a really accurate estimate of total population, little confidence can be placed in any exact figure put forth either for the absolute number of artisans, or the ratio of artisans to other Spaniards. But it can be considered proved that, in Peru in the conquest and civil war period, many hundreds of Spaniards did not hesitate to call themselves tailors, smiths, and carpenters, and work at their trades.

Analysis of the comparative numerical strength of the various trades can proceed on a firmer footing, a list of 800 being, if nothing else, a significant sampling. Most numerous were tailors and shoemakers, the producers of clothing. Next were the several kinds of workers in iron; during the first four or five years of the conquest, smiths were the most prominent group by far. Third came the construction trades, which began serious work in 1535 with the founding of Lima and Trujillo, and were in full swing by 1540. Silversmiths, muleteers, barbers, pharmacists, and confectioners were each a significant group. Musicians, experts in artillery, and candlemakers were not lacking, and Peru had representatives of rarer trades all the way down to bookbinding (see Appendix Tables). There were, then, a great variety of artisans in Peru, of vital importance to the nature of the Spanish presence there. But this should not be allowed to hide the fact that Spain itself had an even greater variety. A loss of specialization took place in artisanry just as in commerce. For Peru's single generalized type of shoemaker, Córdoba had five or six separate specialists.

The regional origins of artisans were as various as their trades. Like all other major groups in the Spanish Peruvian population, they were from every part of Spain. They also shared in another tendency observable in Peru, that wherever groups with special skills are concerned, Andalusia contributed even more than its usual share, and Extremadura, the second-largest group overall, contributed little. In a sampling of the origins of artisans, Andalusia was by far the largest regional group, with a third of the total, while Extremadura fell to fourth among the groups, behind both Castiles.

A newly arriving artisan, possessing only his tools, some training, and debts from the sea passage, would often seek work in an established shop as a temporary expedient before going into business on his own. Or he might join the staff of an encomendero for a time, as both servant and artisan. Many new arrivals worked for a short while in Lima before going off to the highland cities to try their luck. Setting up in business, when that stage came, involved renting a shop in a central location. Rents were high, from 100 to 200 pesos annually, but hardly any artisans, even those who owned other property, could afford to own their shops in the favorable locations near the town square, where property values were so high that practically the only owners were encomenderos, monasteries, and the cities themselves. The lots which were granted to artisans by the municipal councils, when they decided to settle in a community, were on the edges of town, more suitable for gardening, or quick resale, than for a residence or a shop. Artisans' shops huddled close to each other, and there was even, in Lima at least, a discernible tendency for the individual trades to bunch together.[1]

If he at all prospered, an artisan would buy Negro and Indian slaves in order to increase his productivity. If possible, he bought artisan slaves already trained in his trade; if these were not available or too high-priced, he acquired ordinary slaves whom he proceeded to train. Some artisans did not await prosperity, but bought a slave or two on credit when they first started business. As a result of this massive buying, artisans were, as a group, among the largest holders of slaves in Peru, second only to encomenderos, and Negro slaves made up the nucleus of the working force in artisans' shops. Many references in the sources make it clear that Spanish artisans themselves continued active personal work in their shops, but their role as foremen and trainers was equally important. If a whole generation of working Spanish artisans had not devoted themselves to the training of Negro and Indian slaves and helpers, the civil occupation could not have been as dense, or Spanish Peru as Spanish, as it became. For the artisans, training slaves to be resold became a lucrative business (see p. 183).

The Negro slave staff in the shops of successful artisans was balanced by a more quickly shifting force of Spanish helpers of various kinds. In case of need, artisans hired unskilled Spanish workers on a temporary basis, paying them a low daily wage. The system of apprenticeship, too, was far from dying out in Peru, though of course it did not nearly match immigration as a source of new artisans; throughout the 1540's and 1550's a fairly sizable stream of Spanish-born boys and young men became apprentices in the different trades, but particularly the more prestigious ones, such as pharmacy or silversmithery. In the latter 1550's the Spanish apprentices were joined by an increasing number of Indians and mestizos. Apprenticeship arrangements were much the same whatever the origin of the apprentice; the contract ran for a two- or three-year term, the master was obliged to feed and clothe the boy, and teach him all he knew, while the boy performed general service as well as working at the trade. At the end of the time, the boy received a set of tools, new clothing, or money, and sometimes all three.[2]

No formula was ever found for long-term cooperation between individual Spanish artisans. With an expanding Spanish population and possibilities existing in several parts of Peru, no trained artisan was long content to remain in the pay of another, particularly since the yearly wage, usually 150 to 200 pesos, was unreasonably low, hardly more than the cost of renting an artisan slave for a year. Equal partnerships or companies seemed to offer much greater advantages, and artisans of all trades contracted partnerships again and again, only to meet with repressive measures from the city councils, which viewed artisan companies as nothing more than attempts to organize monopolies and raise prices for encomenderos. Similar council opposition failed to stop other things encomenderos did not like, such as the multiple resale of merchandise, but artisans did not have the merchants' talent for organization and manipulation. No artisans' company is known to have lasted more than a year.[3]

Most artisans bought the raw materials of their trade, whether iron, cloth, leather, or sugar, from merchants, in fairly large lots worth from a hundred up to several hundred pesos; the larger transactions were on a credit basis. Tailors often bought cloth, or had the customer buy cloth, for each commission. Artisans also sold their products on credit, like merchants, and steady customers, particularly encomenderos, maintained accounts. This way of doing business could bring quick ruin to a new shop if it did not do well, for the artisan started out with a heavy load of debts for rent, slaves, and materials, and received at first little but promises.[4]

Artisans who were unestablished continued an itinerant mode of life, moving on to Arequipa, Cuzco, then Potosí in search of better opportunities, always tempted to accept positions as majordomos or miners when these appeared more lucrative than artisanry. Those who succeeded in getting their shops well established, however, settled into their communities more firmly than any other group in the Spanish Peruvian population, with the possible exception of the encomenderos. The trade of a successful artisan, based upon a local reputation and clientele, could not be transferred from one place to another. Artisans, like all other Spaniards in Peru, were not without their regional and family ties to the rest of the populace, but they had nothing to compare with the familial business networks which caused merchants to change their place of residence so frequently. The difference in stability of residence between merchants and artisans is striking. Not a single merchant prominent in Lima in the 1530's was still there in 1550. But of eleven established artisans who protested against price-fixing by the town's council in 1539, eight settled in Lima permanently, and four of them were still alive in Lima in 1560.

Tied to the community by the nature of their trade, artisans felt no hesitance about marrying or buying property. Some artisans brought their wives and children to Peru when they first came; others sent for them, or married in Peru. Just what per cent of the artisans had their wives with them must remain unknown, but everything indicates that the absolute number was quite high, and it seems safe to say that a majority of established artisans were married. The first artisan known to have had his wife and children in Peru was a tailor living in Lima in 1536. A glimpse of a portion of the artisan community of Lima in 1546, afforded by an unusual trial record, shows a circle of ten artisans, almost all tailors, both established and unestablished, of whom five had their wives with them in Lima.[5]

Peru's artisans, as a group, owned a large amount of property in and around the Spanish cities. Almost any successful artisan would own a house or two, including his residence, and a piece of agricultural land outside the town. In part, the artisans were attempting to realize the seigneurial ambitions which all Spaniards shared, and some of them succeeded to a surprising extent in the externals, with large houses worth up to a thousand pesos, numerous slaves in their shops and on their land, and a retinue of helpers and apprentices. For some, ownership of property became active speculation, a field where carpenters and masons were quite naturally prominent. Occasionally artisans became involved in the ownership of valuable properties of a type usually associated with encomenderos, such as the water mills that ground wheat and maize for city markets.[6]

The general situation of artisans was such that though they were denied advance into the highest ranks of Spanish Peruvian society, the type of reward available to them was sufficient to cause a large number to take root in Peru. It can be assumed, though statistical evidence is lacking, that a good percentage of artisans who failed to become established went back to Spain. Those who were established, however, had little incentive to return home. Artisans in Spain could accumulate wealth, but could hardly expect to own land and large numbers of slaves, and even in purely economic terms, the prices of artisans' products in Peru were many times what they were in Spain. While Spain still observed some restrictions on the type of dress allowed to the lower classes, artisans in Peru paraded in the town squares in the finest fabrics, within view of shocked governors and viceroys who always threatened to take measures, but never did. Another motive for not returning was that, though there is no reason to think Peru's artisans less than competent, it is clear that many who claimed to be masters had been only apprentices in Spain, and would not have been admitted there by the guilds to the status they already enjoyed in Peru.[7]

While hardly any artisans entered the ranks of the encomenderos after a very early date (see pp. 18–20), there was little to prevent their becoming merchants, if they had certain qualifications, and so desired. In fact, not many desired to exchange artisan status for the somewhat higher, yet dubious status of a merchant. Rather they chose, typically, to become entrepreneurs without being merchants, disassociating themselves from all labels. Many artisans in any case lacked the education to keep complicated accounts and function efficiently in the quickly changing international market. Though a few did actually become declared merchants, they were, with one known exception, local rather than import merchants.

In some cases, an artisan-entrepreneur would merely give a certain amount of money to a merchant to invest for him. But most artisans who invested in merchandise became more directly involved than this, availing themselves of the tight relationships that existed between fellow tradesmen. Though artisans had nothing remotely equal to the organized commercial networks, each trade constituted a spontaneously cohesive group much like a regional origin group. Tailors lived near each other, did business together, were compadres, gambled and fought together, and in every respect made up a community. In the same sense, a community of all artisans existed, though weaker than communities based on single trades.[8] Typically an artisan's first step into commerce took the form of a mixed company between two artisans; one partner would continue to work at the trade while the other took their combined capital and bought merchandise for resale, the total profits of both enterprises to be divided equally. Eventually some of these artisans became far more active in commerce than in their trades, but usually they neither lost their artisan associates nor took on the name of merchant. In Arequipa in the decade of the 1550's one of the most prominent entrepreneurs was Felipe de León, who dealt in livestock and in merchandise going to Potosí, like many merchants of Arequipa, but was not known as a merchant; he had started as a tailor and was still practicing his trade as late as the mid-1540's.[9]

Hardly any generalizations can be made about artisans as combatants in the conquest and civil wars, though their reputation as fighting men was poor. A noble Spaniard who had served in the European wars complained in 1541 that Peru was full of artisans and other low-born people who lacked the skills of war as well as the necessary horses and arms, and were interested in nothing but civil pursuits. Such statements were, however, as ill-founded as the commonly-stated opposite view, that the country was populated exclusively with idle, pretentious wastrels, spoiling for a fight. During the earliest stage of the conquest, the first two or three years, artisans fought along with the rest. After that, some artisans took part in battles, and others did not, along lines that are hard to determine. There was some tendency for smiths, as the producers of muskets and swords, to be expert fighting men, while tailors were less frequently seen in combat. Diego de Cantillana, a tailor, was penalized for not helping in the fighting even at the siege of Lima in 1536, when Indians were running through the streets of the town. But other tailors at the same time and place did fight; it appears that

personal inclination was the final determinant. When they did partici-
pate in battles, artisans were to be found among the infantry.

Artisans were always one of the main components of the skeleton
population left behind whenever, in the course of the civil wars, most
of the able-bodied men were taken from the towns for a campaign. To
keep a campaign going, it was necessary to maintain a flow of money
and supplies, to which artisans, along with merchants and majordomos,
made a large contribution. The artisans and merchants who were left
in the towns were mobilized only in cases of extreme local emergencies; one observer remarked with surprise that Gonzalo Pizarro fielded
all his men near Lima in 1547 "down to the tailors and shoemakers,"
this being, then, an unusual measure.

The real importance of artisans in the civil wars was their feverish
activity in producing munitions and supplies. The paraphernalia of war
could not be brought all the way from Spain; from a very early time,
Peru was amazingly self-sufficient in this respect, and even the royal
emissaries who were sent to put down rebellions did so with equipment mainly produced in Peru. Smiths banded together and produced
muskets, swords, and horseshoes. Carpenters made pikeshafts and
musket stocks; barbers honed pike blades; tailors worked overtime to
turn out the gaudy outfits preferred for war; silversmiths collaborated
in the production of armor; shoemakers and saddlers did their needed
work. Every remotely relevant skill was utilized; even a builder of mu-
sical instruments could make wooden powder flasks. Two considerations were of ultimate importance in the civil wars: politics, and equipment, particularly the quality and number of the muskets. It is hard to
say which was the more decisive factor, but it is noteworthy that in a
long series of major battles, the army with its back to Lima, the center
of Spanish Peruvian artisanry, always won. To the artisans themselves,
war meant a time of boom.[10]

In the top levels of artisanry were practitioners of several trades who
in skill and education were as near to the professional class as to the
other artisans. These were, primarily, pharmacists, barber-surgeons,
and silversmiths, though some of the most skilled stonemasons and armorers also fit the description. Such trades demanded thorough training and elaborate equipment, and the men who practiced them were
usually literate; pharmacists always so. The distinction was not between mechanical and non-mechanical trades; for all their skill, silversmiths were manual workers, yet held public esteem equal to that of

the others, and were consistently the artisan group most successful in obtaining encomiendas, while pharmacists and surgeons, as medical non-combatants, were not eligible.

Pharmacists and barber-surgeons constituted a single group. At least one man in Peru, Maestre Francisco Briceño, practiced all three trades. Each Peruvian town had a pharmacy, and larger towns several, where the pharmacists mixed syrups, potions, and tonics, partly imported from Spain and partly made from materials found in Peru. When hospitals were introduced, pharmacists came to be attached to them in the same manner as physicians. Barbers and ordinary surgeons were almost completely overlapping groups, but there were separate titles for the two functions, so that there were, at the top, a few surgeons who were not barbers. Standards in these lower reaches of the medical profession rose considerably as time went on. In 1552, *prótomedico* Licenciado Torres passed judgment on the titles of six ordinary surgeons then in Lima, finding four of them sufficient and one sufficient for minor cases. But surgeon Francisco Sánchez, who had been practicing in Peru since 1537, was declared incompetent.[11]

"Silversmith" or *platero* was the name Spaniards gave not only to silversmiths but to goldsmiths, jewelers, assayers, smelters, and other experts in non-ferrous metals, since specialization in these fields was not thorough. The various skills of silversmiths were much in demand, particularly for mining, which claimed many of them, but their most responsible task was assaying silver and gold, thus determining the value of the currency and the extent of merchants' profits. The silversmith about whom most is known happens to have been a Fleming, as a good many were. His name, in Spanish, was Juan Renero or Lerrenero, and he first went to New Spain in 1535. He came to Peru, where he was known as Juan de Bruselas, sometime in the 1540's, and by 1549 had become the official assayer of Lima and inspector of the town's silversmiths. Bruselas was a versatile workman, producing seals of silver for the city and chalices for the monasteries, and repairing trumpets for the army. In 1551 he left Lima to go to Potosí, doubtless to try his hand at mining, but soon returned. He was a wealthy man, able to loan the treasury over 2,000 pesos in 1554.[12]

In the ordinary trades, artisans were of a rather different stamp, rougher and less well-educated; the typical artisan in these trades could sign his name, but did not know how to read and write. Yet the range of education was large, and there were many not even capable of signing, along with others who were truly literate. To work in any ordinary trade amounted to an admission of humble birth and renunciation of claims to hidalgo status, though not to a respected position in the community. Ordinary artisans could be and were called honored, rich, trustworthy, peaceful, good citizens, Christians, and family men, anything in short but hidalgos. Until 1560, at least, no practicing artisans in Peru claimed to be hidalgos.

Ironworking, the basic trade that provided the sinews of the conquest, was the most prominent branch of artisanry in the first few years, and continued to be so wherever there were hard frontier conditions, in isolated backwoods communities like Chachapoyas, or on the various expeditions of exploration and discovery sent out from central Peru. Two essential figures always accompanied expeditions, the smith and the *herrador*. In the then current division of labor in smithery, locksmiths, swordsmiths, and gunsmiths were closely related varieties of the ordinary smith; they could and did double as blacksmiths. Blacksmiths did not usually perform one essential task, horseshoeing, which was left to professional horseshoers or farriers, called "herradors." The herrador was part smith and part veterinary expert, in the latter capacity being called an *albéitar*. As general maintenance men for horses, indispensable for communications, war, and the prestige of encomenderos, herradors were in greater demand than any other kind of artisan. Town councils on occasion resorted to forcible detention to assure themselves of the services of at least one herrador.[13]

A forge represented a large capital investment, far more than the tools of a tailor or even a carpenter, so that smiths often worked for some years in forges owned by others before becoming independent. On expeditions, both in the discovery period and later, the commander usually owned the forge and its slave staff, the smith being his employee or junior partner. In Lima a smith named Antón Pérez, though established and a family man, continued to operate forges for others from 1537 to 1542 before acquiring his own forge and going on to become alcalde of Lima's smiths by 1549. Smiths bought imported iron from merchants, and also re-used iron extensively. Their other principal raw material, charcoal, could not be imported, and since wood was scarce near most of the Spanish settlements, procuring charcoal was a major problem. Some smiths bought charcoal from encomenderos, others had a slave responsible for procurement and production, and others made more elaborate arrangements to insure their supply. In

1555 three smiths of Lima had a company in charcoal production, with several slaves working in the valley of Pisco a hundred miles down the coast.[14]

Along with the ordinary smiths, there were highly skilled men, generally locksmiths, who knew how to make items like machine tools for the production of millstones, and could repair intricate machinery such as Lima's large town clock. The most lucrative, and one of the most crucial skills of Peruvian smiths was the production of muskets; yet there was hardly a single individual who freely admitted to being a gunsmith. During peacetime, the whole trade in arms and munitions went on surreptitiously, and gunsmiths were exposed to possible legal action by the authorities; in wartime they and their forges were likely to be seized by rebels. They therefore did their best to hide their identity. When the younger Almagro was planning his revolt in 1541, he could not find an admitted gunsmith in Lima, so he commissioned muskets, supposedly for hunting, among Lima's blacksmiths to discover who would do the best job. Whenever war came, almost all Peruvian smiths proved able to collaborate in the production of muskets, though not all had equal skill.[15]

Just as Peru's largest import was cloth, so its artisans were most numerous in the clothing trades. Even small towns like Huamanga had enough tailors to constitute a group, and when the trades began to be organized as corporations in Lima in 1549, after the end of the Gonzalo Pizarro revolt, tailors and hosiers were the most active guildsmen, contributing the most for processions and receptions, and reelecting their officials with the greatest regularity. (As in the other trades, a few of the richest artisans rotated in office at short intervals.) There would seem to have been about forty Spanish tailors and hosiers in Lima by 1549. Tailors, hosiers, and sederos or workers in silk, the three main specialized groups, produced a wide variety of clothing, much of it luxurious, for the Spanish population and the Negroes, and even some clothing in indigenous style for town Indians. Though tailors worked in small shops with one or sometimes two Spanish workmen, they were inclined to cooperation, sharing the work with a colleague when they received a commission too large to be taken care of quickly by one shop alone. The various specialties also cooperated in production, one man producing the basic garment and another putting on the buttonholes and edgings.

Shoemakers and the related saddlers operated in the same way as tailors, but had to make rather different provisions to secure their raw material, leather, only a portion of which was imported from Spain. More came from Mexico and Nicaragua, and a constantly increasing amount was produced in Peruvian tanneries. In the late 1540's and 1550's, Lima had several tanneries which supplied the local shoemakers and exported hides to Arequipa; the largest of these establishments had a capital of 10,000 pesos.[16]

The construction trades stand out from the others because of the nature of the work. Carpenters and masons were contractors, not often in their shops, who took on a few large projects rather than many small jobs, and made much more lavish use of unskilled labor, both Negro and Indian, than did other artisans. In a typical contract, the encomendero, town council, or church for whom the building was being done would supply the labor, usually of encomienda Indians, and part of the materials. Carpenters and masons were not infrequently in the countryside building mills or parish churches, and since their trade depended less on a regular clientele than the clothing trades they seem to have been rather less strongly rooted in the individual communities.[17]

Construction in conquest Peru was not necessarily the crude affair it is often imagined to be. Without doubt many buildings were thrown up hastily, and churches were not yet such works of art as they later became, though even that branch of construction cannot be dismissed, for the Dominican monastery of Lima was established in the early 1540's with the same basic floor plan it still has, and some churches were partly vaulted over, while others had carved wooden ceilings. Secular works of some magnificence began to be undertaken in the early years; before the death of Francisco Pizarro in 1541, masons had built in his Lima garden a hexagonal pool of brick and mortar with a bower in the middle, in the manner of an islet. The pool and bower still existed and were marveled at in the first decades of the seventeenth century.

But the greatest development was in the construction of pretentious residences for encomenderos and other prominent people, since a large house was at the very heart of the seigneurial ideal. By 1545 the outward aspect of Lima was already what it was to remain for centuries, long lines of bare adobe walls broken by splendid wooden doors. The Lima residence of Accountant General Juan de Cáceres in 1542 had as its principal entrance a double door nine feet high by seven feet wide, with moldings on the outer face. In the patio were several hardwood doors and windows, the largest window grated, with a marble casing. Four years later a brick portal at the entrance and three pools in the patio were added. By 1555, at least, the carpenters of Lima were beginning to build wooden balconies much like the miradors for which the city is famous. In Cuzco and Arequipa all the larger houses had baked tile roofs, and Arequipa must have been striking in appearance, its houses of white volcanic stone roofed with the reddish tile.[18]

A large effort was required to procure the materials for such extensive construction. In the environs of each Spanish city were quarries and kilns for the production of tile, brick, lime, and cut stone. Sometimes the quarries were owned and run by specialists, perhaps in company with encomenderos or other entrepreneurs, but more typically, masons and carpenters themselves took an active part. Production, with Negro labor, could be quite considerable. In the 1550's one mason of Lima owned a quarry for brick and lime, for which he spent more than 5,000 pesos to buy Negroes, carts, and oxen; he was able to deliver 40,000 bricks within a short period of time. Getting wood was a larger problem, sometimes simply insoluble. Carpenters entered agreements with encomenderos to be responsible for cutting and dressing timber, often at great distances from the towns, using the labor of encomienda Indians. As the years went by, carpenters increasingly bought hardwoods imported by merchants from the Guayaquil area for all their better work.[19]

The only aspect of carpentry or indeed of artisanry in general which answers quite well to the notion that the products of the conquest period were crude is furniture making. It was impossible to import from Spain any large quantity of heavy solid wood furniture; the only items commonly imported were vaulted chests and writing desks, though the viceroys managed to obtain more complete furnishings. On the other hand, woodturners and cabinetmakers were hardly known in Peru, and other specialized carpenters such as cartwrights were anything but common. Furniture making was left to carpenters whose main interest was house construction, with the result that furniture was scarce, rudimentary, and crude, as can be seen in the records of the auctions. A few beds, tables, and benches would be auctioned off for a fraction of the price of expensive draperies, bedding, and clothing.[20]

Most practitioners of the trades connected with food production were not artisans in the usual sense of men with special training and equipment. Bakers hardly existed; baking bread and biscuit was the province of women, often Negro women. Millers, often former sailors or foreigners, were merely the hired men of the mill owners (usually encomenderos), and were picked out of the lowest ranks of the unemployed. Each town had a central, municipally-controlled butchery, the man who ran it being more of a contractor than an expert in meat-cutting. The only real artisans in the food trades were the confectioners and pastrycooks, who catered to the Spaniards' insistent demand for sweets, particularly for candied fruit and preserves. Confectioners, as mass producers, tended to have large slave staffs, and some of them sold wholesale as well as retail. There was a strange interpenetration between the two trades of confectionery and candlemaking, apparently because both involved metal pots and boiling.[21]

Since wagon roads were nearly nonexistent, the transportation trades were dominated by the muleteers, who were skilled and equipped, but not ordinary artisans, and certainly not sedentary. They led trains of ten to twenty mules and several Negroes, bearing valuable Spanish merchandise or silver through the highlands. Though muleteers were knowledgeable about their mules, whom they wryly named after priests, Indian women, and dreaded captains of the civil wars, their primary responsibility was the safety of their precious cargo. Above all, they were navigators and guides; a pack train could not proceed without its muleteer. There was some transportation by pack train between Lima and Arequipa, and more between Lima and Cuzco, but the greatest field of activity for muleteers was the triangle bounded by Arequipa, Cuzco, and Potosí. Because of the outlay of thousands of pesos required for mules and Negroes, only a few muleteers were able to own their own trains. Most worked for a yearly salary of 300–400 pesos in the employ of the merchants and large encomenderos who were the main owners. The large-scale carting of goods was restricted to the short trajectory between the port of Callao and Lima proper, but from the 1540's on, large oxcarts, varying in number from twenty to fifty, ground back and forth, driven by Negro slaves, under the general supervision of a few Spanish carters and cartwrights.[22]

Musicians, who were counted artisans, were prominent in Peru, though not really numerous. There were two trumpeters and a fifer at Cajamarca, and they were real musicians, not stand-ins. One of the trumpeters, Juan de Segovia, was later followed to Peru by his relative Diego de Segovia, also a trumpeter. In the 1540's Gonzalo Pizarro had a band of several musicians, famous for their proficiency, who played not only fanfares, but also the noble part music of the Renaissance. Most, but not all music was martial in nature, for battles and public ceremonies. There were a few specialists in chamber or dance music, half dance-masters; one of them, who came to Peru in 1541, brought with him several flutes or recorders, a psaltery, a tambourine, and a *vihuela* or guitar inlaid with ivory and silver. Peru was able to support one or two instrument builders, and an organ builder who constructed an eight-foot organ with several stops for Lima's cathedral in 1552, at the substantial price of 1,800 pesos. Other fine arts or crafts were less well-represented. Lima had a *librero* in the 1550's, who seems to have been more of a bookbinder than a bookseller, and a Portuguese painter who produced some canvases of the mines of Potosí and of a fort in Chile, apparently without the benefit of having been there.[23]

On the edge of the artisan class were a small number of Spanish gardeners and agriculturalists, the only functioning remnants of Spain's peasantry in Peru. An important characteristic of conquest Peru's otherwise complete Spanish society was the virtual disappearance of the lower levels of the agricultural sector, which were taken over by Negroes and Indians. The few Spaniards who deigned to remain in agriculture did so as supervisors, being called *labradores* or farmers rather than *villanos* or peasants. (Above, p. 25, it was seen how Spanish agriculturalists, the originators of the truck gardening that fed the cities, often began as employees of encomenderos and then made themselves independent.) The social position of the farmers and gardeners was low, below that of artisans in general, though wealth could improve their status somewhat. Agriculture was able to attract two kinds of people: first, skilled and dedicated growers, who were willing to accept the stigma of their trade and earn in return the large profits to be had in the Spanish cities, eager for familiar varieties of food; and second, marginal or handicapped people incapable of anything else, like Alejo Rodríguez, a gardener in Lima in the early 1550's, who was lame and slightly demented.[24]

As the subject of a biography which can stand as typical of Peru's artisans, it seems appropriate to choose a tailor, since tailoring, to Spaniards, was the symbol of all artisanry.[25] A man who lived through all the phases of Spanish Peru's development was Domingo de Destre, an Aragonese tailor from the village of Samper de Calanda, southeast of Zaragoza. He was of good stature, robust and well built, with a long scar down the right side of his face from the kick of a mule, facts we know from a description of him sent back to his home town, where he meant to retire. Destre arrived in Peru in 1535, about 22 years old, just in time for the great Indian rebellion, and took an active part in the fighting during the siege of Lima in 1536. When the coastal area quieted down in 1537, he became the junior partner in a Lima tailor shop, and made quick progress in establishing himself. In the late 1530's and the 1540's he was one of Lima's most prominent artisans, his name usually at the head of the petitions of protest sent to the city council. But for some years Destre continued in a dependent relationship to Captain Diego de Agüero, a great encomendero of Lima. He had fought under Captain Agüero in 1536, and afterwards lived in Agüero's house, took care of small business matters for him, and lived with Agüero's Negro slave woman Ana, who bore him a son.

Destre managed to avoid involvement in the battle of Salinas in 1538, but shortly afterward traveled to Cuzco in the entourage of Francisco Pizarro, a trip which was probably the first step in his second career as an entrepreneur. He brought back with him from Cuzco an Indian woman, Catalina, who was to be his mistress for some years. When the war against Almagro the younger developed in 1542, Destre joined the campaign, no doubt meaning to fight (he was present at the battle of Chupas), but also to sell the 1,350 pesos worth of merchandise he took along with him. He was by this time quite wealthy, with six Negro and two Indian slaves, two houses in Lima, and a piece of agricultural land outside the town.

Most of Destre's connections were determined by two factors, his regional origin and his trade. Though Aragon contributed only a tiny minority of the Spanish Peruvian population, Destre could always find four or five Aragonese to bear witness to any important document concerning him. He knew the prominent Aragonese merchants of Lima, had valuables in safekeeping for an Aragonese encomendero of Cuzco, and implored for the life of an Aragonese threatened with execution by ˙ Gonzalo Pizarro. On the other hand, he lived in a close circle of ten or fifteen fellow tailors and hosiers. Two of them, with their wives, sponsored the baptism of one of his mestizo children by his second Indian mistress, Francisca, in 1545. Human beings defy categories, however, and Destre's closest associate of all was neither Aragonese nor a tailor, though he was an artisan, an established mason of Lima named Diego

Hernández. In the mid-1540's a close friendship grew up between them as they joined the same cofradía, became compadres, and together with two merchants helped to found and endow a hospital for Lima.

In 1546 Hernández and Destre undertook their first joint commercial venture by sending 2,000 pesos with a third party to be invested on the Isthmus in merchandise for resale in Peru. Successful in this, the partners decided to enter commerce even more directly. The more active role fell to Hernández, who was a quite well educated man, while Destre, though he learned in 1545 to print his signature crudely, was illiterate. Hernández relinquished construction projects he had already commenced in Lima's Dominican and Mercedarian monasteries, and left for Spain late in 1547, taking with him over 4,000 pesos belonging to Destre, besides his own money. In Seville the next year, Hernández bought a shipment of typical general merchandise and personally brought it back to Lima, arriving in early 1550. The partners' enterprises were now quite extensive and interwoven. Hernández put the merchandise in a store in Destre's house and hired two Spaniards to sell it, which took over a year; meanwhile the two employees lived there, at company expense. The same house contained a tailor shop run by another partner, the tailor Antonio Rodríguez, who was in charge of four slave tailors of Destre's. Destre himself went on a year-long trip through the highlands to Potosí to collect several thousand pesos' worth of debts owed the company.

From this time forward Destre's career cannot be followed closely, but the pattern was already set. After 1542 he participated in no more battles, beyond being called up briefly for a local emergency in 1554. From 1549 he no longer openly called himself a tailor, and he may have stopped actual work at his trade, though he certainly continued to own a tailor shop. His partner Hernández died by 1554, and Destre carried on alone in commerce and money-lending. For the day when he would go back to his home town of Samper in Aragon, Destre bought up large amounts of property there, but he never actually returned. He was in Lima in 1560, still identifying his interests with those of the artisans who wanted no part of a price limit on Negro slaves. Thirty years later, in 1590, Destre still remained in Lima, in his late seventies, honored as one of the few survivors from the early years of the conquest. He was by this time a corporal in the viceroy's company of musketeers; not, significantly, in the cavalry company. Whether or not he ever married, or whether he continued an active interest in tailoring into his later years, is not known, but it may be suspected that he did. At any rate, in the year 1965 there was a Destre tailor shop in operation on Carabaya Street in downtown Lima.[26]

Spanish artisans were among the most constructive, stable elements in the Hispanic Peruvian world, far more so than the transient merchants or the professionals. They may not all have helped found a hospital or lived in the same town for fifty years like Domingo de Destre, but they did tend to be firmly settled, long-time residents, who took the part in their communities that self-interest dictated. Their production made it possible for Spaniards to live in Peru with amenities comparable to those of Spain, and their training of Negro and Indian artisans was one of the principal processes in the acculturation of those groups; both activities were prerequisite to the thorough Hispanization of Peru's urban areas. The two complementary groups of artisans and encomenderos did more than any others to build up and maintain Spanish Peru.

VII SAILORS
AND
FOREIGNERS

One day in 1544 a group of seamen came into Lima from the port of Callao to transact some business. The shipmaster was Greek, the owner Corsican, and the sailors were Genoese, Corsican, Greek, and Slavic.[1] Non-Spanish Europeans were no rarity in the Peru of the conquest period, but they were a specialized group; in fact and in the public mind, the two little-esteemed fringe groups of sailors and foreigners were intertwined beyond unravelling. While perhaps as many as two-thirds of the seamen on the Pacific coast came from within the borders of Spain, they were all from coastal regions, many from the half-foreign Basque country. Of the hundreds of seamen whose origins are established or suspected, one single sailor is known to have been from inland Castile. The only fully Spanish region contributing significantly to the maritime population was the Atlantic coast of Andalusia, the Seville-Huelva area, which was the home of perhaps half of all of the west coast's sailors. All the others, from the point of view of Castilian Spaniards, were foreign or half-foreign.

The bulk of the seamen navigating on the coast from Chile to Mexico, possibly three-fourths of the total, were from the Atlantic coast of the Iberian peninsula, the most coming from Seville-Huelva, very significant groups from Portugal and Biscay, and less from the rest of Spain's north coast. The Mediterranean coast of Spain contributed little, far less than Italy and Greece, which were the source of most of the non-Iberian sailors; relatively few were from the Netherlands. To speak in round numbers and a bit speculatively, it appears that about a fourth of all sailors were non-Iberians, a third non-Spanish, and half from regions speaking other languages than Spanish. Throughout the period of the conquest and the civil wars, and apparently far beyond that time, foreigners continued to be a most active element in the seafaring population. The founder of Lima's hospital for sailors, built in 1573, was a Greek.[2]

While Spaniards were prepared to accord some respect to shipmasters as men in a position of command, they considered sailors and foreigners to be the scum of the earth. Certainly most mariners, both masters and men, both foreign and Spanish, were rough and uneducated, illiteracy being the rule among them, though masters generally learned to make a shaky signature. Their social status was so low that a plebeian mestizo woman of Lima who married a sailor in the late 1550's was thought to have lowered herself. When four followers of Gonzalo Pizarro stole a fishing boat and ran away to join the forces of the viceroy, not much notice was taken of the event, because the renegades were "sailors and Levantines, of little account." Gonzalo Pizarro recruited a large number of sailors to support his rebellion, and they were reputed to be base and cruel, not observing the conventions of war, the worst of the lot, of course, being those who were foreigners.[3]

All European merchandise and livestock, and almost all the people to reach Peru came by the sea route, from Panama and secondarily from Nicaragua and New Spain. Ships to transport them had to be built on the west coast, from materials found there. Despite difficulties, adequate shipping was soon available; by 1533 there were an estimated thirty ships on the South Sea, as the Spaniards called the Pacific. In 1562, after what can be imagined to have been a slow, steady increase, a group of experienced masters agreed that between fifty and sixty ships were navigating the Pacific coast. A more detailed accounting appears impossible, since the registers of the port of Callao have disappeared, and though a great many names of ships can be found in the existing records, it is fruitless to count them. Literally about half of the ships were named "Santiago" or "La Concepción," and most had alternative secular names or nicknames like "La Traidora," "Saltabarrancos," and "La Carpintera."[4]

The largest vessels, called indiscriminately galleons or ships (*navíos*) had a capacity of around three hundred tons, but a smaller size seems to have been the rule, and the category of "ship" included everything above about sixty tons. There also existed a class of smaller boats or frigates, the main use of which was to transport produce for fairly short stretches along the Peruvian coast. Some of the coasting boats were large enough to be confused with ships, while others were very small affairs, manned only by a Spaniard assisted by a Negro and a couple of Indians. One vessel had once been the ship's boat of a galleon. A few frigates, at least, had oars as well as sails, to enable them to make frequent trips against the difficult winds on the west coast, but large galleys for the Panama-Lima voyage never caught on, despite repeated attempts to introduce them.

Practically all Pacific shipbuilding was done outside Peru, in yards in Nicaragua, Guatemala, and Mexico. Though one reliable scholar, Woodrow Borah, maintains that the largest and best vessels were being built in Guayaquil by mid-century, there is nothing in the Peruvian records to indicate that there was any construction at Guayaquil before 1557, when Viceroy Cañete sent a party to build some galleons there. Ships were of cedar, and their usual effective life span, to judge from the time the best shipmasters stayed with the same ship, must have been about five to seven years. Occasional cases of apparent greater longevity may well disguise two ships of the same name. While a large galleon, when new, was worth 6,000 to 8,000 pesos or more, ordinary ships sold for very low prices, most often between 1,000 and 2,500 pesos, and boats and frigates brought only about 500 pesos, hardly the price of a good Negro slave.[5]

Shipowning went through an evolution similar and very closely related to the development of commerce. The first ships on the Pacific coast were built under the sponsorship of the governor of Panama, and governors and officials were still prominent among shipowners at the time of the conquest of Peru. Some of them were the same people who were active as large entrepreneurs, including the Pizarros and the fugitive governors from other areas, like Licenciado Espinosa. Pedro de Alvarado also built a fleet of ships in Guatemala, some of which went to the Pizarros when Alvarado's Peruvian expedition of 1534 was thwarted. The ambitious near-governors in the conquest of Peru, Hernando de Soto and Benalcázar, also owned ships. But just as in commerce, though the governors had a brief period of dominance, they never had anything like a monopoly. Already in 1533, there were six ships waiting off Piura for payment of freight costs, and only one or two of them seem to have belonged to the Pizarros.[6]

By 1540 the governors' dominance of navigation had ended, and with it disappeared, for the most part, ownership of fleets. The Pizarros, Almagro, Licenciado Espinosa, and Alvarado each owned two to five ships at once, but in the 1540's and 1550's the only multiple owner appearing in the records is the Gaitán family of Nicaragua and Mexico. The fleets of ten or twenty sail put together at various times by governors and rebels were simply collections of individually-owned ships. The three main groups of owners were shipmasters, merchants of Peru and Panama, and shipbuilder-entrepreneurs of Central America. While most owners usually retained a given ship for its effective life, merchants bought and sold more quickly according to the needs of their companies. Joint ownership by masters and merchants was extremely common, and most ships appear to have been in one way or the other jointly owned. Peruvian encomenderos owned a certain number of ships, principally the small frigates that brought produce from their coastal encomiendas to the cities.[7]

West coast navigation was strongly influenced by the prevailing south wind, which made it nearly impossible to reach Peru from Panama except during the months of January and February. The great basic voyage from Panama (or Nicaragua or Mexico) to Lima and back was therefore undertaken only once a year, though under optimum conditions there would have been time for several voyages. When the winds were right, a ship could reach Piura from Panama in nine or ten days. Ordinarily the trip took longer, and if the ship left too late it could spend three or four months tacking in the wind before getting as far as Manta, Peru's northernmost port, near Puertoviejo. Progress southward in the latter part of the voyage was so painful that it was common for passengers and livestock to disembark at Paita, the port of Piura, and cross on foot the hot sands toward Lima, while the ship worked its way along with the remaining load of merchandise and personal belongings. Ships had to set out from Panama well supplied for the possibility of a long voyage, yet on arriving in the first ports of Peru they always took on more wood, water, and provisions. Loading and unloading was done at most places by Indians in small boats or rafts. The return voyage from Peru to Panama presented little problem, and could be undertaken at most times of the year, the trip between Lima and Panama, even with frequent stops, lasting usually less than a month.[8]

All ships coming southward made a long stop at Lima, the end of the voyage for many, while some others then went on to Arequipa with merchandise destined for the highlands. It was quite feasible to go from Panama to Arequipa and back the same year, with good luck. The voyage to Chile was another matter; a year was the norm for the trip from Lima to Santiago and back, and some shipmasters specialized in navigation to Chile, while other masters who knew the coast all the way from Mexico to Arequipa had never been to Chile. Until the late 1540's, navigation to Chile remained on an irregular, exploratory basis, getting firmly established only after 1548 and the end of Gonzalo Pizarro's rebellion.[9]

The paying cargo on voyages from Panama consisted of European merchandise, passengers, and Negro slaves. Freight costs were very high, for a ship might net as much as it was worth on a single trip from Panama to Lima. From Nicaragua came livestock, at first horses and mules, and later also cattle and sheep, which were often the property of the same men who owned the ships. To land a full shipload of up to 100 horses or 200 sheep in Peru was an economic triumph, but the business was risky because of the high mortality rate among the stock. New Spain sent both livestock and merchandise to Peru. On the return voyage, the main cargo was silver and gold, belonging to merchants, individuals, and the king. Since navigation was easy and ships were far from full, and not as many Spaniards were leaving Peru as coming to it, passage to Panama was cheaper than in the other direction. The encomenderos of Trujillo and Piura did send a certain amount of wheat, maize, and other provisions to be sold in Panama, which town, however drew most of its sustenance from Nicaragua. A cargo which required a special voyage was the wood of Guayaquil, in great demand in Lima. Having delivered its load of merchandise in Lima in March, a ship would head back for Guayaquil in April or May. There, after a few days of rest and enjoyment of that region's sarsparilla cure, the crew would load the ship with wood and try to get back to Lima and then Panama quickly enough not to miss the next year's return voyage to Peru.[10]

Though many ships could carry a hundred men and more, they rarely did so except in time of war, because of other cargo. One gets the impression that the average number of passengers may have been about twenty. Prominent passengers sometimes occupied the poop cabin, at great expense, while others travelled in less comfort, but still at high rates, which few could afford to pay in cash. (The documents, phrased in terms of debts, do not provide exact price data.) Most passengers went on credit, paying or finding security for payment on arrival in Peru. Collection was usually the task of the ship's notary.[11]

West coast shipmasters were a varied but generally competent and professional group of men. In the very early years, almost all of them had been masters or pilots on the Atlantic, but with time, experience of the idiosyncrasies of the coast came to be the most crucial factor, as seasoned west coast sailors began to rise to the rank of master in the 1540's. Though there was a clear enough distinction between the functions of masters, who commanded and operated the ships, and pilots, who navigated, in practice the two groups were one. A master on one voyage would be pilot on another, according to need, and most frequently one man filled both posts. Some pilots, including the first one to enter the waters of Chile, knew nothing of latitude, relying on instinct and experience, while a Greek master named Juan de Xio, on the other hand, had an astrolabe, a navigating chart, and three mariner's compasses. Not a few had been examined as pilots in Spain and Portugal. The common denominator of shipmasters was experience; of a group of masters testifying at an inquiry in Lima in 1552, most had been navigating the Pacific for ten or twenty years. By the early 1540's there had been built up a nucleus of from twenty to thirty masters well known in Peru, a slowly changing corps which dominated navigation and gave it continuity.[12]

When a master was also owner or part-owner of his ship, his remuneration becomes impossible to calculate, but leaving that added complication out of account, he received two and a half times as much as an ordinary seaman, and if he also acted as pilot, four times a sailor's pay. In absolute amounts, this usually came to 500 or 600 pesos for a year's voyage. The master was also allotted a certain amount of free space to ship merchandise on his own account, and had the use of the main cabin, where he might live in some pomp, with rugs, silver service, and his Negro slave cabin boys waiting on him. Masters had a free hand in freighting the ship and hiring the crew, and bore ultimate responsibility for the fate of the ship and the cargo. In case of a wreck, the shipowner or the shippers whose merchandise was lost would commonly sue the master, usually causing his imprisonment, for he lost as much as anyone else.[13]

Completing the crew were a mate or boatswain (*contramaestre*), who was well on the way to becoming a master; a ship's notary; a ship's carpenter; a caulker; a cook or steward; and as many ordinary seamen as were required. While a master often stayed with a ship for several years, the remaining personnel shifted rapidly, signing on anew at the start of each voyage and being dismissed at the end of it. They were, however, true professionals, drawn from the sailors of the Atlantic and the Mediterranean. Their salaries varied from less than 100 to 300 pesos for a year's voyage, usually paid only at the end of the year, and often not even then if the freightage had not been collected. To increase their bargaining power and assure some continuity in their lives, it was common for seamen to organize partnerships and hire themselves out in pairs or small teams. In 1544, two north coast Spaniards and an Irishman made a joint contract to serve as sailors in the viceroy's fleet, the leader of the group getting two pesos a month more than the others. Separated from the other seamen by their literacy were the ship's notaries; sometimes landsmen had to be hired for this job, but more typically they were real sailors, from Seville-Huelva or the Basque country, for this was one post that foreigners could not fill. At least a few ship's notaries advanced to the rank of master.[14]

The size of crews varied with the ships, up to a maximum of thirty men for a large galleon, but crews were kept as small as possible to save expense, so that even galleons usually had to get along with twenty men or less, the crews of ordinary ships varying from five to fifteen.

There was a strong tendency for sailors to bunch together in groups following the ethnic origin of the master, but the scarcity of manpower kept the trend from reaching its logical conclusion. One case of ethnic bunching actually received mention in the Spanish chronicles, because it was connected with an episode of the civil wars. A small fleet was organized for viceroy Blasco Núñez Vela in 1544, and the two leaders being Basque, the sailors were reputed to be "all Basques." Surviving treasury records reveal a definite tendency in that direction, yet only about half the men were from the Basque country and other parts of the Spanish north coast. Whenever galleys were used, their crews were strongly Mediterranean. Marcos Veneciano (his true name was Marco Negro) was a master of galleys in the 1530's and again in 1548. The galley built in 1547 for Gasca's campaign had a Catalan for a captain, and a crew of ten Mediterraneans, three Flemings, and a Spaniard. From necessity, however, many ship's crews were true ethnic hodgepodges of Andalusians, Portuguese, Basques, Mediterraneans, mulattoes, and Negro slaves. Indian sailors are unrecorded, though a few mestizos from Central America began to appear among the crews in the 1550's.[15]

Seamen supplemented their nominal salaries by side investments which in many cases far outweighed the salaries. When the ship was carrying merchandise, each sailor would bring along fifty or a hundred pesos' worth, free of freight, to be sold on his account. If the cargo was stock, each man would bring a horse. When an Andalusian sailor and caulker named Bartolomé Alonso died in Lima in 1542, he had not been paid his salary for the last two voyages he had made, but had just sold a hundred pesos' worth of wine, and left 400 pesos in cash. With the shipmasters, investment in merchandise became so extensive that often the largest lot the ship carried belonged to the master, and masters sometimes allied themselves with merchants in protests against government regulations. In a few cases masters even gave up the sea to become full-fledged merchants, a course which was open to only a few of the best educated of them.[16]

West coast navigation united adventure and danger with the most mundane and thoroughgoing kind of commercialism, so that the following story of the wreck of the galleon "Santiago" off Manta, though in some ways unusual, has aspects of the typical. It is in any case the only bit of connected maritime narrative the records offer us. Francisco Núñez, an Andalusian entrepreneur and stock raiser based in León, Nicaragua, financed the building of a large ship or galleon, the "Santiago," in a Nicaraguan yard in 1550. On its completion he sold a half interest to Diego Gaitán, a prominent ship owner, for 4,000 pesos, and Gaitán in turn sold a fourth interest to another entrepreneur named Juan López de Aspea. The owners planned for their galleon a maiden voyage to Peru carrying livestock, to be followed by a trip from Lima to Guayaquil and back with a cargo of wood.

After some argument between Francisco Núñez and Juan López, the two active partners, a crew was hired consisting of thirteen men: five Portuguese, five Italians, two Spaniards, and a Greek. To avoid paying a master's salary, the owners gave the post of master to Juan López himself, who was not a sailor and knew little of the Peruvian coast, actual direction of navigation being in the hands of the Italian pilot. When the ship left Nicaragua it carried 60 mares, 150 sheep, 80 casks of water, and provisions for both men and beasts. Most of the stock belonged to Núñez the senior partner, López the master and part-owner, an encomendero of Puertoviejo named Cristóbal de Burgos, and a merchant of Lima, all of whom were on board. López, who as master was allotted the poop cabin, filled it up with his sheep.

By January, 1551, the "Santiago" was standing off Manta, the first port of call for ships coming to Peru, where the livestock belonging to Cristóbal de Burgos were to be disembarked. But the pilot did not know the port, which was like others completely unimproved, and anchored beyond the customary place in shoals where the ship soon went aground. A raft full of Indians came out and told the pilot by signs where the usual anchoring place was, but it was too late. The crew abandoned ship in the boat, also taking off their gear and a few animals, while Burgos went with the Indian raft into Manta, and as an encomendero of Puertoviejo, told the cacique to provide Indians and rafts to help bring the livestock to land. The cacique complied, but the Indians could remove only a few of the animals before the "Santiago" filled up with water, and, while the owners argued over the advisability of cutting the cable, beat herself to pieces.

Both the owners were now ruined. Núñez had to take refuge in the Mercedarian monastery of Puertoviejo to avoid being jailed for debts. From there, in separate actions, he sued the master and the crew for incompetence. The crew was quickly absolved, but the suit against López was appealed to the Audiencia in Lima, where all concerned soon went, the crew to seek further employment, and the owners to litigate. The suit ended without resolution when Francisco Núñez died in poverty in 1552.[17]

Part of the seagoing population, yet a distinct group, were the fishermen operating along the coast, near Arequipa, Lima, and Piura, and perhaps in other places as well. Fishermen came from the same regions as sailors, and had friendships and business connections with them, but did not often move from their specialized trade into long-distance navigation. Generally they were organized into companies owning two or three sea-going boats, which could be as small as eighteen feet, each manned by one Spanish fisherman and a Negro crew, with in some cases the participation of coastal Indians hired from an encomendero. The fisheries of Lima sold their catch locally, while those of the north coast sent at least part of theirs south. One company, owned by a Basque, a Portuguese, and a Spaniard from Granada, in conjunction with an encomendero (see p. 31), fished along the south coast, and periodically sent lots of one or two tons of dried fish inland to be retailed in Arequipa. Successful fishermen tended to take root in their communities. Juan Quintero and Juan Camacho, two fishermen from Huelva, present in Lima from the time of the city's founding, were still operating companies there well into the decade of the 1550's.[18]

Peru or, more specifically, Lima, was the goal and center of west coast navigation, but though most mariners would be there once in the course of any normal year, they could not really be claimed as residents of Peru. Ordinary seamen were nomads, without a fixed residence or base. But masters and pilots, at least successful ones, were more inclined to establish a home where they would enjoy and display their wealth. Some settled in New Spain and Central America, but many chose Lima, where the residences of some of the most influential masters on the west coast could be found at any time after 1540. By the 1550's between fifteen and twenty masters and pilots, at least, owned houses and had their wives (who were usually of plebeian stock) in Lima. Some ship's carpenters also lived in Lima, presumably to do repair and maintenance work, like Maestre Antonio Genovés, a ship builder who moved from Nicaragua to Lima in the 1540's. Masters who specialized in the voyage to Chile usually considered Santiago their home.[19]

A respected master based in Lima was the Greek Antón de Rodas, who came to the west coast very early, being one of the pilots consulted in the border disputes of Almagro and the Pizarros in the years 1535-37. Through most of the 1540's he took his ship "San Jorge" regularly back and forth between Panama and Lima. In the Gasca campaign against Gonzalo Pizarro he held a position of command, and after the end of the war he was one of two masters chosen to convey the king's treasure to Panama. In 1549 he acquired a new ship, the "San Juan," which he kept for several years. Just when he settled in Peru is not clear, but by the late 1550's he maintained a large house in Lima, full of Negro slaves, his Spanish wife's relatives, and the families of his seafaring colleagues. Among the relatives of his wife was one of the labradors who carried on truck gardening near Lima, giving occasion for Rodas himself to invest in this kind of enterprise. Rodas continued to be active as a shipmaster at least until 1563, by which time he was one of the two or three most senior figures in Pacific navigation.[20]

Under normal circumstances a career like that of Antón de Rodas was the most a seaman could hope for, particularly if he was a foreigner. A few foreigners, and several Spanish sailors, managed to become encomenderos, but the line was drawn at foreign sailors. Sailors as a group did not profit much from the age of greatest social mobility, 1532–36; to become candidates for encomiendas they had to leave their ships, buy a horse, and join the conquerors on land, something many seemed reluctant to do, despite the opportunities. Of about fifteen sailors known to have participated in some stage of the 1531–32 conquering expedition, only three came permanently to land. Two others became prominent mariners, and the rest disappeared. The most successful sailor-conqueror was Tomás Vázquez, from Palos, who left the sea in time for the conquest of Cuzco, and went on to be a great encomendero, alcalde in Cuzco, and captain in the civil wars. About the last sailors to become encomenderos in this way were Martín de Garay and Martín de Andueza, master and notary of the same ship, who joined the 1537–38 campaign of the Pizarros against Almagro, and were rewarded with encomiendas in Huamanga.[21]

A procedure for the advancement of mariners to the status of encomendero did exist, but was available to very few. While there were hardly any real sea battles in the Peruvian civil wars, control of the flow of men and supplies along the sea routes was crucial, so that whenever there were hostilities, the available shipping was organized into fleets, and supreme military command was given to one or more seacaptains, over and above the shipmasters. Among others, such command sometimes went to able and experienced masters, who were thereafter eligible for the highest rewards. The first seaman to advance through this avenue was Juan Fernández, who, though illiterate and known to be of very humble birth, had participated in the beginnings of west coast navigation, was involved in the conquest of Peru, and served as chief pilot of the expedition of Pedro de Alvarado. He became captain as well as master of the Pizarros' galleon "San Cristóbal," and eventually acquired the signs of complete success: an encomienda, a coat of arms (being a galleon in full sail) and election as alcalde in Lima. Not many of his colleagues followed him. In 1548, three shipmasters and seacaptains who had aided in the Gasca campaign became encomenderos in Upper Peru, the only other cases known.[22]

In one way or another the sea accounted for most of the foreigners who came to the west coast, but there were many who, seeing the great wealth of Peru, came to land to seek their fortunes. Frequently the civil wars were the occasion, for military manpower was scarce, recruiting vigorous and pay high, if irregular. Numbers of foreigners fought, almost always as infantrymen, on both sides of all the civil war battles from 1537 to 1554. Their importance reached a peak in the years 1546–48, when Gonzalo Pizarro, who presented the most direct challenge to royal authority of all the Peruvian rebels, drew heavily on foreigners, apparently counting on their lack of feeling for the Spanish king. One observer reported that Pizarro's army included two hundred foreigners, most of them previously sailors, and the chronicler Gutiérrez de Santa Clara, who may have been an eyewitness, goes so far as to say that a majority of Pizarro's troops were foreigners. While both statements are doubtless exaggerated, the list of those condemned for the Pizarro rebellion shows that the participation of foreigners was very significant.[23]

A newly landed Italian or Portuguese (often having jumped ship), with the doubly low status of foreigner and sailor, would ordinarily have to be content with a position on the fringes of the Spanish Peruvian world. The humblest niche in Spanish Peruvian society, that of estanciero, or low-level employee of an encomendero, was naturally one function in which foreigners were readily tolerated, and where they came to be quite numerous, though reputed to live badly and be even harder on the Indians than their colleagues. Foreigners, particularly the Portuguese, also were important in the truck gardening that went on near the cities, a type of activity most Spaniards avoided as degrading. Near Lima, Portuguese were overwhelmingly predominant in this role; of eleven labradors or truck gardeners of Lima whose ethnic origin is known, eight were Portuguese. One of them was Baltasar Drago, an illiterate Portuguese, apparently with some admixture of Negro blood, who came to Peru around 1540 when already advanced in age, for in 1555 he claimed to be 85 years old. For twenty years he raised fruits and vegetables for Lima's market, living in a hut on his chácara or plot of ground near the river bank, not far from the city. As he prospered, he accumulated a work force of Negro slaves, and was able to marry his mestizo daughter, with a dowry of 4,000 pesos, to a Spaniard.[24]

The second specialty of foreigners was artillery. Gunnery, the founding of artillery, and the manufacture of gunpowder were the practical monopoly of foreigners and indeed, the Spaniards thought, of Greeks. In fact, there were also Flemish, Italian, and Portuguese artillerymen in Peru, but there is no doubt that the Greeks were the most prominent. Most, if not all, had been naval gunners in the Atlantic or the Mediterranean. The first and most famous of them was Pedro de Candía, a Greek artilleryman, who was vaulted into high rank by his presence among the thirteen companions of Pizarro on the island of Gallo. He received an appointment as royal captain of artillery, took part in the capture of the Inca at Cajamarca, and became a large encomendero of Cuzco. Candía was a metalworker and founder of

professional competence. For the division of spoils at Cuzco in 1534 he
produced a branding iron or stamp to mark the silver and gold, consisting of a castle surrounded by the letters "Carolus I." The end of his career, and the peak of Greek dominance in Peruvian gunnery, came in
1542, when he joined the forces of the younger Almagro in Cuzco.
Gathering together fifteen or twenty Greek artillerymen and making
use of Indian smelters, Candía produced twelve or more bronze cannon, six of them large pieces ten to twelve feet long, and brought them
to the battle of Chupas, where he was killed. Candía's Greeks were not
the only ones at the battle, for there were at least five or six Greek gunners on the other, winning side.

Pedro de Candía was the only artilleryman to attain the status of encomendero in Peru, and even his success had its limits. When he undertook an ambitious expedition east of Cuzco in 1538, he failed miser-
ably, in large part because the Spaniards under him had little respect
for the authority of a foreigner. After Candía, artillery captains were
Spaniards, figures of command rather than artillerymen, and their foreign gunners received lesser rewards, such as the concession of a
tambo, or depot and inn, in the port of Callao, which was granted to a
group of artillerymen in 1548. Greek predominance apparently receded
somewhat with time. While the artillerymen manning the eleven big
guns of the royal army in 1554 were all foreign except for a Basque
and one possible Spaniard, there were only two Greeks among them.

It is clear that Spaniards avoided the artillery, but not completely
clear whether foreigners took over the field because they possessed real
training and skill, as some of them certainly did, or simply because the
Spanish lack of interest left the opportunity open. In 1545 when the
forces of Viceroy Blasco Núñez Vela were pushed far to the north,
outside the limits of Peru, and had no one to manufacture gunpowder,
a Jorge Griego took over the task, though it was not his profession, and
went on a few years later to make large quantities of powder for the
Gasca campaign.[25]

Another skill that could be transferred from sea to land was carpentry, since the step from ship's carpenter to builder of houses was not a
large one. It may be suspected that quite a few of Peru's carpenters
had once been seamen, and in some cases it is a known fact.

The Genoese Rostrán Tujia, who for years called himself simply
Rostrán the carpenter, came to Peru in the 1530's. In 1537 and 1538 he
served as sailor and ship's carpenter on the "Santiago," belonging to the

Pizarros, after which he gave up the sea to work for a time with a Spanish carpenter of Lima. In 1543 he moved to Arequipa and settled down permanently, marrying and becoming a property owner and small entrepreneur, in addition to his artisanry. One of his largest undertakings was building a sugar mill for an encomendero in the valley of Camaná, in 1550. Rostrán continued to be active as a carpenter at least until 1554.[26]

An exception to the rule that foreigners came from the sea were a number of skilled artisans working in Peru, principally silversmiths and tailors. They were of various nationalities, including Portuguese and Italian, but the largest contingent by far was Flemish, despite the fact that the Netherlands contributed only a small percentage of the overall total of foreigners. Foreign participation in silversmithery was extensive, another result of the Spanish weakness in metallurgy; what the proportion of foreigners may have been is a matter for speculation, but it was certainly higher than in any other trade except munitions manufacture. Possibly, however, there were as many foreign tailors as metallurgists, though they were relatively less important, Peru's clothing trade being so large. Flemish tailors were actually able to maintain something like a network, being represented in Trujillo, Lima, Cuzco, and Arequipa. They collected debts for each other and maintained correspondence in which news of their families might be mingled with business, for many Flemish artisans married in Peru.[27]

Peruvian commerce was another area of endeavor which absorbed a significant number of foreigners, at all levels, but most characteristically as the marginal small dealers called tratantes (see p. 84). Since small, miscellaneous entrepreneurial activity was part of the system of remuneration of sailors, it was quite natural for them to continue similar pursuits on land. A seaman like the Genoese Bartolomé Ferrer, who in 1547 had small commercial interests in various places on the coast from Mexico to Peru, owned a boat in Nicaragua, and accepted commissions from people in Trujillo to sell used clothes in Lima, was already on his way to becoming a tratante. Fixed residence on land is about the only point of difference between Ferrer and a tratante of Lima such as Bartolomé Esteves, a Portuguese who still had close connections with the sea and was part owner of a ship.

But more characteristic than the relatively successful Esteves, who was on the verge of becoming a true merchant, was his colleague, Juan Bautista Genovés. Occasionally in jail for debt, Juan Bautista sold sides of bacon and other miscellanea, but specialized in horse-trading. True horse dealers were almost unknown in Peru, because first-rate horses and mules were so expensive that they had to be bought and sold on an individual basis, by the users themselves. The horses Juan Bautista sold were nags, lame or half-blind, which brought prices of only 60 or 70 pesos, compared with 200 to 400 for a good mount, but which might suffice to carry some humble Spaniard who wanted to move to the highlands. In general, there was a strong tendency for foreign tratantes to become involved in the sometimes lucrative, yet most marginal form of Spanish Peruvian commerce, dealing in Indian clothing.[28]

Among long-distance merchants, foreigners were a significant minority, though their numbers and wealth did not count for much in the broader picture of Peruvian commerce, thoroughly dominated by Spaniards. Most foreign merchants traded inside Peru rather than importing, and many were little more than tratantes, like Pedro Alemán, from Augsburg, Germany, who took small shipments of merchandise from Arequipa to Potosí. A figure quite typical of the foreign merchant was Bartolomé Tardín, a Genoese, who traded in Arequipa, Lima, and Upper Peru in the 1540's and 1550's. Illiterate or nearly so, he had probably started as a seaman, and at any rate was not born and raised a merchant. Tardín bought agricultural products in Arequipa to sell in Potosí, and also dealt in Spanish merchandise. Indicative of the size and nature of his operations is a company he made in 1550 with a Genoese tailor, investing 4,000 pesos of his own capital, to buy merchandise in Lima for sale in Cuzco or Arequipa.[29]

True professionals were quite rare among foreign merchants, but did exist. The Florentine merchant Neri Francisqui, active in the years 1534–36, sold Spanish merchandise, livestock, and Indian slaves to the conquerors, and had a particular interest in speculation in precious metals and jewels. A more permanent resident was another Florentine, Nicolao del Benino, reputedly a relative of the Medici. Benino was well-connected among the large Spanish merchants, and such an accomplished letter-writer that a newsletter he sent to Seville was published. From early in the decade of the 1540's, he carried on medium-large commercial operations in Trujillo and Lima. After 1548 he shifted the direction of his business toward Potosí, where he took up residence before 1552, and gradually became more of a mining entrepreneur than a merchant. Benino was still in Potosí as one of the largest miners in 1573, in the era of Viceroy Toledo.

The largest of the foreign merchants were two brothers from Corsica, Juan Antonio and Nicoloso Corso, in Peru from 1543 at least, who from apparently maritime beginnings became large importers of Spanish merchandise and Negro slaves in the 1550's. When Nicoloso died in Lima around 1560, he was preparing to take the improbable sum of 80,000 pesos in profits out of the country. There were prominent Portuguese and Flemish merchants as well, notably the Fleming Francisco de la Cruz, for several years majordomo of Lima's hospital for Indians, but there is no doubt that the Mediterraneans were more numerous and active in the regular channels of commerce.[30]

One type of foreigner, the Portuguese, stood out from all the others who came to Peru. Not only were the Portuguese the largest of the foreign nationality groups, but they were the least foreign. With Spanish nationality so diffuse, foreignness was a vague and shifting concept. On the one hand the word for foreigner (*extranjero*) was used for anyone not a permanent resident in a given community; on the other hand hardly anyone was a complete foreigner, for Sicilians, Milanese, Germans, and Flemings were all subjects of the emperor. Newly combined Castile and Aragon did not stand as a tight unit against foreign Portugal; rather the Iberian peninsula contained a Castilian-speaking core extending from Seville to León and Zaragoza, and three important fringe groups, the Catalans, the Basques, and the Portuguese, who were in their different ways about equally alien to the Castilians. To the Castilians, the Basque was the very prototype of the foreigner.

Portugal and the Portuguese, as part of a first layer of Iberian half-foreignness around Castile, were in some respects widely considered to be simply Spanish. Returning Spaniards, whose ships often first came upon the Portuguese coast, would express their feelings at seeing "Spain" once again. In a trial involving a large number of non-Spanish witnesses, the testimony of Italians and Greeks was challenged as that of foreigners, while the Portuguese witnesses were left unmentioned.[31] Neither did the suspicion of religious heterodoxy, attached to many foreigners, apply as strongly to the Portuguese. The Portuguese ethnic contribution to Spanish Peru included people in typically foreign marginal positions such as sailors, estancieros, and tratantes, but there were other Portuguese settlers who found their equivalents only among the Spaniards themselves. Portuguese priests and friars were a significant and influential minority, being the only foreigners in the Peruvian clergy except for a few Flemings and Italians in the unusual Franciscan establishment in Quito. The only foreign-born women in Peru were a good number from Portugal.

Above all, the Portuguese, like the Spaniards, included among their number representatives of the Iberian upper classes, with characteristic marks of rank, including the title "don," membership in the military orders, and hidalgo status, the meaning of which the Spaniards could readily comprehend. The great majority of foreigners of other nationalities were illiterate plebeians, and even if they were wellborn they did not fit conveniently into the category of hidalgo, unknown outside Iberia. Portuguese noblemen in Peru were not only parallel to, but often actually related to the Spanish nobility. Noble Portuguese and, in the early years, Portuguese commoners as well, were potential candidates for encomiendas in a way no other foreigners were. Though no Portuguese can be identified among the men of Cajamarca in 1532, they were present among the conquerors from 1533 on, and took part in the conquest of Cuzco; two or three of them received encomiendas at the time of the city's founding. Almost any Peruvian city could be expected to have a Portuguese encomendero or two.

Some of the Portuguese who received encomiendas came not from the seacoast like most of their countrymen, but from the interior region bordering on Spain, particularly from Portuguese Extremadura, where Portuguese speech and sovereignty extended farther to the east than they do today, taking in Olivenza, which now is miles inside the Spanish border. Badajoz was the metropolitan center of a region partly Spanish and partly Portuguese, in which family and other relationships took little account of nationality. The chronicler Garcilaso, whose father was from the Spanish part of the Badajoz region, shows a special sympathy for the Portuguese; one of Garcilaso's relatives in Peru, the captain and encomendero Gómez de Tordoya, was certainly related to a Portuguese named Luis Gómez de Tordoya, from Olivenza, who came to Peru in the second decade of the conquest.[32]

The most famous of all the Portuguese in Peru, Lope Martín, a man of humble birth, was from the territory of the Marquis of Villarreal, in Portuguese Extremadura. A conquerer of Cuzco and large encomendero there from the early 1530's, Lope Martín became renowned as a scout and guide, in which function he was prominent in all the civil wars from 1537 to 1554. In 1547 he was made a captain in Gasca's army, and after the defeat of Gonzalo Pizarro went to Europe as the governor's personal emissary to the emperor. From then until he was killed in 1554 at the head of his reconnaissance company of mounted musketers, Lope Martín was one of the most powerful men in Peru.[33]

It was a great rarity for foreigners other than Portuguese to receive encomiendas; only one case is known beyond the Greek Pedro de Candía, whose position as one of the original thirteen conquerors made him a figure of mythical prestige. For foreigners who were ambitious to hold positions of honor and command, the best chance was to go beyond Peru to Chile, where long-continuing frontier conditions resulted in a more open attitude. The Genoese seaman Juan Bautista de Pastene, who started as master of a ship of the Pizarros on the Peruvian coast in 1536, later became Valdivia's captain general of the sea, and alcalde and encomendero in Santiago. Vicencio de Monte, a Milanese, was royal treasurer of Chile. A German, Bartolomé Flores, held the honorific post of procurador general of the city of Santiago. Several foreign seamen received encomiendas in Chile, in recognition of the aid that came from the sea at several junctures of early Chilean history. The greater opportunities for foreigners in Chile were so well known that sailors signing on in Lima for the voyage to Chile had to oblige themselves specifically to make the return trip.[34]

In considering the role of foreigners in Peru, it is well not to forget those who were neither Spanish nor foreign, but were born in Spain of foreign parents. Spain was far from empty of foreign nationals and in some places, such as Seville, Sanlúcar, and Medina del Campo there were cohesive foreign mercantile communities where the second and even the third generation did not lose completely the language and culture of the homeland. The foreign community of Medina del Campo sent second-generation foreigners to Peru, and also served as the channel through which merchants of the first generation, like the chronicler Girolamo Benzoni, made their way. A family of Spanish-born Englishmen from Sanlúcar, the Falers, were prominent in Peru's Arequipa region, where one of them became an encomendero. They were responsible for the presence of one of the few full Englishmen known to have been in conquest Peru, an associate of their father's named David Buston. Some residue of the foreign connection remained even in descendants who had lost the foreign culture completely, a phenomenon often seen in similar circumstances elsewhere. An early conqueror of Peru and encomendero of Lima was Antonio de Solar, born in Medina del Campo of an Italian father and a Spanish mother. He was fully Spanish in every way, and certainly his mestizo daughter could not have been very Italianate, yet she married Iñigo de Bocanegra, himself born in Burgos and at most half Italian, without doubt because of the tie of the original nationality.[35]

The economic and strategic contribution of west coast navigation in supplying men and goods to build up Spanish Peru is a clear part of the record. Harder to assess is the social importance of the diverse maritime population, made up of Spaniards, foreigners, and half-foreigners, that built, owned, and manned the ships, and filtered into various land activities, usually marginal and lowly ones. What foreign mariners did on land has been outlined, and it is to be assumed that their Spanish colleagues did much the same (though no doubt with wider possibilities and a higher upper limit to their progress, since they lacked one of the stigmas of the foreign seamen), but the records do not throw much light on the process. While following the career of a foreigner with a rare name like Rostrán is feasible, it quickly proves impossible to track down an Andalusian sailor named Diego Hernández or Juan García among the scores of Peruvian Spaniards who bore those names. Seamen, both Spanish and foreign, were marginal in more than one sense, occupying the lowest social position imaginable for Europeans, and hardly improving upon it if they came to land as estancieros or peddlers; the active seafarers were hardly even residents of Peru at all. Yet it is clear that the ethnic contribution of seamen to the total European population of Peru was not negligible.

Foreigners, most of them seamen actively or in origin, were doubly a fringe group, but there can be no doubt of the presence of significant foreign minorities in conquest Peru. As usual, it is easier to estimate the relative importance of the component groups than absolute numbers, and in the case of foreigners there is the added doubt as to whether the nomadic seamen among them can be considered as living in Peru. But begging that question, research for the present study produced a list of over five hundred foreigners physically in Peru at one time or another in the years 1532–60—a figure which must be at least tripled or quadrupled to arrive at the probable total when one considers the sources (see p. 96) and the little occasion that obscure seamen and tribute collectors had to have their names recorded anywhere.

Plate 1. Page from a notarial register, signed by merchants of Lima in 1543.

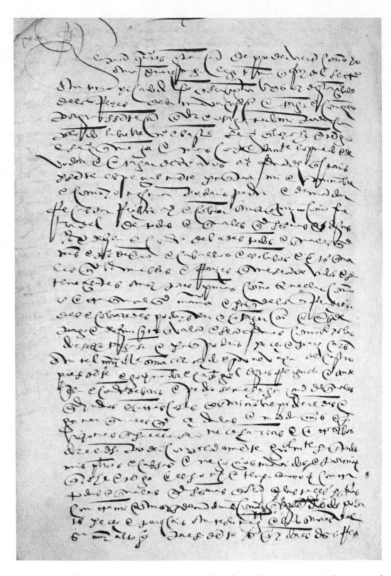

Plate 2. Two pages from a 1542 register of Pedro de Salinas (see p. 72). Most of the document is in the hand of Salinas; the last section is in the hand of his partner, Juan Franco.

que abiendo bra mag e md dur ... de plata ... Bele ... bra del ... q est se ... en todas
... rah dados ... onedas ... en un plato Bele ... bra del y por ... oum tal onis de
... amos bra m l de preyta ... toda la ... la ... on ... del ... a bra mag pziere o pere
me ... ... bra satta Cesarea Catholica m. ... nro ... po bien a ventura de
... con mucha paz ... djenna el bra ... Esta cabdad de cabca Abeynte
dias el mes de Julho año el ... de myle e qny... efreynta e ... año

.J.b.s.r.C. mag.t

bmyl de ... faces los muy ffrales pjes y manos de bra mag besom

Por mandado del ... ... esta cabdad de cabd...

... Jeronymo de alf... ... ... esno mo

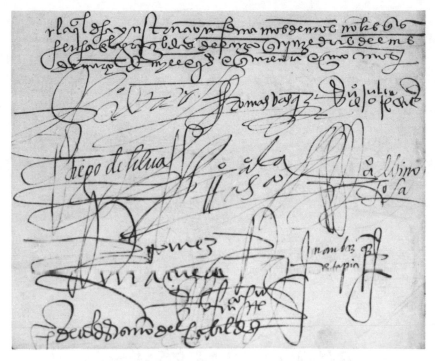

Plate 4 (above). Signatures of the council of Cuzco, 1545. Note differences between these and the signatures in Pl. 3. In 1534 the Spaniards were still restricting council membership to the well-educated, as in Spain, but by 1545 some illiterate plebeians had been admitted to the councils on the strength of their position as first conquerors; their cruder, blockier signatures stand out among the rest. The Jauja signatures show the contained energy and grace of the first years of the conquest, as against the flamboyant arrogance and rebelliousness of the later period, particularly in the highlands.

Plate 3 (left). Last page of a letter of the town council of Jauja, 1534.

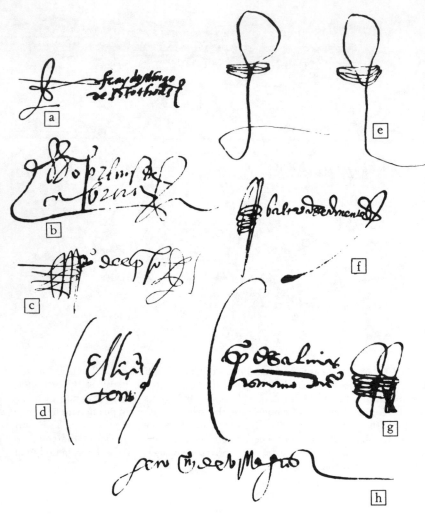

Plate 5. Individual signatures:

    (a) Fray Domingo de Santo Tomás (p. 60)
    (b) Don Pedro Luis de Cabrera, nobleman (p. 42)
    (c) Pedro del Peso, majordomo (p. 23)
    (d) Licenciado Alvaro de Torres, physician (p. 66)
    (e) Martín Pizarro, encomendero (p. 19)
    (f) Baltasar de Armenta, merchant (p. 92)
    (g) Pedro de Salinas, notary (p. 72)
    (h) Jerónimo de Villegas, encomendero (p. 27)

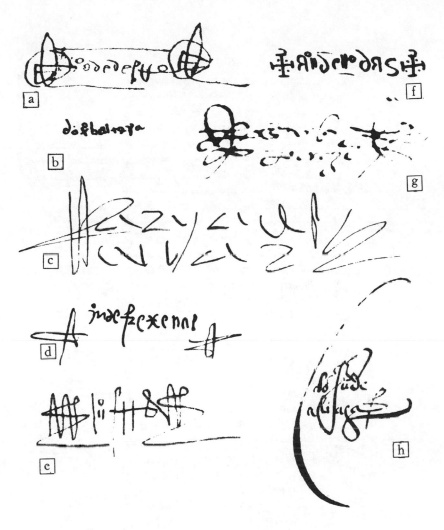

Plate 6. Individual signatures:

(a) Domingo de Destre, tailor (p. 110)
(b) Don Cristóbal Tupac or Paullu Inca (p. 211)
(c) María de Escobar (pp. 44, 158)
(d) Juan de Fregenal, free Negro (p. 193)
(e) Juan Fernández, pilot and seacaptain (p. 124)
(f) Antón de Rodas, Greek shipmaster (p. 123)
(g) Garci Pérez, entrepreneur (p. 147)
(h) Don Juan de Aliaga, son of a first conqueror (p. 39)

Plate 7. First page from a checklist of the merchandise of a company involving
Baltasar de Armenta in Lima, 1542 (p. 93).

All in all, the estimate that the Chilean scholar Thayer Ojeda made for his own country in the mid-sixteenth century appears close to the truth: that about one settler in twenty was a foreigner. Portugal, the Mediterranean, and the Empire were the sources of nearly all aliens, the handful of Englishmen and Frenchmen being no more than an oddity. The Portuguese were the largest group, followed by Italians of all kinds, with Genoa the best represented of the Italian states. Greeks, who were second most numerous among the Mediterraneans in Peru, were a subspecies of the Italians, for most of them came from Greek islands under Italian domination, and had been exposed to Italian linguistic and cultural influence. North and Central Europe, principally the Netherlands, contributed a small but highly skilled minority, less closely identified with the sea than other foreigners. Each ethnic group formed as much of a community as its limited numbers would allow. Members of strong groups like the Genoese were able to have a good part of their friendships and business dealings with their compatriots, while the Florentines had to consider all Italians their countrymen, and Germans fell back on the somewhat distant relationship with Flemings.

The estimate that one of twenty Europeans in and around Peru was foreign gives some idea of their numerical importance, but conveys an inflated impression of how frequently foreigners were to be seen. An observer of the Spaniards parading in the main square of Cuzco would in all probability have seen hardly a foreigner; most were at sea, others in remote Indian villages, and others in lowly positions where they were not much in evidence. Despite the number of foreigners present, Peruvian Spaniards remained in the deepest ignorance about them. They called Irishmen Levantines, and were unable to tell a Hungarian from a Corsican. Foreigners who had any measure of conventional success within Spanish Peruvian society, and came into daily contact with Spaniards in the cities, quickly became thoroughly Hispanized, in the externals at least. It is not too much to say that foreign cultural influence was nil.

The primary contribution of foreigners was in navigation and shipbuilding, not because they were any more competent than the Spaniards from Seville and Huelva, but because the limited Atlantic coast of Castile could not alone supply the naval manpower needed for the Indies. On land in Peru, the foreigners' skills were really needed only in metallurgy and artillery, Spanish weak spots. For the rest, foreigners

were seeking their fortunes rather than filling a need, and the Spaniards tolerated them, as a rule, only in certain more or less degrading
tasks which they did not much want for themselves. But Spanish Peru
was already to a certain extent a melting pot for Europeans, and the
foreigners were a living reminder of the continuous history of colonization as a pan-European phenomenon, from the Eastern Mediterranean to Chile.

VIII TRANSIENTS

The image of life in the Spanish Indies of the conquest period has been distorted in the past by the overuse of official reports as a source of information. It is not that such sources are worthless, for in fact they do contain priceless information, but they are invariably one-sided, often in predictable ways, over and above the persistent tendency to exaggerate that gives them their characteristic style. The reports of royal treasury officials, for example, were mere collections of gossip then current about the activities of the viceroys—as such invaluable, but useless as evaluations or complete accounts. Other kinds of correspondence directed to the Council of the Indies, such as the much-quoted letters of the viceroys and bishops, have equally specific, if somewhat more subtle types of bias.

An example of the partial truths which have been extracted from these sources is the reputed emptying of the Caribbean territories after news arrived there of the riches to be had in Peru. In letters like those collected in Porras Barrenechea's *Cartas del Perú*, the governors complain again and again that their territories are being left unpopulated and will revert to jungle. Yet a census of the city of Santo Domingo in 1528, listing all the important citizens and many less prominent ones, reveals only two or three names familiar in Peru.[1] The development of Hispaniola continued on the path it already had taken, practically unaffected by the discovery of Peru. Governors' reports obscure the differing effect of the discovery of Peru in the various older areas of occupation. Behind the unvarying accounts of depopulation lies the fact that in the more distant areas like Hispaniola and New Spain, all those who had any firm political or economic position stayed on, only the new arrivals and floaters being attracted to Peru, while in the territories of Panama, Nicaragua, and Guatemala, which were closer to Peru and served as a staging area for the conquest, not only men without roots, but encomenderos, council members, alcaldes, and even governors left to seek wealth in the new country.

The greatest of these distortions, or governor's myths, as far as they touch on the history of the conquest period in Peru, is the notion that Peru's Spanish population consisted almost exclusively of idle, turbulent claimants to honors, disinclined to any kind of manual labor or honest commerce. Previous chapters have shown this conception of Peru to be erroneous in a hundred ways. There remains the important task of ascertaining the approximate relation between the steadily growing nucleus of sedentary Spanish Peruvians on the one hand, and the population of transients and malcontents, which existed in every Spanish colony, on the other hand.

The most extreme, and best-known, contemporary statement on the subject is a letter written by Viceroy Cañete in 1555.[2] Commentators have little noted that Cañete wrote the letter from Seville before he had ever been near the Indies. His facts are therefore no doubt based on other reports, probably from the Audiencia, then governing on an interim basis, and his interpretation, while no doubt to a certain extent reflecting the reports, must be allowed to have been made in large part in ignorance. Cañete writes that of approximately 8,000 Spanish inhabitants of Peru, 480 were encomenderos, and about the same number held some kind of governmental post as notaries and functionaries, leaving the country swamped with no less than 7,000 idle pretenders. The number given for the encomenderos is substantially correct, as is known from other sources; the figure presented for total population is the only estimate we have of the population of Spanish Peru in the late 1550's, and being consonant with common sense and projections from earlier estimates, may well be near the truth. But the implication that seven-eighths of the population was engaged in nothing more than fighting for encomiendas must be contested. Though there is no firm basis for estimating Spanish Peru's sedentary population at any given time, by the most conservative minimum estimates that the evidence will allow, Peru's 500 encomenderos by 1555 must have been sharing the country with at least a thousand of their majordomos and other employees, including miners; 350 ecclesiastics; 350 merchants; 300 notaries; 150 lawyers and doctors; 500 artisans; 750 to 1,000 women; 200 to

400 sailors. In other words, there was a core of 4,000, or, to make a realistic rather than a minimum estimate, perhaps 6,000 Spanish people who in one way or another participated in Peruvian civil society, leaving from two to four thousand who were truly rootless and idle. This ratio was further altered by the fact that among those with no visible means of support were an undeterminable number of relatives of encomenderos, who, living as the latter's permanent dependents, were far from dissatisfied with their lot, and were performing a function for the encomenderos by increasing their effective power and prestige. In any case, an unemployment rate of from twenty-five to fifty per cent would be a formidable problem in any society, and it is understandable that idlers and pretenders should have been the overriding, almost exclusive preoccupation of the governors of Peru.

What kind of men made up this floating population which so worried the governors and hindered, though it did not stop, the development of civil life in Spanish Peru? Little enough can be known about them as a group, because they did not constitute a community, and because transients, lacking the epithets or labels that identified almost everyone who had any special qualification or status, cannot be easily identified, followed, or tabulated. It is possible, however, to make at least a calculated guess about their regional origin. In the overall regional distribution of Peruvian Spaniards, Andalusia was the largest single group, and Extremadura second; yet when samples are taken for any one of the specially skilled groups such as artisans or notaries, Andalusia always emerges even farther ahead than usual, while Extremadura sinks back to third, fourth, or fifth place among the regions. If, then, less than the normal proportion of sedentary Spaniards were Extremadurans, Extremadura must have contributed more than the normal proportion of transients. Perhaps Extremadurans were the largest single regional group among transients, though hardly an absolute majority. It does not necessarily follow, however, that all transients were rough and uneducated, qualities which can be fairly applied to Extremadura on a general level, for many of them were men of good birth who knew no trade and were in serious competition for encomiendas. They came from every imaginable social background, in proportions that can only be surmised to be a reflection of the composition of the general populace.

In legal terminology, the transients were called by unspecific terms (*estante, habitante, morador, residente*) indicating various degrees of temporary residence. In everyday speech, repeated in the chronicles of

the civil wars, they were referred to simply as soldiers, giving rise to
much confusion among historians of later generations, for whom the
word soldier called up professional military men and a military hierarchy of a kind then hardly existing even in Europe, and certainly not in
Peru. Starting from the fact that the Spanish conquest of the Indies
was carried out by military force, by the settlers themselves, the Spaniards had fallen into the habit of calling everyone who was not an encomendero or tradesman a soldier, completely regardless of the individual's possession or lack of military equipment, training, or ability.
Two students of the Peruvian scene have already grasped this special
use of the term "soldier," conscientiously putting it in quotes. For the
seventeenth century, when fighting was a thing of the past and no
standing army existed, it is self-evident that the so-called soldiers were
merely vagrants. But the same was already true in the midst of the
Peruvian conquest and civil wars. Without doubt the term "soldier" at
that time still had a good deal of meaning, because under the conditions almost all able-bodied men had to know something about
fighting, and recruiters found the most ready response among transients. Yet the "soldiers" of Peru cannot be accepted as military professionals, not even those of them who fought in the ranks of the civil war
armies.

Indeed, it is no easy task to find, within the framework of conquest
and civil war in Peru, anyone who answers to the description of a
professional soldier. There was neither continuing rank nor steady pay.
When an army was raised, it was organized for that campaign only; all
ranks expired after victory or defeat, though the captains might continue to use their high-sounding and socially meaningful titles. To
speak of "officers," as some have done, is to go too far. There was only
one real rank of leader, the captain; lieutenants, majors, and colonels
were completely lacking. For the campaign, one of the captains would
be chosen captain general or strategic commander, another *maestre de
campo,* or second-in-command and tactical expert. No further hierarchy existed. Captains, and the encomenderos who made up the nucleus
of the cavalry, received no personal pay, their reward being rather the
grant, improvement, or confirmation of encomiendas. Ordinary soldiers
(again, "enlisted men" is inappropriate) received a lump sum at the
time of their recruitment, usually about the equivalent of a generous
year's pay, partly as a remuneration, and partly in order to outfit themselves. No further pay was to be expected unless the campaign

dragged on unduly. Only exceptionally were there small monthly ration payments.[3]

The conditions of conquest in Panama and Nicaragua produced veteran fighting men, skillful in Indian wars, who contributed importantly to the first years of the conquest of Peru. But this did not quite make military men of them; they lacked any but the most pragmatic discipline, and knew little or nothing about troop movements; the difference between the Indian fighter and the professional soldier, after all, is familiar from North American history. The Spaniards were fully aware of the distinction between the two kinds of war. Francisco Pizarro was on the coast south of Lima in 1537 when he got news of Almagro's return from Chile and seizure of Cuzco, but his men were equipped for Indian fighting, and rather than proceed further he returned to Lima to outfit them to fight against Spaniards.

In central Peru Indian fighters soon became an anachronism, but they found a place in the expeditions of discovery and conquest, or *entradas*, which were sent out repeatedly from Peru. The entradas almost invariably failed, but there were many Spaniards who, adventurous and inured to hardship, joined one unsuccessful venture after another. A man who, like Esteban Rodríguez Cabeza de Vaca, had been on eleven separate entradas over a period of twenty years, became in the course of his career a professional explorer and Indian fighter, and can with much justice be called a soldier, but not in the usual meaning.[4]

The infantry in the armies of the civil wars consisted partly of transients, and partly of people drawn from civil pursuits, including artisans, merchants, majordomos, and seamen. Those who had a civil calling tended to be marginal figures, living near poverty and unhappy with their current status, so that certainly a majority of the foot soldiers could be considered transients in a broader sense. An illuminating sample of the kind of men who made up these armies is provided by the interrogation records of a group of soldiers of Francisco Hernández Girón, last of Peru's great rebels. They were anything but professional military men. One, having been a merchant in Mexico and Peru, was in jail for debt at the time of Francisco Hernández' uprising, and joined his army when set free. Another was a working blacksmith. A third made his living from livestock he owned near the highland town of Huamanga. A fourth man had worked as tribute collector, another as lay missionary for an encomendero. Another operated a store in Potosí, where he sold the narcotic coca leaves and other Indian products. The nearest thing to a real soldier was a man who knew no trade, and had spent his six years in Peru living at the expense of relatives and friends, in various towns, waiting for some campaign to develop.[5]

The only true military professionals were those who had experience in the wars of Europe, or "Italy," and therefore knew something of military science. They were in great demand in Peru's civil wars, for the ordinary encomendero-captain, though he had personal valor, qualities of leadership, and a following, knew little about the placement and movement of men on a battlefield. European veterans always received the post of sergeant major, without a direct command, but involving responsibility for such matters as picking the battle site, ordering the companies, and placing the artillery. The same few experts appear in the sergeant major post in one campaign after another. Diego de Villavicencio was sergeant major first for Gonzalo Pizarro, then for Gasca, and later for Marshal Alvarado. Such men were badly needed for their skills, and received encomiendas, but were not esteemed or rewarded in the same fashion as the other captains.

If, however, a military man also had a commanding presence and the gift of leadership, he might leap over the ordinary captains into the position of maestre de campo, taking effective charge of both strategy and tactics, and receiving corresponding rewards. Rodrigo Orgóñoz, a veteran of Italy, became the elder Almagro's second in command, amassed a great fortune, and was named a marshal by the king. The experienced soldier who as Pizarro's maestre de campo presided over the defeat of Orgóñoz, Pedro de Valdivia, received the conquest of Chile as a reward. Years later he returned briefly to Peru to perform the same function in the Gasca campaign against Gonzalo Pizarro, and was confirmed in his governorship. The most dedicated professional of all was Francisco de Carvajal, one of the few soldiers to come to Peru already equipped with a permanent title as His Majesty's Captain. Carvajal was first sergeant major for Vaca de Castro, then became famous as Gonzalo Pizarro's cruel and undefeatable maestre de campo. Carvajal was a master of logistics, troop movements, and ruses. He understood the overwhelming importance of muskets, which he stockpiled. Scornful of all who were not skillful at arms, he drilled his men and tried to instill a spirit of professionalism in them, even writing a treatise on the conduct of war.[6]

Between wars, transients lived as best they could, their main resource being the hospitality of wealthy encomenderos, who were very willing to take in and maintain guests, particularly people from their home town in Spain, partly from charity and custom, and partly because supporting a houseful of guests was important to their prestige. Guests stood in a dependent relationship to the lord of the house, and were expected to follow his lead in politics and accompany him as a part of his retinue. The duties of guests were at times such as nearly to erase the distinction between a guest and a servant. In Cuzco, indeed, it happened that house guests would become so angry, and so bold, as to sue their hosts for wages in return for their services, causing the city council to deny that any wages need be paid in absence of a written contract. When an encomendero's house guests reached twenty or thirty in number, as they sometimes did, they became a very real threat to the peace, the starting point of plots and mutinies. Monasteries played a similar role by serving as a refuge, and source of cheap or free sustenance, for those who would flee civil or criminal justice; the rebellion of don Sebastián de Castilla was hatched in the Dominican monastery of Cuzco. One of the motives impelling the wellborn transients who originated that revolt was that Audiencia regulations were reducing the encomenderos' revenues, and making them less willing to lavish their wealth on guests. Large conglomerations of transients in a single house, while not a rarity, were nevertheless not the rule. In Cuzco around 1550, some of the encomenderos maintained from four to six guests, while others had fewer or none at all.[7]

Among Peru's floating population were no small number of rogues or confidence men, the famous *pícaros* of Spain. A noteworthy example of the class was an incorrigibly argumentative young man named Diego Tinoco, who came to the Indies in 1547 with Gasca. By the later 1550's he was in Quito, planning a hoax with a confederate named Guzmán. The two went to the backwoods community of Pasto and set up a sham ecclesiastical court in which Guzmán impersonated the judge and Tinoco his notary. After hearing cases, imposing penance, and collecting fines, they were detected and condemned to exile. But while Tinoco was in jail in Guayaquil waiting for a boat to take him to Panama, he escaped, first to the local church, and then along the coast to Piura. There he succeeded in convincing an encomendero, wealthy but old and blind, that he was a distant relative, Diego de Mendoza Carrillo, born of noble parents in the southern Extremaduran town of Ribera. Tinoco lived for some time as the guest of his supposed relative, gradually gaining his confidence and taking over responsible tasks, though constantly involved in fights; he once started a fight in church at mass because someone gave him a candle he had not asked for. Eventually Tinoco got into a namecalling altercation which led to his being sued, jailed, and exposed. Once again he escaped and took refuge in church, but then returned, was sentenced, and appealed his case to the Audiencia in Lima. On the way south to carry on the appeal, he managed to be present at a fight in the courthouse of Trujillo. In 1560 the Audiencia confirmed the verdict of the court in Piura, but lightened the sentence of partial exile, leaving Tinoco practically free.[8]

Most transients were neither so novelesque nor so purely without occupation as Tinoco, but had some nominal calling or reason to be in Peru. More typical than Tinoco was Diego Sánchez de Córdoba, the son of merchants of Córdoba, who worked for several years on the Isthmus as a merchant's factor, before being exiled from there for not having brought his wife to live with him. But rather than return to Spain, he went to Cartagena and slowly worked his way along the land route, past New Granada and Quito, to Lima, where he hoped to collect certain debts owed him. In Lima he lived for over a year, without making any strenuous effort to collect the debts, at the house of a Spanish woman who took in roomers, eating usually with a merchant or a silversmith whom he got to know because they were also from Córdoba. In time, some claims left over from Sánchez' commercial activity in Nombre de Dios caught up with him, and he fled to the Mercedarian monastery.[9]

A mainstay of the transients was gambling. The Spaniards gambled mainly with cards, their favorite game being a simple one called *dobladilla,* and with dice; elaborately organized games of chance and professional gamblers were rare or unknown, though of course some men were better at gambling than others, and some of the transients were best of all. On one occasion two of them set up a formal company in card-playing, with much fine print devoted to the proper division of what they would win. When an encomendero of Cuzco once went with friends to his encomienda to amuse himself and collect his tributes of several thousand pesos, a wandering soldier-gambler named Vadillo heard what was going on, came by, and won the whole sum from the encomendero (though he then went into the nearest settlement and quickly gambled away everything he had won). However, transients by no means had a monopoly on gambling, and indeed suffered some handicaps, for, as one encomendero remarked when he turned down a request to gamble, when you gamble on credit, it's hard to collect. Everyone in Spanish Peru gambled, particularly in Charcas, near the great silver mines, and the myth-making feats of gambling were performed by the men who had the resources, the great encomenderos. Pedro de Valdivia and Hernando Bachicao were said to have bet 14,000 pesos on a single hand of dobladilla.[10]

One course open to idlers and fugitives from justice was to retire to some remote village, with or without its encomendero's consent, and live on the Indian economy. Living in the country and eating Indian food was, for the urban-minded Spaniards, a repelling prospect, only considered as a desperation measure, and the enforced country-dwellers were ripe for any kind of turbulence that might bring improvement in their situation. From the early 1540's on, Collao, the lonely region to the south of Cuzco, was the center of this kind of vagabondage. In 1542 Governor Vaca de Castro considered the problem almost beyond remedy, because of the vast size of the area to be policed and the sparsity of Spanish settlement in Upper Peru. The founding of La Paz in 1548, partly to help control the vagabond problem, failed to prevent the danger from becoming even more acute, as fortune seekers flocked into the region, attracted by the riches of Potosí. In 1552 whole bands of renegades were roaming the countryside openly armed and beyond the reach of the law, robbing both Indians and Spaniards.[11]

The classic device used to drain the country of an excess population of claimants and idlers was the sending out of entradas, expeditions of discovery, conquest, and settlement. Pressure was built up at the end of each civil war campaign, when the Cuzco area, where the final battles were always fought, would be overwhelmed with a mixed horde of the victorious and the defeated. The victors were the greater problem, because of their clamor for encomiendas, which were not nearly numerous enough to fill the unlimited demand. In this situation governors, from Francisco Pizarro on, would authorize from five to ten entradas to go out in all directions from central Peru.

The governors were frankly more interested in dispersing a turbulent mob than in developing new territories. Gonzalo Pizarro's expedition of 1541 was the last large-scale, utterly serious attempt to find new riches comparable to those of Peru; after that there was a quite general realization that the limits of the area of silver mining and sedentary Indian populations had been reached. However, wealthy encomenderos could always be found to lead and finance entradas, to have the great honor of command, and on the slim chance of finding a gold mine; some expeditions did stumble onto placer mining areas which gave a good yield for a few years. The rank and file, often less well-informed, went along for the prospect of riches and adventure, the initial pay, and lack of any other opportunity.

The entradas were reasonably effective in achieving the purpose of scattering potential malcontents, but seen in themselves, were mainly sorry episodes. Going into some of the most difficult terrain in the world with little hope of real success, manned by the least responsible elements in Peru, they suffered repeated crises of leadership. Whereas Pizarro, Almagro, Benalcázar, and Valdivia kept their great conquering expeditions under reasonably good control, in the history of entradas murder, mutinies, and chaos are standard fare. The demented violence and rebelliousness of the Amazonian expedition of Pedro de Orsua and Lope de Aguirre in 1560, which have been presented as typical of Peru, were rather the ultimate degeneration of a kind of behavior primarily characteristic of the entradas; it could reach such extremes precisely because it took place beyond the restraining influence of Spanish Peru.[12]

For contemporaries, the most famous of all these expeditions was the so-called entrada of Rojas, which took a group of two hundred Spaniards all over the northern part of Argentina in the years 1542 to 1546. The Rojas entrada was unusual in having three noted captains among its leadership. Diego de Rojas and Felipe Gutiérrez had led an unsuccessful expedition to Veragua on the Isthmus of Panama; Nicolás de Heredia had been a prominent Almagrist. Among the ordinary men were veterans of the Veragua venture, still following their old captains. Heredia brought with him quite a few Almagrists, some of whom had been on the original expedition of the elder Almagro to Chile; these men went, in some cases, from addiction to adventure, but also because central Peru offered few rewards to followers of the Almagros until the advent of Viceroy Cañete in 1556.

As in this case, the men who went on entradas were often caught in a circle. If they survived the almost inevitable failure of the expedition, they nevertheless missed an episode of the civil wars in Peru proper, or arrived there at a late stage of the campaign. They therefore received no reward at victory, and were afterwards forced to enlist for yet another entrada. For this reason, soldiers on entradas were not usually striplings. A sampling of the ages of some participants in the entrada of

Rojas indicated a centering on the late twenties, with numbers diminishing gradually in both directions down to a few teenagers and forty-year-olds. The Rojas expedition, like most entradas, included a few Spanish women (the mistresses of prominent soldiers), a good number of Negro slaves, and a large contingent of friendly Indians.

Despite good auspices, the expedition ran a familiar course. Rojas soon died, under suspicious circumstances, and a young follower of his was raised to the command over the heads of Heredia and Gutiérrez, the last of these being sent home in disgrace. After two years the usurper was assassinated, and Heredia assumed command, causing the group to split in two and return divided to Peru, having accomplished little beyond exploration, but with such a reputation for exploits of bravery that some members of the expedition, like Diego Pérez de la Entrada, thenceforth took their surnames from it.[13]

After entradas, the second main option for the rootless in Peru was to return to Spain. It may seem paradoxical that the poor were more prone to return than the rich, yet, as was seen in the case of artisans, a Spaniard with any kind of an established position found it hard or impossible to transfer his status to Spain, while a man with nothing more than a few hundred pesos could very well hope to get his small fortune intact across the ocean and, with luck, past the danger of seizure at the *Casa de Contratación,* for the officials there tended to be lenient with small shipments. Three hundred pesos was not a large amount in Peru. A Peruvian Spaniard might get that much for a year's work, win it gambling, receive it as a gift from an encomendero patron or earn it at some marginal enterprise. But in Spain, three hundred pesos was enough to invest and live on modestly for many years. Rootless Spaniards in Peru were constantly tempted to take advantage of the greatly differing value of silver in the colony and in the homeland.

In the eyes of the governors and the priests, not some but all of the Spaniards were determined to return quickly to Spain. The prominent Dominican fray Domingo de Santo Tomás wrote that all who came, governors, prelates, judges, priests, encomenderos, merchants, and every other kind of people, had but one purpose in mind, to get rich quickly and return home.[14] This is another of those exaggerated views with some kernel of truth, typical of official correspondence. It was probably literally true that all Spaniards desired, or even intended, to go back to Spain some day. But while with one side of their nature they made plans to return, they continued to get more and more deeply involved in Peruvian affairs. They were like the tailor Domingo de Destre (see p. 110) who never for a moment wavered in his intention to return to Aragon, but lived for more than fifty years in Lima.

Captain Nicolás de Heredia, who as a former notary had a facility for correspondence, in 1534 wrote a touching and apparently sincerely felt letter to his wife in Córdoba, announcing that he had acquired a fortune, was sending money home and would follow as soon as he could get permission to leave Peru.[15] Yet the year 1542 saw him among the leaders of the Rojas expedition into the wilderness, and he was killed in the civil wars on his return to Peru proper in 1546. This pattern is seen so often in Peru as to make it likely that the only field in which really well-established people commonly returned to Spain was commerce, and even there the merchants who had left often still made trade with Peru their principal business.

If, in general, it was among the transients and semi-transients on the margins of the economy that thoughts of returning home were the strongest, such thoughts became a burning fever in the area of Potosí, where a large unsettled population of Spaniards was trying, under the most forbidding conditions of geography and climate, to get some share of the great wealth extracted from the silver mines. Almost like men marooned, the Spaniards at Potosí tried hard to divert themselves (there gambling and bull-fighting reached their fullest development), and talked incessantly of home.

One small trader at Potosí in the early 1550's, Juan Prieto, wrote frequent letters to his wife and family in Valladolid, showing his intense preoccupation with the details of his household there. Prieto sent home amounts of 150 to 200 pesos from time to time with returning friends, and he had very precise ideas as to what should be done with the money. His daughter Sabina was to be cared for and guarded with extreme care, so "even the sun won't see her, much less people." He wanted the orchard and garden to be kept well, and a good stock of rabbits and doves to be bought. Above all he wanted a large wooden double door, framed by a stone portal, to be built at the garden entryway, with a foot-wide iron reinforcement to keep the wood from getting damaged when the cart went through. Prieto must have spent much time dreaming about the door. He and half-a-dozen friends at Potosí, all from Valladolid, meant to return to Spain together soon. Whether or not they actually did return, the plan to do so was their way of justifying to themselves their presence in bleak, cold Potosí.[16]

The field of possibilities in Peru for a Spaniard who, like many of the transients, had little hope of ever receiving an encomienda, but refused to be an artisan, declared merchant, or majordomo, was narrow indeed, yet some few managed to thrive in this limbo, becoming important citizens without being encomenderos. Such men usually got their start from a loan, gift, or other favor from an encomendero relative or friend; anyone with influence among the encomenderos could get the grant of some agricultural land, which often implied the right to use nearby Indian labor. Agriculture, livestock raising, and indirect entrepreneurial activity in the provisioning of Potosí were the principal specialities of those who would be gentlemen but were not encomenderos.

Such a career was most feasible in Upper Peru, where the mines gave the economy a second dimension. In 1552 the non-encomendero Francisco Mejía de Loaysa had an estancia in the jurisdiction of La Paz, where he kept over 600 head of pigs and raised 5,000-bushel crops of grain and potatoes with the labor of Negroes, Indian yanaconas, and Indians whom he rented from encomenderos. He had his own large residence on the estancia, as well as a tambo where he sold to passers-by his produce and other kinds of provisions. Even more impressive was the estate of Gonzalo Silvestre, a famous conqueror and fighting man who had been on Hernando de Soto's Florida expedition, and arrived in Peru too late to get an encomienda, though he fought prominently in several of the civil wars. By 1555 Silvestre was living fully in the style of an encomendero, with two good riding horses, Negro slaves, and a majordomo who administered his mining interests, agricultural land, livestock, and houses in La Plata and Potosí.[17]

Lima, however, rather than Potosí, was the scene of the most striking single example of success outside the encomienda system. There, in a career reminiscent of nineteenth-century North America, a Spaniard with the unprepossessing name of Garci Pérez, from Medellín, became a tycoon in cattle, transportation, and finance. Though Garci Pérez was in Peru by 1535, he was for some reason never considered for an encomienda, while on the other hand he avoided identification as a merchant. Just how Pérez got started is not known, but by 1538 he was already, in company with an artisan from his home town of Medellín, buying a row of shops on Lima's main square. In the same year he was the successful bidder for Lima's butchery concession, which he was to obtain again intermittently over the next fifteen years.

In the 1530's the meat animals he depended on were pigs and llamas, but with the subsequent multiplication of cattle, beef became the staple.

In the early 1540's Pérez, by agreement with the city council, built a cart road from the port of Callao into Lima, and was granted the city's first carting concession. Another of his activities was standing surety on any of the hundred occasions when Spanish law demanded it; he became Lima's principal bondsman. In 1549 Pérez and others bought up the estate of Peru's former royal treasurer, agreeing to take over the large debt the treasurer owed the king. The largest transaction of Pérez' career, and perhaps of the whole civil war period in Peru, came in 1554 when he sold his herd of 3,200 cattle, along with 16 Negro slaves, for 118,810 pesos. In 1556 he undertook an even more ambitious venture, agreeing with Viceroy Cañete to level a road more than fifty miles long between Arequipa and the coast, in return for a ten-year carting concession there.

Overextension prevented the accomplishment of the latter project; Garci Pérez was always somewhat overextended, but this time the consequences were serious. Pérez had to spend long periods in jail (though in the daytime only) for debts, both to the king, for sureties, and to individual creditors. The road in Arequipa got no farther than the construction of some warehouses at the port; Pérez' greatest asset, the debt still owed him for his giant cattle sale, was seized and auctioned off. His rival in the bitter competition for Lima's butchery concession, Alejo González Gallego, whose career was much like Garci Pérez' own, tried to have him murdered, but Pérez fended off this threat, approaching the intended murderer directly and winning him over. Through it all, Pérez lived, in as lordly a style as any encomendero, in a large house in Lima where he sheltered several Spanish families as permanent guests. By 1563 he was back on his feet, though with reduced resources, and was negotiating to have the Arequipa road-building agreement extended for fifteen years.

The episode of Garci Pérez' confrontation with the man who was supposed to murder him can serve to evoke the atmosphere of risk and rascality in which such frontier capitalists operated. At the time, Pérez was under house arrest, so he sent friends for the assassin, Juan Sánchez de Calzadilla, who was a penniless transient, though full of pretensions. When he arrived Pérez addressed him flatteringly as Señor Calzadilla, and asked him to sit down to dine with him. After the meal toothpicks and citrus water were brought, and Pérez and Calzadilla walked alone in the garden, where Pérez, starting out by saying that no one who worked for Garci Pérez had ever been sorry for it, went on to offer to pay Calzadilla if he would testify in court about the murder plot. They reached no conclusion, but Calzadilla's whole attitude was changed, and as he left, Pérez gave him 50 pesos "to buy a pair of shoes."[18]

Spanish Peru, beyond any doubt, was plagued with a large population of transients who took no interest in any constructive activity and were strongly inclined to criminality and rebellion. This element loomed so large in the governors' eyes that for them there was nothing else in Peru. But in a more balanced view, the transients never brought to a halt the steady growth of a sedentary Spanish society. The great value placed on the maintenance of guests as part of a seigneurial way of life made the country able to absorb a relatively large number of hangers-on with little strain, and prevented a potentially dangerous polarization of the rich and the poor. The innumerable entradas did their part to reduce the pressure. Then too, the situation was not the same at all times and places. Turbulent idlers were never a source of preoccupation in Lima, the center of all aspects of Peruvian civil society, and hardly so in Arequipa; Cuzco and Charcas were the principal loci of the problem. The worst years were the early 1550's, when Upper Peru seethed with a series of duels, incidents, mutinies, and robberies. But even this troublesome class of transients made some contribution to the development of Spanish Peruvian society. From their ranks came the first men who achieved wealth and position without being either encomenderos or merchants, constituting by the decade of the 1550's an important group, with many implications for the future.

IX SPANISH WOMEN
AND THE
SECOND GENERATION

Spanish women constituted a large minority of the settlers in Peru in the conquest period, and their significance was even greater than their numbers, for although women from home were not numerous enough to give every Spaniard a wife, they sufficed to keep Spanish Peru from being truly a society without women. The analysis Gilberto Freyre made of Brazilian society, that in the absence of European women, Indian women largely determined early Brazilian culture insofar as it had to do with the household, cannot be applied to Peru. While Indian influence was important, both immediately and over time, Peru even in the first generation had enough Spanish women to preclude the simple loss of any important culture elements.

Nevertheless, assessing the role of Spanish women in conquest Peru is a delicate task. In view of the old tradition among historians of ignoring them, the cultural and biological contribution of Spanish women to the building of a European society in Peru requires emphasis. Spanish women were commonly present at almost all times and places during the early occupation of Peru, and therefore cannot be considered a rarity. On the other hand, there can be no doubt that in Spanish Peruvian society, as in any new community, women were greatly outnumbered by men. Tabulations for the Indies as a whole, based on the *Pasajeros a Indias,* have indicated a ratio of about ten to one. As suggested by Richard Konetzke, however, the actual proportion of women in the Indies must have been higher than it had been at emigration, because of the higher mortality among men.[1] For Peru this was a factor of more than usual significance, with the major Indian rebellion, twenty years of civil wars, and innumerable expeditions of discovery into surrounding jungle areas.

A list of Spanish and apparently Spanish women in Peru during the period of 1532–60, assembled from all sources used for the present study, reached a total of 550, but this figure is even more ambiguous raw material for arriving at an overall estimate than was the similar list of artisans (see p. 96), since women had little occasion to appear in notarial and official records. Therefore, it is reasonable to think that the list of 550 women, brought together from the same archival sources as the more than 800 artisans, is a much smaller fraction of the total than in the latter case; but there is no firm basis for even the rudest approximation of a statistical estimate.

A second element of uncertainty in the listing is the quite broad interpretation Spaniards were willing to give to the concept of a Spanish woman. Women were identified in legal records only as to their marital status, but Spanish women were recognizable as not being specifically called Negro, Indian, or mestizo. The Spanish secretaries were very consistent in specifying Negro and Indian women; with mestizo women, particularly daughters of prominent Spaniards, they were somewhat less so, but this group did not become important until the late 1550's. There was, however, hesitance and inconsistency, both in fact and in the matter of their explicit identification in documents, when it came to two groups who were in the process of being absorbed among the ordinary Castilian women: the *moriscas* and certain light-skinned, Spanish-speaking mulatto women. The moriscas, slave women of Muslim descent, were for the most part Caucasian, Spanish-born, and converted to Christianity, and they spoke Spanish as a native language. Fully acculturated mulatto women were also usually born in Spain or an older colony. Slave-mistresses of both types often obtained their freedom, and married Spaniards or in other ways took their places among the ranks of Spanish women, which they might well do, considering their birthplace. It is particularly hard to find reasons to deny full status as Spanish women to the moriscas, who were simply undergoing a process familiar for centuries in Spain's Christian reconquest.

At any rate, one must keep in mind that Spanish women included a minority of moriscas and mulatto women with, after 1555, the addition of some mestizo women. To define the size of the minority is statistically impossible, but it can hardly have been more than a tenth of all ostensibly Spanish women. To make a rough commonsense estimate, then, of the statistical importance of Spanish women, including the women from ethnic minority groups who were accepted as Spanish, and taking into consideration the *Pasajeros a Indias*, Konetzke, and the implications of the list made for the present study, it appears probable that from the early 1540's on, Peru had one Spanish woman for every seven or eight men, in absolute numbers perhaps three or four hundred women by 1543 and a thousand by 1555.

Few Spanish women, except moriscas, took part in the actual conquest of Peru in the years 1532–35, but followed close behind the fighting. They were present in Piura by 1533 and in Jauja by 1534, as those areas became relatively pacified. According to one account, there were fourteen Spanish women in Lima in 1537.[2] By 1541, the year of the death of Francisco Pizarro, there may have been a hundred and fifty or two hundred Spanish women in Peru, not a large number but enough so that Spanish Peru could not be considered an all-male society, and the basic decision had already been made that encomenderos, and indeed most other Spaniards, would marry Spanish and not Indian women. The number of Spanish women would seem to have grown quite steadily until 1548, when, with the end of the great Gonzalo Pizarro rebellion, they came into the country at a much faster rate than before. By 1548 enough time had elapsed so that a very large number of Spanish Peruvians had roots in the country, were sure they wanted to stay, and sent for female relatives, such a summons being the principal mechanism for the entry of Spanish women.

As the relatives of the male Spanish Peruvians, the women shared the social and regional origins of the rest of the population. A sampling of the regional origins of Spanish women showed all the principal regions in their usual order, and close to their usual proportions of the total. Andalusia was at the head of the list, as was to be expected, but Andalusian women had already lost the overwhelming numerical superiority they apparently had in the Caribbean area in the early years of the sixteenth century. There were only two variations from the pattern normal for men, both of them relatively minor. First, Santo Domingo, as the nearest place where Peruvian Spaniards could find fully Spanish women in any number, contributed a significant minority. Second, the contribution of Biscay fell to almost nothing, rounding out the picture of complete predominance of the Spanish core regions as the place of origin of the European women in Peru. Except for some Portuguese women, the element of European foreigners which was present in the male population had no counterpart among the women.

The social quality of Spanish women in Peru was as varied as that of the men, ranging from the sisters of fishermen to the daughters of counts. Just as with men, there took place over the years a rise in average social status on the Spanish scale, as the wealth of Peru attracted people from an ever broader spectrum of Spanish society. It would be hard to say whether social origin had more or less importance among the men than among the women. On the one hand, a woman who could buy fine clothes and learn to imitate polite behavior could make herself more nearly the equal of high society than could a man, who faced the barrier of literacy. For while some ladies could read and write and play keyboard instruments, such accomplishments were far from universal even at the highest level. On the other hand, the use of the "doña" drew a sharp line down the middle of the female population, based on Spanish peninsular distinctions.

As was seen above (p. 36), usage in the mid-sixteenth century gave a greatly divergent meaning to the terms "don" and "doña," which were in origin merely the masculine and feminine genders of the same word. While "don" in Spain (and for nearly a generation in Peru) connoted high nobility, "doña" had become much more widespread, to the point of being almost synonymous with ordinary hidalgo status. In the process of rapid devaluation in Spain itself, the term "doña" naturally underwent more change in Peru than the conservatively used "don." But there were still limits. Throughout the whole period it remained unthinkable that an artisan's wife or daughter, or any other obvious plebeian, should use the title. Spaniards showed great reluctance to change the way they addressed a given woman once custom was set, even if she was relatively wellborn and reached great prominence. Changes therefore applied mainly to the second generation or to women who arrived in Peru very young. Spaniards felt the incongruity of calling a child "lady," and were never consistent about it, so that age 18 to 20 was the time to introduce the "doña" inconspicuously, if one was going to do it.

Many of the encomenderos' wives in the 1530's, having been married in Spain before their husbands became rich, or picked from the generally plebeian women already in the Indies at that time, did not boast the title "doña." After the 1540's, the encomenderos married practically only doñas, and the older ladies' lack of title was sorely felt, but no change was possible. It could happen that their younger sisters, brought to Peru to share the family's good fortune and to make advantageous matches, would be allowed to assume the "doña" which was

denied the rich and powerful patronesses.[3] For the second generation, the "doña" was standard for the legitimate daughter of any encomendero, whether the mother bore the title or not, and was commonly allowed to the daughters of any prominent and wealthy man.

Two women of wealth and seniority in Peru, desiring external recognition of their real status, in the 1530's applied for and received royal
cedulas granting them the "doña;" but though usage was in many ways
loose and generous, the decisions of unwritten custom were hard to
change by fiat, and it took some time for the theoretical right of the
two new doñas to become reality. The title became effective first with
Inés Muñoz, whose way was eased by her position as sister-in-law of
Francisco Pizarro; the other recipient, Francisca Jiménez, had to wait
ten years for people to call her "doña" with any consistency. Part of
the difficulty was these ladies' last names. The Spaniards considered
"doña" to be almost incompatible with a plebeian surname. Though
there were hidalgo families in Spain with names like Pérez and
Gutiérrez, for their women they sought out any higher-sounding surnames to which they might have some claim, such as Salazar or Maldonado. Poor doña Inés apparently had no noble-sounding name in her
whole family tree; she stopped using her surname almost entirely,
though at times, in a way very uncharacteristic for the age, she resorted to the use of the surnames of her first and second husbands,
Alcántara and Ribera. Francisca Jiménez finally settled upon "doña
Francisca de Pinedo." Such transformations were quite a regular occurrence whenever a woman with an ordinary surname assumed the
"doña," being facilitated by the fact that women in general, and
doñas in particular, were even less firmly tied to their surnames than
were men. A doña's last name was hardly ever used in everyday speech,
being applied mainly in the third person for clarity of reference, and
in formal documents; completely aside from any desire to ennoble one's
name, there were doñas who never quite decided which of two entirely
different surnames they preferred to go by.[4]

Family and regional ties were even more important for women than
for men. The great majority of women either arrived as part of a family, or were sent for by male relatives already in Peru. The motive was
usually to seek marriage or join a husband. If the husband died, as
could happen without a moment's notice in tumultuous Peru, the
woman would be thrown completely on family and compatriots, for
unless she was wealthy, a widow or single woman could sustain herself
only with difficulty or loss of honor.

Probably nine-tenths of all adult Spanish women were married. Previous chapters have indicated how marriage was, though not universal, the rule among encomenderos and established artisans; it was common for lawyers, doctors, notaries, and shipmasters, and not unknown among merchants. All this added up to a formidable demand for marriageable women. The natural desire to form matches was given urgency among the Spaniards by their particularly strong drive to perpetuate and enhance their lineage, and by the importance of an honorable, legitimate wife in the Spanish ideal of life. The official threat to deport all those who, having wives in Spain, failed to have them brought to the Indies, cannot be considered a major factor. Most of the time, and for most people, it was a dead letter, though governors could rid themselves of troublesome individuals by invoking it, and the royal officials could use it to extort money.

There was only one area where official policy had a strong effect in encouraging marriage, though there it was admittedly of utmost importance. While an encomendero could hope to avoid the various royal ordinances threatening to take away the encomiendas of those who did not marry, he had no chance of passing his encomienda on to his heirs unless he married and had legitimate children. At this point official policy became a serious matter, for the deadly competition to secure encomiendas would allow nothing else. Many encomenderos had their mestizo sons legitimated to inherit their property, but legitimation was never allowed to include the right to succeed in the father's encomienda, except for the children of Francisco Pizarro and one other noted captain. The encomendero's incentives to marry were increased even more by the prospect, then still very much alive, that the encomienda could be converted into a perpetual fief and family possession. With these motivations, some encomenderos began to marry or bring their wives to Peru as soon as, or even before, the first phase of the conquest was ended. Ten years after the conquest, a large minority, perhaps a third, had their wives with them; in certain more settled areas like Lima, Trujillo, and Piura the proportion was no doubt greater. By the early 1550's two-thirds of the encomenderos of highland Cuzco were married; and in 1563 there were only thirty-two encomenderos left unmarried in all Peru, of almost five hundred.[5]

Certain aspects of marriage were the same whether the man was an encomendero or an artisan, the wife wellborn or plebeian. Practically all marriages were strategic alliances arranged with a view to improving the partners' wealth or social standing; if a few Spaniards married for love, they were exceptions not indicative of any trend for the nature of marriage to change in the Indies. Both partners were seeking the greatest wealth and the highest lineage possible in the other party; but the classic type of match in the Indies was that in which the man had acquired wealth or power and now wanted to gain matching social prestige by marrying a woman of higher birth, though often poor. In these cases the man contributed a large dowry, perhaps many thousands of pesos, reversing the traditional process. Almost always the fiction was maintained that the dowry originated with the wife or her relatives, but occasionally the man, alleging the "custom of the Indies," would grant the sum openly, in consideration of the lady's virginity and high birth. However, if the higher lineage was on the man's side, the dowry reverted to its traditional form. Some encomenderos paid princely dowries, of 20,000 pesos and over, to have their sisters or daughters marry a member of the Spanish high nobility or a magistrate of the Audiencia.

The dowry had other uses as well. At times it simply represented the total property and money which a widow or wealthy spinster brought into a marriage, and meant to keep under her control. A dowry could also be a hedge against future indebtedness; sometimes husbands acknowledged receipt of a fictional dowry far in excess of the total worth of man and wife, so that if in the future the husband's property were seized for debts, or if claims heaped up after his death, the wife could always retain this large amount in the family as dowry goods.[6]

Spanish Peru, as has been seen elsewhere, was not a place where social mobility was easy, but there were ways a man could, within certain limits, raise his position through his own activity in war or commerce. For a woman, on the other hand, there was hardly anything she could do independently to enhance her position, and much that she could do to lower it. Women took their original status from their family, and it could be altered only through marriage. Practically the only chance for a woman of humble birth to reach the top rank of Peruvian society was to marry an obscure man who later became an encomendero. After the 1530's this was a rare occurrence.

Except for the minority who had married in Spain before leaving, encomenderos chose their wives primarily from among the female relatives of prominent people, other encomenderos or churchmen, in their own Peruvian community. Marriage in the upper levels of society was the first area of life where a new Peruvian regionalism superseded the

Spanish regionalism to which the settlers remained generally faithful when choosing friends and associates. Though it would not be unheard of for an encomendero of Cuzco to seek out a bride from his home town, he would be more likely to choose a sister or cousin of the richest and most powerful of his Cuzco colleagues who would deign to consider a match, regardless of the two men's regional origin in Spain. (Such marriages were often arranged while the brides were still in Spain.) In this way, the encomendero class in each Spanish Peruvian town had by 1560 become a closely interrelated group.

Other encomenderos made matches with the wellborn, and allegedly wellborn, ladies who were imported for that purpose almost as a speculative business venture. An impecunious father with three or four marriageable daughters and some claim to hidalgo status would set out from Spain to Peru with no other assets than the prospective marriages and, in some cases, royal cedulas recommending that the Peruvian governors show favor to whomever the daughters might marry.[7]

The encomenderos' wives were the most important and influential women in Peru, their position as central in its way as that of their husbands. They were the heads of large households of dependents, servants, and slaves. (Alone of all the women in the country, some of them had the luxury of a Spanish woman head servant.) Aside from their household responsibilities, they were often left in charge of their husbands' encomiendas and general affairs. In this broader function they were not thought to perform well; there was general agreement that the most heartless, avaricious, and destructive tribute collectors were Spanish women.[8]

Nevertheless, the encomenderos' wives, always maintaining their homes even when the encomenderos were absent at war, were an important force for social and economic continuity, a continuity which was not broken with the death of the encomendero. The mortality rate in the civil wars among prominent men was high, and one woman might retain the same house, servant staff, encomienda, and landed property through as many as three or four husbands. Because of the pressures of custom, the governors, and the dissatisfied pretenders, no woman who inherited an encomienda could stay unmarried. She might have a limited choice as to her next husband, but had to remarry almost immediately. Some governors merely implored and hinted at reprisal if compliance was not forthcoming, while others straightforwardly informed the ladies concerned that they had arranged their marriage;

but all were adamant. The record for noncompliance was set by María de Escobar, a women of immense wealth, seniority, and political power, who managed to place a three-year interval between her second and third husbands. In cases like these, the encomienda was juridically and in fact more the woman's than the man's.[9]

By the end of the civil war period encomenderos' wives were, in their social origins, a motley group, but could usually accept each other as equals because, as with the encomenderos themselves, the prestige of seniority could compensate for relatively humble birth. Yet among both men and women this rough balance left hidden resentments, which with the women sometimes broke onto the surface in the form of arguments about precedence.

The most famous of these incidents illustrating the tensions between the new and the old nobility was an argument between María de Lezcano and doña Ana de Velasco. María de Lezcano occupied a position of great prominence in the Trujillo region of Peru, on the basis of seniority and regionalism. She was the widow of Juan de Barbarán, a veteran of Cajamarca so powerful and so closely allied to the Pizarros that he was allowed to set up residence in Lima and become alcalde there without giving up his position in Trujillo. María's lineage, with the names of Villafranca and Lezcano, included two or three encomenderos and several of their daughters and sisters who married encomenderos, the whole interrelated clan forming the core of a regional group from the Madrid-Toledo area that was a large factor in Trujillo politics. The Villafrancas came from relatively humble, but not peasant origins in Spain. The men were literate; the women made no pretensions to the "doña," not even María, as one of Peru's most respected women. Probably they had been, in Spain, the kind of family which might produce small merchants, well-to-do artisans, or lower clerics.

Doña Ana de Velasco in 1548 was new to the country. She had recently married Alonso de Alvarado, a veteran captain and a power in Peru, who was returning from Spain with his new wife and the exalted title of Marshal. Doña Ana was the granddaughter of the Duke of Frías, at home among Spain's courtly nobility.

In a church in Trujillo, these two women, approximately equal in wealth and power, María with far more seniority and doña Ana with an infinitely better position in Spanish peninsular society, fell to arguing over a cushion in a pew. Doña Ana felt so insulted by impertinence from a woman of humble birth that she asked her husband, in any case excessively proud and vindictive, to avenge her. Alvarado hired two ruffians who publicly affronted María by stabbing her in the face and cutting off her hair. The courts quickly convicted Alvarado of grave misdoing; at one point, he was condemned to death. After years of litigation Alvarado paid María 12,000 pesos out of court, and received a relatively light fine (which he refused to pay). Both parties continued to maintain their positions in Peru through it all.[10]

The wives of men who were not encomenderos, among whom artisans' wives were the largest group, could not live with as much magnificence as women in the upper rank, but they came nearer to that ideal than might be imagined. In a singular fashion, Spanish Peru preserved most of the social distinctions of the Peninsula, and even invented new ones based on seniority and the possession of encomiendas, yet at the same time, because of the fabulous wealth available to the intruders, and the presence of a large servile population, even those Spaniards who were thought of as poor and plebeian could afford things that in Spain were the perquisites of wealth. Most Spanish women dressed in fine stuffs; none were without servants. An artisan's wife could be expected to have a considerable staff, who would call her "señora" and relieve her of most of the burden of daily housekeeping. In Lima in 1546, the wife of one far from prosperous artisan was waited upon by a Negro woman slave, a freed Indian woman of Nicaragua, and a Peruvian Indian servant, aside from two slaves who aided her husband in his work. In the main, artisans' wives and encomenderos' wives lived in different circles, choosing their confidantes, comadres, and dining companions from among their equals. Yet there were points of contact; often a humble woman stood in a kind of client relationship to an encomendero's wife, and it could happen that the wife of an encomendero would serve as sponsor at the wedding of an artisan.[11]

Independent economic activities of women, carried on either by married women from the base of their dowry goods, to which they retained rights, or by widows and spinsters who had to gain a living, were channeled into certain areas defined by convention. Women owned a great deal of city real estate, both for their own residences and for the purpose of renting out, but were not too often seen as the owners of agricultural land or livestock. A large proportion of Negro slave house servants were the personal property of women, and much speculative buying and selling took place. Like all other elements of Spanish Peruvian society, women who had achieved solvency invested as silent partners in merchandise and loaned money.

There were single women in Lima who over the years acquired great wealth and a solid position, though not much social prestige, through such enterprise. It was not that any stigma attached to these activities in themselves, being practiced by the most patrician of ladies, but if a woman was of humble origin, or had a less than honorable start, such facts were not subsequently forgotten.[12]

Other fields open to women were more in the nature of feminine specialties, and had strongly lower class connotations. The baking of bread and biscuit, both for ordinary city consumption and for the provision of ships and armies, was carried out largely under the supervision of women. Spaniards spoke of the *panaderas* as if male bakers did not exist, which was not quite true, but there is no doubt that the business was mainly shared by Spanish women and free mulatto and Negro women, the bulk of the work in either case being done by Negro slaves and Indians. Women naturally monopolized the occupation of midwifery, which they combined with the general healing of ailments. Poor women, doing as they have always done, sewed and took in boarders. Hospitality by the rich was the principal method of housing and feeding transients in Peru, but some of the women who accepted boarders for a fee began, by the late 1540's and the 1550's, to evolve into regular innkeepers (who also sold odds and ends to the public), not only in Lima but as far into the highlands as La Paz.[13]

The type of woman in charge of these inns varied from the humble but honorable to the definitely shady. Nearer to the second category was Francisca Suárez, generally called la Valenciana, who for two decades from the later 1530's was one of the best-known women of Lima, though always frankly plebeian. To judge by the ambiguity of her own statements about herself, it is possible that she was in origin a morisca. At various times she went by two completely different names, and gave both Valencia and Almería, in the kingdom of Granada, as her birthplace. Her assertion that she was the legitimate daughter of a Captain Pedro Cuadrado who died in Italy can only have been a falsehood, at least the part of it pertaining to legitimacy. It is beyond the realm of practical possibility that the legitimate daughter of one of his Majesty's captains should have been a *curandera*, a practical healer of ailments, and that is what Francisca Suárez basically was.

In Almería she had been married to a Corsican, and had two children, both husband and children still being alive when she left Spain to come to the Indies. In Lima, from a start as a curandera la Valenciana came to operate what amounted to a boarding house, staffed by several slaves and well equipped with provisions, silver service, and wall hangings of damask and velvet. As she prospered, she went into other enterprises common for women; her establishment (probably not she herself) manufactured bread and biscuit for sale, and she owned four or five houses besides her own, all of which she rented out for income.

For their self-protection and for their honor, it was prudent for women who kept inns to marry, and those who could find willing husbands did so. In 1547 la Valenciana married an Antonio de Toledo, who thenceforth helped in the operation of her house. She became deeply committed to Toledo in more than a formal sense, giving him free management of her properties and supporting his relatives. But the relationship came to an end because of a difficulty that plagued marriage in the Indies. Toledo was a bigamist. Presumably la Valenciana's husband in Spain had died before the new match, but Toledo's first wife was still alive. He had succumbed to the temptation that overcame more than one Spaniard in Peru, that of forgetting a poor, distant wife in Spain for a new one who was rich and present. After a year the validity of the marriage was challenged in the ecclesiastical courts, only to be confirmed, until finally around 1554 Toledo's previous marriage was established beyond doubt, he was exiled from Peru, and his marriage with la Valenciana was invalidated.[14]

There is no particular reason to think that la Valenciana's place was ever more than a boarding house. But it is possible; not all adventurers in the Indies were male. Already in 1537 Bishop Berlanga of Panama complained of the presence of too many single women of bad morals. There were always a certain number of women, not necessarily of the very lowest origin but certainly of low repute, who served the Spaniards as prostitutes, camp followers, and mistresses.

Full-fledged prostitutes definitely existed in Lima, the center of all amenities, and in rich Potosí, but there were not enough such women to be organized by the houseful. Nor was there anything like mass demand for the physical woman. Spanish men found Indian women attractive, and any Spaniard could have as many as he wanted. Spanish prostitutes catered more to the need of Spaniards to be near a woman who shared their language and culture. As much as anything else they were entertainers, who might, like María de Ledesma in Potosí, have a fine vihuela or guitar and know how to play and sing well. Jokingly, half in derision, these women were commonly called "doña" by their clients, and this usage has found its way into the chronicles of the civil wars; but they were not so termed in any serious context.

Far more common than true prostitutes were adventuresses who were prepared to form loose relationships, either temporary or quite permanent, with any man who would support them well. They were not averse to an advantageous marriage, but could expect marriage only under unusual circumstances. Often such a woman served in effect as interim or replacement wife for a man whose real wife was still in Spain, or, even more characteristically, for a man who was single and desired female companionship, but did not want to marry until he was in a position to make a match with a wealthy or wellborn lady who could do honor to his lineage. When that time came, if the relationship had been a meaningful one and the man was generous, he might give his former mistress a dowry and marry her to another, less ambitious Spaniard.

In an occasional exceptional case, the pair would form a deep attachment and become married; a man who took his mistress on the Rojas expedition later married her, after they had spent several years in the Argentine wilderness together. In the late 1530's some Peruvian encomenderos, taking seriously the royal threat to deprive all those who were single of their rights, married their mistresses for lack of other women. Later, at the time of the New Laws, these men complained bitterly and publicly that they had married beneath them to retain their encomiendas, which they were now to lose after all.

Very typical of the manner of existence of these women was the career of Violante de Góngora, who lived with a Portuguese merchant in Peru in the 1550's. As his mistress, she accompanied him back and forth to Panama on business trips, something it would not have been considered proper for a legitimate wife to do; the wives of merchants and sailors stayed in Lima while their husbands traveled. Violante had borne the merchant a child, and the relationship was quite a stable one; when he died on the way back from Panama in 1556, he left her in charge of liquidating his affairs. But rather than settle down to a respectable pseudo-widowhood, she drifted and lived loosely. In 1560 she was in highland Huamanga, where she had two Spaniards arrested for beating her.[15]

At the opposite pole from the concubines were the feminine devotees of the church. Peru was slow to develop true convents of nuns, and the ones that began to be organized, as 1560 neared, already belonged to a new era. But they were preceded, in the late 1540's and 1550's, by the *beatas*. Beatas, a specifically Spanish phenomenon, were women living in pious retirement, sometimes individually and sometimes in groups, who wore the habit of an order with which they had some, usually formal, connection.

The Dominican beatas seem to have been the first to organize themselves; in 1548 the Dominican beata Mari Hernández de Pereda donated her house for the purpose, though she soon added the clause that a rival, Leonor del Aguilar, should not be allowed entry. Later the Dominican friars persuaded her to revoke the clause, and the formerly excluded Leonor, who had lived in her own small house with a mulatto slave girl and a mestizo child she cared for, came there to live. Discipline, one can see, was not what might be expected from regular nuns, but the Dominican effort was serious and sustained. Leonor del Aguilar remained a beata for at least ten years; the Dominican house was still in existence in 1557, and even had affiliated members in the coastal valley of Chincha, where the Dominican friars maintained a monastery.

The Dominican beatas were women of modest circumstances; another establishment started under Augustinian sponsorship around 1557 drew from a different stratum of society, its membership being prominent widows and daughters of encomenderos, all of them doñas. After some years the beatas became regular nuns and founded a convent of the same order.[16]

Rich and poor, concubine and beata, Spanish women made their most basic contribution to the development of the country by educating those around them in the ways of the homeland. In their houses Spanish was spoken and learned. They taught their Negro and Indian maids to make beds, sew European clothes, and prepare Spanish foods in Spanish fashion. As irregular as some of their own private lives may have been, they taught religion to their slaves and servants, and encouraged them to form steady unions and marry.

But above all, this influence extended to the second generation, for whose upbringing the Spanish women were responsible, a generation which included not only their own fully Spanish children, but large numbers of mestizo children, fathered by Spanish settlers who were not content to see their offspring raised as Indians. The demand for people to care for such children was large, and any Spanish woman, whether she had children of her own or not, could expect to be importuned to raise mestizos and orphans. Once the children were taken in, personal attachment grew, whatever the original agreement had been. Francisca Suárez la Valenciana, the somewhat disreputable boarding-house keeper, agreed in 1544 to accept a Spaniard's mestizo daughter to raise and instruct, receiving a Negro slave woman toward defraying of expenses. Some years later the Spaniard died penniless in a civil war battle, but la Valenciana kept the girl, and left her a sizable legacy in her will.[17]

When it came to the wives of encomenderos, their collections of children were truly imposing. Isabel de Ovalle, twice married but childless, raised two orphaned Spanish girls, a mestizo girl who had been befriended by her first husband, and two more mestizo girls she had taken in on her own initiative (not to speak of two Negro slave orphans she meant to free). She planned to give them all substantial dowries. Childlessness was not, of course, the rule among encomenderos' wives, many of whom were notably fertile. Doña Francisca Jiménez had, by 1548, ten children alive and with her; two by her first husband, three by her second, and five by her third. She was also raising the mestizo daughter of her second husband, who acted as her maid. This was the fate of many mestizo children who were raised in Spanish homes; they received sustenance, education, and affection, but were seen in the light of servants.[18]

There was, then, growing up in Peru during the 1540's and 1550's, a new generation whose cultural heritage was strongly Spanish, whether they were of pure Spanish blood or mestizo. For the future character of the colony, this group was of immense importance; but in the period before 1560 they remained little more than a potentiality. Hardly any representative of the second generation, either Spanish or mestizo, appeared in any kind of independent role during the whole thirty years from the time the conquering expedition set out for Peru, not even in the humbler fields of endeavor such as artisanry.

Mestizos and Spanish children were born in Peru from 1533 on, but the second generation had its true beginnings only after the Indian rebellion ended in 1537. By 1560 only a small minority of the second generation were over twenty years of age. The new generation also had to contend with the general Spanish reluctance to entrust anything important to the very young; in the Spanish legal tradition, very much in force in Peru, both men and women were minors and required guardians until their twenty-fifth birthday. Emerging into independence was rendered yet more difficult by the crushing prestige of the first generation of settlers, which kept them in command in all walks of life for an abnormally long time.

Almost all apparent exceptions to the rule of the late emergence of the second generation turn out to involve people born in other parts of the Indies. Spanish women born in Santo Domingo were brought to Peru to marry encomenderos as early as the 1530's, and were treated fully as equals, as though Hispaniola were one of the regions of Spain. The only mestizo (aside from the utterly exceptional don Diego de Almagro) to become a captain in the civil wars was Diego de Ovando, fathered in Santo Domingo by Governor Ovando. In the chronicles there are reports of mestizos in the armies of Gonzalo Pizarro and Francisco Hernández Girón, but the only two whose origins are definitely known were Mexican, one of them being the chronicler Pedro Gutierrez de Santa Clara. Wherever one looks, the story was the same. A mestizo who worked as an ecclesiastical secretary in Lima in the late 1550's was from Nicaragua. The mestizo daughter of a Lima shipmaster, who married the mate of her father's ship around 1558, then sank into a career of petty thievery, was born in Panama. The complete foreignness in Peru of these mestizos from the older areas apparently made it easier for them to achieve some acceptance among the Spaniards (though not full equality). The process repeated itself in the 1560's, when some Peruvian mestizos went to Chile and as Indian fighters gained a position that seemed denied them at home.[10]

Since there were so few of them living an independent existence before 1560, there is little more to be said about the Peruvian-born Spanish children than that they grew up in their parents' homes and received a Spanish upbringing, the sons being directed into their fathers' footsteps and the daughters married advantageously at an early age. The mestizo children, on the other hand, knew many fates which will require more extended discussion. But both kinds of children alike were often orphaned by the civil wars and other frontier perils, in which case, if their parents left them anything, both alike were put under the care of legal guardians. The Spanish system of legal guardianship did not function well for the purpose of charity; no legal provision was made for children who were truly abandoned until, in the 1550's, an attorney in Lima was appointed official "father of orphans."

But if a child inherited money or property from his father, one of the city alcaldes, making no distinction between Spanish and mestizo, would seek out and appoint a guardian, who would hold the property in trust and use a stipulated amount of the income to support the child, being liable at all times to inspection of the accounts. Most often the guardian was a family friend who took the orphan into his home, but whether he was or not, the system worked quite well for those who came under it. There were encomenderos' sons who inherited, at three or four years of age, encomiendas and great properties which were held for them successfully for twenty years or more. On a smaller scale, there were quite a number of children who, through a guardian, owned a house or some livestock that assured them of a living.[20]

Those children who lived with their own families or guardians, or otherwise were in some way recognized as belonging to Spanish Peruvian society, got an education apparently not below the Spanish standard, despite the scarcity of formal instruction. Only two or three professional grammar school teachers are known to have come to Peru, but the encomenderos, at least, managed to find someone to teach their Spanish and mestizo sons. Sometimes they hired competent people as private tutors; sometimes they persuaded an ecclesiastic to teach grammar and Latin to a class of boys. What results this education could give may be seen in its most illustrious product, the mestizo chronicler Garcilaso de la Vega, whose perfect Spanish style is still admired. However it was done, the second generation had a better, or at least a more elegant, education than most of the conquerors; their elaborate signatures bespeak an increase in refinement and a loss in strength.[21]

There was in conquest Peru no one standard treatment or fixed social evaluation of the thousands of mestizo children born of Spanish fathers and Indian mothers. Many, never recognized, grew up with their mothers as Indians and were reabsorbed into the indigenous population. In other cases, Spaniards went to great lengths to provide for mestizo offspring. Some Spanish fathers sent for their mestizo children to join them from as far away as Mexico and Nicaragua. Many made plans to send mestizo sons and daughters to Spain, to be raised at home by their own families, and though this did not come to fruition as often as intended, it was no idle thought.[22]

For those who were in one way or another received among the Spanish Peruvians, their condition as mestizos was a handicap, but depending on other factors, did not preclude acceptance at a fairly high level. It is hard to separate the Spaniards' feelings about racial mixture, as it affected the mestizos, from their position on illegitimacy, for nine-ty-five per cent of the first generation of mestizos were illegitimate. To judge by the treatment accorded the few legitimate mestizos, who were accepted fully as equals, the Spanish may have considered illegiti-macy to be a more serious blemish than mixture with Indians. Legiti-mate mestizos could and did inherit encomiendas, and one was consid-ered for an appointment to the city council of Lima. Moreover, there were cases of Spaniards who had both Spanish and mestizo sons out of wedlock and gave them all equal treatment.[23]

But even illegitimate mestizo children of prominent fathers were treated with respect. The children of Pizarro and Almagro were lifted by their exalted parentage right out of the mestizo class into positions of leadership among Spaniards, while still at a tender age. The mestizo sons and daughters of other captains and encomenderos were given a careful upbringing in Spanish homes (often being taken away from their Indian mothers), and received from their fathers enough money to let them live in a certain style. Their position varied with the wealth and power of the fathers, and was enhanced if their mothers belonged to the high Inca nobility. Some mestizos of this type came to enjoy nearly the status of Spaniards, and one of them actually received a small encomienda. When an encomendero had no legitimate heir, his mestizo son, though he could not succeed in the encomienda, might in-herit a large part of his property and become a wealthy figure in the community on that basis. In general, however, there was no very obvi-ous future in Spanish Peru for upper-class mestizo boys; Garcilaso de la Vega was not the only one sent off with a few thousand pesos to Spain to seek further education or a career.[24]

The path was easier for the girls of this class, who could hope to marry within Spanish Peruvian society, perhaps not to their fathers' equals, but to substantial Spaniards of lower degree. To a Spaniard, such a marriage offered the advantages of an alliance with the girl's fa-ther, and a large dowry, which might be enough for him to live on. If the father was exceptionally rich and powerful, his mestizo daughter might be able to marry well by any standards. A daughter of the fa-mous captain Lorenzo de Aldana married a large encomendero of Charcas. Diego Maldonado, called the Rich, married his daughter to a Spanish don, with a dowry of 20,000 pesos. Ordinarily, however, such girls married men from the second rank: majordomos, merchants, entrepreneurs, or gentlemen pretenders without encomiendas.[25]

The pattern seen among the mestizo children of encomenderos repeated itself at the lower levels, but with alteration. Above all, the frequent presence on the scene of the Indian mother reduced the intensity of Hispanization. Ordinary Spaniards often succeeded in marrying their daughters to juniors or inferiors; a shipmaster to one of his sailors, or a merchant to his factor. But the point was soon reached at which the size of the dowry and the prestige of the father did not suffice to attract suitors. Many Spaniards fulfilled their duty to their mestizo children (both boys and girls) by making them a "donation." If the donation was large, perhaps a thousand pesos in value, the child could be assured of a future, but usually it was much less: two or three hundred pesos, or a mare with a colt, or a few goats. A child so endowed would probably succeed in being raised by some Spanish family, but the amount was not enough for a dowry or a start in life.

By the 1550's, therefore, a major problem in Peru was what to do with the many mestizo girls who were growing up Spanish, but were not wealthy enough to find Spanish husbands. It became a favorite form of charity to donate dowries to mestizo orphans. In Cuzco and Lima, philanthropic citizens established houses to shelter them. (Hardly ever did it occur to the charitable to arrange a marriage between two mestizos, partly, no doubt, because men did not marry as young as women, and few mestizo men had come of age). Philanthropy could not, of course, take care of all the Hispanized mestizo girls; apparently very many ended in purely servile positions, or took to loose living, or were abandoned entirely.

Ordinary mestizo boys, like the upper-class mestizos, had a hard time finding a place for themselves, but did have the advantage that they were not above acting as Spaniards' servants or entering the apprenticeship of artisans, so that some of them found avenues of integration into Spanish Peruvian society in a useful position. Not until 1561, however, were there enough trained mestizo artisans for the issue to arise as to whether they should be allowed to operate shops independently (in Cuzco it was decided in the affirmative).[26]

All in all, the Spaniards must be judged to have shown an unusual amount of interest in the fate of their mestizo offspring. Even if many, possibly most, mestizo children suffered neglect, there were many hundreds who were protected, and grew up inside Spanish Peruvian society.

In order to explain the relatively good treatment of mestizos it is not necessary to imagine any unusually strong parental tenderness on the part of the Spaniards, though some had such feelings (they were often struck, it appears, by how much their mestizo children resembled them).[27] Most important was the strong Spanish feeling for lineage, which emphasized solidarity with all one's relatives near and distant, as well as the necessity of carrying on the family name. Another factor was the strict Spanish machinery for legal guardianship. Finally, there was the special sense of responsibility which the Spaniards, in the Arab tradition, felt for the protection of females. At all levels, more care was lavished on mestizo girls than boys, with the probable result that a higher proportion of them were absorbed into the Spanish population, and indeed, with men more numerous in that population than women, they were more needed.

To sum up the substance of the chapter, there were among the settlers of Peru a large minority of Spanish women who, living in the cities, often as heads of the large households of encomenderos, were able to exert a cultural influence on the urban population out of proportion to their numbers. Even humble women had mixed servant staffs to whom they taught Spanish ways. The household of one almost indigent Spanish woman of Lima could stand as a paradigm of Spanish Peru: herself, her Negro slave, her Indian servant, and a mestizo orphan girl.[28] Above all, the Spanish women were responsible for the existence of a second Spanish generation who were to inherit the encomiendas and other wealth of the first, and they provided the surroundings in which a generation of mestizos grew up to be primarily Spanish in language and culture.

But both elements of the second generation, the Spanish and the mestizo, were extraordinarily slow to assert themselves. No nativeborn Spanish merchants, artisans, or influential encomenderos (there were some youths who had inherited encomiendas) were seen in Peru before 1560. The mestizos by that time had not yet come to constitute a community, such as the communities of Negroes, urban Indians, or even Italians or Basques. There was no such thing as a mestizo family of father, mother, and children; but then perhaps there was not later, either. As 1560 approached, some hints of the future began to appear. Vagabond mestizos of Cuzco were trading with, cheating, and robbing the Indians in the coca-growing areas, anticipating the *léperos* who later were such a plague in the Spanish colonies. The first signs of what was to become creole decadence, the fruit of wealth and underemployment, were also showing themselves.[29]

The true emergence of the second generation occurred in the 1560's. That decade saw the first mestizo revolts and the first Peruvian-born members of the city councils. It was then that the very word "creole" as now commonly used, was introduced in Peru, for until that time "creole" had referred only to Negroes, and the Spanish second generation were merely called Spaniards like their fathers. The groundwork had been laid in the period of the conquest and civil wars, but the final definition of the role of the creoles and the mestizos was one of the few essential formative tasks left undone in Spanish Peru by 1560.

X NEGROES

In 1533 Francisco Pizarro, still encamped at Cajamarca after capturing the Inca emperor, sent an advance party on to Cuzco, the first men from the Old World to see the Inca capital. One of the four men to go was a Negro. It is typical of the myth-making process that this group of two Andalusian seamen, a Basque notary, and a Negro should have been transformed in the later chronicles into two captains from Extremadura. As it turned out, the Negro did not get to Cuzco; he returned alone from Jauja, in charge of a train of Indians with a fortune in precious metals.[1]

Among the almost limitless variety of people who helped to conquer Peru, there were always Negro slaves. They were present as servants and auxiliaries on all the early discovery expeditions, from 1524 on; some Spaniards took Negro slaves along as a speculation, hoping to sell the slaves at a great profit if the expedition should strike it rich.[2] In the period before the capture of the Inca, Negroes were not numerous, because the money to buy them was not available, but after the spoils of Cajamarca were distributed, Negroes flooded into the country. They were on the coast, in the highlands, in Chile, on all the subsequent expeditions sent into peripheral areas.

In the very early days the prime function of Negroes was to serve as valuable military auxiliaries. Whenever the Spanish prepared for an expedition against Indians, they bought three things: arms, horses, and Negroes.[3] With the founding of cities, the Negroes' functions expanded rapidly, until they were performing a whole range of tasks essential to building, providing, and maintaining the Spanish settlements.

Basic to an understanding of the role of Negroes in conquest Peru is an appreciation of their intermediate position between the Spaniards and the Indians; they are not to be thought of as beneath the Indians. Negroes assimilated Spanish skills much more rapidly and thoroughly than did the Indians. Militarily, the Negroes were almost as superior to the Indians as the Spaniards were. A small band of Negroes could terrorize a whole Indian countryside; a single Negro could dominate an Indian village. Negroes, even as slaves, showed a tendency in the early period to accumulate servant staffs of cowed Indians. Though some Negroes lived with or married Indian women, and in the cities there was a certain rapprochement between the two poles of the servant class, the relationship between Negroes and Indians was, in the main, one of strong mutual hostility, with the Negroes occupying a position of much greater power.[4]

On the other hand, Negroes were not the equals of Spaniards. Completely apart from the obvious subordination of Negroes in the role of slaves, the Spaniards retained military superiority. When Spaniards fought Indians, Negroes fought along; when the Spaniards went to the civil wars, Negroes went as pages, and stayed in the tents at battletime. It is true that the presence of so many potential fighting men tempted Spanish commanders more than once, and finally in 1554 the rebel Francisco Hernández Girón organized a company of three or four hundred Negro slaves, promising them freedom, but the results were inconclusive, and since this was the last major civil war, Negroes never again had a chance to learn the refinements of the military art.[5] In war as in many other things, Negroes ranked between the Spaniards and the Indians, probably closer to their fellow intruders from the Old World than to the native inhabitants of Peru.

At first, the Spaniards in Peru were unaware of the great complexity of the Africans' ethnic background, or indifferent to it. Sales of Negro slaves in the 1530's hardly ever contained any reference to place of birth or ethnic origin. But early in the decade of the 1540's, buyers and sellers started paying irregular attention to the ethnic-geographic origin of slaves, which they thought of as the Africans' "country" (*tierra*) or *nación,* a loose and general term with several meanings: birth, nation, race, or tribe. From the late 1540's on, reference to origin was a quite regular part of the description of Negro slaves, omitted only through neglect or for the lack of information. Nothing indicates, however, that the Spaniards as yet attached great economic importance to slaves' origin; prices did not vary discernibly with ethnic group.

For the period of about 1548 to 1560, then, information is available to give an indication of the approximate origins of the Africans in Peru. Though exhaustive, methodical research on the subject was not possible for the present study, some spot checks of typical material gave results which are likely to be confirmed by any future investigation. That part of the West African coast called Upper Guinea or the Cape Verde region, and indeed that section of it south of the Senegal River through Portuguese Guinea, was far and away the most important source of Peru's Negroes, though Africans from the Congo region, Mozambique, and elsewhere in West Africa were no rarity.

The terms used in Peru to designate a slave's origin were taken from the Atlantic slave trade, and most of them referred to large ethnic groups, or sometimes to states. Some of them were names the Africans might well have used as their primary designation in their homeland, others not, but the Africans were at least familiar with the terminology, and knew which group they belonged to. The most important groups or designations, with figures for the frequency of their occurrence in a sampling of notarial registers of Lima and Arequipa, are as follows:[6]

CAPE VERDE	Jelof (Wolof)	45	
	Biafara (Biafada, Biafar)	40	
	Bran (Bram)	23	
	Berbesí (Serer)	18	
	Mandinga (the Malinke of the Gambia)	15	
	Bañol (called Banyun by J W Blake)	8	
	Cazanga (Kassanga)	4	
	Fula	1	
	Zape (Sierra Leone region)	8	
			162
OTHER WEST AFRICA	Tierra Nova (not positively identified)	20	
	São Tomé (though possibly proceeding from the south)	3	
			23
SOUTHERN AFRICA	Manicongo (Congo)	13	
	Mozambique	5	
	Enchico (Anzico)	2	
	Anbo (Ambo)	1	
	Angola (Ndongo)	1	
			22
OTHER	Spain, Portugal, Indies, "creole"	49	
			256

These provisional results tally well with impressions gained from reading a large variety of sources not here tabulated. It is reasonably clear that the ethnic spread of the Africans underwent no major change in the period 1532–60.

While so many of them came from a single region, the Africans were ethnically extremely fragmented. No one group formed a majority or a dominant minority. Furthermore, it appears that African slaves somehow got shuffled about and intermingled in transit, before reaching Peru, so that even newly arrived lots had internal diversity. All available lists of relatively large collections of Negro slaves show the same extraordinary diversity, with only two or three slaves from any single group. It is not clear whether the Spaniards consciously strove to break up concentrations of Africans with the same background, or whether the diversity was a natural product of the method of collection and the various resales which most slaves had gone through by the time they reached Peru.

Planned or accidental, ethnic diversity was an element of prime importance in determining the Africans' role in Peru. It meant that Africans lived and acted almost entirely within the Spanish context. Most Africans must have had to speak Spanish to each other. Separated from the Indians by race, culture, and mutual hostility, cut off from one another by their diversity, Africans counted in the conquest and occupation of Peru mainly as so many more Spaniards, so many more spreaders of Spanish language and European ways.

The only African traits that could at all assert themselves were the very general patterns that were more universal than language. African-type dancing was one of these, and appeared wherever Africans could congregate. Kingship was another. The few independent communities of renegade Negroes which managed to exist in certain parts of Peru for a few years operated under that African political institution.[7] It would be of great interest to know what language the renegades spoke. Probably it was Spanish. Or possibly these communities enjoyed some degree of success because they had been able to concentrate enough people from one or another of the ethnic groups to form a strong nucleus. In any case, ethnic diversity was one effective deterrent to slave rebellions.

As seen in the table above, not all Negroes in Peru came directly from Africa. A significant minority were born in Spain and Portugal, where Negro slavery was then common. This group was perhaps comparable in number to one of the second-ranking ethnic groups like Berbesí or Mandinga. Spanish-born Negroes were even more completely dependent on the Spaniards than were the African Negroes; it is unlikely that many of them spoke any language other than Spanish. They were, however, not as prominent, as distinct from the other Negroes, or as highly esteemed by the Spaniards as one might reasonably expect. Only two differences are readily discernible. A fair number of Spanish Negroes were really mulattoes, of mixed African and Spanish parentage. And they provided more than their share, though not nearly a majority, of the important class of Negro artisans.

For years the Spanish Negroes were the only significant group of non-African Negroes in Peru. Though much is hidden behind the all-inclusive term "creole," it appears that very few Negroes born in other parts of the Indies ever reached Peru. Only isolated examples occur, mainly from the Isthmus and the Antilles. The first major addition to the Negroes born outside Africa came in the mid-1550's, when a generation of Peruvian-born Negroes reached saleable age, according to the criterion of the time. In 1556 and 1557 there was an increase in the sale of boys and girls in their early teens, "creoles," who must have been Peruvian-born. One document of 1557 shows 19 creoles, presumably Peruvian, against 42 Negroes from Africa.[8]

The terms used to classify Negro slaves lacked the precision and elaborateness of later times. Buyers and sellers got along with four rough terms, "creole" (*criollo*), "*ladino*," "*bozal*," and "mulatto." The word creole applied, in the time before 1560, exclusively to Negroes. It had a wide but quite exact meaning. Any Negro born outside the African homeland was a creole; not only the Negroes born in Peru and other parts of the Indies, but Negroes born in Spain and Portugal, were creoles. Alongside creoles from Lima and Puerto Rico were creoles from Seville, Jaén, Almagro, Valladolid, and Lisbon. As an isolated case, there was a creole Negro born on the island of São Tomé, in the Bight of Biafara.[9] Since the Portuguese were established there, São Tomé was not considered African.

"Ladino" and "bozal" were two words that did heavy duty in the description of slaves. Buyers wanted to know two things, whether or not a slave was experienced, used to life outside Africa and among Europeans, and whether or not he spoke Spanish. Two sets of terms were really needed to express all this, but, in the peculiar conditions of slavery in the Indies at the time, experience and Spanish speaking so nearly coincided that one set of terms sufficed. "Bozal" basically meant just an inexperienced new arrival from Africa, and "ladino" merely meant Spanish-speaking, but they were used as opposite poles, "bozal" to mean a new slave who therefore knew no Spanish, and "ladino" to mean a Spanish-speaking slave who was therefore experienced. These meanings, already fairly clear from the ordinary use of the words in documents of sale, can be deduced with certainty from their occasional use together, as when one Negro was called "half-way between ladino and bozal."[10]

To express all kinds and degrees of mixtures of Negroes with other races, only one word, "mulatto," was in common use. Mulattoes were not generally thought of as a group distinct from Negroes; a mulatto was a type of a Negro. The word *zambo* for Negro-Indian mixture had not yet come into use. Negro-Indian mixtures were called mulattoes right up to 1560. When the Spaniards found an unusual mixture or hue in a slave, they resorted to direct description. A Spanish-born slave woman, sold in Lima in 1552, was "the color of cooked quince."[11]

This rough classification system was adequate and appropriate in the fluid situation that existed. Africans were still very much an unknown quantity, methods of marketing had not yet reached maturity, and though Africans were numerous, they were not present in the overwhelming numbers that plantations would have required.

Most Negro slaves went through life with no more than a simple Christian name like Pedro, Antón, or Catalina, often qualified by the word Negro. Generally Negroes assumed surnames only when they were freed, but a few Negro slaves (who tended to be from Spain) had complete Spanish names such as Juan Delgado, or Francisco Calderón. There was a real felt need for surnames only when fairly large groups of Negroes worked together. In these cases, African ethnic names and the slaves' occupations or former occupations were the most common surnames, or replacements for surnames.[12]

The international network that brought Negro slaves to the Indies cannot be studied here in any detail. But it is important to have some idea of that part of the slave trade which projected directly into Peru. Above all it should be made clear that in the period of 1530–60 Negro slaves did not yet ordinarily arrive in Peru by whole boatloads, as they did in the Caribbean. Negroes got to Peru by miscellaneous and various means, as the Spaniards themselves did. Many Negroes came with their permanent owners, or with Spaniards who, as a sideline, were speculating on the sale of two or three slaves. Small private activity may have accounted for as many Negroes as the more or less official trade carried on by large merchants.

Even the merchants did not regularly import really large shipments of slaves into Peru. The logistics were staggering, the risks enormous. The few shipments of 50 to 100 slaves of which there is any record were connected with large licenses the Spanish crown gave to certain individuals as a political favor.[13] Direct evidence for the size of lots of slaves, such as once could have been found in the registers of Callao, has disappeared. Indirect evidence indicates that even the largest merchants imported lots of only about ten to twenty slaves at a time, and did even that at quite irregular intervals, so that large buyers could not count on supplying their needs from any one source.

The two largest sales of newly-arrived Negro slaves recorded in the notarial archives of Lima took place in 1543, and involved only twelve slaves each. The merchants were general merchants of Lima; despite a contrary opinion, nothing indicates that there were any specialized slave merchants in Peru in the period under consideration. The man most closely associated with the Negro slave trade was a large merchant named Alonso Pérez de Valenzuela. He made one of the sales of twelve Negroes in 1543, a sale of six in 1551, and numerous smaller sales, but selling slaves could not be said to be his main activity. He was the partner of a great entrepreneur of Seville, Marshal Diego Caballero, in importing and selling merchandise of every kind, and also owned ships and made large loans to the royal treasury. Juan Antonio and Nicoloso Corso, brothers, and Corsicans as their names indicate, also imported slaves as a part of a general commercial activity. Nicoloso imported a lot of eight Negroes in 1550, the only piece of direct evidence presently available on the subject of the size of lots. Some Portuguese merchants participated in the trade, but there is nothing to indicate that they at all dominated it.[14]

Any merchant coming to Peru with a shipment of general merchandise would ordinarily bring a slave or two to sell. Small speculation in Negro slaves was prevalent also among any solvent Spaniards who had occasion to travel. A citizen of Lima, Juan Cortés, took a brief trip to Spain in the mid-1540's to negotiate for favors from the royal court. As a side venture while in Spain, he bought, in company with a priest of Lima, three Negro slaves and some merchandise. In 1546 he returned to Lima with his investments and sold them there.[15] Constant small activity of this kind, whether by merchants or others, was a vital element in the Peruvian Negro slave trade.

Lima, as the country's port, was the center of selling throughout the period. There was a large turnover of Negro slaves in Arequipa and Cuzco, but people seeking anything specific directed themselves to Lima. In 1559 the Cuzco city council felt it had to send to Lima simply to buy a "good" Negro slave woman to serve in the city's hospital for Indians.[16]

Large buyers of slaves supplied themselves as best they could. When in 1542 an encomendero of Cuzco purchased seventeen Negroes in Lima to be used in mining in the gold rush area of Carabaya, he had to buy them from three different merchants and a private individual. Most Spaniards who owned large numbers of Negro slaves accumulated them gradually. When the city of Lima was building a permanent bridge of brick and stone in 1557, it decided to employ Negroes as the main steady work force, and for that purpose bought about twenty Negroes, one or two at a time, from different people.[17]

The vast majority of Negro slaves changed hands in small transactions, mostly sales of one slave, less often of two or three. Many of these sales can be called primary; that is, they represented the sale of a newly arrived Negro, by the merchant or speculator who imported him, to the person who was going to own him permanently. But many other transactions were part of a constant, disturbingly prevalent process of resale. Among various reasons for the frequency of resale, the most basic was the peculiarly insistent demand for Negro slaves. In a general market situation where most prices, despite violent short-term fluctuations, were remarkably stable over the years, and prices of livestock and food staples actually fell, the price of Negro slaves rose steadily, giving owners a constant opportunity to make a profit by reselling. It was very common for a slave to have had two or three previous owners at time of sale. A Negro Francisco, one of the slaves imported by Juan Cortés (above) in 1545 or 1546, had served five masters by 1549.[18]

Some types of resale of Negroes had less negative connotations. When, as often happened, Negro slaves were sold along with the land they cultivated, the livestock they cared for, or the tools they worked with, the slave was an element of continuity while the masters changed. At times this became a conscious process of capital formation. A Spanish artisan could acquire untrained Negroes, equip and train them, and sell them as a highly valuable independent unit. Some of the largest sales recorded were of gradually accumulated, trained teams of Negro slaves sold together with the other assets of the company that owned them. In these cases the lives of the Negroes and the operations of the companies remained largely unaffected by a changeover at the top.

After an initial period of instability, the price of Negro slaves was constantly on the rise during the period from 1530 to 1560. In the discovery, or pre-Cajamarca phase, Negro slaves sometimes could not be sold at all, because the impoverished Spaniards lacked the means to pay even moderate prices. At Cajamarca, prices soared. In 1534 prices were briefly depressed because the Peruvian Indians were killing so many more Negro slaves than Nicaraguan Indian slaves.[19]

When prices settled down in the late 1530's, the general run of Negro slaves cost about 100 to 250 pesos. These prices did not change much until late in the 1540's, when the price range inched up to about 150 to 300 pesos. In the 1550's prices increased more rapidly, and by 1557, they ranged from 250 to 500 pesos.

Negro slave prices were unresponsive to some quite important variables. It did not seem to make much difference whether a slave came from Africa, Spain, or the Indies; what part of Africa he came from; whether he spoke Spanish or not; or even whether or not he could read and write. Prices in the highlands should have been higher than in Lima, but prices in Arequipa, the only highland area for which price information could be tabulated, did not vary much from the Lima standard. The only factor that had an obvious effect on the price of an individual aside from age and infirmity was possession of skill as an artisan. Negro slaves who were competent tailors, blacksmiths, or carpenters brought prices 50 to 100 per cent higher than ordinary slaves.[20]

Negro slave owning was very widespread in Peru; not every Spaniard owned Negro slaves, but it can be said that there was no stratum of Spanish Peruvian society which did not include owners of slaves. A complete list of slave owners would include artisans of many kinds, priests, lawyers, notaries, merchants, sailors, and free Negroes, as well as captains and encomenderos. Negro slaves were never the monopoly of the great captains.[21]

Some examples of typical holdings will serve to give an idea of the extent of slave owning. In Lima in 1546, authorities seized the property of a poor hosier named Juan Vázquez. He was found to have only two items worth seizing: a Negro slave and an Indian slave. In the years

1538 to 1541, Francisco Mejía, a blacksmith, had a forge in Upper Peru, operated by a slave staff of three Negroes, a Negro woman, and an Indian woman from Nicaragua. Francisco de Grecia, a gardener and employee of the Pizarro estate, in 1547 owned a Negro woman servant, with two children, and a Negro to take care of the garden and orchard he owned in Lima.

Francisco de Trujillo, a small merchant and former confectioner of Lima, in 1545 had an imposing staff of seven slaves, partly artisans and partly personal servants. Three encomenderos of Cuzco (all three were substantial men, but only one could be called a great captain) had their estates impounded in 1541, and turned out to have from three to eight slaves each.[22]

In the absence of any census figures, examples like these are the only tools available (aside from some figures on the numbers of Negroes who accompanied Spanish armies) for estimating the relative size of the Negro population. With practically all encomenderos and artisans owning several slaves, and many other Spaniards, from rich to poor, at least owning personal servants, or slaves to care for land and stock, it is apparent that Negroes were present in very substantial numbers. All in all, it seems probable that on the coast at least, there were as many Negroes as Spaniards. In the first coastal censuses, around 1570, Negroes had overtaken Spaniards, and may have already done so by 1560.[23] Since the highland areas, except for Arequipa which has many characteristics of a coastal town, lack the dense notarial records which form the real basis of estimation, all that can be said is that Negroes were present in the highlands in substantial numbers, but less numerous than on the coast.

While there is no sure way of knowing who owned the most Negroes, something can be said about the type of ownership represented by the two most prominent groups of owners, encomenderos and artisans. The encomenderos were purely consumers. The artisans were partly consumers, and partly trainers of slaves, and therefore speculators and sellers. When, in 1560, officials attempted to fix the prices of Negro slaves, forty residents of Lima protested. Of the forty, twenty-one are identifiable as artisans, while not a single encomendero joined the protest.[24]

Whatever else they may have been, most Negro slaves in Peru were personal servants. Though the proportion of full-time personal servants to agricultural workers and artisan slaves is not known, slaves in the latter two categories also performed as servants, and certainly were thought of as such. Personal service was the role most closely associated with Negroes in the minds of the Spaniards. Only those slaves who spent or lost their lives in the migrant gangs organized for gold mining completely escaped the category, and such slaves do not seem to have been really numerous except during the Carabaya gold rush in the Cuzco area in 1542 and 1543. Large encomenderos might own a whole houseful of Negro servants. A notary, priest, or merchant would often have only one, preferably female, as general housekeeper.[25]

Negro slaves were in great demand as servants for two main reasons. The first had to do with their utter foreignness. All ages have understood the value, above all the trustworthiness, of foreign slaves who are isolated from the populace at large and therefore cannot melt into it. Negroes had this quality in extreme, far more than the Nicaraguan Indian slaves who, though they did not understand Quechua, looked just like Peruvian Indians and shared many traits with them.

The second reason why Negroes were desired as servants was that they were one essential part of the general pattern of Spanish ambitions. No encomendero felt happy until he owned a large house, land, livestock and—most to the point here—Negro servants. Most Spaniards could not hope to achieve this goal in its entirety, but they aimed at least for two essentials, a house (which could be rented) and Negroes. One of the most important yardsticks for a Spaniard's contribution to any of the various war efforts was the number of Negro servants he brought to the battle with him.

The household of Francisco Vallejo, a shipmaster turned merchant who lived in Lima in the 1550's, was typical of a good number of long-lasting, family-like establishments. In 1560 Vallejo had three Negro slaves: a man, Diego; a woman, Francisca; and Francisca's ten-year-old daughter Beatriz. The three were almost, but not quite, a family. Diego called Francisca his "companion," but the girl Beatriz was not his daughter, and Francisca openly had to do with other men. They had been with Vallejo for quite a long time; Diego for eight or nine years. Diego's main function was to accompany his master everywhere. Francisca, with her daughter's help, ran the house, cooked meals, and shopped. She had the house keys, and when Vallejo was gone she received visitors, and guarded the chest Vallejo kept in his bedroom, full of gold, silver, and papers.[26]

Other servants were not as lucky as Vallejo's slaves, but were shunted from one master to the next. These slaves often became drunks, gamblers, thieves, or runaways, which only increased their masters' desires to be rid of them. Such a case was Pedro Portugués, a Negro slave and personal servant who was in Peru through most of the decade of the 1540's. There was hardly any place in greater Peru where he had not been. He had a series of at least five masters, including an influential citizen of Quito, a priest of Arequipa, and a noble encomendero of Cuzco. Pedro ran the gamut of common offenses. Addicted to gambling, he would gamble the clothes off his back, then steal to gamble more. When he once ran away, he got about the country freely by virtue of a forged note he carried with him, ostensibly from his master, saying, "Let this Negro pass, he is on business of mine." His fourth master sold him to his fifth in Potosí in 1550 at a good price, by lying about his abilities as butler, cook, tailor, and blacksmith. While Pedro and his new master were accompanying a convoy bearing the king's silver from Potosí to La Paz, Pedro stole a bar of silver, was detected, apprehended, and quickly hanged.[27]

Negro artisan slaves were at the top of the ladder in the slave world, the most highly skilled and the highest priced, with a certain measure of intrinsic freedom. Doubtless they were less numerous than ordinary personal servants and field workers, but there were enough to form the backbone of the skilled labor force working in the shops of Peruvian Spanish artisans.

There were Negro slaves working in all the trades then common in Peru, but their distribution did not necessarily follow the relative numbers of Spanish artisans. Negroes were especially well represented in basic trades like carpentry and tailoring. A disproportionate number of Negro artisans were blacksmiths and swordsmiths, practitioners of those most basic trades of all, which made the whole Spanish conquest and occupation possible. All the trades involving mass production, like tanning or confectionery, needed and employed Negroes. But though there were many Spanish silversmiths, few Negroes were trained to the trade. Silversmiths were more assayers and general experts on metals and mining than producers, and what productive work they did was often of high technical difficulty. Further, silversmiths, like stonemasons, enjoyed a certain social prestige, and the Spaniards wanted to preserve such roles for themselves.

Negroes from the Iberian peninsula contributed more than their share to the class of Negro artisans. Information on the ethnical-geo-graphical origin of artisan slaves is hard to come by, but it proved possible to assemble a list of the origins of twenty Negro artisans, showing Spain and Portugal supplying about a third of the total, with the rest distributed quite normally among the African groups and creoles of the Indies.[28] Though the sampling is ridiculously small, the results seem near the truth. The Spanish Negroes were relatively predominant because they arrived in the Indies already trained. An even spread among the African ethnic groups shows that no one group proved to be more adept or inept at Spanish artisanry than the others.

Every Spanish artisan who had enough capital bought one or more Negro artisan slaves, or, if these were not available, bought ordinary slaves and trained them in the trade. This led to the development of complete shop units which consisted of a Spanish artisan manager and several Negro artisans, with the addition, in some trades, of some less skilled Negroes. A tailor shop in Lima in 1550 consisted of a Spanish hosier and four slave tailors, three Negroes and an Indian. A confectionery in 1552 had a Spanish confectioner, a Negro slave confectioner, and three untrained Negro slaves.[29]

The next step was the development of independent units of slave artisans which could function without the direction of an expert Spaniard. Spanish artisans sold these units, equipped with tools, for a small fortune to wealthy people who lived in remote areas like Upper Peru or Chile, or were undertaking expeditions. Forges were the most common such units. In 1554 a Spanish smith sold a forge, two Spanish Negro smiths, and two African Negro helpers, to a lawyer going to Chile, for 2,000 pesos, enough to buy a mansion or a ship. The Spanish smith continued his operations in Lima. He must have accumulated the forge unit specifically for resale. Other Spanish slave owners participated in this process of training slaves to increase their value, by putting their slave boys into apprenticeship with Spanish artisans, on the same basis as any other apprentice, except that the slaves returned to their owners at the end of the term.[30]

Some very highly skilled Negro artisans carried the tendency toward independence even farther, achieving much of the substance of freedom without its forms. The price of a Negro master artisan, often 700 to 1,000 pesos, alone entitled him to careful treatment. Men of this type sometimes reduced their slavery to the level of an obligation to share their profits. In Arequipa in 1550, two Negro slave artisans were running a shop together and remitting the profits to their respective owners. One Negro carpenter, named Andrés de Llerena, the slave of an encomendero, actually entered into a company with a Spanish carpenter on equal terms, or indeed as the senior partner.[31]

The category of artisan slaves merged imperceptibly into the category of slaves with less valuable skills who were employed in large teams or gangs. On the borderline between these two types were the Negro muleteers. Of the three main carriers of goods in the highlands—Indian porters, llamas, and mules—trains of mules were the fastest and most reliable, and the most valuable goods were generally entrusted to them. A pack train consisted of a Spanish muleteer, several mules, and some Negroes who cared for and loaded the mules; Negro slaves had a practical monopoly of the function of accompanying pack trains. Most trains were of moderate size, with ten to twenty mules and, ideally, one Negro for every three mules. The merchants who were the chief owners of pack trains often sold them as a unit, mules, tackle, Negroes, and all.[32]

Certain types of Spanish enterprises employed semi-skilled Negroes in relatively large teams of ten to twenty. These were, principally, the carting companies of Lima, the coastal fisheries, and some incipient large cattle owners. The teams were overwhelmingly male, with only one or two Negro women cooks.[33] How stable such aggregations were is hard to know, but the records do permit comparison of the assets of a Lima fishing company in three different years, 1554, 1556, and 1557. The company owned two fishing boats, nets and equipment, and some horses and mules to transport the catch into Lima. From 1554 to 1556 a single Spanish entrepreneur was the main owner, with shifting junior partnership; in late 1556 he sold the whole company to new ownership. The labor force consisted of seven or eight Negro slaves, only two or three of whom stayed with the company for the whole four years. Probably the two slaves who stayed on were skilled fishermen, effective commanders of the company's two boats. The other slaves, the ordinary crewmen, changed rapidly.[34]

Large-scale use of unskilled Negro slaves on plantations was not yet a factor of importance in Peru by 1560. Only one such operation is known to have existed, in Nazca, on the southern coast, where a royal official and encomendero ran a sugar plantation and also carried on stock-raising and general agriculture, with the labor of Negro slaves. Even this enterprise used a relatively modest number of Negroes. A seventeenth-century statement that the plantation had more than 300 Negroes is fantastic. Something nearer the truth can be deduced from a contemporary source, which says that a raiding army passing through Nazca in 1554 managed to collect about 40 Negroes.[35] Some sugar production also went on in the area of Trujillo, but nothing is known about the kind of labor used.

The most frequent use of groups of unskilled Negroes was in mining, particularly gold mining. Even this was not of really basic importance; the great silver mines of highland Peru were always worked by Indians, with an exception or two. Gold mining was thought to be appropriate for Negroes because gold mines were mainly in hot, low-lying river areas. Even so, gold mining was far from a Negro monopoly. There were two major gold rushes in Peru within our period, one in Carabaya, a low-altitude area in the jurisdiction of Cuzco, in 1542 and 1543, and the other in the Quito area in 1545 and 1546. Most of the work in Quito was done by gangs of encomienda Indians. In Carabaya, too, Indians were used, but the mortality rate was so frightful that Spaniards using Indians sometimes found difficulty in making a profit despite the richness of the sites. In this situation, the Spaniards brought in numbers of Negro slave gangs. Less intensive gold mining with Negroes took place intermittently in various parts of Peru.[36]

Mining gangs usually consisted of ten or fifteen raw African Negro slaves and a slave woman, Negro or Indian, to cook for them, directed by a Spaniard who might be their owner or part-owner, or just a miner-foreman.[37] Occasionally gangs were larger. In the 1540's Francisco de Barrionuevo, a former governor of Panama, extracted gold in south and central Peru with a large force of forty-five Negroes. Though he at that time had no encomienda, the possession of so much economic power put him fully on the level of an encomendero. At one point Barrionuevo entered into an equal partnership with don Antonio de Ribera, one of the largest encomenderos of Peru, in which Barrionuevo's contribution was his Negroes and mining equipment, don Antonio's his encomienda.[38] That in time Barrionuevo gave up his mining ventures and accepted a relatively small encomienda in La Paz is representative of a general trend, the gradual fading out of Negro mining, after initial high hopes. Negro gold miners had the worst lot of all Negro slaves, tramping in gangs from one steaming river site to the next, out of contact with either the Indian or the Hispanic world, except for their Spanish overseer.

Whenever mining gangs or other kinds of work teams were made up of encomienda Indians, Negroes assumed a different role. In these situations a few Negro slaves became a permanent cadre, aiding the skilled Spaniard who directed the work, guarding the plant or equipment when the seasonal Indians were gone, and probably serving as overseers. A silver mining company in Huánuco in 1548 had a force of eight Negro slaves besides the labor of encomienda Indians. In a similar way, a Spanish carpenter who cut and dressed timber for an encomendero in Huancayo in 1542 received the help of two Negroes and twelve Indians.[39]

Small-scale agriculture was one of the main areas of endeavor of Negro slaves, comparable in importance to personal service and artisanry. In Lima as in other towns, the surrounding agricultural land was divided out to encomenderos and others, in quite small parcels, at the city's founding, in this case in 1535. By the early 1540's at latest, the environs of Lima had become an impressive garden spot, full of closely spaced small holdings where Spanish agriculture was practiced, with irrigation, to supply Lima's markets. Almost every one of these holdings, called chácaras or estancias indiscriminately, had one or more Negroes working on it. In Arequipa the situation was much the same, and apparently in Trujillo as well. It is doubtful that nearly as many Negroes did agricultural work in Cuzco and Upper Peru, but the pattern did extend that far, as shown by the eleven Negroes who were working on various landed properties of a great encomendero of Charcas in 1549.[40]

In Lima, some Negro field workers lived in the city and went out daily to work, while others lived fulltime on the chácaras, to the distress of law-enforcement officers. Many or most of these Negroes were without any direct Spanish supervision. The agriculture they carried on· was totally unspecialized. In accordance with their masters' wishes, they attempted to raise all kinds of grains, vegetables, and fruits on each plot, and if possible, a few animals as well. A fair amount of speculation in land did not affect the field workers greatly, because they were sold with the land they worked on.[41]

The picture of life on the chácaras remains hazy, but it is clear that the Negroes did the daily work required throughout the year, and counted on seasonal help by Indians for harvesting. By the 1550's, some of the holdings were imposingly complete units, like a chácara for wheat and maize in the valley of Surco, maintained by a Negro slave farmer and carpenter, which had a house, garden, dovecot, plows, and two oxen. There were yet more ambitious chácaras where it was apparently intended that Negroes would do the bulk of the work even at harvest time. In 1552 one Spaniard was managing and living on a chácara near Lima, where he grew wheat, maize, beans, and melons, and kept 150 goats and a few horses. To do the work he had four Negroes and a Negro woman, four oxen, a cart, and plows.[42]

Outside the immediate environs of the cities, small landholdings devoted mainly to intensive agriculture gave way to larger, more loosely defined properties where stock raising took precedence over agriculture, and, in distant plains, superseded it entirely. Since even the small plots near town had some animals on them, there was no sharp distinction between the two types. In terminology there were some distinctions; agricultural lands were called either chácaras or estancias, while stock raising enterprises were called only estancias. Whatever they were called, they had Negro slaves working on them.

As large-scale ranching began to develop in the 1550's, whole teams of Negroes worked at cattle herding. Even in the 1540's, there were some good-sized establishments, like the six Negro slave men and women who cared for a herd of cattle and goats in the Lima area in 1547. But most characteristic were the lone Negroes living deep in the country, far from the Spaniards, in charge of several cows, goats, or pigs. Herdsmen were more closely attached to the stock than to the land; whereas field Negroes were sold along with the land they worked, herdsmen were sold together with the herds.[43]

The list of country Negroes is completed by the *tamberos* and the woodcutters. Tamberos were in charge of tambos, the roadside inns of the Incas; in the name of their encomendero masters, they sold provisions to the travelers and provided them with free wood and fodder. (There were Spanish tamberos, too, particularly on well-traveled routes where business was good.) Negroes had the reputation of being particularly hard on the Indians who supplied the provisions. The Negro woodcutters lived in the cities, but went out periodically with a mule or a lame horse to the nearest wooded area to fetch firewood to sell in city markets.[44]

While the great majority of Negro slaves worked directly for their owners, the practice of hiring out slaves did exist. When a special project demanded temporary extra labor, slaves would be rented from any owners who could spare them. At least one owner in Lima kept slaves specifically to be hired out for general labor, such as rowing boats, acting as servants, guarding cattle, or, in one case, digging in Francisco Pizarro's garden for gold presumed to be buried there. The price for hiring unskilled slave labor was exorbitant, as much as a peso and a half a day. A special practice was the hiring out of valuable artisan slaves to Spanish artisans for a year at a time for 100, 150, or 200 pesos, enough to buy an ordinary slave permanently.[45]

Despite occasional disappointments, Spaniards placed extraordinary trust in their Negro slaves. Agricultural slaves had infinite opportunities to run away. Negro herdsmen not only could run away, but were in complete charge of easily movable property that had an especially high value in a country only in the process of being stocked with European varieties. The degree of independence of Negro master artisan slaves has also already been seen.

Some slaves were allowed to lend and borrow money, and it was common for Negro slaves to be entrusted with merchandise to sell. In 1547 at least seven Negro slave women (probably considerably more) were selling foods and other merchandise on the square of Lima, in the names of their owners. A merchant in Potosí in 1550 thought to save himself the expense of a Spanish factor by turning over a whole store to a Negro slave woman. It was too much; the woman ran away with the profits.

When Spaniards knew individual slaves really well, they gave them the kind of absolute confidence they otherwise extended only to close blood relatives. In 1553 a Spanish muleteer fell ill while taking his pack train, loaded with merchandise, from Arequipa to Potosí. He returned to Arequipa for treatment, leaving the senior Negro slave muleteer in charge of the merchandise, the mules, and the other Negroes, with 30 pesos in silver to spend on food and maintenance. The pack train and the merchandise, worth several thousand pesos, represented the Spanish muleteer's life savings and more.[46]

Why Negro slaves in Peru, presented with such multiple opportunity, did not all run away, may seem a mystery. Part of the explanation is the lack of a place of refuge. Most Spanish settlements were far away from such dense tropical forests as protected runaway slaves in Panama and the Antilles. Runaway Negroes could not hope to be received among the Indians, to whom Negroes were merely another type of intruder. In any case, hiding among the Indians was impossible for Negroes because their distinctive physical appearance made them readily identifiable. In effect, runaways had only one place to go, some other Spanish settlement than the one they were in. Slaves who had a specific fear or grievance could at times find temporary refuge in the Spanish monasteries, but this was hardly running away.[47]

In conditions like these, the recovery of runaway Negro slaves was a relatively easy, even a predictable process. The Spaniards were so confident of recovering runaways that it was not at all uncommon for a runaway slave, while still absent, to be sold without conditions, at a good price, to a new owner. A shoemaker of Arequipa gave his own Negro slave plus 200 pesos to acquire rights to a runaway Negro trained in shoemaking.[48]

Since runaway Negroes could not live among the Indians and were quickly detected in the cities, the only way they could hope to maintain themselves was by organizing bands of cimarrons or renegades in the countryside. Geography kept Peru from becoming a land of cimarrons like Panama, but there were usually a few small bands in operation in some part of the country.

Once the cimarrons became a serious threat. In 1545, about 200 renegade Negroes organized an embryo kingdom in an inaccessible reedy marsh at Huara, on the coast a few miles north of Lima. They were equipped with large quantities of Spanish weapons and armor, had allies among the Negro slave population, and were planning to overthrow the Spaniards and take the encomiendas for themselves. The deputy governor in Lima sent a force of 120 Spaniards against them, under an old conqueror and former alcalde, Juan de Barbarán. After heavy fighting the Spaniards killed all the Negroes, for none surrendered. Barbarán and ten other Spaniards lost their lives, and many were wounded.[49]

More typical were smaller bands of fifteen or twenty cimarrons, preying mainly on Indians. A band of about fifteen runaway Negroes operated in the area of Piura all through the decade of the 1540's and well into the 1550's, until caught and defeated by a Spanish expedition. They raided Indian villages, killing the men and abducting the women, and robbed Indians and others on the highways. They had brought the usual commerce of highland with coastal Indians in that area to a complete halt. Their remote base was a real settlement, with houses and fields, and they had many children, "mulattoes," by the Indian women they had abducted. Another group of this size was a robber band of twenty Negroes and two renegade Spaniards which troubled the area of Lima in 1549.[50]

With cimarrons a continuing problem, by the 1550's the Spaniards resorted to a small standing constabulary of *cuadrilleros* to patrol the countryside, recover runaways, and prevent the formation of large bands. Half or more of the patrol were free Negroes themselves.[51] Whether because of the cuadrilleros or for other reasons, renegades never again presented a serious threat to Spanish settlement or to the owning of Negro slaves.

The Spaniards felt little or no reluctance to liberate individual Negro slaves. Negroes in Peru started obtaining their freedom very early, by 1536 at the latest,[52] and the movement continued with increasing momentum right through 1560. Most of the Negroes freed had to buy their liberty in one way or another. Charity played an important role, even when freedom was bought, but it came into full operation only when the owner no longer needed the slave, or the slave was not in the prime of life. Spaniards made true grants of freedom in their testaments, or when they left for Spain; also to aged slaves and to infant children of slaves.[53] Such grants were in their sum effect a significant factor, but they cannot be said to represent the ordinary avenue to freedom.

Slaves somehow managed to accumulate the money to free themselves. If there was any legal obligation on the part of masters to liberate slaves for their just price, the masters did not recognize it. Some owners let their slaves go cheaply as an act of charity, others for a good price. Others held out for exorbitant amounts; in 1538 a Negro slave couple had to raise 1,800 pesos to buy themselves free. Just where such money came from is an interesting question. Either slaves were allowed to earn money on the side, or they received some sort of pay or allowance from their masters. However they did it, it was a difficult process. One Negro bought his freedom on the installment plan, gradually making payments to his owner until the total reached 200 pesos and he was freed. Many slaves could not get the money together, and relied on loans, or worked out the equivalent of the price. The loans came from various sources, often from other Negroes who were already free and solvent. Loans might take the form of an advance in pay from the new freedman's employer.[54]

Along with the flood of the newly freed was a trickle of Negroes who arrived in Peru already free. Beatriz Hernández, a free Negro woman born in Portugal, came to Peru in 1538, bearing a document proving that she was free and the child of free parents.[55]

Free Negroes were an important class of people. Though it is impossible to estimate their absolute numbers, the constant flow of municipal ordinances on free Negroes convinces even one who is a hardened skeptic about the informative value of Spanish legislation that they were numerous indeed. In Lima they were already considered a problem as early as 1538. As was true of Negro slaves, more free Negroes lived on the coast than in the highlands, but they were to be found in the highlands too.

The freedom that Negroes bought was far from absolute. In all kinds of legal records, Spaniards were careful to see that freedmen were specifically called free Negroes, the only ordinary exceptions being some light mulattoes. Spanish legal authorities, often calling free Negroes simply slaves, continued to claim farreaching jurisdiction over them. Freedmen were periodically ordered to register and to take positions with Spanish masters. Once authorities issued a peremptory order for all free Negroes to leave the country; another time all freedmen were to join an unpaid, involuntary street-cleaning force. All such orders and schemes failed, partially or completely, because of the social reality. Though Spaniards as a group were disturbed to see the rise of a class of independent Negroes (whose contribution to slave delinquency is undeniable), Spaniards as individuals tolerated them and found them useful. Not a single free Negro left Peru; the only concrete result of the agitation to get rid of freedmen was that in 1557 Viceroy Cañete sent sixteen free Negroes of Lima, on a semi-voluntary basis, to settle in the gold mining area of Carabaya.

Legislation requiring former slaves to take Spanish masters was more serious. First, it had a strong nuisance value, forcing the freedmen into at least ostensible and sporadic compliance. More basically, such ordinances had a certain shaping effect on the lives of free Negroes; they were the legal precipitation of the Spaniards' determination not to let Negroes take over positions and functions that they desired for themselves. Artisans' shops run independently by free Negroes, for example, were in constant jeopardy. With this upper limit, freedmen enjoyed the legal privileges of Spaniards (and it should be remembered that even Spaniards were subject to orders to find a job or leave town). A freedman could own and bequeath any kind of property, marry, and carry on litigation.

The standard Spanish ambitions of acquiring a house, a wife, land, fine clothes, and Negro slaves were also the ambitions of free Negroes. Successful free Negroes were particularly anxious to enjoy the respectability conferred by marriage; most prominent free Negroes were married, usually to free Negro women, or less often, to Negro slave women or Indian women. The status of free Negroes was judged by the same set of criteria as that of Spaniards. Francisco Hernández, the recognized leader of Lima's free Negro community, was married, propertied, and had been in Peru from the early days of the conquest.

Free Negroes formed a coherent group or community, much like the Basques or foreigners, but even more tightly knit. Negroes married within the community, had their closest friends and worst enemies within it, loaned each other money, and preferred to do all kinds of business with each other. In the late 1540's the free Negroes organized a cofradía or religious brotherhood, over Spanish opposition.[56]

Since practically all free Negroes had been slaves, there was a close relationship between the occupations of the two groups. The activities of freedmen can be described summarily by saying that they merely did all the same things slaves did, except that they did them as independent operators or as wage earners. Personal service, agriculture, and artisanry were the primary occupations for Negroes, whether free or slave. As in other ages and countries, many freedmen maintained a close relationship with their former masters. Slaves ordinarily took their master's surname at the time of freedom; many either continued to work for their masters, or stayed dependent on them indirectly, living on or near the master's properties. The very word "freedman" (horro) could be synonymous with servant. Free Negro servants got a yearly wage ranging from 50 to 150 pesos, which was not much less than the wage of an unskilled Spaniard.[57]

Naturally there were some opportunities denied to slaves but open to freedmen—particularly activities having to do with owning property. Agricultural workers were anxious to have their own fields or chácaras, and often succeeded in getting them, buying land sometimes from Spaniards, sometimes from Indian caciques. The free Negroes sent to Carabaya did not become mere mining employees as planned; soon they were the owners of agricultural land, cultivated by Indian labor.

Many free Negroes bought houses in the cities to live in, and some owned property which they rented out as a source of income. Freedmen also owned their own Negro slaves; a prominent Negro like Francisco Hernández might own several.[58] Negroes loaned money, primarily to other Negroes but also to Spaniards, sometimes in amounts as large as 150 to 200 pesos. Few if any succeeded in becoming long-distance wholesale merchants, but they did speculate on merchandise by having merchants invest money for them.[59]

As independent operators, freedmen might do miscellaneous things, from selling llamas to running a tavern, but tended to concentrate on certain types of enterprises, by operation of the process that has always led to the economic specialization of foreign minorities. Negro women were associated with, though they did not monopolize, the business of baking bread and biscuit to sell in city markets. Since independent Negro artisanry encountered resistance, much Negro effort was channeled into the construction of adobe walls and fences, an activity Spaniards did not resent. (In the highlands, where Spanish artisans were not so overwhelmingly numerous, independent Negro artisans seem to have had an easier time of it.) Many of the town criers and executioners in Peruvian cities were free Negroes, because few Spaniards would consent to hold the post.[60]

In Chile a free Negro became an encomendero; in Puertoviejo a member of the city council and royal official was said to be a Negro and former slave.[61] But these were fringe areas; in central Peru, the kind of complete success and social acceptance represented by encomendero status and high office was far out of the reach of free Negroes, though some did achieve wealth and started to improve their social status outside the Negro community. Catalina de Zorita, a free Negro woman who lived in Lima in the 1540's and 1550's, owned a bakery and confectionery staffed by ten Negro slaves; the total must have been worth several thousand pesos. She was married to a Spaniard (or possibly a light mulatto), and in 1549 she arranged the marriage of her mulatto daughter to a Spaniard from Medellín, with a 3,000-peso dowry. People no longer called her a Negro to her face, though they continued to do so in her absence.[62]

A somewhat fuller outline of the life of one successful freedman, called Juan de Fregenal, will help in the understanding of what was and was not possible to a Negro. Juan de Fregenal was the Negro slave of a notary public of Lima in the 1540's. He achieved his freedom around 1547, and got a start toward economic independence that year by buying, on credit, a lot on the edge of town from his former master. By the late 1550's he was a fixture in Lima, a man of some wealth, one of the few Negroes who could make a signature (though crudely), and to whose name the Spanish secretaries did not studiously attach the affix "freed Negro." Basically a mason, specializing in adobe construction like many other Negroes, Fregenal branched out into real estate and truck gardening.

In 1553, Fregenal built a high adobe enclosure around a lot for the royal treasury, receiving 110 pesos. Carrying out small jobs of this type, probably with a skilled helper or two and some Indian labor, must have been his ordinary economic activity, but his life was affected time and again by the ordinances requiring free Negroes to take Spanish masters. Three times he entered the pay of Spaniards, once specifically saying he did so to meet the legal requirements. It appears probable that Fregenal worked only part-time for his employers, and with his legal position thus assured, continued his independent activity. His first job may have been bona fide; he worked for eight months in 1550 as the helper of a Spanish mason of Lima, receiving a peso for every work day, plus food, which would have been reasonable pay even for a skilled Spaniard. The other jobs were certainly part-time, possibly even mainly legal fictions. In 1553 he worked for a year for the Franciscan monastery, doing building and maintenance, at a salary of 120 pesos, no more than he would get for a single construction job. In 1555 he worked for a notary as a mason and general hired man for the same pay.

Probably Fregenal's most profitable enterprise was the improvement of real estate. He was not just a speculator. He bought property, and using his skill as a mason, built on it so that it could be sold for a large gain. His first acquisition, the lot which he bought from his former master in 1547, cost him 115 pesos. When he sold it to a Portuguese gardener in 1551, it had become a large house or complex of houses with a garden inside, and the price was 800 pesos. In 1552 Fregenal bought another lot from the widow of an encomendero, for 60 pesos. By 1555 he had built a house on it, and was selling it for 250 pesos. There is no doubt that Fregenal carried out other similar operations, particularly among Lima's free Negro community.

Fregenal also ventured into the general agriculture then thriving in the immediate area of Lima, much of it carried on by Negroes, whether slave or free. In 1555 he became the senior partner in a company with Juan de Eslava, apparently a Spaniard, to raise grains, fruits, vegetables, chickens, and pigs on some land near Lima that they rented from a Spanish notary public. (One of the threads in Fregenal's life is a series of connections with notaries, probably because he had once been a notary's slave.) Fregenal's contribution was purely financial. Eslava was to do all the work, including the hiring of permanent and temporary help. Fregenal was to pay the wages, give Eslava a mount to ride, and rent him a house in Lima to live in.

The economic aspect of Fregenal's life is the clearest part of it. Of his private life little can be said. Unlike many freed Negroes, he did not quickly marry on getting his freedom. His main personal tie seems to have been to Francisca, his natural daughter by a free Indian woman of Jauja, where Fregenal had probably been at some time while he was a slave. In 1550, still early in his career as a free man, Fregenal settled 400 pesos on his daughter as her future dowry. In 1555 he had her brought to Lima from Jauja; she must have lived there with relatives until then. Fregenal lived and had his closest acquaintances in Lima's free Negro community, in which he was a figure known to all, and a source of small loans in return for good security.

Fregenal's activities and ambitions were much like those of any Spanish carpenter or mason, and his wealth comparable to what might be expected of a successful Spanish artisan. But of course he remained a Negro. A Spaniard with his drive and ability would have been building brick portals and galleries, not adobe walls. Legal restrictions, the jealous attitude of Spanish artisans, and the meager training slaves often received, combined to make humble adobe construction and rough carpentry the Negroes' province in the construction trades. Working within these limits, Fregenal lived a productive and probably satisfying life.[63]

A career like Fregenal's is typical enough, except that not all free Negroes enjoyed that degree of economic success. Some ended as charity cases, in a context where they were not likely to receive much charity. Others had a tolerable existence, but lived close to financial disaster. Such a man was Jorge Palomino, a free Negro living in Lima all through the 1550's. Palomino lived from chácara agriculture, but in 1553, when he prematurely made his will, he had no land. He had sold the land he owned to another free Negro, at a good price, but had not managed to collect the money. When the authorities of Lima demanded a 6-peso assessment from him as his contribution to the reception of Viceroy Mendoza in 1551, he had to raise the money by pawning a black cape and a goat with Juan de Fregenal. He was never able to redeem his possessions. Palomino's only asset in 1553 was a house in the city, where he lived together with his second wife, who was a free Negro woman, and his son by a previous marriage to an Indian woman from Huaylas. Though he lived precariously, Palomino made his way in some fashion, and was still alive in Lima in 1560.[64]

The fate of the children of free Negroes is little more than a subject for speculation. The records for the period up to 1560 contain remarkably little about them, beyond the facts that their parents could bequeath them property, and that some of them were put into apprenticeship with Spanish artisans.[65] There is little reason to doubt that the second generation was headed into the path marked by the first; but whether free Negroes were a truly self-perpetuating class, or sustained themselves by each generation's contribution of new freedmen, is a question to be answered by research in documents of a later period.

Free Negroes present a double image. In the official municipal records they appear as a band of troublemakers, abetting runaway slaves, covering up thefts, fomenting unrest. In the notarial records they appear an industrious and useful class of people who seized every opportunity given them, and did much to build up the country for themselves and the Spaniards.

In the minds of the Spaniards, Negroes were associated closely with another slave group called moriscos; the ordinances on Negroes always include mention of moriscos as well. The moriscos were the most exotic and mysterious element in the whole broad range of people involved in the Spanish conquest. Just who they were is far from clear. Basically the word morisco designated the Muslim Spaniards and their descendants, but it was also used for slaves from Morocco.[66] Even the race of the moriscos is not certain. Moriscos from Northwest Africa may well have been partially or completely Negroid. The matter is confused further by the way Spaniards frequently, but not always, called moriscos white, leaving it uncertain whether or not they did this to make a distinction. Still, given the fact that moriscos often had Spanish surnames even as slaves, and when free were quickly absorbed into the main body of Spaniards, it appears likely that the great majority of them were born in Spain, spoke Spanish perfectly, and were physically indistinguishable from other Spaniards.

While Negroes were a many-sided, truly major group, constantly growing in importance, moriscos were specialized in function and not very numerous. Certainly there were not more than a few hundred of them. Their main importance was in the early period, the 1530's and early 1540's. Long before 1560, they had for practical purposes disappeared from view.

The most unusual thing about the moriscos was the sex ratio. The ratio of the sexes among Negroes would seem to have been close to the assumed ratio at export from Africa, about two or three to one in favor of men. Among moriscos the ratio must have been at least four or five to one in favor of the women, moriscas. Morisco men were little more than an oddity. The few male morisco slaves who can be identified were highly valuable artisans or trusted bodyguards.[67] Probably the explanation for the rarity of morisco men is that it was easy for a man who looked and talked like any other Spaniard to throw off his slavery in the wide reaches of the Indies. There is some reason to believe that an important citizen, encomendero, and council member of Lima had started as a runaway morisco slave.[68]

Morisco slavery, then, meant female slavery, and in practice, concubinage. Moriscas did not have a broad spectrum of roles; while there was a strong presumption that a Negro woman slave might be her master's concubine, in the case of a morisca it was a certainty. To buy a morisca was to buy a housekeeper and concubine. As a transitional phenomenon, moriscas satisfied the need for Spanish women in the very early period when free Spanish women were still inordinately scarce. The gradual diminishing of the importance of moriscas in the 1540's, and their almost complete eclipse in the 1550's, are parallel to the advent of Spanish women in large numbers. It is not likely that many of the moriscas actually left the country. Morisca slavery disappeared because the moriscas were freed. Nearly half of all the documents in which moriscas appear are grants of freedom.

As free women, moriscas were in a delicate position. They had the disadvantage of belonging to a despised class, but they were, in a fashion, Spanish women, and since most of them had been in Peru since the early days, they had *antigüedad,* or seniority, the quality so highly esteemed by the Spaniards. Some free moriscas remained servants or held other positions on the margins of society.[69] One became a famous fortune teller. Most of them simply assumed the role of Spanish women, among whom they disappeared. Under the right conditions, they could advance to the top rank of society along with the men they married. Juana Leyton, who came to Peru as a morisca slave, married an Italian who subsequently became an encomendero of Arequipa.[70]

The most spectacular success was a morisca named Beatriz, who came to Peru in 1532 as the slave of García de Salcedo, the royal *veedor* or comptroller. In just what year she received her formal freedom, if she ever did, is not clear. Soon she was calling herself Beatriz de Salcedo, and since royal officials were not supposed to be merchants, she carried on a large part of the veedor's commercial dealings for him. Eventually Salcedo married her, and she became one of the great ladies of Peru, wife of one of its highest officials and richest men. The only honor denied her was the title of "doña," and her two daughters (born before her marriage) achieved even that; one of them married a large encomendero, and the other a judge of the royal Audiencia. Late in the 1550's, when her origins were half-forgotten and her son-in-law was on the country's highest tribunal, she actually claimed to have been one of the first Spanish women to come to Peru. She also maintained that she had introduced the cultivation of wheat by planting some kernels she found (an honor claimed by practically every Spanish woman who reached Peru before 1537).[71]

Africans, or Negroes as we must call them, since some of them were born in Spain or the Indies, were a factor of absolutely first importance in Peru in the conquest period. They were an organic part of the enterprise of occupying Peru from its inception. The dominance of Spanish language and culture was never threatened, but in terms of ethnic or racial groups, the conquest of Peru was carried out by an equal partnership. Negroes were in a hundred ways the agents and auxiliaries of the Spaniards, in effect doubling their numbers, making the Spanish occupation a much more thorough affair than it could have been without them. Far from their own roots, apart from the Indians, the Negroes assimilated Spanish culture with amazing speed, and were for the main part the Spaniards' willing allies, in spite of the cimarrons. And this willingness is understandable. Though Negroes were subordinated to Spaniards, they were not exploited in the plantation manner; except for mining gangs, Negroes in Peru counted as individuals.

XI INDIANS

Negroes were the most important, but not the only auxiliaries the Spaniards had in the task of conquering and ruling Peru. Semiacculturated Indians of several types lived among the Spaniards and performed many of the same tasks as the Negroes, constituting, therefore, a segment of Hispanic society in Peru. The group most comparable to the Negroes were the foreign Indians, from Nicaragua, New Spain, and other areas of previous Spanish occupation. In the early 1530's, these Indians, most of them slaves, actually surpassed the Negroes in numbers. As foreigners, they had many of the same qualities as Negroes, and they played an important transitional role during the period of relative scarcity of Negro slaves.

Of far greater ultimate significance is the other main group, made up of Indians of Peru itself. Starting with the earliest irruption of the Spaniards into the Peru of the Incas, numbers of Peruvian Indians were caught up in the growth of Spanish Peruvian society. At Cajamarca and on less memorable occasions, Spaniards appropriated to themselves, as servants and mistresses, Indians who thenceforth traveled about the country in their personal retinue. Torn out of the indigenous social context, many such Indians lost their geographical context as well. A large proportion of them settled down with their masters in parts of Peru remote from their birthplaces, so that even they shared a certain degree of foreignness with the Negroes and foreign Indians. Some Peruvian Indian servants came from the ranks of a pre-Spanish servant class, the yanaconas, which had already lost all clan associations under the Incas; yanaconas, both pre-Spanish and newly created, were important in the Spanish silver mining settlements as metallur-

199

gists and skilled workers. Any Indians who happened to live in or near
Spanish cities were gradually absorbed to some degree within the
Spanish society that dominated those cities. Also, many members of the
Indian ruling classes did their best to emulate Spanish behavior, some
of them actually living in the Spanish cities all or a good part of the
time.

These Peruvian Indians who were directly touched by Spanish society form a group unique within the present book and within the history
of the period. They were both active and passive in the process of the
Hispanization of Peru. As active participants, auxiliaries in the Spanish
occupation, they were a fringe group, increasingly numerous, but less
important, more marginal, and generally at a lower level than the
Negroes and foreign Indians, because less thoroughly Hispanized. As
people passively acted upon, a part of the gradual process of acculturation of large segments of the Peruvian Indian population, the Hispanized Indians were a first example of the way Spanish culture was to
work itself deeply into the lives of the original inhabitants.

Foreign Indians came to Peru mainly as slaves, branded with the "R"
for *Rey* that signified the Spanish king. Some few accompanied Spaniards as free servants, but the majority were products of the Spanish
policy of enslaving Indians who resisted conquest, a policy which in
some places, like Nicaragua and the coast of Venezuela, led to full-
scale slave raiding. One of the reasons why foreign Indians faded in
significance in Peru after a brief period was that the enslaving of Indians ceased in most parts of the Indies by the 1540's.

The greatest single source of Peru's foreign Indian population was
Nicaragua. Guatemala and Mexico also contributed sizable contin-
gents, and in 1548 and 1549, long after the influx of new foreign Indians from other territories had ended, a fair number were imported
from the Venezuelan coast, channeled through the pearl fishery of Cu-
bagua. In a sampling of documents dated from 1531 to 1543, over two-
thirds of the Indians were from Nicaragua, with the rest divided quite
evenly between Mexico and Guatemala. The predominance of Nicaragua may not have been quite so overwhelming as appears in all the
sources. The Spaniards had a tendency to name the whole after the
largest part; they called wars in Europe the Italian wars, and used
"cloth" to mean general merchandise. In the same way Nicaraguan Indians stood for all foreign Indians, particularly those from South Central America.[1]

A question relevant here is whether or not the Spaniards enslaved

Peruvian Indians; there are apparently conflicting statements on the subject in contemporary sources. The most clearly authenticated Peruvian Indian slaves are some hundreds who were in Panama in 1544 and were repatriated by a martinet viceroy. A careful reading of the chroniclers on this episode reveals that the Indians were from the coastal regions north of Piura. Indians from the same area are known to have been kidnapped by passing Spaniards and taken to Lima to be sold as slaves. The truth in the matter appears to be that most of the Peruvian Indians enslaved were from fringe areas held by the Spaniards but not by the Incas before them. The inhabitants of such areas had not been organized into larger units, did not speak any of the main languages, and were therefore, in the Peru of the Incas, foreigners. As semi-foreigners these Indians made better slaves than central Peruvians, and above all, they were easier to enslave. Indians in the fringe area often had no encomendero, or, if they did, had nothing to give him, so that the encomendero had no reason to watch closely over them. In central Peru there were powerful encomenderos, determined not to lose a single tribute-paying Indian. On the one occasion when an attempt was made to enslave rebellious encomienda Indians in central Peru, the Indians' encomenderos made such an efficient protest that most of the slaves were returned to the encomiendas.[2] In sum, it appears that no significant number of central Peruvian Indians were ever enslaved; some Indians from the periphery were, but did not reach central Peru in numbers comparable to the Indians from Central America.

The intensity of the employment of Indian slaves had already reached its peak in the period before Cajamarca, and the relative frequency of foreign Indians compared to Negroes declined steadily ever afterward, until the new input of foreign Indians stopped completely around 1550. To summarize the general population trend for foreign Indians, they were by far the most numerous auxiliaries until Cajamarca, retained a slight edge over Negroes until after the great rebellion of 1536–37, then lost it before 1540. In the early 1540's Negroes became much more numerous than the Indians, and by 1550 the Indians were for practical purposes no longer in evidence. This does not mean that they literally died out or left Peru. The notarial records, the source of the data above, reflect primarily sales. One can gather from isolated references to the presence of foreign Indians even in the late 1550's, that most of those who came in the early period lived out their lives in Peru.[3]

There can hardly be said to have been an organized "trade" in In-

dian slaves, as there was in Negroes. Such a trade had existed between
Nicaragua and Panama, but does not seem to have extended to Peru.
Merchants in Peru did not engage in the import of Indian slaves, at
least not after the very earliest days, though there is some indication
that sailors at times brought Indian slaves with them on voyages to
Peru as an investment. The great bulk of foreign Indian slaves came
with their masters; selling was frequent on arrival in Peru because
prices were so much higher in Peru than in the countries of origin. The
prices of Indian slaves were always lower than those of Negroes, but
not beyond comparison. In the late 1530's an ordinary Indian slave
might cost from 50 to 150 pesos, compared to about 100 to 250 for a
Negro. In the decade of the 1540's Indians' prices pulled up even closer, presumably because by that time most Indian slaves were trained
or experienced.[4]

Indian slaves were not in any way kept separate from Negro slaves;
they lived interspersed among the Negroes, carrying out the same
kinds of tasks. In the early period of Indian predominance, of course, it
was the other way around; some Negroes were to be found interspersed among the Indians, as in a blacksmith's forge staffed in 1537
and 1538 by two Nicaraguan Indian smiths, called Coatl and Diego,
Diego's Nicaraguan Indian wife, a "native" Indian to operate the bel-
lows, and a Negro Sancho to make charcoal.[5]

Since Indian slaves shared the functions of the Negroes, there is no
need to describe those functions in any detail. There were, however,
some differences. As far as can be told, Indian slaves completely escaped agricultural work and employment in teams and gangs, which
were important uses of Negroes. The Indians were definitely a more
specialized group. The great majority of Indian slave women were personal servants or concubines, and most, though not all, Indian slave
men were artisans. There were more of the women than the men,
though not the overwhelming predominance of women found among
the moriscos.[6] Still, foreign Indians had much in common with the moriscos; both groups were specialized in the same areas, had a majority of
women, and played transitory, though important, roles.

Though generally Indians brought lower prices than Negroes, some
foreign Indians had reached a high degree of skill or acculturation, and
were esteemed accordingly. Most of them spoke good Spanish. There
were Indian slaves in all the trades the Negroes practiced; most commanded prices about on the level of a very valuable untrained Negro,

but an exceptional Indian could be sold for near the price of a Negro master artisan.[7] Some of the women seem to have had contact with the Spaniards long enough, at a quite early date, to have picked up some of the refinements of Spanish housekeeping. A Nicaraguan Indian woman, Juana, in 1546 was the senior servant of her Spanish master and mistress in a household that included Negroes and Peruvian Indians. Aside from being Christian, speaking Spanish, and supervising work like the changing of bed linen and the washing of men's shirts, she had mastered embroidery, and sometimes sat in her mistress' room doing embroidery work on a handkerchief.[8]

Something of the career of one Indian artisan slave is known to us through his persistent efforts to free himself. His name was Francisco, and he was born in Tenochtitlán or Mexico City. There he learned the trade of saddle- and harness-making from a Spanish artisan for whom he worked (according to his own claim) as a free man. The artisan gave Francisco away against his will to another Spaniard, who took him to Lima around 1539 and sold him there to a Spanish shoemaker, as a trained artisan slave.

In Lima, Francisco soon began to agitate for his freedom, and the courts pronounced him free in 1541, whereupon he left his master and went to live and work with a rival shoemaker. Apparently there had been a strong presumption, because of his birthplace, that Francisco was enslaved illegally. A fair number of Indian slaves were from New Spain, but very few from the central area around Mexico City. One day when Francisco was walking down a Lima street, two Spanish artisans who knew him started making fun of him, asking how in the world it was possible for an Indian from Mexico City to be a slave.

Political events forced Francisco back into slavery after only a few months of working for wages, when Pizarro was assassinated and the party of Almagro came briefly to power. The shoemaker who had hired Francisco, being from Trujillo, was closely associated with the Pizarros, while the other shoemaker, Francisco's former owner, was in the favor of the Almagrists. In this situation it was possible for the former owner to regain legal possession of Francisco.

Within a year Francisco's shoemaker owner sold him to a Spanish saddler passing through Lima, who took him to Cuzco. There, in 1543, the saddler sold Francisco once again, together with a Guatemalan Indian partially trained as a saddler, and their tools. The circumstances of the transaction throw a good deal of light on these sales of produc-

tive units or shop staffs, which were such a common way of transferring ownership of artisan slaves, both Negro and Indian. Francisco's
prospective buyer was not interested in the tools, and thought that the
Guatemalan Indian knew less than nothing about saddle-making, but
he placed so much value on Francisco's skill that he was willing to buy
both slaves to get Francisco, paying the very substantial total of 850
pesos. Not long after this sale, Francisco sued for his freedom once
more, and court action continued sporadically, in Cuzco and Lima,
through 1548, with the final result unknown, but meanwhile it seems
that Francisco enjoyed his freedom much of the time. Whether he remained a slave or free, Francisco's real skill in a Spanish trade and his
fifteen years of living in Spanish settlements all over the Indies assured
him a certain position in the Hispanic Peruvian world.[9]

Since there were foreign Indian slaves, there were also Indian freedmen. All the avenues to freedom open to Negroes were open to Indian
slaves as well. But nothing is more instructive about the difference between these two groups than the different uses they made of the same
set of legal procedures. While Negroes mainly bought and worked
themselves free, simple charity grants were the most important instrument for freeing Indians. No Indians are known to have bought their
freedom, and only a few received it by negotiating advances on future
services. Most of the Indians freed were women who were the mothers
of their masters' children. It seems clear that the proportion of slaves
attaining formal freedom was much lower among the Indians than
among Negroes. The Indians were without the Negroes' talent for purposeful action under depressing conditions, and perhaps since Indian
slavery after 1545 was an obviously dying institution, some Indian
slaves enjoyed a kind of unofficial freedom without a formal grant.[10]

No community of Indian freedmen, in the sense that there was a
community of free Negroes, can be said to have existed. Indian freedmen often stayed quite closely dependent on individual Spaniards.
Some were personal servants for a very low wage, 30 to 40 pesos a
year, and some Indian women married Spanish men, though never
men of high rank.[11]

Francisco de Herrera, a prominent encomendero and once alcalde of
Lima, who came to Peru not long after Cajamarca, brought with him
two Nicaraguan women slaves, both of them his mistresses. Their
names were Beatriz López and Elvira González. (The Spaniards were
much quicker to give Spanish surnames to foreign Indians than to

Peruvian Indians.) Herrera soon granted them freedom, but continued to live with them and have children by them until he married a Spanish lady in the 1540's. At the time of Herrera's death in 1546 he still had no legitimate heir by his Spanish wife, so he left substantial legacies to the two Indian women and their children. The children received the bulk of the wealth and were taken out of the control of their Indian mothers, to be cared for by a Spanish legal guardian and a hired tutor. The mothers received dowry money to get married, and one of them then immediately married a Spanish tailor.[12] Women like these had gone over completely to the Spanish style of dress, and spoke Spanish of necessity, for there was no one to understand their native tongues.[13]

The foreign Indians who must have been most familiar to the Spanish Peruvian world at large were three Mexican trumpeters named Pedro de Tapia, Francisco Sánchez, and Antonio Bravo. They seem to have arrived with Viceroy Mendoza in 1551, and were probably never slaves. Their work was to perform at all kinds of ceremonial occasions, in Lima's cathedral as well as on its square and streets. Sometimes the city paid them, sometimes the royal treasury, at a rate of 50 pesos each per year; they rode horses that the treasury bought for them. In 1554 they accompanied the royal army on a campaign through the highlands which took them far south of Cuzco. When Viceroy Cañete arrived at Lima in 1556, they were still there to play at his reception.[14]

In sum, the role of foreign Indians stands in contrast to that of the Negroes despite their shared status as intrusive slave groups. Foreign Indians were a phenomenon of transition, while Negroes were a permanent block of the colonial population. The Indians never distantly equalled the massive effort that Negroes directed toward attaining freedom and economic gain. No Indians ever engaged in any of the branches of petty capitalism which were the Negroes' specialty. The Indians' only socio-economic advantage over Negroes was the limited success of Indian women in marrying into the Spanish world at a somewhat higher level than was possible for Negroes.

The vast majority of the population of greater Peru in the conquest period was made up of unacculturated Peruvian Indians living in villages apart from the Spanish settlements; these Indians were distributed to four or five hundred fortunate Spaniards in large encomienda units, a whole valley or ethnic group at a time. The encomienda Indians are the core of Indian society, the opposite pole of Spanish Peruvian society and therefore, though of great ultimate relevance, are not of immediate concern in the present study. Still, there were ways in which some of the encomienda Indians came into direct contact with the Spanish world.

Civil war among the Spaniards brought many thousands of Indians face to face with the intruders. Every three or four years until 1554, major military campaigns swept from one end of greater Peru to the other, ending typically in pitched battles at which hordes of people were present. The number of actual combatants in these wars was never high; most battles were fought with from 400 to 800 men on each side, and never with more than 1,500 to 2,000. But the wars were major operations nevertheless. Each Spanish combatant was accompanied by one or more Negro slaves, if he could manage it, and several Indians of both sexes. Almost all the Spaniards, even those destined to fight on foot with muskets or pikes, rode to battle. The footmen had mules or nags, while the cavalrymen rode first-rate war horses, and the richer encomenderos might bring several good horses each. All of this added up to a camp of thousands of people, many of them local encomienda Indians commandeered on a short-time basis.

In 1538 there was introduced the large-scale use of heavy field artillery, which meant that other thousands of encomienda Indians were employed in carrying the big guns around the country. When Gonzalo Pizarro advanced on Lima at the beginning of his rebellion in 1544, he is estimated to have taken 6,000 Indian bearers along to transport the artillery, munitions, and other supplies.[15]

Encomienda Indians had their most regular link with the people in Spanish towns through the system of tribute delivery. A significant group of tribute collectors and estate managers lived in the country among the Indians, but it is not their role that is to be discussed here; as lone Spaniards in whole valleys and regions they can hardly have had great social or cultural influence. The important thing in that respect was the yearly migration of numbers of Indians to the Spanish towns to deliver their tributes. Encomienda Indians did this in all parts of Peru, the only exception being some groups in coastal valleys, who could deliver their tribute to small ports at the mouths of the valleys.

The tribute delivered by the yearly parties was always of two kinds; the produce brought, and the labor of the Indians who brought it, as long as they stayed in town. The two kinds of tribute formed one inseparable unit, and though the relative importance of the two elements could vary greatly, both were always present. Upper Peru's *mita* labor system for the silver mines and Lima's tribute deliveries were in origin and essence one and the same. In the first fifteen or twenty years of Spanish occupation, the word "mita" referred to the whole unit sent out annually from the encomienda area to the Spanish town, the produce as well as the work done by the Indian bearers.[16]

In most areas a party of encomienda Indians, led by their cacique, brought their tribute, or a substantial part of it, to the city where the encomendero lived, and then settled down on the edges of town for a period lasting from one to three months. Each encomendero owned a large lot with some huts on it to accommodate his Indians. During their time of residence the Indians performed various kinds of tasks which required a large number of workers. In construction, they quarried stone, transported building materials, served as the labor force which under Spanish and Negro supervision built the houses of the Spanish towns, and themselves built enclosures and other types of structures using their own techniques. In agriculture they harvested the crops, grown intensively on surrounding fields, which were a large part of the cities' food supply. They did all this work primarily for their own encomenderos, but the encomenderos also hired them out to other Spaniards.[17]

With time, annual tribute-bearing migrations brought major social change. The tribute parties themselves, working as units under the immediate direction of other Indians, may have undergone no great direct influence other than high mortality rate from new diseases, though they at least saw what Spaniards and Spanish towns looked like. More important was the way the annual migrations stimulated some Indians to move toward the towns as individuals for longer periods of time. Some of the Indians who came with the tribute parties, poorer or more ambitious than most, did not return to their encomiendas, but stayed on in the towns to work as unskilled laborers. As the possibilities became known to more and more encomienda Indians, any economic disaster they suffered would bring numbers of them to the towns seeking work. By 1550 this movement had already reached major proportions.[18] Another related development was the growing tendency of caciques to bypass the encomenderos (with their permission) and rent out Indians directly to Spaniards, in lots ranging from four or five to fifty.[19] At any time from the early 1540's on, the Spanish cities were surrounded by a forest of huts which contained three different kinds of Indians making up a single continuum: organized tribute parties, individual migrants seeking temporary or permanent work, and permanent personal servants of the Spaniards.

Wherever there were rich mines, particularly highland silver mines, the tribute parties were deflected in that direction. The gold rushes of Carabaya and Quito were merely episodes of particularly frightful mortality. Potosí was more typical, and more than typical, because after 1545 Potosí was the goal of tribute parties from all over southern Peru. While smaller parties still went to the place of the encomendero's residence in the southern areas, the main contribution was produce and people sent directly to Potosí. This was true not only for Charcas and nearby La Paz, but also for large sections of Cuzco and Arequipa provinces. The type of contribution varied with the distance from Potosí; areas close to Potosí sent more people to work and less produce, distant areas sent more produce and fewer people.

As a scourge and a factor in disrupting Indian society, the importance of Potosí was immense. As a focal point of acculturation, it could not compare with centers like Lima, Arequipa, and Cuzco. The Indians came in larger units, better equipped to resist outside influence, and Potosí had nothing like the strong ordinary civil life which went on in the other towns. The highlands were always weaker than the coast in this respect, and in any case normal sedentary Spanish life in the province of Charcas was centered more in the capital of La Plata than in Potosí itself, particularly in the early period. Still, a movement similar to that in the towns did take place. It was never possible for the Spaniards and caciques to separate strictly the Indians' tribute activities from their activities as individuals; they worked for themselves as well as for others. While most Indians fared poorly at Potosí, and many died of disease, work, or starvation, there were some who returned from the mita with new clothes, silver bracelets, and supplies of coca. Indians who had this kind of luck were tempted to stay on, and some of them joined the permanent force of yanaconas who were expert miners.[20]

Briefly, then, the tribute system used by the Spaniards had indigenous roots, yet was similar to migratory labor systems used at various times in many other colonial areas. Though disruptive, it had the effect of spreading knowledge about Spanish society among the unacculturated Indians, and set in motion a movement of Indians to the cities that has never ceased.

The traditional Indian nobles and chieftains, whom the Spaniards called "caciques" in Peru as in other parts of the Indies, were the principal intermediaries between the encomenderos and the encomienda Indians. As such they had frequent occasion to be in the towns and communicate with Spaniards, giving rise to widespread, but uneven and superficial acculturation among the cacique class.

As long as a cacique remained pagan, he retained his Indian name, but when he turned Christian he was given a Christian name and the title "don" to indicate his noble condition. This practice makes it possible to judge in a general way the speed of the conversion of Indian nobles. By 1540 most of the large chieftains, responsible for whole valleys or encomiendas, had been formally converted, though baffling exceptions occur until a late date. The sub-chiefs or *principales*, as the Spaniards often called them, lagged far behind, and even as late as 1560 many were unconverted.

The caciques were quite unsuccessful in learning Spanish. In the 1550's neither the cacique of Lima nor the cacique of Huarochirí, up the Lima valley, could speak Spanish well, although their area had been the point of maximum impact of Spanish culture for twenty years. Gradually over the years some caciques began to acquire fluency in spoken Spanish; but hardly any learned to sign their names, though some tried.[21]

Like the nobility of other conquered peoples, the caciques were anxious to imitate the dress of their conquerors. By the 1550's caciques were to be seen in the full costume of fine stuffs that the Spaniards gloried in. But they did not do so well in acquiring the other trappings of the Spaniards. Their war chargers were often nags, mares, or mules; for muskets they had crossbows. The wine that they bought up probably had the same effect on them as brandy on North American Indians in a different age.[22]

A cacique was a welcome guest in the house of his encomendero, for with a good personal relationship to the cacique, an encomendero could hope for more favorable tribute arrangements. The caciques of Huarochirí, for example, succumbed completely to the friendliness of their encomendero. The first and second cacique of Huarochirí both assumed the name of Antonio Picado, their encomendero (not an uncommon thing to do); the cacique's daughter not only took the name of the encomendero's wife and successor, Ana Suárez, but went to Lima to live in her house. The second don Antonio Picado and his sister doña Isabel Suárez both contracted Spanish marriages, arranged for them by their mistress, with dowries raised among the encomienda Indians. Don Antonio married the woman servant of a government secretary (in all probability a morisca), and doña Isabel married a hosier of Lima. As a result of cultivating the caciques, Ana Suárez received such rewards as advances on the following year's tributes.[23]

Though the caciques were pitiful figures, they were not merely that. In the highland areas, caciques exercised considerable real power over Indians even within the borders of the Spanish towns. In economic affairs, caciques everywhere represented their own interests, if not those of their people, very efficiently, dealing with the Spaniards on an equal footing. They had a very considerable income from renting the services of their subjects directly to non-encomendero Spaniards, and from selling Indian products. Some of them, not satisfied with the security of their traditional rights to land, sought to guarantee those rights by converting them into full private ownership of land in the Spanish style, sanctified by the Spanish legal authorities. A few caciques even went over to Spanish methods of economic exploitation; in 1557 the cacique of Huanchuaylas hired an Aragonese estate manager to carry on general agriculture on his lands with oxen, plows, carts, and Indian labor.[24]

To the Spaniards, the Inca emperor was one more cacique. Still, they made some distinction between the class of ordinary caciques, and the high Inca nobility with close connections to the emperor and Cuzco. The distinction is particularly clear in the different treatment accorded the women of the two groups. Where the daughter of the cacique of Huarochirí with effort managed to marry a hosier, many high Indian noblewomen found it possible to make quite good marriages. Three or four Indian women who were close relatives of the Inca emperor received encomiendas in Cuzco, that is, it was made clear that the Spaniards who married them would become encomenderos. Even this, however, did not represent marriage into Spanish society at the very highest level. The husbands of the Indian princesses were all from fringe groups, or of low extraction.[25]

Hardly a single member of the true Spanish Peruvian aristocracy, meaning those who had come to Peru early and had large encomiendas, membership on municipal councils, and good connections in Spain, ever married an Indian woman. Their feeling for lineage was too strong. Even when they were personally attached to their noble Indian mistresses, they renounced them (though making some provision for their future) to marry Spanish women. Garci Laso de la Vega, father of the chronicler, was perfectly typical in this respect. Alonso de Toro, lieutenant governor in Cuzco around 1545, was unable to give up his Indian mistress, but married a Spanish woman anyway, living with both women until his father-in-law killed him for favoring the Indian princess and insulting his Spanish wife.[26]

Outside Cuzco only a very few Indian noblewomen, probably no more than two or three, married encomenderos. In Arequipa, doña Isabel Yupanque married a man who had a small encomienda, in a match arranged and subsidized by her protector, one of the greatest encomenderos of that region. In Lima one Indian noblewoman, doña Inés, was lifted entirely out of her category by virtue of having given birth to the daughter of Francisco Pizarro, doña Francisca. Pizarro married her to Francisco de Ampuero, his employee, and granted them a large encomienda. An intelligent and literate man, Ampuero developed into one of Lima's most prominent citizens.[27]

Not nearly all Indian princesses were able to marry encomenderos; many had to accept a great loss of status in becoming part of the Spanish world. One *palla* or noblewoman of Cuzco married a Portuguese resident of Lima, Enrique Fernández. Fernández was quite respected as an individual, but was not an encomendero, and made his living from small-scale agriculture and various jobs for the municipality of Lima, including the despised post of town crier. A doña Isabel, another palla of Cuzco, lived as the mistress of a tribute collector on a large encomienda in the Arequipa area. (She was Christian and may have spoken some Spanish, but otherwise retained her traditional dress and lived still in the world of Indian Cuzco, where she had all her friends, connections, and property rights.)[28]

The single Indian of the princely class who achieved high position within the Spanish world was Paullu Inca, one of the few noblemen with a plausible claim to succeed on the Inca throne. Whether for his own advantage or for deeper reasons, Paullu decided very early in the conquest period on a policy of collaboration with the Spaniards. He smoothed the way of Almagro's expedition to Chile, opposed the rebellion of Manco Inca, and for many years was an important factor in the loyalty of Cuzco's Indians to the Spaniards rather than to the Inca kingdom holding out in the mountains.

As a reward, Paullu received a large encomienda in the Cuzco area,

on the same basis as any Spanish encomendero, and kept it until his
death, when his son succeeded him. He lived in an Inca palace on the
hill below Sacsahuaman, Cuzco's fortress. Soon after his first contact
with Spaniards he embarked on a life-long process of Hispanization
which went far in some sectors of his life, while leaving him in other
ways practically untouched. He quickly taught himself to handle a
musket or a crossbow, and learned to ride a horse for the trip to Chile.
One Spaniard said he had seen Paullu on horseback lancing Indians "as
if he were a Christian."

Only in 1542, after about eight years with the Spaniards, did Paullu
turn Christian, taking his name don Cristóbal from the then governor.
By 1544 he had learned to sign his name in Spanish letters. He installed
a private chapel in his palace, and hired Spanish servants, including a
Spaniard to educate his son don Carlos. By this time, if not earlier, he
had abandoned Indian dress for a complete Spanish costume. But with
all this he never learned to speak Spanish. He married according to the
Christian rites on his deathbed, and even then only to legitimate his
son to succeed him in his encomienda. At his death in 1549, all the
able-bodied Indians of Cuzco, following an old custom to preserve legitimate succession on the throne, came to his house and guarded it
until he was buried sumptuously as a Christian.

Paullu or don Cristóbal retained real power in the Indian world and
played a significant role in the Spanish world, but in the latter his position was very precarious. While the authorities valued him for his
influence among the Indians, the ordinary Spaniards never learned to
pay him any deference. Getting the Spaniards to respect an Indian
chieftain was as hard as getting a cat to respect a pet canary. Once the
henchman of a prominent Spaniard struck Paullu on the street, pulled
him by the hair and called him degrading names; the Spaniard was
never punished. When Spaniards robbed Paullu's house, the authorities
placed Spanish guards there, but the guards also robbed the house.[29]

Paullu's son don Carlos was much more thoroughly acculturated. His
general level of education was probably not much below that of his fellow student, Garcilaso de la Vega. At very least, he spoke and wrote
Spanish perfectly; his fluent signature is that of a cultivated man. He
married a woman of full Spanish descent and good social position.
Even so, he was very far from full acceptance as an equal in Spanish
Cuzco.[30]

The Indian nobility of Cuzco was still nearly enough intact that its members, even those who married Spaniards, remained resistant to Spanish influence, particularly to linguistic influence. Garcilaso claimed that in all the time he lived in Cuzco before he left in 1560, he knew of only two Indians who really spoke Spanish, and don Carlos Inca was one of them. The Spanish encomenderos of Cuzco who were married to Indian noblewomen were drawn to each other by that common factor, and formed a sub-group of society in which the Indian influence was as important as the Spanish. Doña Beatriz, who had been the mistress of one Spaniard and then the wife of another, still could not speak Spanish when she married for a second time.[31] In other parts of Peru, where the Indian tradition was more fragmented, Spanish influence took hold quicker. The two Indian noblewomen of Lima both spoke good Spanish.

The Indian who came nearest to being absorbed into the world of the Spaniards was don Martín, also called don Martín Pizarro after his protectors the Pizarros, and don Martín, *lengua*, indicating his profession of interpreter. After a large measure of real success, don Martín's life ended pathetically—the fate of so many premature manifestations of full Hispanization.

Whether don Martín was from the class of caciques or had some connection with high Indian nobility is not certainly known; at any rate, he claimed to be noble and a nephew of the cacique of Chincha. He was one of the two boys, possibly twelve or fifteen years old, given to Francisco Pizarro by the Indians in 1528, to be trained as interpreters. In 1529 he went to Spain with Pizarro, and returned to Peru with the conquering expedition. By 1532 he was already an accomplished speaker of Spanish. In the conquest he both fought on horseback using Spanish arms, and conducted negotiations to convince Indian leaders to receive the Spaniards peacefully. Whenever booty was distributed, don Martín received a share, and paid the king's fifth like any Spaniard.

In the years 1535 to 1537 don Martín received impressive rewards for his services. Francisco Pizarro, who had taken a strong liking to him, gave him an encomienda near Lima and married him to a Spanish woman, Luisa de Medina, apparently of good ordinary Spanish stock, and no morisca. When she returned to Spain many years later, she called herself *doña*, which would have been impossible to a woman without at least the appearance of good breeding. The Spanish king granted don Martín knighthood and gave him a coat of arms, an award which for Spaniards signified arrival at the top rank.

Don Martín enjoyed the full prerogatives of a Spanish encomendero. He had a large house in the center of Lima where he received many Spanish guests, both men and women. He owned horses, livestock, Negro slaves, city real estate, and agricultural land outside Lima. Like other encomenderos, he had a Spanish tribute collector and estate' manager.

The peak of his career came in the late years of the life of Francisco Pizarro. Since don Martín was so close to Pizarro, Spaniards cultivated him in hopes of bettering their position with the governor. One Spaniard put all his affairs completely in the hands of don Martín, a gesture of confidence usually extended only to relatives and close friends.

Even after Francisco's Pizarro's death don Martín did not go into any obvious eclipse, though he was no longer so much in the center of things. He served in the 1542 campaign against the younger Almagro, and was among the cavalry at the battle of Chupas, probably the only Indian to fight in the Spanish civil wars. After the war, Governor Vaca de Castro bettered don Martín's encomienda near Lima.

The great rebellion of Gonzalo Pizarro (1544–48) occasioned don Martín's ruin. He could not bring himself to be unfaithful to the Pizarros, who had been the source of his success. Neither could he understand the issues, nor did he have the subtle sense of timing that allowed the Spaniards to change sides at the right moment. Don Martín stayed with Gonzalo Pizarro too long; when he was captured once by the other side, he escaped and returned to Pizarro, whom he followed until his defeat. Afterwards the new governor, Gasca, made use of don Martín on a mission to the renegade Inca. Then, in view of his obvious guilt and the number of Spaniards clamoring for encomiendas, Gasca without ceremony took away don Martín's encomienda, confiscated most of his property, and sent him into exile. Don Martín went to Spain meaning to protest at court, but died on the way in Seville in 1550. His wife and daughter lived on in Spain for many years.

Don Martín represented a formidable degree of Hispanization. He was Christian, wore only Spanish clothes, lived, ate, and slept like a Spaniard and among Spaniards. Around 1540 he learned to sign his name, though probably no more than that. His prime quality was his mastery of spoken Spanish, which struck everyone who met him. Having started so young, he very possibly spoke with no discernible accent. Though he was literally one of the two first Peruvian Indians to come among the Spaniards, don Martín, because his experience began at such an early age, was in a sense a second-generation figure.

There are some examples of don Martín's speech recorded, in some quotations from him and in testimony he translated for court records. His Spanish was strangely flamboyant, a quality stemming mainly from his overuse of idioms and other set expressions; occasionally he fell into a subtle mistake through unnecessary duplication. His vocabulary was large, which makes it all the stranger that he retained the Indian word *Apu* for king or governor, perhaps because the Spaniards expected him to. A most characteristic sentence of don Martín's is "When is the Apu of Castile coming to take us from this captivity?"

However secure don Martín's position appeared at one time, he always existed on sufferance. In any pressing situation, he reverted in the minds of the Spaniards to the status of a mere Indian. This had shown itself early, when Francisco Pizarro promised him 10,000 pesos for his part at Cajamarca, but failed to pay him a penny of it. Don Martín's life shows that certainly the Spaniards, and perhaps the Indians, were not ready for the full Hispanization of the top stratum of Indian society.[22]

Hispanization of the nobility was a premature fruit. Deeper and more lasting acculturation went on among the Indians who, in more humble positions, were thrown into daily household contact with Spaniards.

Of all such Indians none had a better opportunity to learn about Spaniards and the Spanish language than the omnipresent class of Indian servant-mistresses. Without undue cynicism, it is safe to say that practically all Spaniards had Indian mistresses. If they were married, they had mistresses until their wives arrived; if they were single, they had mistresses until they married. Such relationships were often quite stable, partaking of the nature of common-law marriages.

Harem-keeping did exist, and it may be assumed that where it existed it reduced the depth of the relationship and, above all, made the Indian element predominant in the household. Some Spaniards literally had so many mistresses and children that they could not remember them all. Alonso de Mesa, a prominent encomendero of Cuzco, started to make his will in 1544. Announcing that he had five natural children by five Indian women of Cuzco, all then living in his house, he proceeded to list them, and arrived at six children and six women. Then he remembered a seventh woman pregnant by him at the time, also living in his house. Only two women were nominally Christian, and it is doubtful that any spoke Spanish.[33] Had harems been the usual mode, the culture of the Indians might have gone far toward winning out even in the cities, at least in the cities of the highlands. But in fact a kind of monogamy seems to have been far more common.

Indian servant-mistresses generally retained Indian costume, but learned to speak some Spanish, just the opposite of the caciques. They traveled and lived with their masters, though refraining from anything that would imply social equality. If the master married or went back to Spain, he might make some provision for his mistress, in the form of a small house or lot, or a hundred pesos. Men who left their mistresses wanted to see them appropriately married, and might arrange a marriage, generally with a city-dwelling Indian, a mulatto, or a Negro. If the mistress bore the Spaniard's children, the Spaniard sometimes rewarded her because of the offspring, but perhaps more frequently the mother was neglected in concern for the child.

An abandoned mistress could be a pathetic figure, living as an unwanted servant in the second patio of some Spaniard's house, or she might have a modestly adequate situation. One of these women, called only María, lived in Lima in 1557. She was from Cuzco; the vast majority of Peruvian Indian servants in all parts of the country were from the highlands. She spoke Spanish well, was Christian, and belonged to a religious brotherhood. Though she had no real estate, she had a fair amount of money, some chickens, plenty of clothing in the Indian style, some Spanish tools and utensils, and a luxury item or two, such as a religious figurine.[34]

The Indian mistress and servant was important in the evolution of other varieties of town Indians. A very common phenomenon was the Indian servant couple, who might live either with the Spanish employer or on the edge of town where the Indians had their *ranchos* or huts. In these servant couples the woman was generally far the more active partner, and it is often apparent that she got her start as the mistress of a Spaniard. Indian women servants working alone were also often abandoned mistresses. By 1560 some former Indian concubines had become emancipated in a fashion, wearing Spanish clothes, living by themselves, and operating houses of prostitution.

There were, of course, other types of Peruvian Indian servants. In the houses of encomenderos, the lower level of the servant staff was made up of encomienda Indians who rotated on a short-time basis and therefore had only superficial contact with the Hispanic world. Another common form of Indian servant was the servant boy. Young boys entered or were put into the service of Spaniards, in a type of relationship which, though the boy's work was the major factor, still had some flavor of training or apprenticeship.

Peruvian Indian servants were very poorly paid. Servant-mistresses generally received nothing, and couples very little. Some Indian servants got only food and clothing, and those who earned a salary in money rarely received more than 20 or 30 pesos a year. The formalization of arrangements with Peruvian Indians was a late development, belonging mainly to the 1550's; before then it had apparently been so easy to commandeer Indians, and the difference between a trained and an untrained Peruvian Indian had been so slight, that making contracts with them had not occurred to anyone.[35]

The lives of Indian servants showed noticeable regional variation, and between Lima and Cuzco there was quite a strong contrast. The poles of Indian servant life in Lima were the Spanish house and the rancho. Either the servant was able to live directly in a Spanish household, or he lived in the rancho section on the periphery of town, where Indian group life was disrupted by the quick turnover of the migratory population and the diseases and starvation which, one contemporary thought, in the 1540's caused the deaths of two or three thousand Indians in Lima in every year.[36]

In Cuzco, though both rancho living and living with the Spaniards were known, there was a third element of great importance. Many Indian servants in Cuzco lived apart from their masters not as squatters in huts, but in more substantial dwellings in better locations, often on lots they either owned or had other, semi-permanent rights to. The Cuzco servant class was like the Cuzco nobility (the two groups were of course connected with each other) in remaining part of a relatively intact, independent Indian world which existed right within the Spanish city and made the Indians much more resistant to Spanish influence. In 1560 there were still few Indian servants in Cuzco who spoke good Spanish, and even in the matter of Christianization Cuzco lagged far behind Lima, where practically all permanent Indian servants were Christian. Though most of the servants in Lima were highland Indians like those of Cuzco, the difference in rate of acculturation is more than sufficiently explained by the strength of the Spanish impact on the coast and the fragmentation of the displaced highland Indians in Lima.[37]

Peruvian Indian artisans in the Spanish trades were an outgrowth of the Indian servant class, and the distinctions observed between highland and coast are as true for one group as for the other. Like the servants, the artisans came mainly from the highlands, and those on the coast were farther along the path to acculturation.

Spanish artisanry practiced by Peruvian Indians was a late development; there are hardly any known examples of Peruvian Indian artisans until the 1550's, and even in that decade Spaniards, Negroes, and foreign Indians were carrying on the bulk of the work. Little or no transferral of skill took place from the flourishing arts and crafts of the Incas to the Spanish trades. Peruvian Indians could more easily produce Spanish artifacts using their own techniques than they could learn Spanish methods. Time and again Indian metal workers produced usable European-style armor for the Spanish civil wars, employing their traditional methods, with no more instruction than a sample of the helmet or cuirass to be copied. But this did not mean that the Indians found easy entry into the shops of Spanish silversmiths. Late in the period, the archbishop of Lima still thought it something of a miracle, worth writing to the Spanish king about, that one Indian had learned silversmithing in the European style. Moreover, the Indian in question was not Peruvian, but Mexican. The mastery of the Inca architects and masons of Cuzco is world famous. But when the Spaniards built a stone bridge near Cuzco in 1559, they had to import from Jauja seven Indians who had learned something of Spanish stonemasonry during the previous construction of a Spanish bridge there.[38]

In the early part of the decade 1550–60 some Peruvian Indians began to appear in the Spanish artisans' shops, working on the same basis as Negroes and foreign Indians, but invariably receiving low pay and bad terms. Indian boys also began to enter formal apprenticeship under Spanish artisans, so that by 1560 it appears that Peruvian Indians were finally preparing to take a place in Spanish artisanry alongside the Spaniards and the Negroes. In Cuzco (not, apparently, in Lima) some Indians were operating independently in 1560 as carpenters and tailors. Only the highlands could have produced a combination like the Indian of Cuzco who made clothes for Spaniards, but himself spoke no Spanish and continued to wear Indian apparel.[39]

Most of the Indian servile population falls into reasonably distinct categories, but the same clarity cannot be attained for the group termed yanaconas, servant Indians outside the frameworks of clan and encomienda. To some Spaniards, all town Indians were yanaconas; to others, the word meant a personal servant. More specifically, the Indians who were seized as servants in the early stages of the conquest were considered yanaconas, permanently attached by a semi-legal bond to their Spanish masters. During the Gonzalo Pizarro uprising, the rebel authorities granted to some Spaniards legal title to possess such Indians. There is no need, however, to give much consideration to difference of legal status among Indian servants. The power balance between the two peoples so overwhelmingly favored the Spaniards that no Indian servant or employee, whatever his legal status, had much freedom to absent himself from his master.[40]

The only yanaconas who require mention as really somewhat distinct from the general Indian servant class are those of Potosí. For the first year or two after the discovery of the silver mines of Potosí in 1545, the work was done by yanaconas, organized tribute parties from the encomiendas not yet entering into the picture. Some of the yanaconas had already been working in the nearby mines of Porco for their Spanish masters; others appeared spontaneously after news spread of the wealth of the mines. Within a short time there were 7,000 yanaconas in Potosí. By a rough political mechanism, each yanacona was assigned to a Spaniard. The yanacona, operating on his own, extracted ore, smelted it in a native oven or *huayra*, and delivered a set weekly quota of silver to his master. Anything else he earned was for himself. In the early years the surplus could be quite large, and some yanaconas amassed respectable fortunes.

This system was rapidly altered as the encomienda Indians arrived in large numbers and mining became more methodical. Nevertheless, a residue of yanaconas remained at Potosí as relatively expert miners among the untrained mita Indians. They worked for any of various mining companies, and gave a percentage of their earnings to the Spanish masters assigned them by political authorities. Spaniards who had some claim on the authorities but were not in line for an encomienda could be satisfied by the grant of the rights to ten or fifteen Potosí yanaconas.

In origin, some of the yanaconas of Potosí were the traditional miners of the region who had worked under the Incas. Others were general servants of the Spaniards, from various parts of Peru. The Indian who discovered Potosí, a yanacona named Hualpa, or, later, don Diego, was the son of a sub-chief in the Cuzco region. Not long after the conquest he became the servant of a Portuguese; the two went together from place to place before ending up in Porco, where Hualpa began to work at mining. The Portuguese had to leave Porco, but Hualpa stayed on under a new master, soon afterward discovered or was important in discovering Potosí, and worked there the rest of his life as a miner and yanacona. The acculturation of the yanaconas at Potosí seems to have been limited mainly to mining techniques. When Hualpa died in 1572, neither he nor any of his collaborators from the early period had learned to speak Spanish.[41]

While the Hispanization of the caciques was a surface phenomenon, Spanish influence on the ordinary Indians of the towns was part of a process that was to alter Peru profoundly; but in the first generation both were pitiful spectacles. Paullu, the candidate for the Inca throne who was at the mercy of the lowest Spaniard when he went out on the street, had something in common with the superb Peruvian craftsmen who never mastered simple Spanish trades. It took the Indians nearly twenty years to develop any flexibility or initiative within the Spanish world, even to the extent of fulfilling adequately the Spaniards' needs for low-level auxiliaries. In the interim, Negroes, moriscos, and foreign Indians filled the gap. By 1560, the end of the period under study, the moriscos and foreign Indians had disappeared from the scene, but the Negroes still were far more firmly embedded in Spanish Peruvian society than the Indians, by virtue of their greater degree of acculturation, their many-sided activities and their individual drive. In Cuzco and Charcas, where Negroes were less numerous, Indians set the tone in the lower reaches of Hispanic society, but still could not compare with Negroes in prestige and useful skills.

Indians were relatively marginal members of the Hispanic world, but their women were more central as the servant-mistresses and occasionally wives of Spaniards. Indian women—noble, plebeian, and foreign—supplied the Spaniards with sometimes casual, sometimes lifelong companions, and often acquired more than a veneer of Hispanic culture, working their way into the fabric of Spanish society. In this role they were far more prominent than Negro women, and the Spaniards only reluctantly replaced them with Spanish wives for reasons of lineage and shared culture.

XII CONCLUSION

Social history, like biography, cannot be condensed meaningfully beyond a certain point, because rather than a set of principles it is a set of facts with widening circles of implications. To know a man or a society requires a fair amount of contact. Whereas after reading a thousand pages of reasoned argument one can carry off the conclusion like a jewel, the chief profit gained by the reader of social history, though as rich, is more diffuse: the feel for a subject matter. The material to be found in the conclusion of a book like this one, which attempts to be a sort of collective biography of a society, is hardly to be compared in value with the body of it, or with the last chapter of a book built around an advancing argument.

With this disavowal, some generalization may nevertheless be attempted. A great deal of what emerges here can be summed up under the general statement that an essentially intact, complete Spanish society was transferred to Peru in the conquest and civil war period. An enormous variety of people participated in the enterprise of conquest and occupation, and among them every stratum of Spanish society and every region of the Spanish heartland was represented in force. Important nuclei of artisans, professional people, merchants, and Spanish women were present.

This means that a variety of ideas from the time of Prescott, tending to limit the character of the Spanish occupation severely, should now be abandoned once and for all (for Peru certainly and for other comparable areas too, in all likelihood). Artisans participated in the early period, and did not refuse to work in their trades. Spanish women were of course not nearly so numerous as men, but the Spaniards did not come without women. Negro slaves and European foreigners were much more numerous and important than once supposed, representing another element in the transferral of Spanish society to the Indies, for the foreigners came primarily from among the aliens in Spain's own maritime and artisan population, and the uses of Negro slaves were a direct carry-over from the Negro slavery then existing in southern Spain. The nineteenth-century tradition that the conquerors were all peasants, or all petty nobility, or some combination of both, lacks substance.

As to the question of military predominance, that is a more subtle matter. There is no attempt to deny that the Spaniards came into Peru by force of arms, that most able-bodied men could handle weapons, and that large-scale civil wars rocked the country for years. Yet the average Spaniard in Peru was a fighter rather than a soldier, and his position was defined by some non-military calling or function. No kind of permanent military cadre or hierarchy existed, and professional soldiers were so rare that they were sought out eagerly as consultants in the civil wars. As on the North American frontier, the advent of the professional military was a tardy and secondary phenomenon.

The question of commerce, too, is more complicated than the mere presence or absence of a corps of merchants. It has been shown here that large numbers of professional merchants operated successfully in Peru from the beginning, often on the basis of fully developed networks stretching from Seville to Potosí. But beyond the merchants, almost the whole free population, from Negroes through sailors and artisans to encomenderos, engaged in various kinds of entrepreneurial activity, and only on the highest level was there any attempt to act through intermediaries. The Spaniards who came to Peru were no ruffianly adventurers lacking in commercial sense; rather they were a good cross-section of Spanish society, perfectly capable of carrying on the generalized commercial capitalism of the Renaissance which then prevailed in Spain. Certain of the conquerors may have behaved recklessly at the great distributions of spoils in the very early years, but for every man who gambled away his share there were two or three who returned rich to Spain or established positions of power in Peru. These were exceptional episodes, characterized by the prices and atmosphere of a boom, and even then the Spaniards were not indifferent to commercial possibilities. After the division of Atahuallpa's ransom at Cajamarca, the conquerors used their shares of gold to buy up the king's hard-to-transport silver, thus speculating on the currency and realizing a large profit.[1]

When it comes to more general characteristics the picture remains the same; the Spaniards who occupied Peru were a relatively complete cross-section. Reliable compilations of vital statistics for the settlers of Peru are not to be hoped for, but it is quite clear from the records that the Peruvian Spaniards were not all beardless youths. After all, a man twenty years old in 1532 was thirty in 1542 and forty in 1552. But even at the beginning, very young men were not clearly predominant. All the principal leaders of the Cajamarca expedition were in their late thirties or forties; about half of the body of men were veterans of Nicaragua, almost all over thirty; the rest were fresh from Spain, but not even they were all terribly young. Teenagers were very few among them; of the two known one, about eighteen, was left behind in Piura, while the other, about nineteen, took part in the capture of the Inca, but the value of his participation was later contested on the ground that he was a mere boy.

While the most common single type of settler was a young man in his early twenties setting out to seek his fortune, people with skills or education often came at a later age. The innumerable trial records and interrogatories left in the archives can never provide the basis for a statistical estimate of age grouping, because men of established reputation and maturity were chosen as witnesses; but they suffice to show that most people in responsible positions as town council members, captains, large encomenderos, lawyers, priests, even successful artisans and notaries, were thirty years old or more. The Spaniards in any case tended to give prestige and responsibility to older men and scoff at youths, who remained legal minors until twenty-five years of age, and this tendency was enhanced by the position of power held by the first conquerors, so that from about 1545 to 1560 Peru was dominated by men in their maturity or even, toward the end of the period, frank old age. The very young were never lacking in Peru, but neither were mature men of all ages up to fifty and beyond. In general, the settlers of Peru seem to have been young, in the broader sense of the word, but the controlled vigor and purposefulness of the years twenty-five to forty-five played a greater role than the erratic behavior of the first flush of youth.

In the matter of education, Spanish Peru had the illiterate plebeian, the doctor of law, and all the intermediary stages. Placing great importance on legal formulas and the written word, the Spaniards were never, even in the most remote settlement or smallest expedition, without a notary or two; at Cajamarca there were ten men with notarial training. Education was centered in the professional classes (the clergy, lawyers, physicians, notaries) and the merchants, but did not stop there, since the ability to read and write was common among wellborn laymen, and extended to a certain part of the artisan population. Peru, far from being in danger of losing the refinements of Spanish culture, was in a position to improve on Spain in certain respects, for many illiterate Spaniards learned in Peru at least to sign their names, and there is no doubt that the sons of the conquerors knew more Latin and grammar than their fathers.

Also in regional origins the Peruvian Spaniards were a representative group, representative at least of the great heartland of Spain, the kingdom of Castile. Past characterizations of the settlers as coming primarily from one region or another seem inappropriate in the case of Peru, given the strength of the groups from all the main regions. Work on the *Pasajeros a Indias* has established an overwhelming predominance of Andalusians in the Caribbean in the first years of the sixteenth century, but by the time of the conquest of Peru this had receded to a plurality, Andalusia remaining merely the largest of the regional groups, very far from forming a majority. Mario Góngora in his work on Panama suggested a predominance of the south, meaning Extremadura and Andalusia, but in Peru the two together are hardly more than half of the total. The more remarkable thing remains the number who came from the north despite the geographical handicap. This was seen by Guillermo Céspedes, who in a general statement asserted what would be true for Peru as well, that the great majority came from the central plateau of Spain. But this unnecessarily sets off the largest single group, the Andalusians of Seville, Córdoba, and Huelva, from the rest.[2]

The most important fact would seem to be that the settlers of Peru were an amalgam of Castilians, in which no one regional group had a clear predominance. In order of size the groups were Andalusia, Extremadura, Old Castile, New Castile, and Leon, but there is no need to dwell on the relative size of entities which, though they represented real divisions, were far from clearcut, and not yet very conscious of themselves. The real distinction was between the Castilian majority and the minority groups from the semi-alien fringe areas of Spain. Biscay and Portugal contributed large minorities, the remaining north coast and the kingdom of Aragon far less.

Not only was Spanish Peruvian society relatively complete, it was also relatively unchanged from its Old World original. Spanish social distinctions were retained, and rapid social mobility for individuals was increasingly rare after a short period of hardly five years, during which certain artisans and other plebeians rose to the top rank by virtue of their participation in nation-founding events like the capture of Atahuallpa and the taking of Cuzco. After that time, and to some extent even during it, entry into the upper level of society, as defined by encomendero rank, was denied to artisans, merchants, and indeed anyone without the special qualifications of either association with the first years of the conquest or good birth in Spain. There were artisans in Lima in the year of its founding, 1535, who stayed there through 1560; by then they were wealthy and respected, but still artisans. With every year advancement became more difficult for those of humble birth, as the educated and wellborn continued to arrive in strength, attracted by Peru's reputation, forcing social standards ever upward. Long before 1560, the possibilities open to the newly arriving Spaniard, while wide, were severely limited in their social potential. He could work at his own calling, or in the employ of an encomendero, or possibly in mining or commerce, and while he could hope, in Spanish peninsular terms, for quick wealth in any one of these endeavors, none would bring him any social improvement, and some had definitely negative connotations.

Though Spanish usages underwent a certain process of loosening in Peru, it would be more nearly correct to say that they were unmodified than that they were transformed. Arriving peasants did not become hidalgos on landing, much less claim the still very weighty title of "don." The centuries brought transformation, but the first generation was very conservative in modifying the social distinctions of the Peninsula. Typical of the first generation was a premature creeping over the line; the Bachiller became a Licenciado, the descendant of prominent merchants an hidalgo, the wellborn courtier perhaps a don. But working artisans, sailors, and many others made no pretension to hidalgo status, and even those of humble birth who were propelled into positions of wealth and power by their participation in the events of the first few years were long reticent about equating themselves with the hidalgos of Spain. The presumption of the Indies showed itself more in externals (titles were too important to the Spaniards to be considered externals). All who could afford it, and most could, dressed themselves in finery that, in Spain, implied high social status, and surrounded themselves with as many servants, slaves, and followers as possible. In the first generation, that is, plebeians appropriated some of the trappings of Spanish nobility, but there was no serious challenge to the groupings into which Spanish society was organized.

The completeness which characterized Spanish Peru was of course not perfect in every respect, nor was the retention of the Peninsular structure absolute. The society was unbalanced by the presence of far too many single, unemployed young men, and though a complete civil population existed, comparison with other transplanted European communities would show that indubitably every single element of it (except possibly the professional) was stronger in such a settlement as New England than in Peru. Yet it is important to modify the older view of the conquest period. If a whole generation of Spanish artisans had not practiced their trades in Peru, Negroes and Indians would never have learned those trades, and the Spanish colonial period would have been a very different thing. Desirable both for an adequate view of Peru in itself and for the perspective of world history is the recognition that though Spanish Peru differed in degree from New England, and was set down in a vastly different environment which altered everything, the two settlements seen in themselves are essentially the same thing, the transfer to a new continent of a viable reproduction of the old society, which though not identical with it, contains it all in germ, and is capable of transmitting a whole civilization. In William McNeill's more than respectable synthesis, *The Rise of the West*, there appears an illustration in which a North European settler is leaving home with his wife, while a "Mediterranean" settler in the other half of the picture is bidding farewell to his womenfolk.[3] This does justice to the important fact that the English settlements had far more European women than the Spanish, but not to the even more basic fact that both New England and Spanish Peru had enough European women to retain their traditions intact, as opposed, for example, to many Portuguese settlements literally without European women, where Portuguese language, religion, and culture were diluted or even lost. Negatively, the completeness of Spanish Peruvian society means abandoning definitively a host of one-sided ideas; positively, it means that centers of pure Hispanic culture existed in Peru as a first step toward transforming the country, and though these centers underwent immediate change and mixture, they were capable of recreating in Peru anything that Spain possessed, from folk customs to court etiquette, from blacksmithery to theology.

The emphasis in these remarks has been on continuity between Spain and Peru, on the degree to which an intact Spanish society was established in Peru. But there are many aspects of Spanish Peruvian society as seen in itself that call for comment, and some of these may be discussed briefly, without any attempt to be exhaustive.

Spanish Peruvian society, far more even than its parent, was urban-centered. There was much travel about the country, but the only Spaniards domiciled outside the cities were tribute collectors, miners, and doctrineros who instructed the Indians in the faith. All three types enjoyed but low esteem, and were for the most part involuntary exiles from the cities.

The real builders of Spanish Peru, therefore, were the people who, living on a long-term basis in one city and taking an interest in local affairs, provided continuity and stability, thickening and strengthening the web of social organization. The most important groups in this respect were the encomenderos, the artisans, the Spanish women, and the Negroes. Encomenderos as a group included both men of civic virtue and pugnacious wastrels, but in any case their positions were irrevocably situated in the cities to whose jurisdiction their encomiendas belonged, and their social prestige depended to a large extent on the size and splendor of the household they maintained there. Artisans were tied to one place by the nature of their practice; that their activity was constructive in the most literal sense is unnecessary to say. Spanish women were of all the groups the most closely bound to a single community. They usually lived out their lives in one town or indeed in one house, hardly ever returning to Spain. Despite the absence or death of their husbands they maintained their households, instructing servants, slaves, and children in Spanish ways. Negro slaves were willy-nilly an important part of the growing civil population because of the work they were pushed into—personal service, agriculture, and artisanry—but they adapted well to their tasks and, displaying surprising industry, came, whether as slaves or freedmen, to dominate humble, useful fields of endeavor abandoned to them by the Spaniards.

Merchants, on the other hand, though they were peaceful, substantial, and of great importance on a country-wide scale, played a small role in the individual communities; they were reluctant to identify themselves closely with any one town, or invest in real property, because their way of business kept them constantly traveling, and as parts of far-flung networks, they hoped for promotion from Arequipa to Lima, or from Lima to Seville, rather than for local prominence. Ecclesiastics in the main were as itinerant as the merchants, except for the dignitaries of the cathedral chapters and the two or three senior friars rotating in the priorate of each monastery who were sedentary and built up community relationships. The rest of the professional class —lawyers, doctors and notaries—showed no marked tendency as a group, but took root or failed to do so according to the individual case. In general, though, they lacked any strong structural tie to the individual community, and even the notaries public, who had such a tie, tended to move or return to Spain after a certain number of years of service.

This whole urban civilization of the deeply rooted and the semi-rooted was overlaid, and in certain times and places almost submerged, by a large turbulent population of floaters and pretenders, who, however, could generally be in some manner absorbed by the hospitality, either temporary or permanent, of the encomenderos, and the numerous entradas, the expeditions of discovery and conquest.

The only Spanish class which contributed really almost nothing, as a functioning group, to Spanish Peruvian society, were the peasants. This is not to say, of course, that none of the settlers were peasants, for we may be sure that a large, though undeterminable, proportion were of peasant origin. Moreover, Spanish plants, animals, and agricultural techniques were quickly transferred to Peru, so that in a sense the agricultural sector was not lost. Yet working directly with the land almost disappeared as an activity for Spaniards; even those who were skilled gardeners and labradors or agriculturalists were more supervisors of Negro and Indian labor than workers themselves.

Though the flood of immigration into Peru came, as was emphasized above, from all over greater Castile, the regions did not contribute quite so equally to the skilled and sedentary elements which were so important to Peru's development. Andalusia figured even larger than usual in all the groups with special skills, whether artisans, merchants, churchmen, notaries or sailors, while in these departments Extremadura's contribution fell to relative insignificance, faithfully reflecting that region's backwardness in Spain. Conversely, Extramadurans were apparently more than usually prominent in the turbulent, idle, or unskilled population. It would not be right to say, however, that Extremadura sent the "soldiers" and the rest of Spain the "civilians." Wherever there is opportunity to analyse the regional origins of an army or an expedition, the pattern is found to be quite normal, with Andalusia the largest group, even in the rebel army of Trujillan Gonzalo Pizarro. Nor were the Extremadurans necessarily the most valiant; Pedro Pizarro's list of the young men who did most at the siege of Cuzco shows a normal distribution. Still, Francisco Pizarro and Pedro de Valdivia were from Extremadura, and so were most of the finest military leaders in Peru, the hard-headed, cruel, efficient men who won battles. In this sense it may be said that Extremadurans fought and others settled the country.

While the Spanish social distinctions based on birth and calling were retained almost intact in Peru, two new important organizing principles were introduced: seniority in the conquest and the encomienda. The magic of association with the nation-founding events transformed the often humble men who took part in them into a dominant group, and from this start seniority gradually became a positive characteristic which could compensate for the lack of other qualities not only for the actual first conquerors, but for everyone who was in Peru in the early period. After a time even those who were on the losing side of the early civil war battles acquired prestige, and the representatives of artisans and freed Negroes were chosen on the basis of longest residence in Peru.

An even more basic new criterion independent of the Spanish distinctions was the encomienda. Peru was organized first into municipal jurisdictions and then into great county-sized encomiendas. Anyone who possessed one of these was by that fact alone in the very top rank of Peruvian society, and anyone without one was not, whatever his Spanish social rank at birth. As time went on, new encomienda grants came to be given more and more to those who were wellborn in Spain, so that the old criteria and the new coincided to a certain extent, but there still remained many of the plebeian encomenderos from the earliest time.

The encomienda system gave scope for a very full development of the seigneurial ideal in Peru. That ideal was already common to all Spaniards, but encomenderos in Peru could live as lords and be the center of all things to an extent impossible to all but dukes and counts in Spain. They were the principal customers of artisans and merchants; their lands and livestock fed the cities; their Indians worked the mines; their followings of relatives, guests, servants, employees, and Negro slaves made them the leaders of independent bands of men; in their large compound city houses were not only their residences, but stores, shops, and the dwellings of a good part of the population, over all of whom the encomenderos wielded a patriarchal influence.

But all these types of organization did not suffice. The newly settled Spanish inhabitants of Peru, mostly arriving as individuals and strangers to one another, sought out and emphasized all available principles of cohesion. The bonds of professional groups were very strong, each calling, from tailor to lawyer, forming a community and a spontaneous network throughout the country. The Spanish regions functioned in the same way, and were of even more basic importance in determining people's actions and associations. (It is noteworthy that the important groupings in this respect were not the large regional entities such as Extremadura and Andalusia, of which the settlers were hardly aware, but the subjectively felt smaller communities, like Badajoz or Huelva.) The settlers also seized upon the cofradías and the compadre relationship, both to reinforce existing ties and to make new ones. Gradually the new Spanish Peruvian communities themselves became capable of generating cohesiveness; in some civil war battles the encomenderos of each Peruvian town formed a separate company of horse. By 1560 each community had intermarried extensively, and there were significant intra-Peruvian regional differences.

A striking characteristic of the Spanish occupation of Peru was the lavish use made of semi-acculturated auxiliaries, in the first instance of Indians from Nicaragua and then increasingly of Negro slaves, who by the end of the period must have been at least as numerous as Spaniards. Uprooted from their own cultures, yet energetic and adaptable, the Negroes rapidly became Hispanized and served Spanish Peru in a hundred useful functions. Intermediary between the Spanish and the Indian populations, they greatly increased the rate of acculturation of the Indians, and by in effect doubling the number of the Spaniards, made the occupation much more dense and thorough in nature than it could have been without them.

In its ensemble, Peru during the first thirty years of Spanish rule presented a singular spectacle of complexity. Strongly concentrated in the cities, with outliers in the countryside, was a population of from

five to ten thousand Spaniards, constituting a coherent society or settlement colony in themselves. Beneath them was an auxiliary population
of about the same size, consisting of foreign slaves assimilated to Spanish culture. And beneath these was the great Indian mass, acted on by
the others. It is not much exaggeration to say that Peru was a settlement colony inside a plantation colony inside an administration colony.
Only South Africa with its whites, coloreds, and Negroes offers a ready
parallel. Social status in a country organized in this fashion has a very
ambiguous quality. The Negroes were at the bottom of the Hispanic
world, but in a position of power compared to the Indians. The Spanish lower classes all had Negro and Indian servants who called them
"señor" and waited on them hand and foot, but this does not mean that
they had gained anything in the still intact Spanish society where their
superiors continued to treat them as in Spain. Another fruit of the peculiar Peruvian structure was the distinct separation of the society from
the more basic aspects of the economy. While the cities teemed with
Spanish life, the activities which made this flourishing possible went on
in distant mining camps and encomiendas.

It would be premature to compare Peru with most other Spanish settlements, but research for the present study brought to light some
significant differences between Peru and contiguous areas. The Peru
which has been treated here is central Peru, the heir of the Inca empire, characterized by precocious civil development, conservative retention of Spanish social distinctions, and organization around the encomienda system. In the poorer fringe areas around Peru like Puertoviejo or Chachapoyas (even though they were part of the same administrative setup) the situation was different. The encomiendas, often too
poor to support their recipients, were far from all-important, and society was more rudimentary and more democratic, encomendero status
and municipal office being accessible to people quite low on the Spanish social scale. The province of Chile was midway between Peru and
the poor fringe areas in these respects; encomiendas were important,
but went to foreigners and others who were not eligible in Peru. Panama stood apart as an area completely dominated by merchants trading
with Peru, who in addition to directing commerce, practically monopolized the town councils, in contrast to Peru, where hardly a single full-
fledged merchant had gained entry to any town council by 1560. Even
within central Peru itself there were significant differences. The coast
and particularly Lima experienced the strongest civil development,

and Upper Peru from Cuzco to Potosí was most affected by vagrancy and turbulence.

What are the implications of the present study for the field of Spanish American history? The discovery of a series of complex social and economic developments in Peru immediately arouses curiosity about Peru's great sister colony, Mexico. The peculiarities of Peru, its internal diversity, and its rate of change within a thirty-year period serve as warnings against a facile generalization of conclusions drawn from the Peruvian experience. Yet there can be hardly any doubt that Mexico's path was roughly analogous. At any rate, the social history of Mexico's conquest period cries out for investigation. Both differences and similarities with Peru should prove instructive. Since Mexico was closer to Spain, was well governed, and did not suffer an extended period of civil wars, that country presumably should prove to have had an even stronger civil development than Peru. But though apparently a logical, this is not a foregone conclusion. The motor of Peru's development was an immense wealth in precious metals not then matched in Mexico, and in many ways Peru throve more because of than in spite of its civil wars.

Likely subjects for further research do not stop with conquest Mexico. Certainly research, at as deep a level as possible beneath the political surface, on the social and economic state of Peru and Mexico in the later sixteenth century, the mid-seventeenth century or the early eighteenth century would reveal each time a whole new picture of complexity and change. The need to get beyond politics cannot be emphasized more urgently than by the case of Peru, where a nation was founded while no one was looking, during twenty-five years of unmitigated political disaster.

An important task of research is to separate the permanent from the transient. By 1540, for example, highland encomenderos were beginning to turn over their affairs to managers and spend much of their time in Lima, a lasting pattern, for the owners of haciendas still do the same. Other things change quickly; in the Caribbean phase of the conquest, the Spanish ethnic stock was overwhelmingly Andalusian; by the time of the conquest of Peru, less so. In the Caribbean, Basque, North Spanish, and Italian merchants were predominant; in Peru, Andalusian merchants took over. There are some things that can be expected to change constantly, while other aspects remain unaltered. Not until the long strands are separated from the short will it be possible to construct a concise yet realistic picture of the colonial period.

A severe handicap to the social history of the Spanish Indies is the lack of works on the social history of Spain. The rate of change between Spain and the Indies is of great interest, but cannot be calculated as long as Spain is a relative unknown. At times the Indies can serve as a good mirror for Spain; regional rivalries and differences, for example, are readily visible in the Indies where the various groups came into close contact. But in general one must fervently hope for more work like that (unpublished at this writing) of Vicenta Cortés and Ruth Pike in the Spanish notarial archives, establishing the prevalence of Negro slavery in southern Spain. And if historians want to find out the specific details of the kinds of people that came to the Indies, there is no other place to search than in the Spanish notarial archives.

The great task, for the present, would seem to be simply to find out what went on in the Spanish colonies, to explore in the notarial archives, trial records, and any other sources that do not have the character of official reports, and construct broad factual syntheses; the abstraction necessary for schematic interpretation or for universal history should come only later. Comparing the detailed picture available of the English settlements with the foggy notion we have of the Spanish settlements is as likely to lead to false results as comparing a photograph of one man with a painting of another.

Social and economic history aside, another necessary undertaking will be to revise the narrative history of the conquest and, in Peru, of the civil wars. One simply cannot appreciate those events properly by imagining them as the actions of a few soldiers rattling around in an empty country. Furthermore, most histories, following Prescott and the later chronicles, are full of unseparated fact and fancy. The standard accounts of the more heroic exploits of the Spaniards in Peru not only come from chronicles rather than documents, but from late chronicles like those of Garcilaso and Montesinos rather than from contemporary ones (which though one-sided are simple and truthful). Oral traditions well over fifty years old were recast by the seventeenth-century chroniclers into set speeches and other rhetorical conventions of historical writing in the Greek tradition, and the results have sometimes been mistaken for factual accounts.

Raúl Porras Barrenechea has already convincingly shown that the famous tripartite pact of Pizarro, Almagro, and Luque was an invention.[4] But that is only the beginning. All the heroic episodes of early Peruvian history are still known to us in mythical versions which it will be well to modify in the direction of truth as far as that is possible, not only because of the general duty to truth, but because the real greatness of the Spanish conquerors emerges more clearly when their deeds are plainly told. It now appears that the commonly repeated version of Peruvian history's most famous episode, Francisco Pizarro's speech to the thirteen who stayed with him on the isle of Gallo, is badly garbled. None of the early accounts say anything about a sword or drawing a line, and in Cieza's simple and short version of the speech, taken from an eyewitness, Pizarro simply reminds his followers that he has shared all their hardships, and warns them that they will starve in any case if they return to Panama.[5] To those who know Francisco Pizarro, this rings much truer than the traditionally reported grandiloquence and arm waving. Peru was conquered by hard-bitten, taciturn Spartans, not by glib Athenians, and the conquerors were men so automatically valiant that they literally gave no thought to death, but obliviously continued business as usual in the face of it, trading horses and making commercial agreements in the midst of the most extreme dangers.

The deeds of the Spaniards may in the end be as unique as Prescott thought they were; but in a more subtle way. The Spanish conquest is comparable to the Arab conquest; the Spanish Peru of the cities to the English settlements; and other aspects of the Peruvian colony to administrative colonies all over the world. The settlers of Peru had much in common with settlers of other times and places. If a man did well, he sent for his brothers, then perhaps for female relatives and others from his home town. People came looking for opportunities in general, often meaning to strike it rich quickly and return home, but usually in the end spent their whole lives in the new country, or only returned to live out their retirement. Spanish Peru had mining booms, it was a melting pot of regions and nationalities. In these and many other ways it fits into the general history of colonization and settlement, as future historians of the conquest will certainly take into account.

As the last third of the twentieth century begins, Spanish American colonial history needs studies that will tread the middle ground between the older tradition of institutional and narrative history and the newer generalizing approach of the social sciences, for which the field is not now and long will not be ripe. But whatever kinds of studies are made, they can profit from an awareness of the social context in which men, ideas, and institutions had to function and in which they must be understood.

REFERENCE
MATTER

APPENDIX

TABLES

Following are statistical totals of some lists assembled by keeping all relevant references from all sources used in the course of research for the present study. There is no space here for extensive discussion of the methods employed, but the bare essentials may be explained. While the absolute numbers involved are much smaller than in the *Pasajeros a Indias,* these lists have two advantages over lists taken from the permits issued at Seville: first, the wide variety of sources used means that a correspondingly wide variety of people, many of whom never received permits, are included; second, all the people listed here actually came to Peru, as opposed to many people with permits who went somewhere else, died on the way, or never left Spain.

As to the actual criteria for inclusion in the lists, on the Peruvian end mere physical presence in Peru in the time from discovery through 1560 was deemed sufficient. For the lists of regional origins, Peru was stretched to take in Chile, since all who were in Chile must have passed through Peru, and it seemed advisable to get as large a sampling as possible. The list of artisans, however, in which absolute numbers are more important, was restricted to Greater Peru proper. On the Spanish end, an individual was considered connected with a Spanish place if he was *natural* (native or born there); "from" there, when the indication did not form part of his name; a *vecino* or citizen there; and also if his brother or father fitted any of these categories. Of these criteria, only the inclusion of vecinos calls for comment. Citizenship in a town need not imply regional identification, but in the course of research the vecino category proved so often to overlap with the others (with no known exceptions outside of Seville) that it was included. Seville, then Spain's fastest growing city, goal of migration from all over Spain, and no more than nominal base for many merchants, is a special case. Where statistically significant, the category "vecinos of Seville" has been used, to take into account the fact that people about whom nothing more is known than their status as vecino of Seville may have come from anywhere in Spain, with only formal roots in Seville; yet it is probable that over half even of this group were true Andalusians, and others were in the process of becoming so.

To organize the data on regional origins, it was necessary to have recourse to the crude method of using as units the regions of Spain in terms of twentieth-century provinces. No works of reference are presently available which would allow one to place given villages reliably in their sixteenth-century political units, and some of those political units did not themselves fit well into regions. Despite some anomalies, such as the fact that Fregenal, then in the jurisdiction of Seville, must be counted with Extremadura, use of the modern regions should not lead to major distortions, if it is only realized that to the Spaniard of the sixteenth century the important unit was the small municipality, not the larger region, which is mainly a unit of intellectual convenience.

Foreigners, often illiterate and in marginal occupations, had much less frequent occasion than Spaniards to state formally where they were from. Yet their names stand out in the records, and advantage was taken of this fact to assemble a list of foreigners in Peru. The results are not scientific; wherever a foreign name came together with surroundings and occupations typical of foreigners, that name was included. But there is little real doubt; the repertory of Spanish names in the sixteenth century was extremely restricted and conventional. If some half-foreigners, people of foreign parentage born in Spain, were inadvertently included in the list, their presence is probably more than made up for by the absence of scores of true foreigners hiding behind such a name as "Juan Griego."

Foreign-sounding names, however, forsake the researcher when it comes to the largest foreign group, the Portuguese. As transcribed by Spanish notaries, most Portuguese names are indistinguishable from Spanish names. In this situation it was decided not to take advantage of those Portuguese who could be distinguished by name only, but to include only those who could qualify as Portuguese under the same criteria used for Spaniards, so that the resultant figure could be compared with the master origins list of Spaniards, and the Portuguese could be considered as one of the Spanish regional groups, which in one sense they were. If everyone in some way recognizable as Portuguese had been counted, the Portuguese would easily have been more numerous than all of the Mediterraneans put together, and the total of the list of foreigners would have been correspondingly larger.

TABLE 1 REGIONAL ORIGINS OF SPANIARDS
IN PERU, 1532–60

PLACE OF ORIGIN	NUMBER OF SPANIARDS
Andalusia	877
Vecinos of Seville[a]	116
Extremadura	603
Old Castile	532
New Castile	486
Leon	270
Biscay	221
Aragon	71
Galicia	27
Canaries	20
Murcia	19
Navarre	16
Indies	12
Asturias	2
Total	3272[b]

[a] See above, p. 237.

[b] A list of Portuguese compiled using the same criteria reached a total of 171, less than Biscay but more than Aragon.

TABLE 2 REGIONAL ORIGINS OF SPANIARDS[a] IN PERU, 1532–60, BY OCCUPATION OR STATUS[b]

PLACE OF ORIGIN	ECCLESIASTICS	ECCLESIASTICS WITH ACADEMIC TITLES	TITLED LAWYERS AND PHYSICIANS	NOTARIES	MERCHANTS	ARTISANS	SEAMEN	WOMEN
Andalusia	41	8	14	31	54[c]	32	46	36
Extremadura	24	1	11	12	12	11	0	27
Leon	12	1	8	7	2	10	0	10
New Castile	19	3	11	17	20	14	0	17
Old Castile	22	7	16	18	16	17	2[d]	18
Aragon	1	0	0	0	7	4	1	2
Asturias	0	0	0	0	0	0	2	0
Biscay	6	0	1	14	12	6	12	2
Canaries	1	0	0	1	0	2	0	0
Galicia	0	0	1	0	0	0	1	0
Indies	0	0	0	1	1	0	0	7[e]
Murcia	1	0	0	0	0	0	1	1
Navarre	1	0	0	0	1	2	0	0
Portugal	1	0	0	0	0	0	21	2
Totals	128	20	62	101	125	98	86	122

[a] Including Portuguese.

[b] This table is compiled from the same master origins list that forms the basis of Table 1. The numbers therefore have significance only relative to each other, and not absolutely.

[c] Of these, 16 were only vecinos of Seville. See above, p. 237.

[d] 1 inland, 1 coastal.

[e] All from Hispaniola.

TABLE 3 APPARENT ORIGINS OF SHIPMASTERS AND
PILOTS IN PERU, 1532-60[a]

Fully Spanish and apparently Spanish	156
Basque	36
Catalan	5
Portuguese	25
Other foreign	67
	—
Total	289

[a] These totals are completely independent of the list on which Tables 1 and 2 are based. The totals have more significance for their absolute numbers, and origins were assigned by rough commonsense criteria, mainly the appearance of the names. There is no doubt that many of the apparently Spanish masters were actually Portuguese. See above, p. 238.

TABLE 4 FOREIGNERS IN PERU, 1532-60[a]

PORTUGAL			171[b]
MEDITERRANEAN	Italy		
	Genoa	59	
	Naples	21	
	Savoy	15	
	Venice	14	
	Milan	10	
	Florence	2	
	Italy (not further identified)	36	
		157	
	Greece	52	
	Corsica	23	
	Slavonia	5	
	Sardinia	3	
			240
NORTH AND CENTRAL EUROPE	Netherlands	43	
	Germany	7	
	Hungary	7	
	Burgundy	2	
			59
ENGLAND AND FRANCE	Ireland	3	
	England	2	
	France	2	
			7
UNIDENTIFIED FOREIGNERS			39
TOTAL NUMBER OF FOREIGNERS			516

[a] This listing is independent of the others. See above, p. 238.

[b] See above, p. 238, for explanation of the principles by which the Portuguese were identified. Despite these figures, they were actually the largest group.

TABLE 5 ARTISANS IN PERU, 1532–60[a]

Clothing trades	Tailors (and hosiers, sederos, hat-makers, etc.)	154	
	Shoemakers (and saddlers)	80	
			234
Ironworkers	Smiths (including swordsmiths, lock-smiths, etc.)	104	
	Herradors or farriers	43	
			147
Construction trades	Carpenters	102	
	Masons	33	
			135
Silversmiths			70
Muleteers			47
Barber-surgeons			36
Pharmacists			25
Confectioners and bakers			24
Musicians and instrument makers			20
Artillerymen and powder manufacturers			15
Carters			9
Gardeners			9
Candlemakers			9
Miscellaneous			44
Total number of artisans			824

[a] This listing is independent of the others. See above, p. 237.

NOTES

A word may be said about the use of references in the present study. Since there is more reliance on direct evidence than on reports, substantiating references are very numerous, and despite great care, may occasionally be in error. But the fact that a single reference in a given note has no apparent relevance to the matter at hand does not necessarily mean that it is a mistake. Many of the notes yield their full sense only with the assembly of all the individual elements, drawn perhaps from archives on three continents and publications rarer than documents. The full potential of the notes will be realized only by those who can consult all the sources in the course of full-time work on related subjects, and while they are designed as the fullest possible substantiation of the text, their greatest usefulness may be as leads for future research. To facilitate such use (and in order to avoid turning the text into an impenetrable forest), in most parts of the study notes are placed only at the ends of paragraphs or short sections, giving the totality of references for that subject matter in one location and in some order.

ABBREVIATIONS

AGI	Archivo General de Indias, Seville.
AHA	Archivo Histórico de Arequipa.
AHC	Archivo Histórico Nacional del Cuzco
ANP	Archivo Nacional del Perú, Lima.
APS	Archivo de Protocolos, Seville.
BNP	Biblioteca Nacional del Perú, Lima.
CDIAO	*Colección de documentos inéditos relativos al descubrimiento, conquista y colonización de las posesiones españolas en América y Oceanía.*
CDIHE	*Colección de documentos inéditos para la historia de España.*
HC	Harkness Collection, Library of Congress.
Juzgado	Libro del Juzgado de la ciudad de Los Reyes, 1535–37, in ANP.
PA	The "Protocolo Ambulante," a collection of notarial documents issued in various parts of Peru in the years 1533–37, in ANP.

RANP   *Revista del Archivo Nacional del Perú.*
RA PC   Real Audiencia, Procedimientos Civiles, a section in ANP.
RA PP   Real Audiencia, Procedimientos Penales, a section in ANP.

A proper name following AHA, AHC, or ANP denotes the register of a notary of that name, contained in that archive. A number following the name denotes the year or years of the register, where that is necessary for identification. All archival sources are cited first in order in the notes. In dates given, the first two digits of the year are omitted and are understood to be 15–. Many of the documents used had neither foliation nor date, but where possible the number of the folio (f.) is given, or failing that, the date of the document.
Full publication details on all books cited are given in the Bibliography.

I. INTRODUCTION

1. For some statements of the view that little colonization took place in Peru before Toledo, see William Lytle Schurz, *This New World*, 139–40; Juan Pérez de Tudela, *Crónicas del Perú*, lxxv; Guillermo Lohmann Villena, *El corregidor de indios*, 4; George Kubler, "The Neo-Inca State," *Hispanic American Historical Review*, XXVII (1947), 189; Rubén Vargas Ugarte, S. J., *Historia del Perú: Virreinato*, 15. For some statements of the importance of peaceful social and economic development during the Spanish conquests generally, see Edward Gaylord Bourne, *Spain in America 1450–1580*, 190–201; C. H. Haring, *The Spanish Empire in America*, 206; Richard Konetzke, "La emigración de las mujeres españolas a América durante la época colonial," *Revista Internacional de Sociología*, III (1945), 123–50; Bailey W. Diffie, *Latin American Civilization: Colonial Period*, 54. Of these, Diffie specifically points to the precocious economic development of Peru
2. *Libros de cabildos de Lima*, VI/1, 338, 381, 424, 428, 438.

II. ENCOMENDEROS AND MAJORDOMOS

1. J. H. Parry, *The Establishment of the European Hegemony: 1415–1715*, 68.
2. Appendix III of Diego Fernández, *Historia del Perú*, II, 124; José Toribio Medina, ed., *Colección de documentos inéditos para la historia de Chile*, VII, 84; Roberto Levillier, ed., *Gobernantes del Perú*, I. 252.
3. AGI, Patronato 93, no. 8, ramo 1; Juan Pérez de Tudela, ed., *Documentos relativos a don Pedro de la Gasca*, I, 415.
4. The synthetic account preceding this note is based mainly on hundreds of individual documentary passages which it would be both impossible and pointless to refer to in detail.
5. Medina, *Colección*, VIII, 422.
6. BNP, A555, f. 1; Raúl Porras Barrenechea, ed., *Cartas del Perú*, 465–68; Pedro Gutiérrez de Santa Clara, *Quinquenarios o historia de las guerras civiles del Perú*, III, 374; Víctor M. Barriga, ed., *Documentos para la historia de Arequipa*, III, 31–36, 136, 173–75, 184–88, 200–2, 221, 223,

226–29, 302–3; Gonzalo Fernández de Oviedo, *Historia general y natural de las Indias*, III, 77.

7. ANP, PA 229; *Libros de cabildos de Quito*, II², 348.

8. AGI, Justicia 467; Rafael Loredo, *Los Repartos*, 268, 293; *Colección de documentos inéditos relativos al descubrimiento, conquista y colonización de las posesiones españolas en América y Oceanía* (abbreviated as *CDIAO*), XX, 352.

9. ANP, Salinas 46–48, f. 578; Gutiérrez de Santa Clara, *Quinquenarios*, IV, 171.

10. AGI, Justicia 467; Patronato 98, no. 2, ramo 2.

11. ANP, Juzgado, 30 Dec 35.

12. HC 1441.

13. AGI, Patronato 98, no. 3, ramo 1; 93, no. 8, ramo 1.

14. Diego Fernández, *Historia del Perú*, I, 128.

15. AGI, Patronato 98, no. 3, ramo 1.

16. AGI, Justicia 1124, no. 6, ramo 7; BNP, A554; ANP, Castañeda, reg. 2, f. 30; PA 2, 178, 300, 301, 669, 783; Barriga, *Documentos*, I, 84–86, 107–9; Pérez de Tudela, *Gasca*, I, 196.

17. BNP, A510, ff. 438–41; A528, f. 984; A30, ff. 399–401; A538, 12 Aug 56; ANP, Salinas 38–40, ff. 54, 145, 445, 484; Salinas 46–48, ff. 306, 407; Castañeda, reg. 4, f. 37; PA 504; AHA, Gaspar Hernández, 18 June 51; Barriga, *Documentos*, I, 110; Porras, *Cartas del Perú*, 332; *Libros de cabildos de Lima*, V, 660.

18. ANP, Salinas 46–48, f. 264; BNP, A153, f. 42; A30, f. 399; AGI, Patronato 101, ramo 19; 113, ramo 1; Barriga, *Documentos*, II, 109; Pérez de Tudela, *Gasca*, II, 159.

19. ANP, Gutiérrez 45–55, f. 241; AGI, Justicia 425, no. 13; Pérez de Tudela, *Gasca*, II, 230, 542; Diego Fernández, *Historia del Perú*, I, 180, 369–70; Gutiérrez de Santa Clara, *Quinquenarios*, III, 96; Pedro de Cieza de León, *Guerra de Chupas*, 145; Juan Cristóbal Calvete de Estrella, *Rebelión de Pizarro*, V, 23, 48.

20. Pérez de Tudela, *Gasca*, I, 509–11.

21. AHC, Vitorero, 16 Nov 59; ANP, RA PP, I, trial of Diego de Mendoza Carrillo, ff. 30–33; E. Pérez 57, f. 1961; AGI, Lima 204, probanza of doña Lucía de Padilla; Contratación 198, ramo 16.

22. BNP, A398; A32, f. 107; A35, f. 538; A31, f. 455; ANP, E. Pérez 57, f. 1961; Salinas 38–40, ff. 312, 601; Salinas 46–48, f. 825; Gutiérrez 45–55, f. 827; Alzate, f. 820; AHC, Vitorero, 16 Nov 59.

23. AHC, Libros de cabildos, I, f. 190; AHA, García Muñoz, 19 Oct, 25 Oct, 26 Oct, 8 Nov 57; ANP, Martel 55–58, f. 431; Salinas 46–48, ff. 134, 934; BNP, A525, f. 844; A33, f. 156; AGI, Patronato 116, no. 2, ramo 4; Garcilaso de la Vega, *Obras completas*, II, 366; IV, 102.

24. ANP, Salinas 42–43, f. 314; Pérez de Tudela, *Gasca*, I, 266, 368; Barriga, *Documentos*, II, 105.

25. AGI, Lima 92, letter of Audiencia, 10 June 51; Pérez de Tudela,

Gasca, I, 447, 453; *Libros de cabildos de Quito, passim;* "Libro de cabildos de Chachapoyas," ed. by Raúl Rivera Serna, in *Fénix,* XII (1956–57), 329.
26. ANP, Salinas 42–43, f. 61; Salinas 46–48, f. 806; BNP, A591, f. 387; Barriga, *Documentos,* II, 101–3.
27. AGI, Patronato 114, ramo 1.
28. AHA, Valdecabras, 8 June 51; BNP, A33, f. 279.
29. ANP, Salinas 38–40, f. 425; Salinas 42–43, f. 314; AHC, Vitorero, Sept-Nov 60; Gutiérrez de Santa Clara, *Quinquenarios,* III, 176; Barriga, *Documentos,* II, 105; Rolando Mellafe, *La introducción de la esclavitud negra en Chile,* 257.
30. ANP, Salinas 46–48, f. 1157; Alzate, ff. 398, 406, 758; PA 272; BNP, A542, ff. 29, 30, 202; AGI, Contaduría 1683.
31. AGI, Contaduría 1680; Justicia 401, 402; Patronato 110, ramo 2; 95, no. 1, ramo 1; Lima 118, letter of Pedro Rodríguez Puertocarrero, 30 Sept 57; letter of Lucas Martín Vegaso, 9 Dec 55; Lima 567, vol VII, 16 Sept 51; Lima 92, letter of Fray Pedro de Toro, 18 Dec 53; letter of Villegas and the cabildo of Arequipa, 18 Dec 53; Lima 119, probanza of Hernando de Santillán; BNP, A510, f. 458; A32, ff. 98, 102; A33, ff. 277, 297, 298, 304; AIIA, Valdecabras, 9 March 51, 5 Oct 52, 9 June 53, 27 Nov 54, 1 Dec 54; Cerón, 7 Apr 49, 17 July 49; Gaspar Hernández, 16 March, 22 March 53, 4 Apr, 17 Apr, 22 Apr 53, 2 May, 3 May, 16 May, 31 May 53; HC 456; Barriga, *Documentos,* III, 67–101, 123–27, 310; II, 244; *CDIAO,* XXV, 244–302; Gutiérrez de Santa Clara, *Quinquenarios,* II, 310; IV, 129; Pérez de Tudela, *Gasca,* I, 448; Enrique Otte, "La flota de Colón," *Revista de Indias,* XXIV (1964), 480; Cieza, *Chupas,* 289; Cieza, *Tercero libro de las guerras civiles del Perú, el cual se llama la Guerra de Quito,* ed. by Jiménez de la Espada, 152.

III. NOBLEMEN

1. AGI, Patronato 116, no. 1, ramo 1.
2. Oviedo, *Historia,* V, 227.
3. R. Cúneo Vidal, *Francisco Pizarro,* 98; Miguel Muñoz de San Pedro, "Doña Isabel de Vargas, esposa del padre del conquistador del Perú," *Revista de Indias,* XI (1951), 27.
4. BNP, A35, f. 395; Tomás Thayer Ojeda, *Formación de la sociedad chilena,* I, 121; III, 355.
5. Pérez de Tudela, *Gasca,* I, 431, 435, 469.
6. Thayer, *Formación,* III, 94.
7. ANP, PA 712; Salinas 38–40, 16 Dec 38; Salinas 46–48, f. 886; BNP, A510, f. 427; AGI, Patronato 94, no. 1, ramo 2.
8. AHA, Valdecabras, 17 July 51; AGI, Patronato 92, no. 3; Cieza, *Chupas,* 97.
9. AGI, Patronato 110, ramo 7; 112, ramo 2; HC 740.
10. ANP, E. Pérez 57, f. 1977.
11. Don Alonso Enríquez de Guzmán, *Vida y costumbres,* 127, 148,

and *passim;* Raúl Porras Barrenechea, *Los Cronistas del Perú (1528–1650)*, 122.

12. AGI, Lima 92; Contaduría 1680; Lima 566, vol VI, 22 May 49; Garcilaso, *Obras*, IV, 76; Thayer, *Formación*, I, 121; don Pedro Mariño de Lobera, *Crónica del reino de Chile*, 323.

13. AGI, Patronato 98, no. 4, ramo 1; Lima 119, petition of Hernán Mejía de Guzmán; Garcilaso, *Obras*, IV, 74.

14. Portocarrero: ANP, RA PC, I, cuaderno 3; Martínez 49–53, f. 3; PA 603. Ribera: *Libros de cabildos de Lima*, V, 467; BNP, A31, f. 27. Sandoval: AGI, Lima 204, probanza of don Juan de Sandoval; Patronato 100, ramo 3.

15. AGI, Justicia 1082, no. 1, ramo 1; Justicia 487; Patronato 114, ramo 10; Diego Fernández, *Historia del Perú*, I, 286 ff.; Garcilaso, *Obras*, IV, 42; *Colección de documentos inéditos para la historia de España* (abbreviated *CDIHE*), XCIV, 142; Roberto Levillier, ed., *Audiencia de Lima*, 100.

16. ANP, Salinas 38–40, f. 123; Salinas 42–43, ff. 23, 25, 14a, 181, 183, 206; Salinas 46–48, f. 706; RA PC, I, cuaderno 3; AGI, Justicia 467; Oviedo, *Historia*, III, 262; Gutiérrez de Santa Clara, *Quinquenarios*, II, 173, 254.

17. AGI, Lima 566, vol V, 18 Aug 48; Patronato 102, ramo 5.

18. AGI, Patronato 110, ramo 11; Cieza, *Chupas*, 365.

19. Pérez de Tudela, *Gasca*, II, 303–18; Diego Fernández, *Historia del Perú*, I, 172.

20. ANP, Salinas 42–43, ff. 81, 174; BNP, A35, f. 361; A34, f. 80; Mariño de Lobera, *Crónica*, 283, 286; Gutiérrez de Santa Clara, *Quinquenarios*, II, 263, 267; Porras, *Cartas del Perú*, 346, 485; Diego Fernández, *Historia del Perú*, I, 39.

21. ANP, PA 466; Salinas 46–48, f. 579; Castañeda, reg. 4, f. 30; AHA, Gaspar Hernández, 19 Feb 49; BNP, A591, f. 394.

22. Garcilaso, *Obras*, III, 147, 207; IV, 69, 72, 74; Calvete, *Rebelión de Pizarro*, IV, 393.

23. AGI, Patronato 116, no. 1, ramo 1; 94, no. 1, ramo 2; Lima 119, letter of Gómez Arias, 31 Oct 59; José Armando de Ramón Folch, *Descubrimiento de Chile y compañeros de Almagro*, 144; Víctor M. Barriga, ed., *Los Mercedarios en el Perú en el siglo XVI*, II, 210; see also fn. 14.

IV. PROFESSIONALS

1. Oviedo, *Historia*, V, 181.

2. AGI, Lima 313, letters of Domingo de Santo Tomás, 1 July 50, 10 Dec 63; Porras, *Cartas del Perú*, 193, 313; Pérez de Tudela, *Gasca*, II, 297.

3. *CDIHE*, XCIV, 172.

4. AHA, Valdecabras, 3 June 51, 1 Dec 54; Barriga, *Documentos*, II, 206.

5. AGI, Patronato 101, ramo 19; *Libros de cabildos de Quito*, II, 314.

6. ANP, Salinas 42–43, f. 595; Salinas 46–48, f. 415; Alzate, f. 392;

Gutiérrez 45–55, f. 203; AHA, Valdecabras, 9 Nov 54; AGI, Patronato 97, no. 1, ramo 1; Pérez de Tudela, *Gasca*, I, 359.

7. ANP, E. Pérez 57, ff. 2016, 2017; AGI, Patronato 97, no. 1, ramo 1; 101, ramo 19; 97, no. 1, ramo 8; Pérez de Tudela, *Gasca*, II, 571; Barriga, *Mercedarios*, IV, 45.

8. BNP, A532, 1 Jan 57; *Libros de cabildos de Quito*, II², 73; Barriga, *Mercedarios*, II, 196.

9. AGI, Patronato 101, ramo 19; Lima 118; Contaduría 1824; Pérez de Tudela, *Gasca*, I, 249.

10. AGI, Contaduría 1679–83, 1784, 1824–25.

11. AGI, Patronato 101, ramo 19.

12. AGI, Contaduría 1680; BNP, A542, f. 604; Juan Meléndez, O. P., *Tesoros verdaderos de las Indias*, I, 126.

13. AGI, Lima 313, letter of Domingo de Santo Tomás, 1 July 50; Gutiérrez de Santa Clara, *Quinquenarios*, IV, 196.

14. Rubén Vargas Ugarte, S. J., *Historia de la iglesia en el Perú*, I, 127; Pérez de Tudela, *Gasca*, I, 249.

15. BNP, A203, f. 58; A528, f. 1011; AGI, Contaduría 1670.

16. ACI, Justicia 1126, no. 2, ramo 1; Indiferente General 1801; ANP, PA 44, 198, 659, 666, 727; Gutiérrez 45–55, f. 23; HC 67.

17. BNP, A556, ff. 14, 22, 40; A34, f. 29; A524; A542, f. 455; A35, f. 320; ANP, Salinas 42–43, ff. 125, 638; Salinas 46–48, ff. 218, 494; Gutiérrez 45–55, ff. 137, 495; AIIA, Cerón, 8 March 49; Gaspar Hernández, 3 June 51, 12 June 53.

18. ANP, Castañeda, reg. 5, f. 12; Martel 55–58, f. 289; Salinas 42–43, f. 166; Salinas 46–48, f. 256; Barriga, *Mercedarios*, II, 65.

19. Guillermo Céspedes del Castillo, "La sociedad colonial americana en los siglos XVI y XVII," 433; Fernando de Armas Medina, *Cristianización del Perú*, 32, 146–47.

20. ANP, Salinas 46–48, ff. 78, 461–64; BNP, A221, 28 Feb 60; AHC, Libros de cabildos, I, f. 76; Calvete, *Rebelión de Pizarro*, V, 58; Gutiérrez de Santa Clara, *Quinquenarios*, II, 164; Loredo, *Los Repartos, passim*.

21. ANP, Salinas 42–43, ff. 1, 302, 693; Salinas 46–48, ff. 511, 538, 789, 1003, 1088; Martel 55–58, f. 455; Gutiérrez 45–55, f. 160; BNP, A524, f. 692; A33, f. 240; A35, f. 245; AHC, Libros de cabildos, I, f. 123; AGI, Contaduría 1680; Barriga, *Mercedarios*, II, 127, 156, 191; Marcos Jiménez de la Espada, *Relaciones geográficas de Indias*, I, 196–99.

22. ANP, Martínez 49–53, f. 31; Salinas 38–40, f. 199; Salinas 42–43, 24 July 42; BNP, A35, ff. 245, 251, 513; A591, f. 375; A400, f. 915; AGI, Contaduría 1824; AHA, Cerón, 1549; Valdecabras, 10 March 51, 9 Nov 51; Calvete, *Rebelión de Pizarro*, IV, 393; Gutiérrez de Santa Clara, *Quinquenarios*, III, 5–6; Barriga, *Mercedarios*, I, 290; *Libros de cabildos de Quito*, II², 296; *Revista del Archivo Nacional del Perú* (abbreviated *RANP*), VII, 204.

23. AGI, Patronato 122, ramo 2; Lima 313; Antonio Calancha, *Corónica moralizada del orden de San Agustín*, 81, 140, 149.

24. BNP, A35, f. 298.

25. ANP, Gutiérrez 45–55, f. 541; "Libro de cabildos de Chachapoyas," ed. by Rivera Serna, in *Fénix*, XI (1955), 302.

26. ANP, Salinas 42–43, ff. 186, 611, 619; Salinas 46–48, f. 306; Gutiérrez 45–55, f. 83; AHA, Gaspar Hernández, 7 Oct 50; AGI, Patronato 109, ramo 5.

27. ANP, RA PP, I, trial of Pedro de Salinas; Salinas 46–48, f. 618; BNP, A35, f. 513; A222, f. 182; AGI, Lima 300, letter of Archbishop Loaysa, 9 March 51.

28. ANP, Salinas 42–43, f. 470; AGI, Patronato 101, ramo 16; HC 507; *CDIAO*, XX, 517; Calancha, *Corónica moralizada*, 200; Diego de Córdoba Salinas, *Crónica Franciscana de las provincias del Perú*, 293, 305, 692, 710.

29. ANP, Salinas 42–43, f. 303; BNP, A538, 30 Jan 53.

30. AGI, Contaduría 1680.

31. ANP, Salinas 38–40, f. 570; RA PP, I, trial of Pedro de Salinas; Porras, *Cartas del Perú*, 353; Oviedo, *Historia*, III, 226, 352; *Libros de cabildos de Lima*, III, 115; Cristóbal Bermúdez Plata, ed., *Catálogo de pasajeros a Indias*, II, 290.

32. Raúl Porras Barrenechea, ed., *Cedulario del Perú*, I, 50.

33. AGI, Patronato 109, ramo 3; ANP, Gutiérrez 45–55, f. 416; Oviedo, *Historia*, II, 106–7, 208; III, 352; Calvete, *Rebelión de Pizarro*, V, 33, 74; Porras, *Cartas del Perú*, 225.

34. ANP, E. Pérez 57, f. 1924; Gutiérrez 45–55, f. 763; Salinas 42–43, ff. 115, 116, 256; AGI, Patronato 187, ramo 15; Lima 566, vol IV, 11 Aug 40; Porras, *Cartas del Perú*, 334; Calvete, *Rebelión de Pizarro*, IV, 247, 328; Pedro Pizarro, *Descubrimiento y conquista de los reinos del Perú*, V, 229; Garcilaso, *Obras*, IV, 22–25; Cieza, *Chupas*, 119; *Libros de cabildos de Lima*, I, *passim*.

35. Calvete, *Rebelión de Pizarro*, IV, 386; Gutiérrez de Santa Clara, *Quinquenarios*, IV, 161, 162; Francisco López de Gómara, *Hispania victrix*, I, 272; Agustín de Zárate, *Historia del descubrimiento y conquista de la provincia del Perú*, II, 503.

36. AGI, Lima 92, letter of Audiencia, March 60; Justicia 1124, no. 5, ramo 3; 1082, no. 3, ramo 3; Lima 566, vol VI, 27 Feb 49; Diego Fernández, *Historia del Perú* (appendix), II, 109; Gutiérrez de Santa Clara, *Quinquenarios*, IV, 155; Calvete, *Rebelión de Pizarro*, V, 87; Garcilaso, *Obras*, IV, 78; Zárate, *Historia*, Diego Fernández, *Historia del Perú, passim*; José Antonio del Busto Duthurburu, *El Conde de Nieva*, 168–210.

37. AGI, Patronato 99, no. 1, ramo 7; AHA, Valdecabras, 17 July 51; HC 788; Barriga, *Documentos*, I, 301.

38. AGI, Contaduría 1824; BNP, A31, f. 5; Calvete, *Rebelión de Pizarro*, V, 73–74; *Libros de cabildos de Lima*, III, 13.

39. ANP, Salinas 38–40, ff. 4, 7, 11, 81, 82, 242, 246, 321; Salinas 42–43, f. 693; PA 235, 492, 619; Oviedo, *Historia*, I, 171; V, 222, and *passim*.

40. AGI, Contaduría 1824; *Libros de cabildos de Lima,* IV, 516; Oviedo, *Historia,* Calvete, *Rebelión de Pizarro, passim.*

41. ANP, Salinas 42–43, ff. 37, 257; Salinas 46–48, ff. 793, 1032; Alzate, ff. 725, 924; Gutiérrez 45–55, f. 535; BNP, A538; A400, f. 913; A221, 8 June 60; AGI, Patronato 132, no. 2, ramo 1; HC 676, 677, 1446; *Libros de cabildos de Lima,* IV, 535–38; V, 122–23; VI/1, 338.

42. AGI, Lima 177, the series of notaries' *probanzas* that makes up the bulk of that legajo; Justicia 1057; Patronato 120, no. 1, ramo 3; 93, no. 9, ramo 1; 110, ramo 1; ANP, Salinas 46–48, f. 594; Alzate, f. 705; BNP, A34, f. 47; AHA, Valdecabras, 4 Aug 53; *CDIAO,* XX, 378.

43. AGI, Lima 566, vol VI, 27 June 50; *Libros de cabildos de Lima,* III, 97; V, 672.

44. ANP, Salinas 38–40, *passim;* Alzate, f. 843; BNP, A34, *passim;* A36, f. 230; AHA, Gaspar Hernández, 5 Aug 50; Cerón, 5 Jan 49; AGI, Lima 177; *Libros de cabildos de Lima,* V, 302.

45. ANP, PA 796, 797; Gutiérrez 45–55, f. 658; BNP, A556, 2 Sept 42; A32, f. 201; A394, f. 161; A400, f. 908; AGI, Justicia 1067, no. 2, ramo 2; Lima 119, 177.

46. ANP, Alzate, f. 311; BNP, A203, 1557; A36, f. 411; ACI, Lima 565, vol III, 30 Apr 40; Justicia 467; Contaduría 1679.

47. Calvete, *Rebelión de Pizarro,* V, 85, 87.

48. ANP, Salinas 42–43, *passim;* Martínez 49–53, f. 44; *Libros de cabildos de Lima,* IV, 288; VI/1, 74.

49. See *passim Libros de cabildos de Lima; Libros de cabildos de Quito;* AIIC, Libros de cabildos del Cuzco.

50. ANP, Salinas 38–40, ff. 160, 505; Salinas 42–43, ff. 301, 312, 647, 717, 760, 762, 768–89; Salinas 46–48, ff. 10, 106, 606, 684, 690, 727, 787, 877, 899, 921, 926, 939, 970, 1022, 1034, 1175; Alzate, ff. 473, 669; PA 688; RA PC, I, cuaderno 14; RA PP, I, trial of Pedro de Salinas; BNP, A36, ff. 27, 164; A35, ff. 590, 591; A32, f. 51; A31, f. 99; AHA, Valdecabras, 1552; AGI, Lima 566, vol V, 19 Oct 40; vol IV, 7 Sept 40; Lima 567, vol VII, 23 Nov 51; Lima 565, vol III, 5 Feb 40; Lima 204, probanza of Juan de León; Lima 177, probanza of Alonso de Luque, petition of Bartolomé Arvallo; Patronato 123, ramo 3; 114, ramo 9; 185, ramo 1; 128, ramo 5; Justicia 429, no. 1; 1067, no. 2, ramo 4; Contaduría 1679, 1680, 1681; Lima 118, power of Francisco Pérez Lezcano, 1 Feb 50; APS, 1550, oficio XV, libro II; HC 496; *CDIHE,* XXVI, 193–203; Calvete, *Rebelión de Pizarro,* V, 102; *RANP,* VIII, 87; XIV, 205; Pérez de Tudela, *Gasca,* I, 444; *Libros de cabildos de Lima,* I, 249, 266, 272, 285, 301, 355; III, 52, 74, 79, 82, 110; IV, 147.

V. MERCHANTS

1. AGI, Contratación 2723, no. 4, ramo 1.

2. ANP, Salinas 42–43, ff. 251, 317, 427, 550, 631; BNP, A35, f. 94; A510, f. 475; AHA, Valdecabras, 17 July 51; AGI, Justicia 9, no. 3; 1074.

no. 9; Oviedo, *Historia*, III, 77; Cieza, *Guerra de Salinas*, 330; Santiago Martínez, *Fundadores de Arequipa*, 260.

3. ANP, Salinas 42–43, f. 500; PA 596; and the notarial registers of Lima in general, the source of most of the information on which this chapter is based up to this point.

4. ANP, Salinas 42–43, ff. 243, 496, 504, 520; Alzate, f. 354; E. Pérez 57, f. 1910; BNP, A404, f. 398; A33, f. 193; A542, f. 3; A37, f. 81; AHA, Gaspar Hernández, 14 Feb 50; Cerón, 28 Feb 49; AGI, Justicia 1067, no. 1, ramo 4.

5. ANP, Gutiérrez 45–55, f. 504; Salinas 46–48, f. 1113; BNP, A542, ff. 34, 158; AHA, Gaspar Hernández, 7 June 53, 12 June 53; AGI, Justicia 1054, no. 2, ramo 3; Cieza, *Guerra de Quito* (Serrano y Sanz), II, 185; see also fns. 20 and 23.

6. ANP, RA PC, I, cuaderno 14; Salinas 46–48, f. 827; Alzate, f. 513; and registers of Lima generally; BNP, A335; Diego Fernández, *Historia del Perú*, I, 150; Pedro de Valdivia, *Cartas*, 48.

7. ANP, RA PP, I, trial of Isabel Gómez; registers of Lima; AGI, Patronato 187, ramo 9; Loredo, *Los Repartos*, 56; Enrique Otte, "Mercaderes vascos en Tierra Firme a raiz del descubrimiento del Perú," in *Mercurio Peruano*, nos. 443–44 (Libro Jubiliar de Víctor Andrés Belaúnde), 81–89; see also fn. 20.

8. ANP, RA PP, I, trial of Isabel Gómez; Gutiérrez 45–55, f. 313; registers of Lima; BNP, A335; AHA, Gaspar Hernández, 9 Dec 51; García Muñoz, 19 Oct 57; AGI, Patronato 187, ramo 9.

9. ANP, Alzate, f. 854; Gutiérrez 45–55, f. 264; BNP, A280; AGI, Contaduría 1680; Medina, *Colección*, IX, 187–90; Calvete, *Rebelión de Pizarro*, IV, 409; see also fn. 20.

10. AGI, Justicia 1126, no. 2, ramo 1; Patronato 95, no. 1, ramo 5; 185, ramo 33; 110, ramo 2; HC 673; Gutiérrez de Santa Clara, *Quinquenarios*, III, 5; Cieza, *Quito* (Serrano y Sanz), II, 184; Diego Fernández, *Historia del Perú*, I, 111, 150; see also fns. 20, 23.

11. AGI, Contaduría 1679–83, 1824–25; Porras, *Cartas del Perú*, 466–67; Cieza, *Quito* (Serrano y Sanz), II, 118; Gutiérrez de Santa Clara, *Quinquenarios*, II, 195; IV, 198; Zárate, *Historia*, II, 571; see also fns. 20, 23.

12. AGI, Patronato 97, no. 1, ramo 8.

13. ANP, Gutiérrez 45–55, f. 253; RA PP, I, trial of Isabel Gómez; AHA, Gaspar Hernández, 15 Nov 53; Valdecabras, 19 Aug 53; *Libros de cabildos de Lima*, IV, 295, 470; V, 65, 149, 194, 252, 480.

14. ANP, E. Pérez, f. 1991; Gutiérrez 45-55, f. 3; BNP, A404, f. 472; A221, 24 Apr 60; A510, f. 426; A36, f. 267; AHA, Gaspar Hernández, 1 Jan 54, 30 Jan 53; *Libros de cabildos de Lima*, V, 84, and similar references in fn. 13.

15. ANP, Juzgado and registers before 1540; AGI, Justicia 467.

16. AGI, Lima 565, vol III, 23 May 39, 7 June 39; HC 413, 419; Bernabé Cobo, S. J., *Obras*, II, 304.

17. AGI, Patronato 95, no. 1, ramo 7; 150; no. 3, ramo 2; ANP, PA 674; Salinas 42–43, f. 127.

18. ANP, PA 651, 664; Salinas 42–43, ff. 55, 89, 256, 361; Alzate, ff. 227, 868; HC 215, 216, 222, 482; AGI, Justicia 1053, no. 5; 1174; Contratación 2723, no. 3; *Libros de cabildos de Lima*, I, 254; Thayer, *Formación*, I, 288; *Catálogo de fondos americanos del Archivo de Protocolos de Sevilla*, III, 115; Medina, *Colección*, IX, 187–90.

19. ANP, Castañeda, reg. 8, f. 48; Salinas 38–40, f. 473; Salinas 42–43, ff. 32, 41, 77, 208, 210, 242, 263, 281, 348, 351, 378, 594, 735; BNP, A556, ff. 3, 4, 7; A591, f. 401; A555; AHA, Gaspar Hernández, 14 June 53; AGI, Patronato 185, ramo 33; Contaduría 1824, 1825; Lima 566, vol IV, 7 Oct 41; vol V, 29 Apr 44; Justicia 467; 1053; 1074, no. 9; 1054, no. 2, ramo 3; HC 383, 513, 538, 617; *Libros de cabildos de Lima*, I, 297, 310; V, 465; Cieza, *Quito* (Jiménez de la Espada), appendix, 90; Pérez de Tudela, *Gasca*, II, 554; Barriga, *Documentos*, II, 130.

20. ANP, Castañeda, reg. 2, f. 10; Salinas 38–40, f. 338; Salinas 42–43, f. 272; Salinas 46–48, ff. 584, 587, 644, 684, 685, 687, 727, 748, 1058, 1156; Alzate, ff. 290, 397; BNP, A591, f. 380; A33, ff. 116, 242, 263; A222, f. 162; A335, f. 823; AGI, Justicia 758, no. 2; 402, no. 2, ramo 1; Lima 567, vol VII, 19 March 52; HC 673; Barriga, *Documentos*, I, 228; Pérez de Tudela, *Gasca*, I, 505; Calvete, *Rebelión de Pizarro*, V, 64; *Catálogo de fondos americanos*, IV, 287, 366; Bermúdez Plata, *Pasajeros*, III, 139, 156, 168, 251, 256, 291, 297, 340; *Libros de cabildos de Lima*, V, 141; Lino G. Canedo, introduction to his edition of *Crónica Franciscana* by Córdoba Salinas; Medina, *Colección*, XII, 260; Valdivia, *Cartas*, 8, 19; Mariño de Lobera, *Crónica*, 283.

21. Valenzuela: AGI, Contaduría 1680, 1681; Contratación 2146; Patronato 95, no. 1, ramo 2; 102, ramo 4; Archivo de la Audiencia Territorial de Sevilla, legajo 59; ANP, Salinas 42–43, f. 723; Gutiérrez 45–55, f. 40; Salinas 46–48, f. 941; Alzate, ff. 349, 747, 819, 866; Villarreal 55–57, ff. 140, 151; RA PC, I, cuaderno 3; RA PP, I, trial of Pedro de Salinas; BNP, A32, f. 57; A35, ff. 184, 254, 283; A538, 3 Feb 53; A516, ff. 148, 154; AIIA, Cerón, 2 March 49; HC 474, 731, 754; *RANP*, XVII, 47; *Libros de cabildos de Lima*, V, 345; Thayer, *Formación*, III, 81, 319. Illescas: AGI, Contaduría 1679, 1680; Contratación 2723, no. 4, ramo 2; Justicia 402, no. 2, ramo 1; Lima 313, probanza of Archbishop Loaysa, 1564; ANP, Gutiérrez 45–55, ff. 92, 93; Salinas 46–48, ff. 929, 1034; Alzate, ff. 41, 295, 305, 307, 468, 478, 530, 545, 657, 740, 850, 925–37; Martínez 49–53, ff. 22, 29; Gutiérrez 45–55, ff. 128, 379, 508, 790; E. Pérez 57, f. 1910; BNP A397, f. 448; A32, f. 154; A607, ff. 3, 522; A33, f. 242; A35, ff. 81, 478; A607, f. 9; A335, f. 907; A222, f. 148; A404, f. 487; A522, 27 May 53; A36, f. 50; A201; A541; A335, f. 806; A34, f. 124; AHA, Cerón, 28 Dec 48, 26 Feb 49, 17 July 49; Valdecabras, 27 Nov 51; Gaspar Hernández, 6 Dec 51, 22 Dec 51, 26 July 53, 31 Oct 53; *RANP*, XII, 106; HC 627, 649, 673; *Catálogo de fondos americanos*, II, 56; III, 115, 147; IV, 204, 357, 358, 399; *Libros de cabildos de Lima*, IV, 509; V, 173, 193, 227, 273, 282.

22. AGI, Contaduría 1680; Lima 313, probanza of Archbishop Loaysa, 1564; ANP, PA 521; Gutiérrez 45–55, ff. 51, 174, 487, 627; Martel 55–58, f. 471; Alzate, f. 860; Salinas 46–48, f. 78; BNP, A33, f. 240; A524, f. 696; A542, f. 392; A221, 19 Jan 60; A35, ff. 303, 502; A542, f. 330; A538, f. 989; see also fns. 19, 21.

23. AGI, Contaduría 1679, 1680, 1824, 1825; Justicia 833, letter of Hernando Pizarro, 8 March 45; Lima 112; Lima 313, letter of fray Pedro de Cepeda, 15 Nov 63; Contratación 2146; 2723, no. 3; Patronato 110, ramo 2; 123, ramo 11; ANP, PA 337, 570, 627; Juzgado, 9 Apr 37; Castañeda, reg. 7, f. 17; Salinas 38–40, ff. 134, 225, 245; Salinas 42–43, ff. 41, 61, 96, 119, 120, 152, 155, 206, 215, 472, 513, 550, 558, 634; Alzate, f. 840; Martel 55–58, ff. 43, 487, 488; Salinas 46–48, f. 594; BNP, A31, f. 99; A33, ff. 98, 118, 135; A34, f. 3; A35, ff. 162, 315, 385; A542, ff. 1, 403; A274; A510, f. 474; A36, f. 187; AHA, Gaspar Hernández, 2 Sept 51, 7 Oct 51, 22 Oct 51, 14 June 53, 22 March 53, 14 Nov 53, 30 Jan 53, 28 July 53, 19 June 53, 15 Nov 53; Valdecabras, 10 Oct 51, 5 Nov 54, 12 Sept 51, 2 Nov 51, 18 Sept 51; Cerón, 22 Dec 48, 31 Dec 48, 2 March 49, 6 March 49; García Muñoz, 3 Nov 57; HC 224, 226, 413, 419; Santiago Martínez, *Fundadores de Arequipa*, 260; Barriga, *Documentos*, I, 57, 63–65; II, 379; *RANP*, X, 183; Porras, *Cartas del Perú*, 467; Pérez de Tudela, *Gasca*, II, 223, 466, 534; Calancha, *Corónica moralizada*, 646.

VI. ARTISANS

1. ANP, Salinas 42–43, ff. 99, 703; Salinas 46–48, ff. 427, 601, 627, 1042; Gutiérrez 45–55, ff. 458, 471, 474, 574, 618; Alzate, f. 934; Martínez 49–53, f. 113; BNP, A542, ff. 82, 126, 432, 472, 645; A36, f. 58; A35, f. 418; A516, f. 122; A538, f. 1033; A400, f. 981; A34, ff. 6, 16; A33, f. 38; A530; AHC, Vitorero, 27 Sept 60; AHA, Valdecabras, 1 Aug 51, 3 Oct 51; Gaspar Hernández, 20 Apr 50, 14 Apr 50, 7 Dec 51; Gutiérrez de Santa Clara, *Quinquenarios*, III, 40; Barriga, *Documentos*, I, 124, 134; see also fn. 26.

2. ANP, Salinas 42–43, ff. 637, 656; Salinas 46–48, ff. 347, 466, 641; Gutiérrez 45–55, ff. 369, 371; BNP, A221, 22 May 60, 15 Feb 61; A524, f. 689; A542, f. 505; A538, 7 Aug 56; A404, f. 394; A222, f. 147; A36, f. 315; A400, f. 1007.

3. ANP, Alzate, f. 821; Salinas 42–43, f. 49; Salinas 38–40, f. 73; Salinas 46–48, ff. 724, 780; Gutiérrez 45–55, ff. 479, 490, 774, 852; Villarreal 55–57, f. 220; RA PP, I, trial of Pedro de Salinas; BNP, A33, ff. 64, 161; A35, ff. 371, 597; A208; A221, 24 Oct 60; A400, f. 972; A528, f. 999; AGI, Contaduría 1679, 1680; AHA, Gaspar Hernández, 7 Aug 50, 5 Nov 50; Cerón, 24 Apr 49.

4. ANP, Martel 55–58, f. 462; Villarreal 55–57, f. 69; Alzate, f. 812; Gutiérrez 45–55, f. 796; BNP, A221, 2 July 60, 1 March 60; AHA, Gaspar Hernández, 8 July 51, 1 Dec 53, 17 Feb 53; Valdecabras, 22 Dec 52; Pérez de Tudela, *Gasca*, II, 548.

5. ANP, RA PP, I, trial of Pedro de Salinas; Martel 55–58, f. 466; Martínez 49–53, f. 101; Gutiérrez 45–55; ff. 501, 858; Salinas 42–43, f. 684; BNP, A542, ff. 75, 326, 449, 551, 611; A336, 10 Apr 59; A538, f. 1045;

A524, f. 710; A525, f. 1004; A152; A400, f. 994; A516, f. 146; HC 227, 722, 804; AGI, Contaduría 1680, 1681, 1784; Porras, *Cedulario*, II, 339; Barriga, *Mercedarios*, III, 45; *Libros de cabildos de Lima*, IV, 435, 461; V, 43; *Revista del Instituto Peruano de Investigaciones Genealógicas*, X, 92.

6. ANP, Alzate, ff. 8, 474, 475, 575; Salinas 42–43, ff. 21, 99, 690; Salinas 46–48, ff. 746, 941; Martel 55–58, ff. 347, 481; Martínez 49–53, f. 114; BNP, A221, 20 Apr 60, 13 July 60; A35, f. 356; A524, f. 679; A36, f. 441; A400, f. 947; A397, ff. 410–17; A33, f. 192; AHA, Cerón, 17 Apr 49, 2 Jan 49; Gaspar Hernández, 2 Feb 49; *Libros de cabildos de Lima*, V, 48; VI/1, 282; Barriga, *Documentos*, II, 281.

7. AGI, Lima 567, vol VII, 24 Apr 53; Gutiérrez de Santa Clara, *Quinquenarios*, II, 199.

8. ANP, Martel 55–58, f. 472; Salinas 42–43, ff. 99, 236, 389, 546, 563; Juan de Padilla 60–61, f. 776; Salinas 46–48, f. 1122; RA PP, I, trial of Pedro de Salinas; Gutiérrez 45–55, f. 770; Castañeda, reg. 7, f. 28; reg. 8, f. 30; Gutiérrez 55–56, f. 447; Martínez 49–53, f. 14; BNP, A538, 31 July 56; A402, f. 489; A221, 15 Feb 61; A419, f. 118; A222, f. 169; A36, ff. 92, 234; A522, 3 July 53; A30, f. 405; A522, 16 May 53; A525, f. 841; A532, 16 June 56; AHA, Gaspar Hernández, 5 Dec 51, 25 May 53, 17 Jan 53; Valdecabras, 11 March 51.

9. ANP, PA 241; Villarreal 55–57, f. 57; Martel 55–58, f. 400 ff.; Salinas 46–48, ff. 302, 523; RA PC, I, cuaderno 3; Alzate, f. 470; E. Pérez 57, f. 1984; Salinas 38–40, f. 255; BNP, A525, f. 825; A532, 28 Apr 56; A36, f. 212; A528, f. 969; A335; A542, ff. 328, 442, 539; A33, f. 152; A221, 27 March 60; AHA, Valdecabras, 21 March 51, 18 March 51, 20 Oct 52; Gaspar Hernández, 11 Apr 53, 9 May 50, 21 Feb 49, 19 March 50, 2 Nov 53; Cerón, 6 Apr 49; AGI, Contaduría 1784.

10. ANP, Juzgado, 12 Feb 37; Salinas 46–48, f. 887; BNP, A36, f. 6; IIC 673; AGI, Contaduría 1679, 1680, 1681; Patronato 101, ramo 14; Pérez de Tudela, *Gasca*, I, 456; II, 230, 362; Medina, *Colección*, VII, 84; Cieza, *Quito* (Jiménez de la Espada), 147; Diego Fernández, *Historia del Perú*, I, 83; Zárate, *Historia*, II, 554; Gutiérrez de Santa Clara, *Quinquenarios*, III, 341; Porras, *Cartas del Perú*, 423; CDIHE, XLIX, 96; Garcilaso, *Obras*, IV, 120.

11. ANP, Salinas 46–48, ff. 343, 615, 904, 1028, 1081; BNP, A35, ff. 315, 368, 375; A35, f. 227; AHC, Libros de cabildos, I, f. 97; *Libros de cabildos de Lima*, IV, 520, 616; V, 511; Barriga, *Documentos*, II, 266.

12. ANP, Alzate, f. 342; Villarreal 55–57, f. 3; Salinas 46–48, f. 133; BNP, A538; A404, f. 451; AGI, Contaduría 1680; Bermúdez Plata, *Pasajeros*, II, 25; *Libros de cabildos de Lima*, IV, 128, 164, 214, 363.

13. ANP, Juzgado, 1 Oct 36, 6 Nov 36; PA 285; AHC, Libros de cabildos, I, f. 82; AGI, Patronato 120, no. 2, ramo 2; *Libros de cabildos de Lima*, IV, 127.

14. ANP, PA 631; Castañeda, reg. 11, f. 9; Salinas 42–43, ff. 653, 659, 504; BNP, A528, f. 983; AGI, Contaduría 1784; Justicia 1067, no. 3; RANP, VII, 13.

15. BNP, A35, f. 176; A221, 1 Apr 60; AGI, Contaduría 1679, 1680,

1681, 1824, 1825; Diego Fernández, *Historia del Perú*, I, 80, 323; *Libros de cabildos de Lima*, VI/1, 124, 153; Calvete, *Rebelión de Pizarro*, IV, 375; Gutiérrez de Santa Clara, *Quinquenarios*, II, 194–95.

16. ANP, Salinas 46–48, f. 491; BNP, A208; A404, f. 402; A542, f. 215; A538, 31 Aug 56; AHA, Cerón, 5 Apr 49; AGI, Justicia 487; *Libros de cabildos de Lima*, IV, V, VI, *passim*.

17. ANP, E. Pérez 57, f. 2027; Gutiérrez 45–55, f. 363; Salinas 42–43, f. 688; BNP, A525, f. 840; A516, f. 141; A201; AGI, Contaduría 1679, 1680.

18. ANP, Villarreal 55–57, f. 221; Salinas 42–43, f. 276; Salinas 46–48, f. 1; BNP, A36, f. 399; AHC, Libros de cabildos; *RANP*, XII, 223–28; Barriga, *Documentos*, I, 203; Cobo, *Obras*, II, 420; don Alonso Enríquez, *Vida y costumbres*, 148.

19. ANP, Salinas 42–43, ff. 86, 616; Salinas 38–40, ff. 43, 383, 999; Salinas 46–48, f. 743; Martel 55–58, f. 461; BNP, A36, f. 364; A37, f. 26; A337, 7 Jan 61; A221, 29 July 60; A32, ff. 58–74; AHC ,Vitorero, 11 Feb 60, 17 Feb 60; AHA, Cerón, 31 Dec 48; García Muñoz, 28 Oct 57; AGI, Contaduria 1682, 1680; *Libros de cabildos de Lima*, V, 201, 482, 532.

20. ANP, E. Pérez 57, f. 2042; RA PC, I, cuaderno 9; BNP, A263; AGI, Justicia 667, no. 2; Contaduría 1682.

21. ANP, Salinas 42–43, f. 28; Salinas 46–48, ff. 44, 62; Gutiérrez 45–55, f. 774; BNP, A412, 3 Dec 52; A542, f. 124; A221, 8 Apr 60; A538, f. 1031; AHA, Valdecabras, 31 Aug 51; AGI, Contaduría 1680; *Libros de cabildos de Lima*, IV, 330, 486, 565.

22. ANP, Martínez 49–53, ff. 73, 110; Alzate, ff. 887, 915; Salinas 46–48, f. 938; BNP, A528, f. 981; A532, 19 Nov 58; A542, f. 314; AHA, Cerón, 24 May 49, 28 May 49, 7 March 49, 21 Feb 49; Gaspar Hernández, 3 June 50, 26 Feb 51, 12 Feb 49, 26 July 53, 4 Feb 53; 15 Nov 53, 21 Nov 53, 6 Dec 51, 10 June 53, 2 July 53, 9 Dec 53; AGI, Contaduría 1680, 1683; Justicia 429, no. 1; *Libros de cabildos de Lima*, IV, 2, 184, 347, 672; V, 529.

23. ANP, Alzate, f. 279; Gutiérrez 45–55, ff. 254, 828; Villarreal 55–57, f. 57; BNP, A524, f. 690; A542, ff. 554, 555; AGI, Lima 118; Contaduría 1680; Lima 566, vol. IV; HC 453; *CDIAO*, XX, 487–537; Barriga, *Mercedarios*, I, 180; Garcilaso, *Obras*, IV, 23.

24. ANP, RA PC, I, cuaderno 13; RA PP, I, trial of Isabel Gómez; Salinas 46–48, f. 889; Gutiérrez 55–56, f. 429; Martel 55–58, f. 431; BNP, A538, 1 Aug 56; A221, 19 Sept 56; A525, f. 844; Garcilaso, *Obras*, II, 368.

25. ANP, RA PP, I, trial of Diego de Mendoza Carrillo; *CDIAO*, XX, 295.

26. ANP, Castañeda, reg. 2, ff. 39, 52; Salinas 42–43, ff. 217, 236, 442, 785; RA PP, I, trial of Pedro de Salinas; Salinas 46–48, ff. 107, 915, 917, 922, 983, 1081; Martínez 49–53, f. 76; Alzate, f. 8; Gutiérrez 45–55, f. 894; Gutiérrez 55–56, f. 384; BNP, A556, f. 225; A591, f. 363; A33, ff. 121, 279; A35, ff. 42, 476; A36, ff. 45, 188, 205, 212; A28; A542, ff. 278, 564; A337, f. 281; A541; A335; AGI, Contaduría 1679, 1680, 1682, 1824; Patronato 98, no. 3, ramo 1; 132, no. 2, ramo 1; 114, ramo 5; 99, no. 1, ramo 6; Lima 204,

probanza of Diego Hernández, Seville, Aug 48; Justicia 432, no. 1, ramo 2; no. 2, ramo 2; HC 121, 670; *RANP,* VI, 117; VII, 187; VIII, 89; XIII, 99; XIV, 97; *Libros de cabildos de Lima,* I, 338; V, 20.

VII. SAILORS AND FOREIGNERS

1. BNP, A 36, f. 79.

2. Cobo, *Obras,* II, 450.

3. ANP, RA PP, I, trial of Isabel Gómez; RA PC, I, cuaderno 11; Gutiérrez de Santa Clara, *Quinquenarios,* II, 310; Diego Fernández, *Historia del Perú,* I, 140.

4. AGI, Lima 205, petition of Laurencio Paggi; ANP, Martel 55–58, f. 318; BNP, A36, f. 317; A542, f. 139; Porras, *Cartas del Perú, passim.*

5. Lists assembled from all sources; BNP, A33, f. 186; A394, f. 168; A221, 19 Feb 57; AGI, Contaduría 1680; ANP, RA PC, I and II, trial of Juan López de Aspea; AHA, Cerón, 7 Apr 49; Woodrow Borah, *Early Colonial Trade,* 68; Diego Fernández, *Historia del Perú,* I, 159; Porras, *Cartas del Perú,* 199; Medina, *Colección,* VII, 83.

6. AGI, Contaduría 1679, 1825; HC 154; Francisco de Jerez, *Verdadera relación de la conquista del Perú,* II, 324–25.

7. ANP, Castañeda, reg. 1, f. 23; Gutiérrez 45–55, ff. 127, 142, 161, 334, 363, 529, 764; Alzate, ff. 360, 444, 507, 787, 837, 839; PA 715; Salinas 46–48, ff. 160, 541, 985; Martel 55–58, ff. 27, 77, 290, 306, 323, 434, 435, 447; Villarreal 55–57, f. 140; BNP, A35, ff. 4, 40, 184, 420, 443, 526; A404, ff. 405, 485; A530, 8 Jan 55, 6 May 55; A531, 10 May 55; A221, 26 March 57; A524, f. 605; A542, f. 126; A33, f. 178; A532, 29 July 57; A556, f. 13; AGI, Justicia 467; Gutiérrez de Santa Clara, *Quinquenarios,* II, 340; Calvete, *Rebelión de Pizarro,* V, 71; Thayer, *Formación,* II, 241; Pérez de Tudela, *Gasca,* I, 421; II, 116.

8. ANP, Salinas 42–43, f. 32; Martel 55–58, f. 504; AGI, Justicia 429, no. 1; Calvete, *Rebelión de Pizarro,* IV, 305; Porras ,*Cartas del Perú,* 99, 104, 412; Gutiérrez de Santa Clara, *Quinquenarios,* II, 342; don Alonso Enríquez, *Vida y costumbres,* 137; Pérez de Tudela, *Gasca,* I, 159, 551.

9. AGI, Contaduría 1680; Lima 205, petition of Laurencio Paggi; Mariño de Lobera, *Crónica, passim;* Thayer Ojeda, *Formación, passim.*

10. ANP, E. Pérez 57, ff. 1934, 1957; RA PC, I, cuaderno 10; Gutiérrez 45–55, f. 150; Salinas 46–48, f. 1076; BNP, A530, 17 Apr 55, A542, f. 577; AGI, Justicia 467; Contaduría 1679–82, 1824; Lima 112; Pérez de Tudela, *Gasca,* I, 549; Gutiérrez de Santa Clara, *Quinquenarios,* III, 40; Girolamo Benzoni, *History of the New World,* 246.

11. ANP, Juzgado, 13 Sept 36; Martel 55–58, f. 304; PA 339, 518; BNP, A222, ff. 142, 144, 145; A34, f. 67; A552, 27 May 53; A542, ff. 75, 93–98, 174, 447; A33, f. 1; A396, f. 61; don Alonso Enríquez, *Vida y costumbres,* 137; Barriga, *Documentos,* II, 128.

12. ANP, RA PC, II, trial of Juan López de Aspea; Salinas 42–43, ff. 496, 568; Castañeda, reg. 12, f. 6; Gutiérrez 45–55, ff. 408, 815; Martínez

49-53, f. 10; Martel 55-58, f. 418; AGI, Patronato 185, ramo 15, Contaduría 1679, 1680, 1784; Lima 205, petition of Laurencio Paggi; Oviedo, *Historia*, V, 144; Calvete, *Rebelión de Pizarro*, V, 65; Pérez de Tudela, *Gasca*, II, 84.

13. ANP, Martel 55-58, f. 320; Salinas 38-40, f. 602; BNP, A404, f. 395; A221, 22 Feb 60; AGI, Contaduría 1782; HC 254.

14. ANP, Castañeda, reg. 4, f. 7; Salinas 46-48, f. 742; Martel 55-58, f. 44; Alzate, f. 408; Salinas 42-43, ff. 60, 461; Juzgado, 9 March 36; Salinas 38-40, f. 472; BNP, A33, f. 52; A35, f. 80; A542, ff. 139, 561; A36, ff. 218, 229; A404, ff. 423, 494; AGI, Patronato 187, ramo 6; Contaduría 1680; Justicia 429, no. 1.

15. ANP, Salinas 42-43, f. 469; Martel 55-58, f. 289; Castañeda, reg. 2, ff. 1, 16-22, reg. 4, f. 24; Salinas 46-48, f. 999; RA PC, I, cuaderno 11; II, trial of Juan López de Aspea; BNP, A36, ff. 344-47; AGI, Contaduría 1679, 1680, 1784; Justicia 429, no. 1; Calvete, *Rebelión de Pizarro*, IV, 252, 358; Zárate, *Historia*, II, 518; Diego Fernández, *Historia del Perú*, I, 345; Pérez de Tudela, *Gasca*, I, 527.

16. ANP, Salinas 42-43, ff. 427, 559; Pérez de Tudela, *Gasca*, I, 549.

17. ANP, RA PC, I, cuaderno 11; II, trial of Juan López de Aspea.

18. ANP, Salinas 42-43, ff. 12a, 477, 611, 729; Salinas 46-48, ff. 400, 624; Alzate, f. 293; AHA, Gaspar Hernández, 4 March 49; 16 March 53; 22 Apr 53; Valdecabras, 5 June 53; AGI, Contaduria 1679; HC 439; BNP, A36, f. 152; A35, f. 22; *Libros de cabildos de Lima*, IV, 669; Cobo, *Obras*, II, 304.

19. ANP, Villarreal 55-57, f. 17; Alzate, f. 852; Gutiérrez 55-56, f. 503; BNP, A35, ff. 408, 584; A522, 24 May 53; A528, ff. 973, 1002; A542, ff. 139, 438; A221, 19 Apr 60; AGI, Contaduría 1680; Patronato 93, no. 6, ramo 4; Lima 566, vol VI, 9 Oct 49; HC 582, 746; *Libros de cabildos de Lima*, I, 317; *Revista del Instituto Peruano de Investigaciones Genealógicas*, X, 91.

20. ANP, Salinas 42-43, f. 173; Gutiérrez 45-55, 1545; Alzate, ff. 352, 373, 977; RA PP, I, trial of Isabel Gómez; BNP, A342, f. 462; A412, 10 Nov 52; AGI, Patronato 116, no. 2, ramo 5; Lima 112; Liam 205, petition of Laurencio Paggi; Contaduría 1679-81; Calvete, *Rebelión de Pizarro*, V, 53, 84.

21. ANP, PA 339, 388, 599; Castañeda, reg. 1, f. 30; AGI, Contaduría 1825; Patronato 185, ramo 7; HC 199; Loredo, *Los Repartos*, 213.

22. ANP, Salinas 42-43, f. 433; Castañeda, reg. 2, f. 41; PA 245, 249, 717; BNP, A35, f. 401; AGI, Lima 565, vol III, 8 Nov 39; Diego Fernández, *Historia del Perú*, I, 198; Medina, *Colección*, VIII, 29, 83; *Revista Histórica*, VIII, 197; Porras, *Cartas del Perú*, 112; Mariño de Lobera, *Crónica*, 387.

23. ANP, PA 430-53; AGI, Patronato 187, ramo 10; Gutiérrez de Santa Clara, *Quinquenarios*, IV, 109, 139; Calvete, *Rebelión de Pizarro*, IV, 317; Oviedo, *Historia*, V, 195, 300.

24. ANP, Alzate, f. 38; Salinas 46-48, ff. 319, 737; Martel 55-58, f. 375; Gutiérrez 45-55, ff. 1, 421; Salinas 42-43, ff. 88, 459; BNP, A30, ff. 314, 315; A524, f. 685; A35, ff. 383, 399; A36, ff. 115, 140, 141; A33, ff. 16, 106; A335, f. 817; A35, f. 217; AHA, Gaspar Hernández, 6 July 53; AGI,

Patronato 98, no. 1, ramo 1; Contratación 198, ramo 12; *CDIHE*, XCIV, 202; *Libros de cabildos de Lima*, V, 31.

25. ANP, Salinas 38–40, ff. 589, 780; BNP, A221, 20 March 60; AGI, Contaduría 1679, 1680, 1784, 1824, 1825; Patronato 105, ramo 11; 90, no. 2, ramo 13; Loredo, *Los Repartos*, 132; Garcilaso, *Obras*, III, 196; Porras, *Cartas del Perú*, 503; Gutiérrez de Santa Clara, *Quinquenarios*, III, 341; IV, 25; *CDIHE*, XCIV, 202; Oviedo, *Historia*, V, 303; Medina, *Colección*, VII, 84; Cieza, *Salinas*, 339.

26. ANP, Castañeda, reg. 2, f. 18; reg. 11, f. 6; reg. 12, f. 18; Salinas 42–43, f. 20; BNP, A591, f. 392; A521, 17 Nov 54; A33, f. 139; AHA, Cerón, 25 Feb 49, 7 March 49, 15 March 49, 16 March 49; Valdecabras, 3 Oct 51; Gaspar Hernández, 12 Feb 50, 23 Sept 50, 29 Dec 50, 22 Jan 51, 13 Apr 51, 23 July 51, 12 Oct 51, 14 Nov 51, 20 Feb 53; AGI, Contaduría 1680; HC 187.

27. ANP, RA PC, II, trial of Juan López de Aspea; Salinas 38–40, ff. 74, 598; Salinas 42–43, ff. 74–171; Salinas 46–48, ff. 133, 359; Gutiérrez, 45–55, f. 477; Villarreal, f. 74; BNP, A35, f. 212; A404, ff. 444, 459; A394, f. 156; A36, f. 82; AGI, Contaduría 1680, 1824, 1825; Pérez de Tudela, *Gasca*, II, 548.

28. ANP, Martel 55–58, ff. 24, 298, 412, 428, 438; Villarreal 55–57, ff. 57, 59, 190; Salinas 46–48, f. 606; Gutiérrez 45–55, f. 170; Martínez 49–53, ff. 74, 87; BNP, A221, 9 Aug 60, 7 Sept 60; A538, 3 Feb 53, 6 Feb 53; A516, f. 133; A412, 17 Nov 52; A522, 23 June 53; A539, 9 Jan 55; A404, ff. 433, 475, 490, 495; AGI, Contaduría 1680.

29. AHA, Cerón, 4 Jan 49; Gaspar Hernández, 28 June 49, 13 May 49, 19 March 50, 22 Apr 50, 19 Apr 50, 30 Aug 50, 9 Oct 50, 24 Nov 51, 2 July 53; AGI, Contaduría 1680, 1681, 1784, 1825.

30. Francisqui: ANP, PA 267, 761; Juzgado, 9 Oct 35; AGI, Contaduría 1824, 1825; Patronato 185, ramo 11; Justicia 734, no. 6; HC 75; *Libros de cabildos de Lima*, I, 21. Benino: ANP, Salinas 46–48, f. 973; BNP, A335, f. 793; AHA, Valdecabras, 14 Dec 51; AGI, Patronato 97, no. 1, ramo 1; 99, no. 1, ramo 5; Contaduría 1680; Lima 92, report of Marshal Alvarado; Jiménez de la Espada, *Relaciones geográficas*, I, 362–71; Nicolao de Albenino, *Verdadera relación;* Héctor López Martínez, "El cronista florentino Nicolao de Albenino en la rebelión de Francisco Hernández Girón," *Mercurio Peruano*, XLI (1960), 297–301. Corso: ANP, Alzate, ff. 454, 618; Martel 55–58, f. 459; E. Pérez 57, ff. 1847, 2053; Villarreal 55–57, ff. 39–40; BNP, A538, f. 1024; A36, f. 61; A335, f. 821; HC 508; Lizárraga, *Descripción*. De la Cruz: BNP, A36, f. 76; AHA, Valdecabras, 6 June 53; ANP, RA PC, I, cuaderno 1; AGI, Lima 313, probanza of Archbishop Loaysa, 1564.

31. ANP, RA PC, I, cuaderno 11.

32. ANP, RA PC, I, cuaderno 1; Garcilaso, *Obras*, III, 147, 401, and *passim* (particularly the repeated favorable mention of the Portuguese with Soto in vol. I, and of Lope Martín in vols. III and IV.)

33. BNP, A35, f. 167; AGI, Patronato 187, ramo 7; Lima 567, vol VII, 11 Aug 52; Contaduría 1680; Cieza, *Salinas*, 281, 284–85; Cieza, *Chupas*, 256; Cieza, *Quito* (Serrano y Sanz), 150; Gutiérrez de Santa Clara, *Quin-*

quenarios, IV, 106; Diego Fernández, *Historia del Perú,* I, 285; and references to Lope Martín listed in indices of Garcilaso, *Obras,* and *Crónicas del Perú,* ed. by Pérez de Tudela.

34. BNP, A32, f. 80; AGI, Patronato 109, ramo 1; 120, no. 2, ramo 10; 187, ramo 6; HC 115; Medina, *Colección,* IX, 6, 206.

35. ANP, Alzate, f. 537; BNP, A337, f. 35; AHA, Gaspar Hernández, 30 June 53, 4 July 53; AGI, Justicia 1073, no. 3; Lima 177, probanza of Antonio de Solar: HC 394; Benzoni, *History of the New World,* 1.

VIII. TRANSIENTS

1. Enrique Otte, "Carlos V y sus vasallos patrimoniales de América," *Clio,* XXVIII (1960), no. 116.

2. *CDIAO,* III, 561.

3. AGI, Contaduría 1680; Albenino, *Relación;* Cieza, *Quito* (Serrano y Sanz), 108; Pérez de Tudela, *Crónicas del Perú,* prologue, xxi, lxxiii; Inge Wolff, "Die Stellung des Extranjero in der Stadt Potosí vom 16.–18. Jahrhundert," 78–109.

4. AGI, Patronato 114, ramo 3; Zárate, *Historia,* II, 489; Oviedo, *Historia,* III, 350.

5. AGI, Justicia 487.

6. Orgóñoz: Raúl Porras Barrenechea, "Medina y su contribución a la historia Peruana," *Mercurio Peruano,* XXXIII (1952), 491–523; Porras, *Cedulario,* II, 213; Medina, *Colección,* VI, 126–32. Valdivia: Alonso Góngora Marmolejo, *Historia de todas las cosas que han acaecido en el reino de Chile,* 82; Mariño de Lobera, *Crónica,* 287; Gutiérrez de Santa Clara, *Quinquenarios,* IV, 114. Carvajal: AGI, Justicia 1074, no. 3; ANP, Castañeda, reg. 11, f. 33; Porras, *Cartas del Perú,* 500–501; Gutiérrez de Santa Clara, *Quinquenarios,* III, 73 ff., 336 ff.; IV, 108, 209–17.

7. AGI, Patronato 114, ramo 6; AHC, Libro de cabildos, 59–60, f. 12; Diego Fernández, *Historia del Perú,* I, 276, 286; Garcilaso, *Obras,* III, 362; IV, 33.

8. ANP, RA PP, I, trials of Diego de Mendoza Carrillo and Juan de Zárate.

9. BNP, A280.

10. ANP, RA PP, I, trials of Isabel Gómez and Pedro de Salinas; BNP, A30, f. 351; *CDIAO,* VII, 361–62; Pérez de Tudela, *Gasca,* II, 16, 71; Mariño de Lobera, *Crónica,* 325; Porras, *Cartas del Perú,* 182; Gutiérrez de Santa Clara, *Quinquenarios,* II, 194–95; Diego Fernández, *Historia del Perú,* I, 303.

11. AGI, Patronato 94, no. 1, ramo 2; Porras, *Cartas del Perú,* 507; Garcilaso, *Obras,* IV, 43–44.

12. BNP, A591, f. 399; Porras, *Cartas del Perú,* 507; Calvete, *Rebelión de Pizarro,* V, 43, 44, 50, 70, 74, 75, 89; Gómara, *Hispania victrix,* I, 242–43; Garcilaso, *Obras,* IV, 160.

13. AGI, Patronato 105, ramo 16, ramo 18; 101, ramo 5, ramo 15; 96,

no. 1, ramo 2, ramo 3; Lima 119, probanza of Pablo de Montemayor; Justicia 1126, no. 4, ramo 1; Diego Fernández, *Historia del Perú*, I, 97 ff.; Gutiérrez de Santa Clara, *Quinquenarios*, III, 119 ff.; Roberto Levillier, *Descubrimiento y población del norte argentino; CDIHE*, XCIV, 137, 138, 141.

14. AGI, Lima 313, letter of 1 July 50.

15. Porras, *Cartas del Perú*, 119.

16. AGI, Justicia 1126, no. 3; Barriga, *Mercedarios*, IV, 41.

17. AGI. Patronato 101, ramo 18; 109, ramo 6; Garcilaso, *Obras*, IV, 148–49.

18. ANP, Castañeda, reg. 8, f. 17; reg. 10, f. 19; Salinas 38–40, ff. 70, 527; Salinas 42–43, f. 50; Gutiérrez 45–55, ff. 80, 130, 274; Salinas 46–48, ff. 11, 90, 92; Alzate, ff. 441, 592, 742, 864, 869, 913, 928; Gutiérrez 55–56, ff. 494, 498; RA PP, I, trial of Alejo González Gallego; BNP, A556, f. 9; A31, f. 126; A33, f. 153; A35, f. 294; A36, f. 65; A412, 18 Aug 52; A280; AHA, Gaspar Hernández, 28 July 53; AGI, Lima 118, probanza of Juan de Saavedra; Lima 92; letter of Licenciado Fernández, 8 Dec 55; Contaduría 1679, 1680; Justicia 400; HC 361, 362, 478, 717; *Libros de cabildos de Lima*, I, 191, 193, 200, 237, 248; IV, 54, 154, 164, 215, 236, 242, 341, 379, 523, 545, 548, 634; V, 148, 474, 501.

IX. SPANISH WOMEN AND THE SECOND GENERATION

1. Richard Konetzke, in *Revista Internacional de la Sociología*, III (1945), 123–24, 146; J. Rodríguez Arzua, "Las regiones españolas y la población de América," *Revista de Indias*, VIII, 695–748; Peter Boyd-Bowman, "The Regional Origins of the Earliest Spanish Colonists of America," *PMLA*, LXXI (1956), 1152–72; Céspedes, "La sociedad colonial," 394–95.

2. Raúl Porras Barrenechea, in his edition of *Relación del descubrimiento del reino del Perú*, by Diego de Trujillo (Seville, 1948), n. 59.

3. Barriga, *Documentos*, II, 311.

4. Doña Inés Muñoz: BNP, A31, f. 62; A221, 12 March 60; AGI, Patronato 93, no. 9, ramo 2, 192, no. 1, ramo 32; *RANP*, VII, 186, 189. Doña Francisca Jiménez: ANP, Salinas 42–43, f. 271; AGI, Contaduría 1680; Lima 565, vol III, 9 Aug 38.

5. AGI, Lima 118, petition of Rodrigo de Esquivel; *CDIHE*, XCIV, 170.

6. ANP, Gutiérrez 45–55, f. 535; Villarreal 55–57, f. 17; Castañeda, reg. 7, f. 28; BNP, A37, f. 31; A33, f. 72; A35, f. 491; A528, f. 1002; A538, 8 July 56; A31, f. 120; A542, f. 22; A201; AHA, Gaspar Hernández, 14 Feb 50, 4 July 49.

7. AGI, Lima 565, vol III, 8 Nov 39; Gutiérrez de Santa Clara, *Quinquenarios*, III, 177–78.

8. AGI, Justicia 467; Lima 204, probanza of doña Lucía de Padilla; *CDIHE*, XCIV, 178.

9. ANP, Salinas 42–43, ff. 3, 16a, 116; Alzate, f. 42; AGI, Lima 28, letter of Viceroy Cañete, 3 Nov 56; Justicia 467; Pérez de Tudela, *Gasca*, II,

154–55; Garcilaso, *Obras*, IV, 138; Gutiérrez de Santa Clara, *Quinquenarios*, III, 113; Loredo, *Los Repartos*, 266; Barriga, *Documentos*, I, 366; see also chapter II, fn. 6.

10. ANP, Salinas 42–43, f. 48a; BNP, A396, f. 81; A35, f. 20; AGI, Lima 565, vol III, 7 March 39; Lima 567, vol VII, 23 Feb 52; Lima, letter of Licenciado Altamirano, 6 Oct 52.

11. ANP, RA PP, I, trial of Pedro de Salinas.

12. ANP, Salinas 42–43, f. 577; Salinas 46–48, ff. 26, 495, 531, 749, 927, 966, 972; Alzate, f. 861; Gutiérrez 45–55, f. 528; RA PC, I, cuaderno 1; Martínez 49–53, f. 61; BNP, A397, f. 444; A404, f. 493; A542, f. 452; A516, f. 590; A35, f. 276; AHA, Gaspar Hernández, 8 Nov 50; HC 502. For the career of Isabel Rodríguez, prominent property owner of Lima: ANP, PA 293; Salinas 38–40, ff. 244, 498; Salinas 42–43, ff. 249, 540, 632, 690; BNP, A528, f. 986.

13. ANP, Gutiérrez 45–55, ff. 585, 628; Salinas 46–48, ff. 14, 1040; BNP, A221, 15 June 56; A419, f. 100; A227, 21 Jan 51; A542, f. 519; A37, f. 6; A533; A524, f. 670; AHC, Libros de cabildos, I, f. 75; AGI, Contaduría 1680; Justicia 429, no. 1; *Libros de cabildos de Lima*, I, 310.

14. ANP, Salinas 38–40, f. 468; Salinas 42–43, ff. 463, 695; Salinas 46–48, ff. 36, 613, 1023, 1024, 1159; Martínez 49–53, f. 2; Gutiérrez 45–55, f. 300; Villarreal 55–57, f. 135; RA PP, I, trial of Pedro de Salinas; BNP, A30, f. 335; A34, f. 140; A33, f. 81; A528, f. 1001; A221, 23 Feb 57; A541; AGI, Justicia 429, no. 1.

15. ANP, Salinas 42–43, f. 366; RA PP, I, trial of Pedro de Salinas; BNP, A30, ff. 308–13; Cieza, *Chupas*, 291; Diego Fernández, *Historia del Perú*, I, 99, 114; Gutiérrez de Santa Clara, *Quinquenarios*, II, 158, 165; III, 182; *Revista del Instituto Peruano de Investigaciones Genealógicas*, X, 93; Porras, *Cartas del Perú*, 236. Career of Violante de Góngora: ANP, RA PC, I, cuaderno 1; BNP, A37, f. 39; A538, f. 1042; A336, 13 Jan 60.

16. BNP, A35, ff. 532, 533, 593; A542, f. 258; A221, 19 Apr 60; A524, f. 682; A404, f. 468; Garcilaso, *Obras*, II, 372; Cobo, *Obras*, II, 428.

17. BNP, A30, f. 335; A33, f. 81.

18. BNP, A542, f. 481, A34, f. 99.

19. ANP, Gutiérrez 45–55, f. 363; RA PP, I, cuaderno 11; BNP, A33, f. 148; A542, f. 5; AGI, Patronato 123, ramo 9; 109, ramo 5; Contaduría 1680; Calvete, *Rebelión de Pizarro*, IV, 329; Garcilaso, *Obras*, IV, 23; *CDIHE*, XCIV, 172; Mariño de Lobera, *Crónica*, 395.

20. ANP, Gutiérrez 45–55, f. 363; Salinas 46–48, ff. 803, 1091, 1163, 1148; BNP, A510, f. 461; A35, ff. 29, 137; A542, f. 43; AHA, Gaspar Hernández, 18 Feb 49, 31 July 53, 10 July 51.

21. ANP, Martel 55–58, f. 393; J. Fernández 57–98, f. 132; AGI, Contaduría 1680; HC 790; Garcilaso, *Obras*, II, 83–84.

22. AGI, Lima 313, letter of Domingo de Santo Tomás, 1 July 50; BNP, A591, f. 386; A36, f. 410; A33, f. 60; Porras, *Cedulario*, I, 121.

23. ANP, Castañeda, reg. 6, f. 30; BNP, A538, f. 1019; AHA, Gaspar Hernández, 11 June 50.

24. ANP, Salinas 46–48, ff. 12, 589, 866; BNP, A221, 19 Apr 60; A516, f. 132; A542, ff. 456, 564; A538, f. 1047; AGI, Patronato 99, no. 2, ramo 3; 102, ramo 2; 93, no. 5, ramo 1; Lima 205, probanza of Juan Sierra de Leguízamo; Garcilaso, *Obras, passim.*

25. ANP, Salinas 46–48, f. 285; BNP, A337, f. 35; A525, f. 861; AGI, Patronato 93, no. 11, ramo 2; 109, ramo 4; 110, ramo 9; 112, ramo 1 and ramo 14; 114, ramo 8; Lima 118, letter of Pedro Rodríguez Puertocarrero, 30 Sept 57.

26. Service: ANP, Gutiérrez 45–55, f. 627; Salinas 42–43, f. 656; Diego Ruiz 57–63, ff. 183, 813; Martel 55–58, f. 458; BNP, A542, ff. 160, 449; AHC, Libros de cabildos, 61–64, f. 7. Donations and marriage: ANP, Salinas 42–43, f. 29; Salinas 46–48, ff. 196, 559; Alzate, f. 910; Gutiérrez 45–55, ff. 575, 612, 613; RA PP, I, trial of Isabel Gómez; BNP, A512, f. 223; A404, f. 440; A35, f. 324; A37, f. 59; A33, f. 198; A221, 5 May 60; AHC, Vitorero, 6 Feb 60; Libros de cabildos, I, f. 153; AHA, Gaspar Hernández, 7 Aug 50, 26 May 53; AGI, Contratación 198, ramo 12; Contaduría 1680; HC 246.

27. AGI, Patronato 110, ramo 9; 99, no. 2, ramo 3.

28. ANP, RA PP, I, trial of Isabel Gómez.

29. ANP, RA PP, I, trial of Juan de Zárate; AHC, Libro de cabildos, 59–60, f. 14.

X. NEGROES

1. Jerez, *Verdadera relación,* II, 337; Pedro Pizarro, *Descubrimiento,* V, 183; Garcilaso, *Obras,* III, 56.

2. Porras, *Cartas del Perú,* 7.

3. ANP, Castañeda, reg. 4.

4. ANP, Salinas 46–48, f. 1090; BNP, A538, 1 Aug 56; AGI, Lima 566, vol IV, 28 Oct 41; *Libros de cabildos de Lima,* I, 23; Mariño de Lobera, *Crónica,* 285–86; *CDIAO,* VII, 381.

5. Diego Fernández, *Historia del Perú,* I, 384; Garcilaso, *Obras,* IV, 91.

6. Registers on which this tabulation is based: ANP, PA; Juzgado; Castañeda; Salinas 38–40; Salinas 42–43; Salinas 46–48; Gutiérrez 45–55; Gutiérrez 55–56; Alzate; Martínez 49–53, Sebastián Vázquez 51–54; Villarreal 55–57; J. Fernández de Herrera 57–98; E. Pérez 57; Martel 55–58; BNP, A33; A34; A35; A542; A400; A37; A538; AHA; Cerón; Valdecabras; Gaspar Hernández, 49–53. For further discussion of the ethnic groups and their names see J. W. Blake, *European Beginnings in West Africa,* and Gonzalo Aguirre Beltrán, *La Población negra de México, 1519–1810.* Some of the ethnic names in the list, such as the Kassanga, were identified through use of G. P. Murdock's *Africa: Its Peoples and Their Culture History.* Professor Philip D. Curtin of the University of Wisconsin gave me valuable suggestions in connection with the list, including a positive identification of the Berbesí as the Serer.

7. *Libros de cabildos de Lima,* IV. 55; Gutiérrez de Santa Clara, *Quinquenarios,* II, 374.

8. ANP, Martel 55–58.

9. BNP, A404, f. 436; A528, f. 1003; A221, 4 May 60; A542, f. 499.

10. BNP, A34, f. 38.

11. ANP, Gutiérrez 45–55, f. 125; RA PP, I, trial of Isabel Gómez; AHA, Gaspar Hernández, 16 May 49; AGI, Lima 204, probanza of Juan Delgadillo.

12. ANP, Alzate, ff. 913; BNP, A36, f. 50; AHA, Gaspar Hernández, 9 Apr 50, 17 Apr 50.

13. AGI, Lima 566, vol VI, 5 Sept 50; Porras, *Cedulario*, I, 22, 161, 185.

14. ANP, Salinas 42–43, f. 723; BNP, A556, ff. 5, 36; A36, f. 61; AGI, Lima 566, vol VI, 5 Sept 50; Mellafe, *La esclavitud negra*, 41; see also chapter V, fn. 21, Valenzuela.

15. ANP, RA PC, I, cuaderno 3.

16. AHC, Libro de cabildos, 59–60, f. 34.

17. ANP, Gutiérrez 55–56, f. 494; BNP, A556, ff. 8–12; A538, f. 1031; A542, ff. 302, 313, 325, 338, 427, 428.

18. ANP, RA PC, I, cuaderno 3; Alzate, f. 762; BNP, A556, f. 15.

19. ANP, PA, *passim;* Porras, *Cartas del Perú*, 17, 100.

20. ANP, J. Fernández 57–98, f. 32; based in general on the sources listed in fn. 6.

21. Mellafe, *La esclavitud negra*, 41.

22. ANP, Salinas 46–48, f. 889; RA PP, I, trial of Pedro de Salinas; BNP, A31, f. 145; A505; AGI, Patronato 185, ramo 33.

23. Céspedes, "La sociedad colonial," 402; Jiménez de la Espada, *Relaciones Geográficas*, I, *passim.*

24. AGI, Justicia 432, no. 1, ramo 2.

25. ANP, RA PP, I, trial of Pedro de Salinas.

26. ANP, RA PP, I, trial of Isabel Gómez.

27. BNP, A153.

28. ANP, Sebastián Vázquez 51–54, f. 959; Martel 55–58, f. 460; Juan de Padilla 60–61, f. 776; Salinas 46–48, f. 420; Gutiérrez 45–55, f. 619; BNP, A538, f. 1023; A221, 31 Oct 60, 3 Feb 61; A33, f. 9; A32, f. 166; A36, ff. 103, 148; A525, ff. 675, 827; A542, ff. 238, 215; A35, f. 31; AHA, Gaspar Hernández, 21 June 53.

29. ANP, Gutiérrez 45–55, f. 774; BNP, A36, f. 212; HC 603.

30. ANP, Gutiérrez 45–55, f. 466; Salinas 46–48, f. 466.

31. ANP, Alzate, f. 34; AHA, Gaspar Hernández, 4 June 50, 8 Nov 50, 10 Dec 51, 24 May 53.

32. ANP, Alzate, f. 925; AHA, Cerón, 7 March 49; Gaspar Hernández, 5 Sept 50, 3 June 50; AGI, Contaduría 1680.

33. BNP, A542, f. 314; ANP, Gutiérrez 55–56, f. 494; Alzate, f. 913; see also fn. 34.

34. ANP, Martel 55–58, f. 41; BNP, A221, 6 Dec 56; A525, f. 833.

35. Diego Fernández, *Historia del Perú*, I, 384; Antonio Vázquez de Espinosa, *Compendio y descripción de las Indias*, 441.

36. AHA, Valdecabras, 8 June 51; Zárate, *Historia*, II, 507, 544; Pérez de Tudela, *Gasca*, I, 201, 212, 218, 302, 511; II, 525; Cieza, *Quito* (Serrano y Sanz), II, 80; Cieza, *Chupas*, 304; Mellafe, *La esclavitud negra*, 62, 257.

37. ANP, Salinas 42–43, f. 723; BNP, A556, ff. 8–12, 36, 40.

38. BNP, A31, f. 27; AGI, Patronato 116, no. 1, ramo 3; 113, ramo 9; Lima 566, vol VI, 28 Nov 48; Cieza, *Salinas,* 115; Oviedo, *Historia,* V, 209–10.

39. ANP, Salinas 42–43, f. 383; BNP, A33, f. 54.

40. AGI, Patronato 101, ramo 12; Zárate, *Historia,* II, 467; Diego Fernández, *Historia del Perú,* I, 16.

41. ANP, Martel 55–58, f. 352; Juan de Padilla 60–61, f. 775; BNP, A524, f. 703; AGI, Patronato 187, ramo 9; see also fn. 42.

42. ANP, Gutiérrez 45–55, f. 840; BNP, A37, f. 81.

43. ANP, Gutiérrez 45–55, ff. 145, 355; Salinas 46–48, f. 584; BNP, A404, f. 427; A221, 19 Apr 60.

44. ANP, Martel 55–58, f. 362; E. Pérez 57, f. 1844; AHA, Valdecabras, 7 Sept 51; Barriga, *Documentos,* I, 392–402.

45. ANP, Alzate, f. 827; Gutiérrez 55–56, f. 509; BNP, A538, f. 1051; A542, ff. 320–22; A221, 7 June 60; AHA, Gaspar Hernández, 3 Jan 51; AGI, Justicia 429, no. 1; Contaduría 1784; HC 463.

46. BNP, A538, 1 Aug 50; A32, ff. 106, 118, 172; ANP, Salinas 46–48, f. 453; AHA, Gaspar Hernández, 3 Aug 50, 2 July 53.

47. ANP, Salinas 46–48, f. 493.

48. ANP, Gutiérrez 45–55, ff. 346, 814; BNP, A33, f. 144; AHA, Gaspar Hernández, 21 June 53.

49. AGI, Patronato 113, ramo 8; Gutiérrez de Santa Clara, *Quinquenarios,* II, 374.

50. AGI, Lima 204, probanza of Juan Delgadillo; *Libros de cabildos de Lima,* IV, 112.

51. *Libros de cabildos de Lima,* IV, V, *passim.*

52. ANP, Juzgado, 7 Nov 36.

53. ANP, Gutiérrez 45–55, f. 500; Salinas 46–48, ff. 345, 1075; BNP, A556, f. 20; A34, f. 113.

54. ANP, Salinas 46–48, ff. 416, 936; Salinas 42–43, f. 547; BNP, A37, f. 74; A542, f. 532; A524, f. 707; HC 374.

55. ANP, Castañeda, reg. 8 ,ff. 1–2.

56. ANP, Gutiérrez 45–55, ff. 125, 507; Martel 55–58, ff. 327, 329; BNP, A419, f. 99; A538, 1 Aug 56; A221, 1 July 60; A516, ff. 144, 148, 152; AHA, Valdecabras, 10 Nov 54; AHC, Libros de cabildos, *passim;* AGI, Contaduría 1680, 1825; *Libros de cabildos de Lima,* I, 297; IV, 28, 55, 75, 403, 581; V, 266, 356 and *passim;* Barriga, *Documentos,* II, 216.

57. ANP, Salinas 38–40, f. 258; RA PP, I, trial of Isabel Gómez; BNP, A35, ff. 384, 592, 612.

58. ANP, Martínez 49–53, ff. 112, 134; Martel 55–58, f. 16; Salinas 46–48, ff. 779, 795; Alzate, f. 327; Villarreal 55–57, f. 169; BNP, A525, f. 557; A32, f. 148; A221, 26 Apr 60, 26 Feb 60; A35, f. 578; A528, f. 981; AHA, Gaspar Hernández, 25 May 53; AHC, Libro de Cabildos, 59–60, f. 66; HC 576.

59. ANP, Salinas 46–48, f. 981; J. Fernández 57–98, f. 125; Villarreal 55–57, f. 65; BNP, A221, 2 Apr 60; A36, f. 159; AHA, Cerón, 9 March 49.

60. ANP, Martel 55–58, f. 475; A542, f. 501; Salinas 46–48, ff. 605, 1058; BNP, A542, f. 501; A35, f. 200; AHA, Valdecabras, 10 Nov 54; AHC, Libros de cabildos, I, f. 160; AGI, Contaduría 1681; Justicia 429, no. 1; *Libros de cabildos de Lima*, III, 73; Barriga, *Documentos*, I, 277, 299–301.

61. AGI, Justicia 467; Tomás Thayer Ojeda, *Valdivia y sus compañeros*, 58.

62. BNP, A35, ff. 200–3; AGI, Contaduría 1680.

63. ANP, Gutiérrez 45–55, ff. 533, 589, 591–92; Gutiérrez 55–56, ff. 350, 389, 421; Salinas 46–48, ff. 449–51; Martel 55–58, f. 71; Nicolás de Grado 59–60, 8 Jan 60; BNP, A35, f. 555; A36, f. 150; A222, f. 140; A404, f. 474; AGI, Contaduría 1680, 1681.

64. ANP, Gutiérrez 45–55, f. 589; Nicolás de Grado 59–60, 8 Jan 60; AGI, Contaduría 1680.

65. ANP, Martel 55–58, f. 36; BNP, A542, f. 505.

66. Gómara, *Hispania victrix*, 265; Garcilaso, *Obras*, I, 389; IV, 87.

67. ANP, Salinas 38–40, f. 81; Salinas 46–48, f. 905; HC 379; Garcilaso, *Obras*, IV, 87.

68. *RANP*, III, 15; Gutiérrez de Santa Clara, *Quinquenarios*, II, 372; *Libros de cabildos de Lima*, III, 15.

69. BNP, A32, f. 206; A419, f. 106; AGI, Justicia 1074; Diego Fernández, *Historia del Perú*, I, 357.

70. BNP, A32, ff. 45, 84; AGI, Patronato 116, no. 1, ramo 1; Lima 204, probanza of doña Lucía de Padilla; HC 399; Garcilaso, *Obras*, III, 302–3, 346–47; Santiago Martínez, *Fundadores de Arequipa*, 423.

71. ANP, Juzgado, 4 Dec 36; Salinas 38–40, ff. 223, 487–88; Castañeda, reg. 11, f. 50; BNP, A607, f. 11; AGI, Lima 566, vol V, 22 Feb 45; Lima 118, probanza of Licenciado Mercado de Peñalosa; Patronato 109, ramo 4; Justicia 467; Contaduría 1679, 1680; HC 656, 799; *CDIAO*, XX, 354; *CDIHE*, XCIV, 162, 223, 224, 225.

XI. INDIANS

1. ANP, Salinas 46–48, f. 1063; BNP, A31, f. 145; sampling based on sources listed in chapter X, fn. 6.

2. ANP, PA 489; AGI, Justicia 1067, no. 2, ramo 1; Pérez de Tudela, *Gasca*, I, 507; Medina, *Colección*, VII, 91; Diego Fernández, *Historia del Perú* I, 11; Gutiérrez de Santa Clara, *Quinquenarios*, II, 157; Porras, *Cartas del Perú*, 322; Oviedo, *Historia*, V, 168, 178.

3. Based on ANP, PA; Castañeda; Salinas 38–40; Salinas 42–43; Salinas 46–48; Alzate; HC 1–31.

4. ANP, Juzgado, 28 Aug. 37; PA 674; and sources listed in fn. 3.

5. ANP, PA 631; Castañeda, reg. 11, f. 8.

6. *RANP*, Libro de bautismos de la iglesia mayor, VII–VIII, X–XIV; and fn. 3.

7. ANP, Salinas 42–43, f. 347; Salinas 46–48, ff. 22, 139, 333; BNP, A208; A581, 30 July 43; and sources listed in chapter X, fn. 6.

8. ANP, RA PP, I, trial of Pedro de Salinas.

9. BNP, A208.

10. ANP, Salinas 38–40, f. 450; Salinas 46–48, f. 668; Castañeda, reg. 11, f. 37; Alzate, f. 374; BNP, A34, f. 117; A35, f. 447.

11. AHC, Vitorero, 28 Feb 60; BNP, A396, f. 84.

12. ANP, Salinas, 38–40, f. 450; Castañeda, reg. 6, f. 30; Salinas 46–48, ff. 24, 151, 164, 184, 325, 841.

13. BNP, A542, f. 273.

14. AGI, Contaduría 1680, 1824; *Libros de cabildos de Lima,* V, 482.

15. Gutiérrez de Santa Clara, *Quinquenarios,* II, 219; IV, 108.

16. AGI, Justicia 401, will of Jerónimo de Villegas; Pérez de Tudela, *Gasca,* II, 309 (where "mita" is misprinted as "mitad").

17. BNP, A547; A542, f. 49; A404, f. 474; A538, ff. 1047–54; AHA, Gaspar Hernández, 53; AGI, Lima 204, probanza of Diego Hernández; Barriga, *Documentos,* II, 215; *Libros de cabildos de Lima,* I, 285.

18. AGI, Patronato 187, ramo 9.

19. ANP, Salinas 42–43, f. 729; BNP, A516, f. 153; AHC, Vitorero, 6 Apr 60, 16 Feb 60, 9 Feb 60; Diego Fernández, *Historia del Perú,* I, 343; *Revista del Archivo Histórico del Cuzco,* IV (1953), 25.

20. AGI, Justicia 667, no. 1; Lima 313, letter of Domingo de Santo Tomás, 1 July 50.

21. BNP, A36, ff. 262, 449; A221, 17 June 60.

22. ANP, Martel 55–58, ff. 329, 380; BNP, A542, ff. 107; A36, ff. 262–63.

23. ANP, Gutiérrez 45–55, f. 598; BNP, A36, ff. 279, 449, 501.

24. ANP, Gutiérrez 45–55, f. 363; BNP, A37, f. 18; AHC, Vitorero, 31 June 60; Libro de Cabildos, 59–60, f. 63; *Revista del Archivo Histórico del Cuzco,* IV (1953), 41.

25. Porras, *Cartas del Perú,* 323; Garcilaso, *Obras,* II, 381; Gutiérrez de Santa Clara, *Quinquenarios,* III, 118; Oviedo, *Historia,* I, 223.

26. Gutiérrez de Santa Clara, *Quinquenarios,* III, 177.

27. ANP, RA PC, I, suit of doña Isabel; Castañeda, reg. 1, f. 15; Salinas 42–43, f. 329; AGI, Lima 204, probanza of Francisco de Ampuero.

28. ANP, J. Fernández 57–98, f. 120; AGI, Lima 205, probanza of don Jerónimo; AHA, Gaspar Hernández, 21 March 52, 22 March 53.

29. BNP, A33, f. 295; AHC, Vitorero, 9 Feb 60; AGI, Patronato 28, ramo 12; Justicia 467; Lima 566, vol IV, 29 Nov 41; Gutiérrez de Santa Clara, *Quinquenarios,* III, 229; Calvete, *Rebelión de Pizarro,* V, 69.

30. Garcilaso, *Obras,* II, 198, 381; III, 48–49; see also fn. 29.

31. AGI, Patronato 93, no. 11, ramo 2; Garcilaso, *Obras,* IV, 11.

32. ANP, Castañeda, reg. 8, f. 45; Salinas 38–40, f. 365; RA PP, I, trial of Pedro de Salinas; Salinas 46–48, f. 208; Alzate, f. 41; BNP, A29, f. 37; A36, f. 8; AGI, Lima 566, vol IV, 20 Aug 40; Justicia 467; Patronato 114, ramo 9;

Contaduría 1679, 1680; Porras, *Cedulario*, II, 340; *Revista Histórica*, XVI, 128; *CDIHE*, XLIX, 231; Pérez de Tudela, *Gasca*, I, 153; II, 266; Calvete, *Rebelión de Pizarro*, V, 30; Cieza, *Tercera Parte*, in *Mercurio Peruano*, XXXIV (1953), 314.

33. BNP, A397, f. 410.

34. ANP, Salinas 46–48, f. 889; E. Pérez 57, f. 2055; BNP, A538, 1 Aug 56; A30, f. 367; AHC, Vitorero, 11 Feb 60; AHA, Gaspar Hernández, 16 Feb 53, 9 Dec 53, 25 May 53, 16 March 53.

35. ANP, RA PP, I, trial of Isabel Gómez; trial of Pedro de Salinas; Villarreal 55–57, ff. 70, 77; Sebastián Vázquez 51–54, f. 961; Gutiérrez 45–55, f. 652; BNP, A538, 2 Sept 56, 16 Sept 56; A222, f. 136; A404, f. 396; A524, f. 705; AHC, Libro de Cabildos, 59–60, f. 73.

36. AGI, Lima 204, probanza of Diego Hernández.

37. AHC, Vitorero, 22 Jan 60, 14 Nov 59, 19 Sept 60, 7 Oct 60, and *passim;* Libros de cabildos, I, f. 14; *Revista del Archivo Histórico del Cuzco*, IV (1953), 33–35.

38. AHC, Libro de cabildos, 59–60, f. 42; AGI, Lima 300, letter of Archbishop Loaysa, 9 March 56; Pérez de Tudela, *Gasca*, I, 313–20; II, 362.

39. ANP, Gutiérrez 45–55, ff. 461, 835; BNP, A538, 11 Aug 56; A524, ff. 672, 679, 690; A525, f. 843; A337, f. 415; A222, f. 147; AHC, Vitorero, 14 Nov 59; AGI, Contaduría 1825.

40. ANP, Salinas 46–48, ff. 119, 202, 267, 272; BNP, A30, f. 322; A32, ff. 40, 84; AHC, Vitorero, 7 Oct 60, 23 March 60; Libro de Cabildos, 59–60, f. 5; AHA, Cerón, 17 Dec 48, 24 May 49; AGI, Contaduría 1825.

41. BNP, A34, f. 147; Jiménez de la Espada, *Relaciones geográficas*, I, 357–60, 362–71, 373; Pérez de Tudela, *Gasca*, I, 206; *Relación de las cosas del Perú*, V, 297.

XII. CONCLUSION

1. AGI, Patronato 185, ramo 11; Porras, *Cedulario*, II, 187–88; Loredo, *Los Repartos*, 9–63.

2. J. Rodríguez Arzua, in *Revista de Indias*, VIII (1947), 695–748; Peter Boyd-Bowman, in *PMLA*, LXXI (1956), 1152–72; Céspedes, "La sociedad colonial," 394 ff.; Mario Góngora, *Los grupos de conquistadores en Tierra Firme*, 77.

3. William H. McNeill, *The Rise of the West*, 602.

4. Raúl Porras Barrenechea, "El nombre del Perú," in *Mar del Sur*, VI (1951), no. 18, 26.

5. Cieza, *Tercera Parte*, in *Mercurio Peruano*, XXXII (1951), 148.

BIBLIOGRAPHY

The present study is based ultimately on notarial registers of the cities of Lima (in both the National Archive and the National Library) and of Arequipa. The registers of Cuzco are missing until the year 1559, and it was not possible within the framework of the project to investigate important centers like Quito, La Paz, Sucre, and Potosí, though it appears that there too notarial documents from the early period are sparse or altogether missing. While many other sources were consulted and have been referred to abundantly, it was in the notarial documents of Peru that the presence and importance of artisans, merchants, and Spanish women first came overwhelmingly to my attention. For the social and economic history of the Spanish Indies, the archives of the Western hemisphere seem to take precedence over those of Spain.

Since this is the first book-length study in the field of Spanish colonial history to give such importance to notarial documents, perhaps it would be well to state briefly some provisional conclusions about techniques of their use. A high degree of skill in reading the notaries' script is absolutely necessary, but such skill can come quickly after total immersion in actual work with the documents. Few notarial documents, except wills and large transactions, appear at first glance significant in themselves; the scholar must familiarize himself with a given time and locality, and then follow threads of interest, often the lives of people.

This means that notarial documents can be used more readily for broad subjects (in a limited time and space) than for highly specialized projects. To assemble a single one of the biographies contained in the present book—that of the merchant Baltasar de Armenta—it would have been necessary to search through most of the sources used for all twelve chapters. To do the necessary notarial research for a specialized study covering a longer time period, such as for example "Artisans in Colonial Peru," appears a sheer impossibility, not to speak of the wasted effort that would be involved, scanning so much material which would be irrelevant to the immediate purpose. (And notarial records are not easy to scan.) A more fruitful approach would be to build up a series of broader studies covering shorter time periods (forty or fifty years at a maximum). After their completion, it would be possible to write an adequate history of artisanry or the encomienda, or some other special subject, for the whole Spanish Indies over the whole colonial period. Though limitation in the time period to be studied is a practical necessity in notarial research, extreme geographical limitation is not. In the present project, Arequipa and Cuzco proved readily comprehensible in terms of patterns learned in Lima; the materials there gave a new country-wide perspective, and filled out the lives of people only partly rooted in Lima.

The range of information to be drawn from sixteenth-century Spanish notarial documents is very broad. Above and beyond sales, wills, work contracts, dowry agreements, companies, and powers of attorney, the legal-minded Spaniards notarized many other insignificant personal dealings which a different society or a later age might never have committed to paper. With some supplementing from the more traditional sources, one can construct from the Peruvian notarial records coherent, detailed pictures of the main branches of the social and economic life of the colony, including the encomienda system, commerce, navigation, artisanry, and even, to an extent, family life. There is detailed information on all strata of society, even including the careers of slaves and freedmen.

But of course there are sharp limits to what can be learned from the notaries. Aside from such obvious limitations as the lack of information relevant to intellectual history as usually conceived, the notarial records are characterized by a very strong urban bias. In the case of a society which itself had an extremely strong urban bias, this characteristic need not debilitate research. But if Chapter II of this book contains much more about encomenderos than about majordomos, or if the picture of miners and rural priests is hazy, it is because the notarial records reflect above all the life of the urban centers. (There still may prove to be records in Bolivia that will throw light on miners and mining in the early period; mining camps had notaries, though the chances of their records being preserved were less than in the cities.) Another characteristic of the notarial records is their great unevenness in matters of factual detail. They provide coherent detail on basic contractual relationships, on the careers of all kinds of individuals, on the things in general that the social historian is interested in. For the economic historian, who wants to know specifics of materials and techniques and prices, notarial documents can be frustrating. Despite occasional spectacular windfalls, the economic historian will usually have to infer how blacksmiths worked from documents referring only to the purchase of "certain tools," or the sale of "certain iron" for a hundred pesos.

The notarial archives seem to have a good deal of potential for statistical research, if the results are viewed with caution. One can collect instances of the occurrence of any given type of person, thing, or situation, and the result will at least represent a minimum figure from which to arrive at some rough commonsense estimate of absolute quantities. Such collected lists also represent significant samplings which probably reflect relative numbers, such as the proportion of smiths to tailors, quite faithfully. Accumulating such lists, however, is almost prohibitively laborious, unless the task is undertaken as a byproduct of other research. In the present study, the appendix represents the sum total of what could be accomplished in the way described without seriously hampering the main part of the work.

Other types of sources also proved useful for the social historian. The Archive of the Indies contains in the sections "Contaduría" and "Justicia" materials which yielded much the same kinds of information as the Peruvian notarial documents. Also the more familiar matter in the sections "Lima" and "Patronato" was interesting, but more for bits of social detail than for the ostensible principal subject. A Spaniard's *probanza de méritos* may say less than nothing about his loyalty, bravery or military ability, but usually contains evidence of his regional and political affinities and general social status. For a fairly rounded picture of the upper strata of society and the merchants, the Archive of the Indies was essential.

A large number of printed contemporary sources were used in the same fashion as was "Patronato," as social history despite themselves, for the chronicles are the purest kind of military history, and the editors of the collections of documents published in the past chose according to narrow criteria. Though a multitude of such sources are in some way relevant, the most important are the chronicles published in the *Biblioteca de Autores Españoles,* and the standard collections of published documents. (Among the standard collections should be included the publications of Porras Barrenechea, Barriga, and Loredo, which are little used outside Peru, and the Gasca papers published by Pérez de Tudela.)

Modern works bearing on the early social and economic history of Peru are few indeed, and mainly either insubstantial or peripheral, but some deserve mention. In Chile the work of Thayer Ojeda and his successors Mellafe and Góngora is impressive, but necessarily tangential to the present study. Thayer Ojeda had many deep insights, some of them applicable to Peru, which have been little noted because they were smothered in genealogy and buried in individual biographical articles. Excellent, but also peripheral, are the work of Enrique Otte on the early period in the Caribbean, and Woodrow Borah's study of trade between Mexico and Peru. The Spaniard Juan Pérez de Tudela, aside from extremely useful activity in publishing chronicles and documents, has made a major statement on conquest Peru in the long prologue to his *Crónicas del Perú.* Though he confines himself mainly to the moral evaluation of prominent individuals, his judgments, particularly of the Pizarros, are often profound, and rest in part on an increased awareness of the complex social and economic realities of Peru.

In Peru, Emilio Harth-Terré has done good work with notarial documents, taking an interest in the humbler elements of society, but has stopped short of an extended, methodical effort. One of the finest minds ever to occupy himself with the history of Peru, Raúl Porras Barrenechea, worked on the edges of the field of interest of the present study, devoting much of his time to textual criticism and the publication of documents. He came to realize that something very basic happened in the first years of the Spanish occupation, but his attempt to express this through the deification of Francisco Pizarro and vilification of Diego de Almagro was misguided, and led him far from matters of greater concern.

In the bibliography of printed sources, no distinction is made between contemporary source materials and modern works. Most of the publications contain both documents and modern interpretation, and even those which are primarily interpretation were often used, in the present project, for the documents they contain.

ARCHIVAL SOURCES

Archivo de la Audiencia Territorial de Sevilla.
Legajo 59.
Archivo General de Indias, Seville (AGI).
Contaduría 1679–83, 1784, 1824, 1825; Contratación 198, 576; Indiferente General 1204; Justicia 400–2, 425, 429, 432, 467, 487, 667, 719, 720, 723, 724, 734, 746, 758, 1052–57, 1074, 1082, 1124–26, 1160, 1164, 1166, 1178; Lima 28, 92, 108, 110–12, 118, 119, 204, 205, 300, 305, 313, 565–67; Patronato 28, 90–120, 124, 128, 132, 135, 150, 185, 187.
Archivo Histórico de Arequipa (AHA).
Notarial registers from the years 1548 to 1556.
Archivo Histórico Nacional del Cuzco (AHC).
Notarial registers from the years 1559 and 1560; Libros de cabildos.
Archivo Nacional del Perú, Lima (ANP).
Sección Notarial, notarial registers from 1533 through 1560.
Sección Histórica, Libro del Juzgado de la ciudad de Los Reyes; Real Audiencia, Procedimientos Penales, legajos I and II; Real Audiencia, Procedimientos Civiles, legajos I and II.
Archivo de Protocolos, Seville (APS).
1550, oficio XV, libro II.
Biblioteca Nacional del Perú, Lima (BNP).
Notarial registers, trial records, and other documents through 1560.
Library of Congress.
Harkness Collection (HC).

PRINTED SOURCES

Albenino, Nicolao de. *Verdadera relacion delo sussedido enlos reynos y provincias del Peru desde la yda a ellos del virey Blasco Nuñes Vela hasta el desbarato y muerte de Gonçalo Piçarro.* Ed. by José Toribio Medina. Paris, 1930.
Armas Medina, Fernando de. "El clero en las guerras civiles del Peru." *Anuario de Estudios Americanos,* VII (1950), 1–46.
———. *Cristianización del Perú (1532–1600).* Seville, 1953.
Barriga, Víctor M., ed. *Documentos para la historia de Arequipa.* 3 vols. Arequipa, 1939–55.
———, ed. *Los Mercedarios en el Perú en el siglo XVI. Documentos inéditos*

del Archivo de Indias. 5 vols. Vol. I, Rome, 1933; vols. II–V, Arequipa, 1939–54.

Belaúnde Guinassi, Manuel. *La Encomienda en el Perú.* Lima, 1945.

Beltrán, Gonzalo Aguirre. *La Población negra de México, 1519–1810.* Mexico City, 1946.

Benzoni, Girolamo. *History of the New World.* Tr. and ed. by W. H. Smith. London, 1857.

Bermúdez Plata, Cristóbal, ed. *Catálogo de pasajeros a Indias.* 3 vols. Seville, 1940–46.

Blake, J. W. *European Beginnings in West Africa, 1454–1578.* London, 1937.

Borah, Woodrow. *Early Colonial Trade and Navigation between Mexico and Peru.* Los Angeles, 1954.

Borregán, Alonso. *Crónica de la conquista del Perú.* Ed by Rafael Loredo. Seville, 1948.

Bourne, Edward Gaylord. *Spain in America, 1450–1580.* Ed. by Benjamin Keen. New York, 1962.

Boyd-Bowman, Peter. "The Regional Origins of the Earliest Spanish Colonists of America." *Publications of the Modern Language Association,* LXXI (1956), 1152–72.

Busto Duthurburu, José Antonio del. *El Conde de Nieva, Virrey del Perú: primera parte.* Lima, 1963.

Cabello Balboa, Miguel. *Historia del Perú.* Ed. by Horacio H. Urteaga and Carlos A. Romero. Lima, 1920.

Calancha, Antonio. *Corónica moralizada del orden de San Agustín en el Perú.* Barcelona, 1639.

Calvete de Estrella, Juan Cristóbal. *Rebelión de Pizarro en el Perú y vida de don Pedro Gasca.* Juan Pérez de Tudela, ed. *Crónicas del Perú.* 5 vols. Madrid, 1963–65.

Carvajal, Gaspar de, O. P. *Relación del nuevo descubrimiento del famoso río grande de las Amazonas.* Ed. by Jorge Hernández Millares. Mexico City, 1955.

Catálogo de fondos americanos del Archivo de Protocolos de Sevilla. 5 vols. Madrid, 1930–35.

Céspedes del Castillo, Guillermo. "La sociedad colonial americana en los siglos XVI y XVII." Jaime Vicens Vives, ed. *Historia social y económica de España y América,* Vol. III. Barcelona, 1957.

Cieza de León, Pedro de. *La Crónica del Perú.* Enrique de Vedia, ed. *Historiadores primitivos de Indias.* 2 vols. Madrid, 1946–47.

———. *Guerra de Chupas.* Madrid, n. d.

———. *Guerra de Quito.* Manuel Serrano y Sanz, ed. *Historiadores de Indias.* 2 vols. Madrid, 1909.

———. *Guerra de Salinas.* Madrid, n. d.

———. *Tercera parte de la crónica del Perú,* Chapters I–LIV. Ed. by Rafael Loredo. *Mercurio Peruano,* XXVII (1946), 409–40; XXXII (1951), 148–59; XXXIV (1953), 305–17; XXXVI (1955), 456–73; XXXVII (1956), 77–95; XXXVIII (1957), 247–68; XXXIX (1958), 565–85.

————. *Tercero libro de las guerras civiles del Perú, el cual se llama la Guerra de Quito.* Ed. by Marcos Jiménez de la Espada. Madrid, 1877.

Cobo, Bernabé, S. J. *Obras.* Ed. by Francisco Mateos, S. J. 2 vols. Madrid, 1964.

Colección de documentos inéditos para la historia de España. Madrid, 1842–95.

Colección de documentos inéditos relativos al descubrimiento, conquista y colonización de las posesiones españolas en América y Oceanía. Madrid, 1864–84.

Córdoba Salinas, Diego de, O. F. M. *Crónica franciscana de las provincias del Perú.* Ed. by Lino G. Canedo, O. F. M. Washington, 1957.

Cúneo-Vidal, R. *Vida del conquistador del Perú, don Francisco Pizarro, y de sus hermanos.* Barcelona, 1925.

Diffie, Bailey W. "Estimates of Potosí mineral production, 1545–1555." *Hispanic American Historical Review,* XX (1940). 275–82.

————. *Latin American Civilization: Colonial Period.* Harrisburg, Pa., 1945.

Durand, José. *La transformación social del conquistador.* 2 vols. Mexico City, 1953.

Enríquez de Guzmán, don Alonso. *Libro de la vida y costumbres de don Alonso Enríquez de Guzmán.* Ed. by Hayward Keniston. Madrid, 1960.

Estete, Miguel de. *El descubrimiento y la conquista del Perú.* Ed. by Carlos M. Larrea. Quito, 1918.

Fernández, Diego. *Historia del Perú.* Juan Pérez de Tudela, ed. *Crónicas del Perú.* 5 vols. Madrid, 1963–65.

Garcilaso de la Vega. *Obras completas.* Ed. by Carmelo Sáenz de Santa María, S. J. 4 vols. Madrid, 1960.

Gómara, Francisco López de. *Hispania victrix: Historia general de las Indias.* Enrique de Vedia, ed. *Historiadores primitivos de Indias.* 2 vols. Madrid, 1946–47.

Góngora, Mario. *Los Grupos de conquistadores en Tierra Firme (1509–1530).* Santiago de Chile, 1962.

Góngora Marmolejo, Alonso. *Historia de todas las cosas que han acaecido en el reino de Chile y de todos los que lo han gobernado.* Francisco Esteve Barba, ed. *Crónicas del Reino de Chile.* Madrid, 1960.

Guitiérrez de Santa Clara, Pedro. *Quinquenarios o historia de las guerras civiles del Perú.* Juan Pérez de Tudela, ed. *Crónicas del Perú.* 5 vols. Madrid, 1963–65.

Hanke, Lewis, and Juan Pérez de Tudela, eds. *Relaciones histórico-literarias de la América meridional.* Madrid, 1959.

Haring, C. H. *The Spanish Empire in America.* New York, 1963.

The Harkness Collection in the Library of Congress. See U.S., Library of Congress.

Harth-Terré, Emilio, and Alberto Márquez Abanto. "Las Bellas artes en el virreinato del Perú: perspectiva social y económica del artesano virreinal en Lima." *Revista del Archivo Nacional del Perú,* XXVI (1962).

Harth-Terré, Emilio. *Cauces de españolización en la sociedad indoperuana de Lima virreinal.* Pamphlet published by Editorial Tierra y Arte. Lima, 1964.

―――. "El esclavo negro en la sociedad indoperuana." *Journal of Inter-American Studies,* vol. III, no. 3 (July, 1961).

Helmer, Marie. "Notas sobre la encomienda peruana en el siglo XVI." *Revista del Instituto de Historia del Derecho* (Buenos Aires), no. 10 (1959), 124–43.

―――. "Notes sur les esclaves indiens au Perou (XVIᵉ siècle)." *Tilas* (Travaux de l'institut d'études latino-américaines de l'université de Strasbourg), V (1965).

―――. "Visitación de los Indios Chupachos (1549)." *Travaux de l'Institut Français d'Etudes Andines,* V (1955–56), 1–50.

Jerez, Francisco de. *Verdadera relación de la conquista del Perú y provincia del Cuzco, llamada la Nueva Castilla.* Enrique de Vedia, ed. *Historiadores primitivos de Indias.* 2 vols. Madrid, 1946–47.

Jiménez de la Espada, Marcos, ed. *Relaciones geográficas de Indias.* Vol. I, *Perú.* Ed. by José Urbano Martínez Carreras. Madrid, 1965.

Konetzke, Richard, ed. *Colección de documentos para la historia de la formación social de Hispano-América.* Madrid, 1953.

―――. "La Emigración de las mujeres españolas a América durante la época colonial." *Revista Internacional de la Sociología,* III (1945), 123–50.

―――. "La esclavitud de los indios como elemento en la estructuración social de Hispanoamérica." *Estudios de Historia Social,* I (1949), 441–80.

―――. "La formación de la nobleza en Indias." *Estudios Americanos,* III, no. 10 (July, 1951), 329–57.

Kubler, George. "The Neo-Inca State." *Hispanic American Historical Review,* XXVII (1947), 189–203.

Lavalle, José Antonio de. *Estudios históricos.* Lima, 1935.

Levillier, Roberto, ed. *Audiencia do Lima. Correspondencia de presidentes y oidores; documentos del Archivo de Indias.* Madrid, 1922.

―――. *Descubrimiento y población del norte argentino por españoles del Perú.* Buenos Aires, 1943.

―――, ed. *Gobernantes del Perú. Cartas y papeles, siglo XVI; documentos del Archivo de Indias.* Vols. I–III. Madrid, 1921–26.

LIMA. *Libros de cabildos de Lima.* Vols. I–VI. Lima, 1935–.

Lisson Chávez, Emilio, ed. *La Iglesia de España en el Perú.* 5 vols. Seville, 1943–47.

Lizárraga, Reginaldo de. *Descripción de las Indias.* Ed. by Carlos A. Romero and Franciso A. Loaysa. Lima, 1946.

Lohmann Villena, Guillermo. *Los Americanos en las órdenes nobiliarias.* 2 vols. Madrid, 1947.

―――. *El corregidor de indios en el Perú bajo los Austrias.* Madrid, 1957.

López Martínez, Héctor. "Un motín de mestizos en el Perú (1567)." *Revista de Indias,* XXIV (1964), 367–81.

―――. "El cronista florentino Nicolao de Albenino en la rebelión de Francisco Hernández Girón." *Mercurio Peruano,* XLI (July 1960), 297–301.

Loredo, Rafael. *Alardes y derramas.* Lima, 1942.

———. *Los Repartos.* Lima, 1958.

Mariño de Lobera, don Pedro. *Crónica del reino de Chile.* Francisco Esteve Barba, ed. *Crónicas del reino de Chile.* Madrid, 1960.

Martínez, Santiago. *Fundadores de Arequipa.* Arequipa, 1936.

———. *Gobernadores de Arequipa colonial (1539–1821).* Arequipa, 1930.

McNeill, William H. *The Rise of the West.* Chicago, 1963.

Maticorena Estrada, Miguel. "Cieza de León en Sevilla y su muerte en 1554. Documentos." *Anuario de Estudios Americanos,* XII (1955), 615–74.

Medina, José Toribio. *Bartolomé Ruiz de Andrade (sic), primer piloto de la Mar del Sur.* Santiago de Chile, 1919.

———. *Colección de documentos inéditos para la historia de Chile.* Santiago de Chile, 1888–1902.

———. *Diccionario biográfico colonial de Chile.* Santiago de Chile, 1906.

Meléndez, Juan, O. P. *Tesoros verdaderos de las indias en la historia de la gran provincia de San Juan Bautista del Perú, de el orden de Predicadores.* 3 vols. Rome, 1681.

Mellafe, Rolando. *La introducción de la esclavitud negra en Chile.* Santiago de Chile, 1959.

———, and Sergio Villalobos. *Diego de Almagro.* Santiago de Chile, 1954.

Mendiburu, Manuel de. *Diccionario histórico-biográfico del Perú.* 2d edition. 11 vols. Lima, 1931–35.

Montesinos, Fernando. *Anales del Perú.* Ed. by Victor M. Maurtua. 2 vols. Madrid, 1906.

Montoto, Santiago. *Nobiliario hispano-americano del siglo XVI.* Madrid, n. d.

Muñoz de San Pedro, Miguel. "Doña Isabel de Vargas, esposa del padre del conquistador del Perú." *Revista de Indias,* XI (1951), 9–28.

———. *Tres testigos de la conquista del Perú.* Buenos Aires, 1953.

Murdock, G. P. *Africa: Its Peoples and Their Culture History.* New York, 1959.

Otte, Enrique. "Carlos V y sus vasallos patrimoniales de América." *Clio* (organ of the Academia Dominicana de la Historia), XXVIII (1960), 1–27.

———: "La flota de Diego Colón." *Revista de Indias,* XXIV (1964), 475–503.

———. "Mercaderes vascos en Tierra Firme a raiz del descubrimiento del Perú." *Mercurio Peruano,* nos. 443–44 (Libro Jubiliar de Víctor Andrés Belaúnde), 81–89.

———, and Miguel Maticorena Estrada. "La isla de la Magdalena en el segundo viaje de Pizarro y Almagro para el descubrimiento del Perú." *Mercurio Peruano,* XLI (June 1960), 259–70.

Oviedo, Gonzalo Fernández de. *Historia general y natural de las Indias.* Ed. by Juan Pérez de Tudela. 5 vols. Madrid, 1959.

Parry, J. H. *The Establishment of the European Hegemony (1415–1715).* New York, 1961.

Pérez Bustamante, C. "Las Regiones españolas y la población de América (1509–34)." *Revista de Indias,* II (1941), no. 3, 81–120.

Pérez de Tudela, Juan, ed. *Crónicas del Perú*. 5 vols. Madrid, 1963–65.
———. ed. *Documentos relativos a don Pedro de la Gasca y a Gonzalo Pizarro*. 2 vols. Madrid, 1964.
Pizarro, Pedro. *Relación del descubrimiento y conquista de los reinos del Perú*. Juan Pérez de Tudela, ed. *Crónicas del Perú*. 5 vols. Madrid, 1963–65.
Porras Barrenechea, Raúl, ed. *Cartas del Perú (1524–1543)*. Lima, 1959.
———, ed. *Cedulario del Perú*. 2 vols. Lima, 1944–48.
———. *Los Cronistas del Perú (1528–1650)*. Lima, 1962.
———. "Francisco Pizarro." *Revista de Indias*, III (1942), 5–41.
———. *Las relaciones primitivas de la conquista del Perú*. Paris, 1937.
———. "Medina y su contribución a la historia Peruana." *Mercurio Peruano*, XXXII (1952), 491–523.
———. "El nombre del Perú." *Mar del Sur*, VI (1951), no. 18, 2–39.
———. *El testamento de Pizarro*. Paris, 1936.
Prado y Ugarteche, Javier. *Estado social del Perú durante la dominación española*. Lima, 1940.
Prescott, William H. *History of the Conquest of Peru*. (The Modern Library.) New York, n. d.
QUITO. *Libros de cabildos de la ciudad de Quito*. Vols. I–III. Quito, 1934.
Ramón Folch, José Armando de. *Descubrimiento de Chile y compañeros de Almagro*. Santiago de Chile, 1953.
Relación de las cosas del Perú. Juan Pérez de Tudela, ed. *Crónicas del Perú*. 5 vols. Madrid, 1963–65.
Revista del Archivo Histórico del Cuzco. Cuzco, 1950 ff.
Revista del Archivo Nacional del Perú. Lima, 1920 ff.
Revista Histórica (organ of the Instituto Histórico del Perú, later variously renamed). Lima, 1906 ff.
Revista del Instituto Peruano de Investigaciones Genealógicas. Lima, 1946 ff.
Rivera Serna, Raúl, ed. "Libro primero de cabildos de San Juan de la Frontera de Chachapoyas." *Fénix* (review of the Biblioteca Nacional del Perú), XI (1955), 292–330; XII (1956–57), 280–336.
Roa y Ursua, Luis de. *El Reino de Chile (1535–1810)*. Valladolid, 1945.
Romero, Carlos A. *Los héroes de la isla del Gallo*. Lima, 1944.
Salinas y Córdoba, Buenaventura de, O. F. M. *Memorial de las historias del nuevo mundo Perú*. Ed. by Luis E. Valcárcel and Warren L. Cook. Lima, 1957.
Schurz, William Lytle. *This New World*. London, 1956.
Thayer Ojeda, Tomás. *Formación de la sociedad chilena y censo de la población de Chile en los años de 1540 a 1565*. 3 vols. Santiago de Chile, 1939–41.
———. *Valdivia y sus compañeros*. Santiago de Chile, 1950.
Tibesar, Antonine. *Franciscan Beginnings in Colonial Peru*. Washington, 1953.
Trujillo, Diego de. *Relación del descubrimiento del reino del Perú*. Ed. by Raúl Porras Barrenechea. Seville, 1948.

U.S., Library of Congress. *The Harkness Collection in the Library of Congress. Documents from Early Peru.* 2 vols. Washington, 1936.

Urteaga, Horacio H., and Carlos A. Romero, eds. *Colección de libros y documentos referetes a la historia del Perú.* 2 series. Lima, 1920–35.

Valdivia, Pedro de. *Cartas.* Francisco Esteve Barba, ed. *Crónicas del reino de Chile.* Madrid, 1960.

Vargas Ugarte, Rubén, S. J. *Ensayo de un diccionario de artífices coloniales de la América meridional.* Buenos Aires, 1947.

———. *Historia de la iglesia en el Perú.* Vol. I. Lima, 1953.

———. *Historia del Perú: Virreinato (1551–1600).* [Lima], 1949.

Varias relaciones del Perú y Chile. Colección de libros españoles raros o curiosos, XIII. Madrid, 1879.

Vázquez de Espinosa, Antonio. *Compendio y descripción de las Indias Occidentales.* Ed. by Charles Upson Clarke. Washington, 1948.

Wolff, Inge. "Negersklaverei und Negerhandel in Hochperu, 1540–1640." *Jahrbuch für Geschichte von Staat, Wirtschaft und Gesellschaft Lateinamerikas,* I (1964), 157–86.

———. "Die Stellung des Extranjero in der Stadt Potosí vom 16.–18. Jahrhundert" *Europa und Übersee. Festschrift für Egmont Zechlin.* Hamburg, 1961.

Zárate, Agustín de. *Historia del descubrimiento y conquista de la provincia del Perú.* Enrique de Vedia, ed. *Historiadores primitivos de Indias.* 2 vols. Madrid, 1946–47.

INDEX

Age: related to responsibility, 28; of
professional men, 68, 70–71, 73; of
men on entradas, 144–45; of settlers
generally, 164–65, 223
Agriculture: livestock, 21, 31, 54, 55,
74, 80, 83, 105, 109, 118, 121, 128,
147, 184, 186; products, 21, 24–25,
31, 118, 127, 147, 108; labor, 22, 25,
110, 125, 147, 184–85, 186, 192,
194–96, 207, 228; description of
Spanish, 24–26, 186–87. *See also*
Chácaras; Gardeners; Majordomos
Agüero, Diego de, 111
Aguirre, Lope de, 144
Alcaldes: individuals mentioned, 19, 42,
67, 69, 72, 105, 124, 131
Aldana, Lorenzo de, 107
Alemán, Pedro, German merchant, 128
Almagro, Diego de: expedition to Chile,
3, 34, 35, 87, 144, 211; civil wars
and, 3, 5, 14, 15, 106, 139, 140;
titles of, 38; mentioned, 69, 72
Almagro, don Diego de, mestizo, 39,
165
Alvarado, Alonso de, 28, 29, 32, 38,
42, 140, 158
Alvarado, Pedro de, 15, 116, 124
Ampuero, Francisco de, 211
Andagoya, Pascual de, 38
Arequipa: role in Gonzalo Pizarro rebellion, 30; merchants' row in, 83;
houses in, 108; place in Peruvian
commerce, 109, 117; projected road
to, 148; slaves in, 178, 179, 183;

chácaras in, 186–87; mentioned, 6,
64, 88, 91, 92, 93, 94, 102, 131, 198,
208
Armenta, Baltasar de, merchant, 92, 94
Artillerymen, 125–26
Artisans: role in conquest period, 13,
15; and encomienda grants, 18–19,
22; various backgrounds of, 50, 69,
125–27, 160, 168, 169, 192, 202–4,
218; and commerce, 78, 87; main discussion of, 96–113; and Negroes,
175, 179, 180, 182–84, 189, 191,
192, 195; role in community, 221,
225, 227; mentioned, 58, 68, 153
Arvallo, Bartolomé, notarial aide, 74
Atahuallpa. *See* Cajamarca
Audiencia, 42, 61, 63–64, 122, 141
Avendaño, don Martín de, nobleman,
37, 42

Bachicao, Hernando, 37, 143
Barbarán, Juan de, 158, 189
Barber-surgeons, 50, 97, 103–4
Barrionuevo, Francisco de, former gov-
ernor of Panama, 185
Beatas, 163
Beltrán, Dr., of Council of Indies, 45–46
Benalcázar, Sebastián de, 14–15, 116,
144
Benino, Nicolao del, Florentine mer-
chant, 128
Benzoni, Girolamo, chronicler, 131
Bocanegra, Iñigo de, majordomo, 32,
132

PAPERBACKS FROM WISCONSIN

SLAVE SOCIETY IN CUBA DURING THE NINETEENTH CENTURY: By Franklin W. Knight. (Received 1970 Black Academy of Arts and Letters Prize for scholarly work in the humanities.) 250 pages, 4 maps. 1970. $4.50.

THE POLITICAL ECONOMY OF MODERN SPAIN: Policy-Making in an Authoritarian System. By Charles W. Anderson. 298 pages, 6 figs. 1970. $5.00.

THE ATLANTIC SLAVE TRADE: A Census. By Philip D. Curtin. 358 pages. 1969. $4.50.

THE POLITICAL ECONOMY OF MEXICO: Two Studies. By William P. Glade, Jr. and Charles W. Anderson. 256 pages. 1963. $4.25.

JOSEPHUS DANIELS IN MEXICO. By E. David Cronon. 384 pages, 15 illus. 1960. $5.25.

SPAIN AND THE WESTERN TRADITION: The Castilian Mind in Literature from *El Cid* to Calderón. By Otis H. Green. 1963-1966. In 4 vols. $4.75 ea.

AFRICA AND THE WEST: Intellectual Responses to European Culture. Edited by Philip D. Curtin. 272 pages. 1972. $5.00.

AFRICA REMEMBERED: Narratives by West Africans from the Era of the Slave Trade. Edited by Philip D. Curtin. 376 pages, 20 illus., 16 maps. 1967. $4.75.

THE IMAGE OF AFRICA: British Ideas and Action, 1780-1850. By Philip D. Curtin. (Received the 1966 Robert Livingston Schuyler Prize.) 1964. In 2 vols. $3.75 ea.

BLACK MOSES: The Story of Marcus Garvey and the Universal Negro Improvement Association. By E. David Cronon. 302 pages, 14 illus. 2d ed. 1969. $3.50.

THE MILITANT BLACK WRITER IN AFRICA AND THE UNITED STATES. By Mercer Cook and Stephen E. Henderson. 150 pages. 1969. $2.75.

TIME LONGER THAN ROPE: A History of the Black Man's Struggle for Freedom in South Africa. By Edward Roux. 488 pages. 2d ed. 1964. $6.25.

U S EXPANSIONISM: The Imperialist Urge in the 1890s. By David Healy. 326 pages, 5 illus. 1970. $4.95.

A HISTORY OF SPAIN AND PORTUGAL. By Stanley G. Payne. 1973. In 2 vols. $5.95 ea.